Road To

The Sikh Way

Renounce both praise and blame, seek the state of *Nirvana* – O
Servant Nanak,
this is such a difficult game, only a few understand
(Sikh Scripture pp.293)

Satwinder Singh
M.A (Econ), PhD (Econ)

This book written in memory of my parents
Sardar Jagat Singh Matneja and Sardarni Pritam Kaur Matneja
sister Gurdeep and brother Sarabjit

is dedicated in all humility to

All Sikh Martyrs Who Sacrificed their Present so
That We Will Have a Future

ਦੇਹ ਸ਼ਿਵਾ ਬਰ ਮੋਹਿ ਇਹੈ ਸ਼ੁਭ ਕਰਮਨ ਤੇ ਕਬਹੂੰ ਨ ਟਰੋ ॥
ਨ ਡਰੋ ਅਰਿ ਸੋ ਜਬ ਜਾਇ ਲਰੋ ਨਿਸ਼ਚੈ ਕਰ ਅਪਨੀ ਜੀਤ ਕਰੋ ॥

Verse reads
Shiva, grant me the boon that I be never afraid of the righteous acts|
I battle with foes without fear and clinch victory with determination||
(Guru Gobind Singh)

From Top Row L-R: 1. Maharaja Ranjit Singh 2. Baba Deep Singh 3. Banda Singh
Bahadar 4. Hari Singh Nalwa 5. Jassa Singh Ahluwalia; 6. Baaj Singh Bandai 7. Akali
Gurbaksh Singh Nihang 8.Akali Phula Singh Nihang
9. Shaam Singh Attari 10. Baghel Singh Singhania 11. Sukha Singh & Mehtab Singh
12. Bota Singh & Garja Singh 13. Deep Kaur 14. Mata Bhag Kaur

In Memoriam

Late Parents
Sister Gurdeep and Brother Sarabjit

Mother's contribution to our lives is explicit in her lifetime; Father's
becomes so after his demise
Siblings (as brother used to say) are there to prove that 'blood is
thicker than water'

Dr Satwinder Singh
M.A (Econ), PhD (Econ)

ISBN   9798843653781

This book is published by the author in conjunction with Amazon.

The e-book, paperback, and hardback of this book are distributed by Amazon.

Cover photos:

Steps to Hazur Sahib (at Nanded city in Maharashtra State, India), also known as Takht Sachkhand ('Region of Truth'). This term was used by Guru Nanak to mean the 'Abode of God'.

Sikhs have five Takhts, thrones, or seats of authority, where matters of importance to Sikhs are decided. Three Takhts are in Punjab - Akal Takht in Amritsar, Keshgarh Sahib in Anandpur, and Damdama Sahib at Talwandi Sabo in Bhatinda district. Two outside Punjab are: Takht Patna Sahib at Patna, Bihar, and Takht Sri Hazur Sahib at Nanded, Maharashtra.

Second photo: Author's son in 2017 on way to Mount Kilimanjaro. At 5895 meters, Kilimanjaro is the highest mountain in Africa and 4th highest in the world. Difficult pebbled climb to the mountain top mirrors real life situations to be overcome with determination and discipline to attain *Nirvana*.

First photo Purchased from Alamy
Second photo from personal collection

The only impossible journey is the one you never begin
(Tony Robbins)

Selected Reviews

An objective and well-articulated study that will open avenues of future research. Chapter on modelling Nirvana is a feat.

Dr Saeed Heravi, Professor in Quantitative Methods
Cardiff Business School, Cardiff University, Wales.

As a non-Sikh, I found the book very easy to follow and whereas before I knew little to nothing of the Sikh religion, I can now class myself as well informed.

Adam Lomond, A1 Proofreading, UK.

This book beautifully explains the growth of Sikhism within the framework of theories of religion and leadership found in the management literature. Readers new to the topic will find the first two chapters and a lucid explanation of central tenets of the Sikh scripture very useful. A landmark.

Dr Rahul Singh,
Professor in Strategy
and Globalization
Birla Institute of Management Technology, Greater Noida,
India.

As an independent film maker, I have travelled and interacted extensively with Sikhs; at one time covered all major gurdwaras in UP for a documentary, 'A Golden Pathway,' made for the UP-Tourism Board. In my close dealings with Sikhs, I have noticed their selfless service with total dedication, with no expectations in return. This book will illuminate the reader to the source of their ethos and moral codes of behaviour that makes them what they are. Here is a race that not only wishes well in theory for all but does step in wherever help is required, sometimes at the risk of their own lives, as their devoted service to communities in COVID pandemic amply showed. This book will enrich readers' understanding of their religion and Sikh route to ultimate bliss and happiness that Nirvana is.

Shashi Saxena, Delhi, India.

Sikhism is a secular religion that treats all human beings as equal and wishes well for everyone. Sikhs' dedication to community service is legendary. This book traces the history of Sikhism and its philosophy. It will delight the reader with its easy to read, yet academically rigorous writing style.

Dinanath Thakur
National President, Sahakar Bharti, India

For someone who has little or no knowledge of Sikh religion, this book will work a treat. Written in an easy to read language, it traces the origins of Sikh religion and then explains logically its growth under the tutelage of 10 Sikh Gurus. Also explained in the book are features of Sikh's Holy Scripture and its central message on how to live a meaningful life of bliss and happiness. Scripture is now over 400 years old but the message it conveys for the physical and mental well-being of human beings is surprisingly practical, modern and doable. A wonderful read.

Dr Ambika Upadhyay
Professor & Principal Scientist (Retd.)

Foreword

Sikh religion is secular in nature and has its origins in the Punjab region of India. It wishes the well-being of the whole of mankind - *Sarbat Da Bhala.* Sikhs believe that the path to blissful living and ultimate happiness and salvation or *Nirvana* as it is sometimes called, can be achieved by residing within the community and inculcating virtues of truth, hard work, and by being of help to communities. Beginning with the birth of the first Guru of Sikhs, Guru Nanak in 1469, Sikhism has grown into a full-fledged religion and is presently the world's fifth largest with about 25 million adherents. Sikhs are recognised all over the world as the race that professes love and care for the humanity.

This book will acquaint the reader with the background, history, and moral philosophy of Sikhs which will help understand Sikhs better. It opens by providing a short but carefully researched historical background of Punjab state as we know it today. Following on, it traces the origin and growth of Sikh religion within the lifetime of ten Gurus of Sikhs and their philosophy, which culminated in written form in their Holy Scripture - *Guru Granth Sahib.* Subsequent chapters lucidly explain the tenets of Sikh philosophy within the framework of Greek philosopher Aristotle's ethical doctrines. This I believe, has been done for the first time in Sikh literature. Similarly, the book's seminal contribution lies in studying the growth of the Sikh religion and their leader Gurus within the framework of 'Theories of Religion' and 'Theories of Leadership.'

The author has also summarised the teachings in Sikh Holy Scripture which would be adequate for non-Sikh readers and those who have only an elementary knowledge of the Scripture's contents. A helpful glossary, as a supplement, and a list of key dates has been added by the author in the beginning of the book. Several detailed volumes are available for those who seek deeper understanding of the contents of the Scripture at a spiritual level. More importantly, staying focused on of how to reach '*Nirvana*'- the Sikh way', the author shows that the code of conduct dictated by Sikh Gurus and embedded in their holy Scripture is practical and possibly the shortest route to it.

Being an academic, the author does not stop here, and has added an innovative appendix chapter for research students seeking to measure an individual or a group's proximity or distance to reaching *Nirvana*. This should delight students registered for college courses that require a research project in partial fulfilment of the degree.

Written in a clear, objective, and matter of fact style, this is an amply readable modern book which will give the reader a very good understanding of Sikh religion. I am sure this book will soon find its rightful place in Sikh literature.

Dr Balbir Singh Bhatia
Pro Vice-Chancellor, RIMT University
https://rimt.ac.in/dr-b-s-bhatia/
Ex-Professor & Dean Research
Sri Guru Granth Sahib World University
Ex. Dean Academic Affairs,
Panjabi University

Contents

6

9

List of Tables and Figures

Key Dates and Glossary

Key Dates

712 - 1526	Afghan, Mongol, Turkish, and Mughals raid India 61 times. With them came Islam in India. Forcible conversions and cross breeding helped nurture it. Prior to AD 712 there were no Mohmadans in India.
1526 - 1857	Babur lays foundation of Mughal Empire in India that lasts 331 years.
1469 - 1539	Birth of Sikh religion with the birth of first Sikh Guru, Guru Nanak.
1539 - 1708	For 169 years after Guru Nanak's death, Sikh religion grows under 9 more Sikh Gurus. Guru Angad (1504-1552), Amar Das (1479-1574), Ram Das (1534-1581), Arjan Dev (1563-1606), Hargobind (1595-1644), Har Rāī (1630-1661), Hari Krishen (1656-1664), Tegh Bahadur (1621-1675), and Gobind Singh (1666-1708).
1604	Sikh Holy Scripture compiled by 5th Guru Arjan Dev and installed at *Harimandir Sahib*.
1608	Entry of East India Company (EIC) in India when its ship docks in Surat, Gujrat.
1608 - 1858	EIC makes gradual inroads into India. In 1858 control of India passes to British crown and India becomes a British colony. EIC ceases as a legal entity in 1873.
1699	Tenth Guru Gobind Singh establishes *Khalsa,* the pure race, and gives Sikhs the identity in which we see them today.
1708	Sikh Holy Scripture declared future Guru by the 10th Guru, Guru Gobind Singh, ending the succession line of living Gurus.
1670 - 1716	Banda Singh Bahadur. He was first Sikh warrior to wage an offensive against the Mughals and

defy them for 8 years. He was captured with his men after an eight-month siege of the fortress town of Gurdas Nangal, and executed by, the then, Mughal emperor Farrukhsiyar (1683-1719).

1801 - 1849   Ranjit Singh (1780-1839) establishes a Sikh empire that extended from *Khyber Pass* in the west, to *western Tibet* in the east, and Mithankot in the south, to Kashmir in the north. Empire had four provinces: Lahore (capital), Multan, Peshawar, and Kashmir. It spanned over 100,00 sq. miles and had 12 million inhabitants. With his death in 1839 empire began to crumble owing to in-fighting. Empire was annexed by British in second Anglo-Sikh war in 1849 (first war 1845-46).

1925   Sikh Gurdwara Act passed giving Sikhs control of gurdwaras.

1947   Partition of India happens; Pakistan as a separate nation formed. Punjab, the border state is divided into two Punjabs - larger one remains in Pakistan.

Glossary

Adi Granth *(AG)*   Another name for *Guru Granth Sahib* (GGS), Sikh Holy Scripture (1430 pages). A *Granthi* is reader of *AG*.

Ahankar   Ego, Excessive pride.

Amrit: Amritdhari   Drink considered Divine; prepared in sugary water, stirred with double edged sword with the recitation of religious hymns. This elixir is taken during baptism. A baptised Sikh is called *Amritdhari* (one who has taken Amrit) and who vows to observe all 5 *K's* (see

	below). A *Sehajdhari Sikh* is a non-baptised liberal Sikh.
Amrit Vela	Time between 3am - 6am (time for Sikhs to rise for morning prayers).
Akal Purakh	'The Timeless One' - used to denote God. Akali is a follower of *Akal Purakh*.
Akhand Path	A non-stop read, by a team of readers (usually in 2 hour shifts), of entire *AG*, followed by *Ardas*, *Kirtan*, and *Langar*. *Sahaj Path* is non-continuous read of entire *AG* at one's pace, over a period of time.
Anand Karaj	'Ceremony of Bliss', name given to a Sikh wedding recognised legally under Anand Marriage Act of 1909. *Lavan* is an act of 4 times circumambulation around the holy Scripture (fire for Hindus) to complete the wedding.
Anandpur Sahib	Located 82km north of Chandigarh is this historic and sacred city of Sikhs on the edge of Shivalik hills near river Sutlej. *Khalsa Panth* was founded here by Guru Gobind Singh in 1699; he also built five forts (Quila or Garh) around the borders of the city: fort Anandgarh, Holgarh, Lohgarh, Fatehgarh, Taragarh.
Ardas	A Sikh prayer. *Antim* (last) *Ardas* is prayer at a funeral.
Ashtapadi	A *Shabad* (religious poem) with eight verses.
Atma	Soul - considered immortal by Sikhs.
Baba	Baba as a noble title is reserved as a prefix (or suffix) as mark of highest respect for ascetics or persons of similar calibre (Baba Deep Singh e.g.).
Bala, Mardana	Life-long companions of Guru Nanak. Bhai Bala (1466 - 1544) from Jat family

	was a childhood friend of Bhai Mardana (1459 - 1534). Bhai Mardana was a Muslim *Mirasi* minstrel who played *Rubab* - a musical instrument.
Bhai	Adjective for a highly learned person (e.g., Bhai Vir Singh; Bhai Gurdas).
Bhai Gurdas	First cousin of 3rd Guru Amar Das, Bhai Gurdas (c.1558 - c.1637) was a scholar, proficient in several languages and assisted Guru Arjan Dev in the compilation of *AG*. His prominent poetic contribution is 40 vars (ballads) that cover a wide range of topics related to Sikhism.
Bhaini Sahib	26 km to the east of Ludhiana city in Punjab is the sacred place of sect *Namdhari* Sikhs who have a living Guru, are vegetarians, tie white turban horizontally across forehead, believe in *AG* and also in *Dasam Granth* from where *Chandi ki Var* is their *Nitnem* (everyday prayer).
Brahamgiani	From *Gian* (knowledge); a highly learned person.
Buddhism	Followers of the teachings of Gautam Buddha (c563C–c483BC). Three *universal truths* of Buddhism are: everything changes; all living things suffer; the law of *Karma* (cause and effect) exists. *Four noble truths* in Buddhism are: sufferings exist; there is a cause of suffering; there is an end to sufferings; there exists a righteous path of living to end the sufferings.
Chandoa; Chaur	Chandoa is canopy hung over *Guru Granth Sahib* in gurdwaras; Chaur is a feather stuffed handheld fan, waved over the Scripture to purify the air.

Chardi Kala	'Buoyant mood/demeanour'. In acceptance of God's will, Sikhs are expected to be in this feeling of mental state of well-being.
Culture	Shared beliefs, norms, and values of a group.
Dastaar	Another name for turban.
Dasam Granth	*'Dasven Pādśāh kā Granth'*, shortened to *Dasam Granth*, is a compilation of philosophical writings, hymns, Hindu mythological tales, and autobiography of 10th Guru Gobind Singh. It is written in Braj, Hindi, Persian, and Gurmukhi languages. It was compiled in 1737 by Bhai Mani Singh, lifelong companion of Guru Gobind Singh.
Dera	Encampment/Habitation (e.g., Dera Baba Nanak).
Dharm	Moral, ethical, and religious code of conduct of a religion.
Dharm Yudh	War in the cause of religion and righteousness.
Ethics	Ethics or moral philosophy is concerned with what is good for individuals and society. It addresses concepts such as right and wrong, virtue and vice, good and evil. Ethics broadly addresses the question: "how should we live?"
Game theory	Models in which players (parties) to a transaction make decisions that are interdependent; each player tries to predict other's reaction or strategy before formulating his own, for the best outcome. Game theory models are used in social sciences to predict large number of behaviours.
Gatka	Sikh martial arts practiced with swords and other battle weapons. It was

	initiated into the culture by 6th Guru Hargobind after the torture and demise of 5th Guru Arjan Dev in 1606 which was the tipping point in Sikh Gurus thinking.
Ghallughara	Massacre. First in 1746 when Mughal army systematically killed 7000 Sikhs around Lahore. In second massacre in 1762, 10000 - 20000, mostly women and children, accompanying retrieving Sikh fighters were massacred by Afghan forces of the Durrani Empire. State engineered third massacre happened in 1984 when around 10,000 Sikhs were massacred in India.
Gurbani	Guru's divine hymns; sometimes shortened to Bani.
Gurdwara	Sikh place of worship. From Guru + Dwar (door).
Gurmukhi	Written language of Sikhs. Spoken language is called Punjabi.
Gurmukhi numerals	0 (੦); 1 (੧); 2 (੨); 3 (੩); 4 (੪); 5 (੫); 6 (੬); 7 (੭); 8 (੮); 9 (੯);10 (੧੦).
Gurpurab	Celebration of Guru's birth anniversary.
Harimandir Sahib	Also 'Darbar Sahib'; known as Golden Temple to non-Sikhs. Built in 1604 by 5th Guru Arjan Dev. It is open on all 4 sides to signify its openness to all castes. Built at lower level so all step down to enter it. Temple's foundation was laid by Mian Mīr, a Muslim Pir (holy man) of Lahore. Temple occupies a small island in the centre of a pool, called Amrit-sar (pool of nectar). Destroyed by Mughal and invading Afghan armies, it has been re-built/repaired several times.

Hinduism	Hinduism is the oldest religion in the world; source of its philosophy is ancient texts, prominent of which are 4 *Vedas* (meaning knowledge). Hindus believe in the law of *Karma*; righteous living can lead to *Nirvana*.
Hukamnama	A written order to an individual or community issued by a Guru or a Sikh religious authority.
Hola Mohalla	Initiated by 10th Guru Gobind Singh in 1680, it is an annual springtime gathering of Sikhs at *Anandpur Sahib* for sports contests, music, and poetry.
Inderiyan	Sense organs. A human being has 5 *Karmendriyas* i.e., organs of action: speech; hands; feet; excretory organ; organ of reproduction. There are 5 sensory organs, *Gyaninderiyans*, used to gather knowledge: eyes, nose, tongue, ears, and touch (skin).
Jainism	Jainism developed c500 BC as a religious sect and taught that path to salvation was by living a pious life through Ahinsa (non-violence) - extreme form of which Jains observe. Jain's honour 24 Tirthankaras (spiritual leaders), most influential of which is Mahavira (c599-c527BC).
Janam Sakhis	Life stories of Guru Nanak written by devotees after Guru Nanak's death.
Janeu	A sacred band of threads worn by upper caste Hindu males (Brahmins, Kshatriyas, and Vaishyas).
Jhatka	Meat slain in one strike versus Halal meat which is a slow process with recitation of *Tasmiya* (Allah's name).

Jizya tax	Protection tax on life and property levied on non-Muslims during Mughal raj.
Karma	Causal relationship between good and bad actions. Good actions result in good outcome: bad actions result in bad outcome - in present as well as in reincarnations. In Sikhism and sister religions - Hinduism, Buddhism, Jainism, good actions result in *Mukti* or *Moksha* i.e., release from cycles of re-births.
Katha	Narration of a tale, usually a religious one.
Khalsa	A baptised Sikh. From Arabic *Khalis* meaning 'pure'.
Kiratpur Sahib	75km north of Chandigarh, and 10km from historic Anandpur Sahib, is located this sacred city of Sikhs, on the banks of river Sutlej. It is the birthplace of 7th and 8th Guru Har Rāī, and Guru Harikrishen. Sixth Guru Hargobind spent last few years of his life here. In 1675 Guru Gobind Singh received here the Head of his father, 9th Guru Tegh Bahadur (who was beheaded for non-compliance to accepting Islam) and cremated it in Anandpur Sahib.
Kirpan	A dagger Sikhs wear on their body as part of *5K*'s.
Kirtan	Singing of religious hymns usually with Tabla *(drums) and Harmonium*.
Kaur	Meaning 'Princess' - middle name of Sikh females.
Laṇḍā	Script used by shopkeepers in northern India to keep accounts.
Langar	Community meal which is always vegetarian.

Miri and Piri	Spiritual and Worldly matters; 6th Guru Hargobind introduced the concept of Sikhs maintaining a balance between the two; Guru Hargobind famously carried two swords representing the two concepts.
Misl	Between 1716 and 1799, to effectively counter Mughals, Sikh leaders divided Punjab in 12 semi-autonomous centres, each under a warrior leader. Ranjit Singh combined the Misls and formed a Sikh empire in 1799 that lasted till 1849.
Mahant (Masand)	Appointed manager of a gurdwara prior to SGPC Act 1925. Tradition of Mahants was abolished when they became all too powerful and corrupt.
Manji	A religious administrative unit (dioceses); 22 were created by 3rd Guru Amar Das, to better run the admin, and preaching of Guru Nanak's gospel.
Minas	Derogatory term for splinter group formed by Prithi Chand (1558-1618), (eldest son of 4th Guru Ram Das, and brother of 5th Guru Arjan dev), when he was not selected for Guru-ship.
Mool Mantar	Basic chant of Sikhs: *Ek Onkar Satnam Karta Purakh Nirpau Nirwair Akal Murat Ajuni Sabhang Gur Prasad.* Meaning: (There is) One Universal Creator God. The Name Is Truth. Creative Being Personified. No Fear. No Hatred. Image of the Undying, Beyond Birth, Self-Existent. By Guru's Grace.
Nihangs	Attired in blue fabrics, Sikhs who follow the warrior lifestyle of the time

	of Guru Gobind Singh. They habitually carry swords and other battle weapons.
Nirvana	A state of ultimate bliss and happiness. Freedom from cycles of re-births.
Nishan Sahib	Saffron colour triangular flag of Sikhs with Sikh emblem, outside a gurdwara. It is raised high so that anyone can recognise a gurdwara from a distance.
Panj	Number 5 - considered auspicious by Sikhs.
Panj Gun	5 virtues expected of Sikhs – compassion, humility, love, contentment, truth.
Panj Kakke	5 K's Amritdhari Sikhs maintain on their body - *Kesh* (uncut hairs), *Kanga* (small comb behind knotted head hairs), *Kara* (steel/cast iron bangle), *Kirpan* (a dagger), *Kachhera* (lengthy drawer up to the knees).
Panj Piare	First five baptised Sikhs by Guru Gobind Singh in 1699 (Daya Singh; Dharam Singh; Himmat Singh; Mohkam Singh; Sahib Singh).
Panj Parā'a	5 stages of life: In *Japuji*, Guru Nanak describes 5 stages to reach the spiritual planes of *Nirvana* - a Dutiful Life *(Dharam Khand)*, Knowledge (*Gian Khand)*, Efforts (hard work - *Shrm Khand), Grace (Karam Khand),* Truth *(Sach Khand - abode of God)*.
Panj Tat	*AG* mentions 5 elements of which life is made - space, air, water, fire, earth; particular mention of air, water, and earth *Pavan Guru, Pani Pita, Mata Dharata Mahata* is made in *AG*.
Panj Vikar	5 vices/evils are listed in *AG* - *Kam* (lust), *Krodh* (anger), *Lobh* (greed), *Moh* (attachment), *Ahankar* (ego).

Panth	A Sect usually a religious one.
Philosophy	Quest for wisdom and knowledge. In philosophy we explore life's big questions to understand what we should do and how we can live a good life. A philosophical enquiry aims to understand something rather than just know it.
Qila / Garh	A fort. Five forts were built by 10th Guru Gobind Singh at Anandpur (city on the edge of Shivalik hills); Lohgarh (fort of steel); Holgarh (fort of colour); Anandgarh (fort of bliss); Fatehgarh (fort of victory); and Taragarh.
Rāga; Rāgi	In Indian classical music, Rāga is a melodic framework based on a scale with a set of notes. *AG* hymns are adorned in 60 (31main+29 sub) Rāgas. Rāgi is one who sings the hymns in Rāgas (see also *Kirtan*).
Religion	A unified system of beliefs and practices which unite people in one single moral community.
RCT	Rational Choice Theory. Theory states that individuals choose a course of action that is in alignment with their personal preferences.
Rehat Maryada	Sikh code of conduct.
Sahib Singh	Sikh studies scholar (1892-1977). Major work: completed in 1972, after thirty plus years of work and over 6000 pages long is line-by-line translation and meaning of hymns in *AG*.
Sangat	Sometime *Sadh (or Sat) Sangat;* a pious congregation – usually for religious purposes.
Scripture	A body of sacred writings.

Sat Sri Akaal	This is Short Greeting when two Sikhs meet; full form is: '*Jo Bole So Nihaal, Sat Sri Akaal,* meaning 'Blessed is he, who says 'God is Truth'. Also: *Vahiguru ji ka Khalsa, Vahiguru ji ki Fateh,* meaning 'Khalsa belongs to Almighty; Victory be to Almighty.
Sati	Tradition in parts of India where a widow self-immolated on husband's funeral pyre. Tradition was abolished by British in 1829.
Sikh Emblem	Imprinted on Sikh flag is Sikh emblem depicting a double edged sword flanked by two side swords and a circle.
Sikh prayers	*Japuji* (morning); *Rehraas* (evening after sunset); *Sohila* (before retiring for the night).
Singh	Meaning 'Lion' - middle name of Sikh males.
Seva	Service - Sikh are expected to perform service to fellow human beings, and to community, with dedication of mind, body, and financial means.
Salok	A stanza.
Sigmoid function	A *S*-shaped curve used to describe the growth pattern of a phenomenon.
Siropa	Honour given by the Sikh community to someone. It is usually a length of cloth (mostly white, saffron, or blue in colour) for use as scarf around the neck.
Sufi	A Sufi in Islam is one who seeks spiritual goal by direct personal experience of God by reciting religious hymns, poetry written in Allah's praise, and dancing in a trance. Sufism is a mystical branch of Islam.

SGPC; DSGMC	Shiromani Gurdwara Parbandhak Committee (SGPC) is the central committee founded by a Govt of India Act in 1925 for the management of gurdwaras. Delhi Sikh Gurdwara Management Committee (DSGMC), also formed by an Act in 1971, manages gurdwaras within the union territory of Delhi.
SPA	Trinity of Greek philosophers and father of modern philosophy - Socrates (c.470BC-399BC); Plato (c.428BC-424BC); Aristotle (384BC-322BC). Socrates was teacher of Plato and Plato was teacher of Aristotle.
Sukhmani Sahib	(*Sukhan di Mani*). Hymn of Peace - a much-loved lyrical soothing composition in *AG* by 5th Guru Arjan Dev.
Shabad	A religious hymn.
Takht	A throne, or seat of authority. Sikhs have 5 Takhts. Three Takhts are in Punjab - *Akal Takht* in Amritsar; *Keshgarh Sahib* in Anandpur; and *Damdama Sahib* at Talwandi Sabo in Bhatinda district. Two are outside Punjab: *Takht Patna Sahib* at Patna, Bihar; and *Takht Sri Hazur Sahib* at Nanded, Maharashtra.
Taksal	Made of two words, Taka (coin)+Shaala (place); place where coins are carved/minted. Metamorphically, in *AG* Taksal is used for Satsangat where Guru's word is carved (e.g., ਅਤੀਐ ਸਬਦੁ ਸਚੀ ਟਕਸਾਲ ॥ meaning 'The Shabad is carved in the true Taksal (of Guru's Satsangat). Famous *Damdami Taksal* founded by

	Guru Gobind Singh, is located 2.3km to the south-east of Amritsar.
Tankhaiya	From 'Tankha' meaning salary. Insulting word, with origin in Mughal raj when a Sikh was found to be on Mughal's payroll. In present time, a Sikh can be declared *Tankhaiya* if found disrespectful to religion.
Theory	A theory helps us understand a phenomenon and predict its likely outcome.
Udāsī	A Stoic - one indifferent to worldly attachments. A sect within Sikhism started by Sri Chand (elder son of Guru Nanak). Sect members do not observe *5 K's,* wear orange or red robes. Their beliefs tilt towards Hinduism.
Vedas: Hindu texts	Vedas are 4 texts of knowledge (Rigveda, Yajurveda, Samaveda, Atharvaveda). There are also 108 known *Upanishads* (philosophical and moralistic texts); 3 *Dharma* texts: Bhagavad Gita, Mahābhārata, Rāmāyaṇa; 18 *Maha Purāṇas* (books of received wisdom with 400,000 Saloks); and 213 *Āgamas* (on teachings on Yoga, Tantra, etc.); and 29 *sub- Purāṇas.*
Waheguru Satnam	Basic chant meaning 'Wondrous God' *is* 'The True Name'.
Zakat	In Islamic world, donating money for the needy.

Preface

It is your road and yours alone,
others may walk it with you, but no
one can walk it for you
(Rūmī)

I conceived the idea of this book in 2017. My intention was to condense the teachings on moral principles in Sikh Holy Scripture and those taught by Sikh Gurus, and to discover how they can help us reach *Nirvana.* But it soon dawned on me that some basic information on Sikh history and growth of its religion would be a useful backdrop, especially for a non-Sikh reader of the book. Secondly, it would also help if the book can stand on theoretical underpinnings of growth of Sikh religion, the leadership role of its Gurus, and their philosophy.

Chapter-1 on Demography and History; chapter-2 on the Lives of Sikh Gurus; chapter-3, on Theories of Religion and Leadership, and chapter-5 on Moral Principles in the Sikh Scripture vis-à-vis Greek philosopher Aristotle's classic work *Nicomachean Ethics* are the result of this thought. Chapters 4 sums up the features, and key messages in the Scripture. Material of these five chapters funnels into chapter-6 which shows in a succinct way how the *Road to Nirvana* can be traversed following Sikh moral principles. Appendix chapter (Modelling *Nirvana*) is for researchers who wish to undertake applied work (possibly in part-fulfilment of a degree program) on Sikh studies. I was trained as an economist; hence, some bias of my profession would be visible in the book.

Five novel features of the book add value to existing literature on the subject. It is the first time that the growth of Sikh religion is explained within the framework of theories of religion. Secondly, theories of leadership have been applied to explain the leadership traits of Sikh Gurus. Thirdly, the tenets of Sikh philosophy have been explained within the theoretical framework of Aristotle's model of moral philosophy. Fourthly, key messages in the Sikh scripture are summarised in a succinct manner (Ch-5). Fifthly, Appendix chapter on modelling *Nirvana* shows how a complex topic of determining the proximity to *Nirvana* can be statistically modelled. I have also sought to add value in chapter 1 by objectively analysing the topography and demography of the Punjab state. In chapter 2 the commonalities and distinctive qualities of 10 Sikh Gurus are also explained.

I confirm that I am not aligned to any political, social, or religious organization. I have worked independently and solo on this project which was self-funded, and I have met all costs related to it, and that I have not taken any funding from private or public sources[1]. I would also like to state that whatever material and interpretations have been used in the book is without any prejudice or malice whatsoever against any individual or a sect. A totally objective academic approach has been adopted. I will urge the readers to read and interpret the material as such.

It was my wish to keep the price of the book the lowest possible so that it is in the reach of a wider audience. Hence the decision to self-publish with Amazon, which

---

[1] Items of expenditure included equipment, printing, photocopying, books, in particular pricy handbooks, other reference material, copyediting, proof reading, travelling (I reckon total cost would be in the region of £10k).

also has a global reach. Surplus, after Amazon takes its cut, will be used for charitable purposes.

I urge my Sikh brethren to encourage their youngsters to read the book to get acquainted with the magnanimity of Sikh heritage. Youngsters would also appreciate the objective fact-based approach, to which they are used to in their college courses, and which has been adopted throughout this book. I am confident that after having read the book they will be happy to recommend it to their non-Sikh acquaintances seeking an understanding of Sikhism. Appendix chapter should also make the survey-based research work in the spiritual realm of Sikh studies easier, should they wish to pursue their degree in this area.

To those who are about to read the book for the first time on the Sikh world, I hope their experience turns out to be a thrill similar to seeing a shining star, or their first date - (or a secret date, dare I say!) - *Bon voyage*, this is the thrill you can experience only once.

Reading, (UK)   Dr Satwinder Singh
July 2022   M.A (Econ), PhD (Econ)

Acknowledgements

Knowledge is in the end based on
acknowledgement
(Ludwig Wittgenstein)

My intellectual gratitude goes to all Sikh and non-Sikh scholars who have spent a lifetime in Sikh studies and published extensively in this field and from whose work I learnt a great deal as a new entrant to the field. During the course of this research, I also discovered and benefitted from the works of several Western, English and Scottish civil servants who worked for the Crown in India and who produced elaborate pieces of written work in the form of reports and books with great attention to detail[2].

My spouse needs to be thanked profusely for her support and for putting up with the habits of an academic. I also acknowledge past help and support of my deceased brother Sarabjit and sister Gurdeep. Eldest sister Harbeer, who has always supported us all, is keenly looking forward to this long-awaited work from me. I hope she will be delighted with it.

Ranbir Kashap and Dr Tapas Sen (a friend from doctoral days) two dedicated readers gave generous

---

[2] Bibliography at the end of this book lists selected works of Charles Stewart (1764-1837); David Shea (1777-1836); Mountstuart Elphinstone (1779-1859); Henry Beveridge (1799–1863); Joseph Davey Cunningham, (1812-1851); Max Arthur Macauliffe (1838-1913); William Wilson Hunter (1840-1900); Stanley Edward Lane-Poole (1854-1931); William Durant (1861-1947); Duncan Greenlees (1899-1966).

amounts of their time in reading the drafts and provided valuable feedback. I am indebted to them.

The penultimate draft of the book was completed in February in Seattle at the picturesque house on the water of our son Gagan and spouse Jill and final draft in May in brother-in-law Ranbir and spouse Linda's home in the woods in Philadelphia. We are indebted to both the families for their warm hospitality and facilities provided.

I am ever so grateful to lifelong friends Dr and Mrs Ajit Bhatia who have always been of help whenever I have approached them. I also thank my ex-Gokhale Institute of Politics and Economics (GIPE) friends for their ever-present support and humour. Dr Sudha Kothari, also an ex-GIPEian, has always been there to assist with her ever-present equanimity and cheerfulness. For technical support thanks are due to Adnan Zaman and Manasi Misal. Cheers to Reading Punjabi Society friends and high school buddies - Manjit, Harbhajan, Kuljit, and Inderpal who have lately added so much colour to our sunset years.

I take full responsibility for the views expressed and for errors and omissions in the book and welcome feedback, comments, suggestions for improvement. Please send them at: awellwisher369@gmail.com.

Executive Summary of the Book

Chapter 1 (Demography and History) gives a brief but essential description of the demography of Sikh populace and the geographical layout of Punjab state within India. Punjab, a border state between Afghanistan and, the then India, and which was in the path of invaders, bore the brunt of Mughal, Persian, Afghan, Turkish, and Mongol invaders from mid-10th century onwards, until the British East India Company took control in 1757, and the British crown took charge of India in 1858. Passages quoted graphically display the brutality of plunder, massacres, slavery, desecration of temples, forcible conversions to Islam, abduction of women - all of which continued, almost unchecked for centuries. Atrocities meted have left scars on Hindu and Sikh psyche that linger till this day.

In the chaos of this milieu was born the Sikh religion. A key point that is made here is that until the entry of invaders in mid-10th century AD there were no Mohammedan in India. Mohammedan population (presently 200 million - third largest cluster in the world, after Indonesia and Pakistan) gradually swelled with the forcible conversion, and soldiers from invading armies taking local brides and settling down in the region. It is argued that invaders when settled to rule left a rich legacy of art, culture, and monuments and that now it is time to move on.

Chapter 2 (Evolution of Sikhs under 10 Gurus) traces the origin of Sikh religion to AD 1469 with the birth of first of 10 Sikh Gurus, Guru Nanak, and describes the steady growth it witnessed in the lifetime of Sikh Gurus. Each of the 10 Gurus had unique strength, respectively, in humility, obedience, equality, service, self-sacrifice, justice, mercy, purity, calmness, and royal courage. They also had some common traits - foremost of which was their long-term thinking for the community. This resulted in them choosing successors purely on merit. They were also instrumental in devising Gurmukhi - the written language of the Sikhs; stressed on physical and mental well-being and helped build centres of learning, gurdwaras, and related infrastructure, essential for the growth of a religious institution, most prominent of which is *Harimandir Sahib*, commonly known as the 'Golden Temple'.

All Gurus were multi-linguists, had intimate knowledge of several languages - Sanskrit, Persian, Braj, Hindi, among others. They were also literary geniuses and had in-depth knowledge of Indian classical music in which they penned their verses. All Gurus were also men of strict moral principles, and never wavered from the righteous path.

A key point for the reader in this chapter would be an understanding as to how a religion that began peacefully came to adopt a militant stance owing to atrocities by the then Mughal rulers on their Gurus and the ordinary folks. The militant stance at one time culminated in the establishment of a Sikh empire with capital at Lahore; empire that lasted 50 years (1801-1849), spanned 100435 sq. miles and had in it 12 million inhabitants. It extended "from the *Khyber Pass* in the west to the river Satluj in the east, from the northern boundary of Kashmir to the deserts of Sindh in the south, comprising the provinces of Lahore, Multan, Peshawar, and Kashmir. It was a liberal and benevolent empire that included Sikhs, Hindus, and Muslims in the ruling class"[3].

Chapter 3 (Rise of Sikhism, Culture Shift, and Leadership) provides theoretical underpinnings to the growth of Sikh religion. Focus on this chapter is to understand the theory that best explains the growth of a new religion that Sikhism was. I reason that the *Rational Choice Theory* appropriately describes the growth of Sikh religion, which was secular in its approach and was understanding on issues of equality, caste system, status of women, and a plethora of rituals from birth to death observed by Hindus of the time. With regard to the speed of growth, I propose that it took an elongated *S* shape, with the growth at first steeper, then somewhat flatter, then peaking and stabilizing in the times of 9th and 10th Gurus. With regard to the analysis of Sikh Gurus' leadership qualities, I propose that since Gurus first considered themselves as servers of the people, the 'Servant-Leader (SL)', paradigm best explains the leadership style of Sikh Gurus.

Chapter 4 (Features of Sikh Holy Scripture) summaries the stylized facts of the *Scripture* - its size, layout, contents, distribution of hymns in various *Rāgas*, and other characteristics of the 1430-page Scripture. Key point we make in this chapter is the amazing precision with which fifth Guru Arjan Dev was able to compile the *Scripture* with the help of just one subordinate and a myriad of constraints - in operations research parlance, the problem he solved is equivalent to finding an optimal solution in a linear programming model. The dexterity with which the tunes of underlying *Rāgas* are matched with each hymn is an exceptional feat of a genius mind.

---

[3] https://doi.org/10.1002/9781118455074.wbeoe314

Chapter 5 (Sikh Scripture and the Aristotelian Model of Moral Philosophy) summarizes key messages in Sikh scripture on how to live a virtuous life. The scripture grants supreme importance to the '*control over mind*' that steers us into doing all that we do in our lives. A controlled and composed mind, full of righteous traits can put us on the path of a virtuous life. Threats to the composure of mind come from five adversaries – anger, greed, excessive attachment to worldly entities, and ego; these in turn are influenced by what we see, hear, smell, taste, and touch. For a person seeking path to a virtuous life, search should begin with keeping in check the adversaries affecting the mind, so that it can take virtuous decisions. To help us in this, Scripture advises us to be in the company of righteous persons. The end-result of leading a virtuous life is the innate happiness it can generate. 'Happiness' which we all intuitively understand is an elusive construct that has been extensively researched.

The 'Sikh model' of moral philosophy has uncanny similarities with the Greek philosopher 'Aristotle's model' of moral philosophy. Both models profess that, with the goal of true happiness in mind, the primary aim of a human being should be to nurture a soul full of good virtues. A person should keep his vices e.g., love for bodily pleasures under check. Both schools of thought also recognize that a virtuous person would also be courageous; believe in justice and fairness; will be charitable; and will make all attempts to harness intellectual virtues. Both schools believe that the highest form of virtue should be the pleasure of contemplation i.e., a truly contemplative person would be on (constant) guard of virtuous and non-virtuous acts in life. The Sikh scripture extends the road map of happiness (leading to *Nirvana*) by urging us to be early risers, observe a disciplined life, make an honest living by dint of hard labour, and reminisce in, and always keep God's memory in mind.

Chapter 6 (Road to Nirvana – the Sikh Way) addresses, head on, the question as to how we can be on the *'Road to Nirvana'* which is also is the title of this book. Principles of Sikh moral philosophy, embedded in their Scripture, and shown by real life examples of their Gurus, reveal an easy way for us to be on this road. The 'system' or 'model' that emerges from a study of the Sikh scripture and the lives of Sikh Gurus and clarified by Sikh scholars in the (written) code of conduct, is remarkably logical and simple in its approach. It goes something like this.

Our 'mind' is the ultimate driver of everything we do in our lives. It is essential that we keep our mind healthy and populate it with good virtues. Since a healthy mind is very much linked with a healthy body, 'system' urges us to work towards habiting ourselves in a healthy body. This begins with an early rise, undertaking exercise, meditation, and prayers. 'System' then urges us to practice and inculcate in us, on a day-to-day basis and making it a part of our disposition, the virtues of humility, obedience, equity, service, self-sacrifice, justice, mercy, purity of service, calmness, and courage.

For us to get a gradual mastery over these virtues, the 'system' urges us to seek, and be in the company of virtuous people, and keep a control over underlying weaknesses of humans - sexual urges, anger, greed, attachment to worldly objects, and ego. We can do this by keeping a check on our channels of interface with the world i.e., what we choose to see, hear, smell, taste, and touch.

Alongside, to be a truly virtuous person, we also need to pay attention to our family life, by teaching good, the religious (and non-religious) virtues to our children, by being faithful to our spouse, and looking after family elders. Final stage to become a truly virtuous person and a candidate for *Nirvana*, we ought to serve the community we live in and share our life with. We can do this by donating part of our earnings for charitable purposes and extending physical help whenever required.

Rationale and ingredients of '*Road to Nirvana*' dictated by the Sikh 'system' of virtues becomes clear and begins to make sense if we ponder a little deeper into its suggestions. Making an honest effort to perfect each element of the 'system' takes us a step closer to *Nirvana*. 'System' also tells us that journey towards it should begin from an early age - this is the reason it urges us to pay attention to our family life. As we grow older, and enter into the complex web of the modern world, we need strong and consistent moral virtues and convictions, to see us through a peaceful journey into work life, retirement, old age, and departure from this world - if we have led a virtuous life in *this* world, we have done well to achieve state of *Nirvana* in *this* as well as in the *next* world. The heartening issue, the 'System' tells us, is that for us to achieve all this we need not renounce anything and journey into forests or mountains to live in solitude; *Nirvana* can be achieved by being in the midst of family and community.

Appendix Chapter (Modelling Nirvana) is for researchers and post-graduate students (MSc, MPhil, PhD) who wish to undertake statistical work to determine how close or far off one is from his mark of reaching *Nirvana*. I propose that with the help of a survey, it is possible to determine (say, on 10 a point scale) the level at which we all are operating on our virtuous traits index - humility, obedience, equality, service, self-sacrifice, justice, mercy, purity of thought, calmness, royal courage, and others; the list can be extended. To facilitate the research process, I have drawn a conceptual model and suggested control and mediator variables. For each of the traits, I have also provided selected survey questions which can be developed further with help from co-researchers and thesis advisers.

Experience of this author as first adviser to fifteen or so doctoral students shows that all three parts of a survey - drafting a good survey instrument, administering it, and analysing data thereof are essential components of a successful research project and it is easy to make mistakes if the basics of these components are not clearly understood. As a result, I have also provided basic terminology attached to these three components. I have also included here some material on data and its analysis - basic concepts, but on which I have found students lacking clarity and making mistakes. Material here would be of help to prospective researchers.

Prologue

*For a man to conquer himself is
the first and noblest of all
victories (Plato)*

Nirvana is a concept found in Indian religions and stands for a state of ultimate bliss – a transcendent state in which a person has been released from the effects of *Karma* and the cycle of rebirths. The term is also synonymous with *Mukti* (or *Moksha)*. In day-to-day parlance the term is taken to be a state of highest peace and happiness having been liberated from attachments and worldly sufferings.

For Sikhs and for devotees of sister faiths - Hinduism, Jainism, Buddhism, ultimate goal of life is the attainment of *Mukti*[4]. To attain *Mukti*, a person must rid himself of all bad *Karma* and focus on gaining good *Karma*. This is what Indian religions focus on, and Sikhism is no exception. It is a job, however, easier said than done. To achieve *Mukti* and to arrive at a state of *Nirvana* is a road most wish to travel but find difficult. This book is no panacea, but it does show that *Nirvana* can be achieved by following some simple moral principles advocated by the

---

[4] An easy to understand the world of Hinduism, Buddhism, and Jainism is respectively (Das, 2019); (Harris , 2009); and (Cort , Dundas, Jacobsen, & Wiley, 2020).

Sikh scripture and Sikh Gurus. The philosophy of Sikhs embedded in their Holy Scripture and a code of conduct dictated by their Gurus is possibly the shortest and simplest route to achieving *Nirvana*.

For us to understand this route, the Sikh way, it would help if we had at least an elementary knowledge of Sikh history, its origins, and the teachings of ten Gurus, each one of whom made a distinctive contribution to Sikhism. We do this in the first two chapters. We then list unique features of Sikh's sacred Scripture, affectionately addressed by Sikhs as *Guru Granth Sahib*[5] before arriving at suggestions for *Road to Nirvana*. Also discussed in the book are the commonalities of ethos of Sikh religion with Greek philosopher Aristotle's treatise on ethics, and relation of theories of religion and leadership with the growth of Sikh religion and leadership styles of Sikh Gurus. A guide to ascertain how near or far off we are to our goal of *Nirvana* is also provided in the appendix chapter.

---

5 Granth is commonly understood as a hefty book of sacred writings; word 'Sahib' meaning 'Master' is added as a mark of respect.

CHAPTER 1 DEMOGRAPHY AND HISTORY

Those who do not remember
past are condemned to repeat it
(George Santayana)

People and the Punjab State

This chapter provides the reader with a brief but essential overview of the people of Punjab, the Sikhs in particular, its topography and history as a background for subsequent discussion. Given its geographical location of a border state, for centuries, Punjab bore the brunt of invaders' ferocity of loot, massacres, abductions, and such atrocities associated with invasions in those times[6]. An understanding of these brutal incursions is essential to understand the present-day Sikh psyche and the emergence of their religion which, despite all the viciousness it endured, is surprisingly unique in its trait of universal love and peace. It though justifies the use of arms to safeguard oneself and those who are wronged and seek protection.

The word 'Sikh' has its origin in Sanskrit word śiṣya , meaning a 'disciple'. The name Punjab means five waters (panj=5, aab=waters) which is a Persian term for five waters. In historical texts (Ramayana and Mahabharata) the region has been addressed as Panchnad - Land of the Five Rivers. The region was originally called

---

[6] Details on the historical records of invasion have been presented as they are without any malice or partisan thought.

Sapta Sindhu, the land of the seven rivers (two having since dried).

Punjab state in which Sikhs predominantly reside accounts for about 1.60% of India's land mass, and 1.72% (20.90 million) of India's population[7]. Within Punjab, people of *Sikh faith* are 16 million or 77% of the total. Unofficial figures put world-wide people with *Sikh faith* at 25 million. Countries with the largest concentration of Sikhs outside India are US (0.70million), Canada (0.45m), UK (0.43m), Australia (0.13m), Malaysia (0.10m), East Africa (primarily Kenya, Uganda, Tanzania: between 50-100,000), Thailand (70,000), and Philippines (50,000)[8].

When we refer to Punjab in this book we refer to 'Indian Punjab'. There is a Punjab province in Pakistan as well that borders Indian Punjab. 'Pakistan Punjab' has 26% of Pakistan's land mass and 50% (110 million) of Pakistan's population. 'Pakistan Punjab' was bifurcated from composite Punjab in the 1947 partition of the country. In this partition, 56% of mostly Muslim dominated areas remained in Pakistan. Present Punjab is a relatively smaller state compared to other Indian states (Figure 1.1, 1.2)[9]. Punjab as we know today shrunk further in size in 1966 when Hindi speaking areas were carved out from it to form an additional state, Haryana.

---

[7] https://censusindia.gov.in/ (Office of the Registrar General & Census Commissioner, India, Ministry of Home Affairs)

[8] https://www.worldatlas.com/articles/countries-with-the-largest-sikh-populations.html

[9] There are 28 states and 9 union territories in India. Under Article 12 of the Indian constitution, a State is defined as the Government of India or the Central government; the Parliament of India (the upper and the lower house); State-based governments and legislative bodies; local Authorities such as municipalities, panchayat, port trusts.

Per person, per year income of people of Punjab in 2019-20 was estimated to be Rs1, 66,833 (app. US $2,383) which was higher than the India's national average of Rs1,35,050 (app. US $1,929). In 2018-19 Punjab contributed more than 1/4th and 1/3rd to the central pool of rice and wheat respectively. Agriculture and allied activities contribute 28%, industry 25%, and services 47% to state's income[10]. Literacy rate is 77%; 63% population resides in rural areas; there are 893 females per 1000 males; population growth rate per annum is 1.4%[11].

Figure 1. 1 Indian States and Union Territories

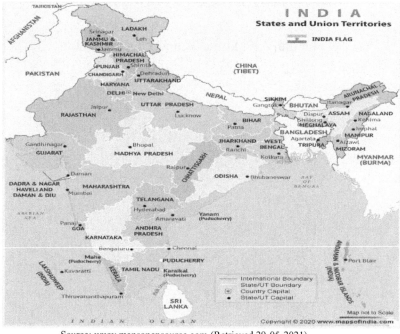

Source: www.mapsopensource.com (Retrieved 29-05-2021).

10 https://www.esopb.gov.in/static/PDF/EconomicSurvey-2019-20.pdf
11 https://punjab.gov.in/state-profile/ Note: Data relates to years 2011 census.

Figure 1. 2 Indian Punjab and Pakistan Punjab

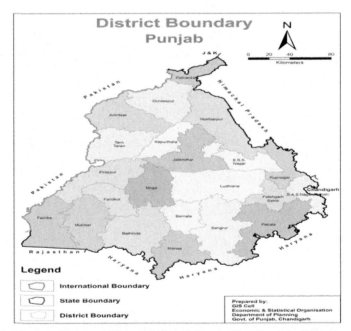

Figure 1. 3 Map of Punjab Districts

Figure 1.3 shows 22 Districts of Punjab. Number of Districts in Punjab increased from 22 to 23 in 2021. The 23rd District, Malerkotla (not shown in Figure 1.3), created in 2021, has been carved out of Sangrur district.

A District (or Zilā) is an administrative division, sometimes further subdivided into sub-divisions (tehsils). A District Magistrate or Deputy Commissioner (DC) is responsible for the administration in the District, and a Superintend of Police or a DC of police, for law-and-order situation.

Three commonly known regions of Punjab are **Majha** - meaning 'middle' lies between rivers Ravi and Beas on the north-west side of the State (comprising 4 Districts of Amritsar, Gurdaspur, Pathankot, Taran Taran); **Doaba** - lying between rivers Beas and Sutlej on the north-east side of the State (comprising 4 Districts of Hoshiarpur, Jalandar, Kapurthala, Shaheed Bhagat Singh (SBS) Nagar (previously Nawanshahr); **Malwa** Lying to the south of river Sutlej (comprising 15 Districts of Barnala, Bathinda, Faridkot, Fatehgarh Sahib, Fazilka, Firozpur, Ludhiana, Malerkotla (new), Mansa, Moga, Muktsar, Patiala, Rup Nagar, Sangrur, SAS Nagar (commonly known as Mohali). The demonym used for inhabitants of these three regions are respectively, Majhel, Doabia, and Malwai.

Crucial Demographic Trends[12]

A look at demographic data shows that compared to Indian average, *the growth of population in Punjab is in*

---

12 Data for this section has been compiled from various tables in Govt of India (2020). *Population Projections for India and States 2011-2036*. Report of the Technical Group on Population Projections, National commission on Population, Ministry of Health & Family Welfare.

decline. Additionally, compared to Indian average, *death rate is higher, and the life expectancy low at birth*. Net migration into the state is positive[13]. Data provides indirect support of social trends such as emigration, influx of labour from other states, in particular from UP, preference for fewer children, and drug misuse.

Present and Projected Population of India vis-à-vis Punjab is presented in Table 1.1.

Table 1. 1 Present and Projected Population of India vis-à-vis Punjab ('000) (m=millions)

Year	India	Punjab	Punjab as Percent of India's Population
2011	1210855 (121.09 crores/1210m)	27743 (2.77crores/27.7m)	2.29
2016	1291074 (129.10 crores/1291m)	29140 (2.91crores/29.1m)	2.25
2021	1363006 (136.30 crores/1363 m)	30339 (3.03crores/30.3m)	2.23
2026	1425908 (142.59 crores/1426m)	31318 (3.13crores/31.3m)	2.20
2031	1478775 (147.88 crores/1479m)	32087 (3.21crores/32.1m)	2.17

---

[13] Migration rate is positive when more people settle into the state than those who leave the state. European Commission defines Migration as "Movement of a person either across an international border (international migration), or within a state (internal migration) for more than one year irrespective of the causes, voluntary or involuntary, and the means, regular or irregular, used to migrate" https://ec.europa.eu/home-affairs/pages/glossary/migration_en (Accessed 11-4-2022).
In the case of Punjab, the Migration into the state is inter-state i.e., between the states – mostly from UP and Bihar.

2036	1522288 (152.22 crores/1522m)	32658 (3.27crores/32.7m)	2.15

Source: Govt of India (2020). Census of India 2011. Population Projections for India and States 2011-2036. Report of the Technical Group.

A crucial indicator of population growth is the fertility rate. If the fertility rate is at the replacement level, population remains stable i.e., it is neither growing nor declining. If the fertility rate is above the replacement level, it causes population to grow; if it is below the replacement level, it causes population to shrink. Assuming no net migration and unchanged mortality, a total fertility rate of 2.1 children per woman ensures a broadly stable population (OECD)[14].

Projected fertility rates of India vis-à-vis Punjab (in brackets) are as follows:

2011-15	India	2.37	(Punjab 1.73)
2016-20	India	2.13	(Punjab 1.60)
2021-25	India	1.94	(Punjab 1.53)
2026-30	India	1.81	(Punjab 1.51)
2031-35	India	1.73	(Punjab 1.50)

Another important piece of statistics related to demographic trends is the *Crude Birth Rate (CBR)* and *Crude Death Rate (CDR)* defined as people born and died in a year per 1000 population. Data related to these measures for India and Punjab (in brackets) is as follows:

2011-15	India	CBR	20.1	(Punjab 14.7)
	India	CDR	7.2	(Punjab 6.8)
2016-20	India	CBR	17.9	(Punjab 13.3)

14 https://data.oecd.org/pop/fertility-rates.htm (Retrieved 21-10-2021).

	India	CDR	7.1	(Punjab 7.2)
2021-25	India	CBR	16.0	(Punjab 11.9)
	India	CDR	7.0	(Punjab 7.5)
2026-30	India	CBR	14.4	(Punjab 10.8)
	India	CDR	7.1	(Punjab 7.9)
2031-35	India	CBR	13.1	(Punjab 9.9)
	India	CDR	7.3	(Punjab 8.4)

Present and projected level of *expectation of life at birth* in India in 2011-15 was 66.9 years for males and 70 years for females; this is expected to go up in 2031-35 to 71.2 years for males and 74.7 years for females. Corresponding figures for Punjab in 2011-15 are 70.3 years for males and 74.2 years for females, which is expected to go up to be 73.2 years for males and 77.6 years for females.

Present and projected *net migration rate* (per 100) into Punjab has been forecast to be consistently positive throughout the period 2011-2035; this rate is expected to be 0.22 for males and 0.18 for females in 2031-35. With a projected population of 3.21 crores in 2031, Punjab can expect net migration of about 7 lac males and 5.75 lac females in Punjab. Interestingly, owing to migration of labour into Punjab from mostly Uttar Pradesh, the net migration rate in Uttar Pradesh is consistently negative for the same period standing at -0.24 for males and -0.17 for females[15].

---

[15]

file:///C:/Users/singh/OneDrive/Desktop/Population_Projections_for_India_and_States_2011-2036.pdf (Table 7 p. 42) (Accessed 2-5-2022)

Punjab in the Context of Indian Topography

Ancient Punjab was the primary geographical extent of the Indus Valley Civilisation (also known as the Harappan Civilisation) which is deemed to be one of oldest civilisations that thrived along the Indus River. The Indus Valley Civilisation, lasted from 3300 BC to 1300 BC, and in its mature phase, from 2600 BC to 1900 BC (Fig 1.4)[16]. Counting backwards from present times, Indus Valley Civilisation is over 5000 years old.

Indus river, which is 2900 km (1800m) long, originates in Western Tibet, flows northwest through the Ladakh region of India and Pakistan, before emptying into the Arabian sea[17]. The name Indus has its origin in the Sanskrit word *Sindhu* meaning a stream. Country 'India' also has its origin to this name.

India's frontier bordered by six countries (China, Pakistan, Myanmar, Afghanistan, Nepal and Bangladesh) is 15,168km (9,425m) long, of which 5,686 km i.e., 40% is coastline.

It is believed that the earliest trace of human habitation in Punjab began in Soan valley between the Indus and the Jhelum rivers. In addition to Indus, five rivers from which Punjab derives its name are Jhelum, Chenab, Ravi, Beas and Sutlej. Of these five snow-fed rivers that originate in the Himalayas, Jhelum (725km in length), Chenab (974km), and Ravi (725km) flow through both

---

[16] https://www.britannica.com/place/India/Agriculture-and-animal-husbandry (Retrieved 9-3-2022)

[17] As a perspective, African River Nile is the longest river in the world at 6650km (4132m), followed by Amazon River, which is 6,437km (4000m).

India and Pakistan. Beas (470km) flows only through the Indian part of the Punjab. Sutlej (1450km) flows through China, Pakistan, and India. Figure 1.5 shows flows and mergers of these rivers at some point. Area between the rivers is popularly known as *'Doabs'* (between two waters Do=two: abs=waters).

An Overview of Indian History Timeline

As stated previously, the Indus valley civilisation in its earliest form, and in its relatively modern form, began, respectively, in 3300 BC and 1900 BC. In its modern form, the civilisation mastered the art of handicrafts and the use of metals such as copper and bronze and had a well-developed system of urban planning. Vedic periods in which famous Indian classics (Mahabharata, Ramayana, Bhagavata-purana and others) were written began around 1500 BC ending in 600 BC. Spiritual teaching followed with Mahavira (c.599 BC-c.527BC) and Buddha (c563BC-c.486BC). Later periods were dominated by selected dynasties.

A dynasty is a series of rulers who are all from the same family, or a period when a country is ruled by them. Prominent dynasties in India were Nanda (in Ganges River valley: c.343BC - c.321BC); Mauryan (Most of India, barring present day Karnataka: c.321 BC-185 BC); Kushan (northern India and central Asia: 2nd century BC - 3rd century AD); Gupta (northern India: early 4th - late 6th century AD); Harsha (northern India: AD606 - AD647); Pallava (Tamil Nadu: early 4th - late 9th century AD); Western Chalukyas (western and central Deccan: AD543 - AD757); Eastern Chalukyas (Andhra Pradesh: c.AD624-c.AD1070); Pala (Bihar and Bengal: 8th century - 12th

century AD); Chola (Tamil Nadu: c.AD850–AD1279); Pandya (Tamil Nadu: 4th - 14th century AD)[18].

Prominent Muslim rule in India can be categorised as follows (all dates in AD): conquest of Sind (712); post-Muhammad Bin Qasim (715-1206); Ghaznavid dynasty (977-1186); Ghurid dynasty (mid-12th to the early 13th century). Beyond this, other prominent dynasties that have come to be known as 'Delhi Sultanate' (13th to the 16th century) and include the Slave dynasty[19] (1206-1290); Khilji dynasty (1290-1320); Tughlaq dynasty (1325–1351); Jaunpur Sultanate (1394-1479); Sayyid dynasty (1414-1451); and Lodī dynasty (1451-1526). Mughal empire dominated in various forms from 1526-1857 when it was taken over by the British crown (1858-1947)[20] (Encyclopaedia Britannica, 2005); (Robinson, 2007).

---

[18] https://www.britannica.com/biography/Gilbert-John-Elliot-Murray-Kynynmound-4th-earl-of-Minto (Retrieved 9-3-2022)
[19] So called because the kings had their origin in slavery.
[20] https://www.britannica.com/list/6-important-mughal-emperors (Retrieved 9-3-2022)

Figure 1. 4 Indus Valley Civilisation in its Mature Phase

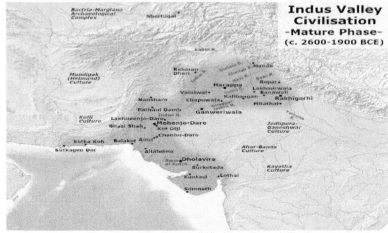

Figure 1. 5 Rivers and Doabs of Punjab

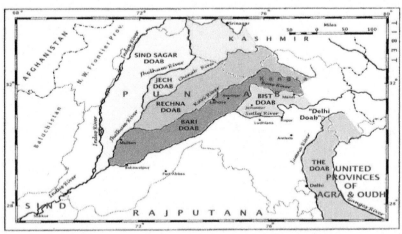

Foreign Raiders Within the Selected Timeline

In the literature it is generally accepted that Aryans who were Caucasians[21] came to India from Central Asia (which consists of Kazakhstan, Kyrgyzstan, Tajikistan, Turkmenistan, and Uzbekistan) where they had first settled on the Iranian plateau and later travelled to northern India and who greatly influenced Indus valley civilisation, Indian Vedic philosophy and thinking[22]. In Sanskrit terminology word *ārya* has come to mean a person of noble birth. After Aryans, Persian king Darius I (550BC-486BC) conquered and ruled over northern Punjab. He was followed by Alexander in 326BC[23].

Save for some pillaging expeditions in Tana (near the present Mumbai) as early as 637AD during the reign of caliph Omar, first concerted effort by Arabs was in 712AD (Lane-Poole, 1903, pp. 6-7) after which incursions into India never stopped for centuries[24]. Gupta (Gupta, 1984, p. 12) has estimated that since the close of the 10th century and up to the time of Guru Nanak (the first Guru of the Sikhs- born 1469), 61 invasions had taken place from the north-

---

21 Anthropologists use Caucasian to refer to someone from a racial grouping from Europe, North Africa, and western Asia.
22 This view, however, is questioned by some authors. See e.g., (Gautier, 2003).
23 Aryan name was originally used for people who spoke an archaic Indo-European languages and who were thought to have settled in prehistoric times in ancient Iran and the northern Indian continent (https://www.britannica.com/topic/Aryan).
[24] Stanley Lane-Poole (1854–1931), a British orientalist and archaeologist was Professor of Arabic at Trinity College, Dublin. In this author's opinion, his book 'Medieval India Under Mohammedan Rule (A.D. 712-1764)' (Lane-Poole, 1903) is a well-researched scholarly work which could be on a compulsory reading list in all high school history courses in India.

west. Table-1 lists these invasions. Invaders were of the Turkish, Afghan, Persian, or Mongol descent. Mughals originated in Central Asia and were descended from the Mongol ruler Jenghiz Khan and Timur (Tamburlaine), the great conqueror of Asia. The name Mughal or Moghul is the distorted Persian word for Mongol, the Central Asian tribe after whom Mongolia is named.

Table 1. 2 Invasions into India c10AD - c15AD

Raider	Number of Raids	Description
Alp-Tegin	01	Alp-Tegin (901-963) was a Turkish slave commander of the Samanid Empire (a Sunni Iranian empire from 819 to 999) which at its height encompassed modern-day Afghanistan, parts of Iran, Turkmenistan, Uzbekistan, Kyrgyzstan, Tajikistan, parts of Kazakhstan and Pakistan.
Sebüktigin	03	Abū Manṣūr Sebüktigin (942-997) once a Turkish slave, founder of the Ghaznavid dynasty, was the son-in-law of Alp-Tegin after whose death, Sebüktigin, as new ruler, expanded the kingdom up to present day Pakistan.
Maḥmūd Ghaznavi	17	Maḥmūd Ghaznavi (971-1030), son of Sebüktigin, was first independent ruler of the Turkic dynasty of Ghaznavids. At the time of his death in 1030,

		his kingdom had become an extensive military empire, which extended to all the way eastward into Punjab.
Shihab-ud-din Ghauri	10	Shihab-ud-din Ghauri (1149-1206), was the sultan of the Ghurid Empire. He laid the foundation of Muslim rule in the Indian subcontinent, which lasted for several centuries.
Mongols	25	Mongol Empire launched several invasions into the Indian subcontinent from 1221 to 1327; many of the later raids made by the unruly Qaraunas of Mongol origin; Mongols subjugated Kashmir as a vassal* state and occupied most of modern Pakistan and Punjab for decades. Dynastic ruler in India with lineage related to Mongols (cf. Figure 1.8). *a holder of land by feudal tenure on conditions of homage and allegiance.
Babur	05	Born Zahīr ud-Dīn Muhammad, Babur was the founder of the Mughal Empire in India. He was a descendant of Timur and Genghis Khan through his father and mother respectively. (cf. Figure 1.8)
Total	61	--

Sources: (a) Based on (Gupta, 1984) footnote on p1; (b) (Lane-Poole, 1903); (c) https://www.britannica.com/place/Punjab-state-India (d) Wikipedia various sites; (e)

(Sarkar, 1932-1938); (f) (Majumdar, 2018); (g) (Thapar, 2002). (h) (Hunter, 1907); (i) https://military-history.fandom.com/wiki/Mongol_invasions_of_India.

An Overview of Afghan and Mughal Empires

In 1526, Babur crossed the *Khyber Pass* and decisively defeated the forces of the Delhi sultan Ibrāhīm Lodī at the First Battle of Panipat. The very next year in 1527 he defeated the Rajput confederacy under Rana Sanga of Mewar, and in 1529 defeated the remnants of the Delhi sultanates. By 1530 when he died, the Mughal Empire had encompassed almost all of Northern India.

Babur's son Humayun who reigned from 1530 to 1556 (and 1555-56) was followed by Akbar from 1556-1605. Akbar's son Jahāngīr (1605-1627) further consolidated the Mughal Empire through conquest. Jahāngīr's (born Salim) son Shah Jahan (famous for building the Taj Mahal) reigned 1628-1658. Shah Jahan's son Aurangzeb, known for his religious intolerance, reigned from 1658 to 1707.

Several Mughal emperors penned or recorded an account of their rule in India [cf. e.g., (Abu-l-Fazl, 2002); (Thackston, 2002); (Jahangir, c.1622); (Khan , 1990)]. Some interesting and candid accounts of Mughal rule in India also exist (Badauni, c.1590-1615). During the reign of Muḥammad Shah, 1719-48, the empire began to decline (see below), accelerated by warfare and rivalries, and after Muḥammad Shaha's death in 1748, the reign passed to Marathas (1785) and then to the British (1803). The last of the Mughal emperor, Bahādur Shah II who ruled from 1837-57 was exiled to Burma by the British who took over the command of India in 1858.

Route Invaders Took to Invade India

Portuguese, the earliest entrants into India came in 1498 with the arrival of Vasco da Gama at Calicut (present day Kozhikode, Kerala). French arrived in 1673 at Chandan Nagar in, the then, Calcutta. The British first landed at the port of Surat in 1608 for the purpose of trade. All these entrants into India came via the sea route. Contrary to this, all Muslim invaders came into India via the land route through Afghanistan which then bordered unpartitioned India.

In 1893 British civil servant Mortimer Durand reached an agreement with Afghan Emir and drew a line demarcating the boundary between Afghanistan and India. This 1660-mile-long border division between Afghanistan and India (now Pakistan) has since come to be known as 'The Durand Line'. This line dividing the boundaries of the two countries has always been controversial, as also, is half of the Pashtu homeland that came to the side of, the then India, and half remained in Afghanistan.

Present day Afghanistan is a landlocked country that shares its boundaries with Iran, Turkmenistan, Uzbekistan, Tajikistan, and China, along with Pakistan with whom it is has the longest border. Afghanistan enjoys natural mountain barriers with Pakistan, India, China, and Tajikistan whereas borders with Uzbekistan, Turkmenistan, and Iran do not have mountain barriers. The border with Pakistan cuts through some of the roughest terrains and is not manned very effectively. As a result, the border remains a hub of drugs smuggling, illegal migration, and terrorism; skirmishes between the army personnel of two countries are not uncommon.

In addition to the unofficial border crossing points, there are also a few official border crossings[25]. Two important such crossings are *Bolan Pass* in the southern side of the border and the *Khyber Pass* in the northern side. *These passes are the routes taken by invaders throughout the history.* Both passes are 600km apart (Fig 1.6). Bolan Pass is 60 miles in length and 6000 feet high at places. It originates at Rindli in Afghanistan and ends at Darwāza near Kolpur (Balochistan) in Pakistan. In 1897 in a great feat of engineering the British built a railway track that originates in Sibi in Afghanistan and ends in Quetta in Pakistan. *Khyber Pass* is 33 miles long; it originates at Landi Kotal in Afghanistan and ends at Jamrud in Pakistan. Khyber railway, a 58km track opened in 1925 by the British is presently non-functional owing to lack of interest in maintaining it.

In 1748, the Afghan king Ahmad Shah Durrani invaded India via the Bolan Pass and the *Khyber Pass*. In 326BC Alexander the Great marched his army through the *Khyber Pass* in his invasion of India. Babur the founder of Mughal Empire in India also came through *Khyber Pass.* During the times of the Kushan Empire the Pass became a key trade and migration route between India and China. 'The Silk Road', as it was then known, became the major thoroughfare for the movement of people and goods such

---

25 There are six official border crossings and trade terminals between Afghanistan and Pakistan: Angur Adda, between Wana and Ghazni, is a border crossing used only for border trade. Chaman, between Quetta and Kandahar, is border crossing station which is used for both border trade and border crossings. Between Ghulam Khan, Miramshah and Khost, (north Waziristan) which is mainly used for border trade. Torkham, between Peshawar and Jalalabad, is a major border crossing. Kharlachi: on July 2020 Pakistan announced reopening of Kharlachi border crossing with Afghanistan for bilateral border trade. Badini Trade Terminal, opened in 2020 is for bilateral border trade. (Source: Wikipedia various sites).

as wool and cotton. Invaders with waves of plundering forays into India mostly came through the *Khyber Pass.* Both the passes complement each other - *Khyber Pass* is located to the north side of the border and Bolan Pass to the

Figure 1. 6 Locations of Khyber Pass and Bolan Pass

Source:http://www.allempires.com/article/index.php?q=First_Afghan_War_-_Part_One
(Retrieved 5-1-2022: map truncated by author)

Figure 1. 7 Topography of Khyber Pass

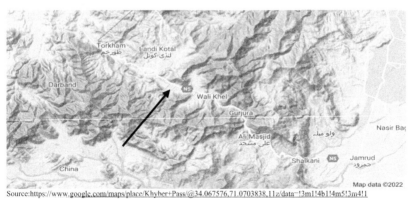

Source:https://www.google.com/maps/place/Khyber+Pass/@34.067576,71.0703838,11z/data=!3m1!4b1!4m5!3m4!1
s0x38d90a93fe057a9b:0xf329767ca6afbbd5!8m2!3d34.0941356!4d71.1574839!5m1!1e4 (Retrieved: 12-3-2022)

south side. A peep into the actions on the *Khyber Pass* can be had from the following passage (from the Imperial Gazette of India 1908):

"The Khyber has always been one of the gateways into India. Alexander of Macedon probably sent a division under Hephaistion and Perdiccas through the Khyber, while he himself followed the northern bank of the Kabul river, and thence crossed the Kunar valley into Bajaur and Swat. Mahmud of Ghazni only once used the Khyber route, when he marched to encounter Jaipal in the Peshawar valley. The Mughal emperors Babar and Humayun each traversed it more than once. Nadir Shah, advancing by it to attack Nasir Khan, Subahdar of Kabul under the Mughal government, was opposed by the Pathans; but he led his cavalry through Bazar, took Nasir Khan completely by surprise, and overthrew him near Jamrud. Ahmad Shah Durrani and his grandson Shah Zaman, in their invasions of the Punjab, also followed the Khyber route on several occasions."

"The Mughal emperors attached great importance to the control of the Khyber, but were singularly unsuccessful in their attempts to keep the route open. Then, as now, it was held by the Afridi Pathans, a race implacably hostile to the Mughals. Jalalabad, first fortified by Humayun in 1552, was further strengthened by his son Jalal-ud-dln Akbar, after whom it was named; and the latter emperor so improved the road that wheeled carriages could traverse it with ease. But even in his reign the Khyber was infested by the Roshania sectaries, who wielded great influence over the Afghan tribes; and the Rajput general Man Singh had to force the pass in 1586, when Akbar desired to secure possession of Kabul on the death of his brother Mirza Muhammad Hakim. In 1672, under Aurangzeb, the tribes waylaid the Subahdar of Kabul, Muhammad Amin Khan, in the pass, and annihilated his army of 40,000 men, capturing all his treasure, elephants, women, and children."

"The first British advance into the Khyber was in 1839, when Captain Wade was deputed to conduct Shahzada Timur to Kabul via Peshawar, while his father Shah Shuja was escorted thither by the army of the Indus via the Bolan Pass and Kandahar. During the first Afghan

War the Khyber was the scene of many skirmishes with the Afrldis and of some disasters to our troops. Captain Wade, with from 10,000 to 11,000 of all arms, including the Sikh contingent, moved from Jamrud on July 22, 1839, to Gagri; here he halted a day and entrenched his position; on July 24 he again marched to Lala China; on the 25th he moved to the attack of Ali Masjid, sending a column of 600 men and 2 guns, under Lieutenant Mackeson, to the right, and 11 companies of infantry, one 6-pounder gun, and one howitzer to the left, while below a column was placed to watch the mouth of Shadi Bagadi gorge. Both columns drove the enemy before them, the right meeting with some opposition, and the left getting into a position to shell the fort. On the 26th all the enemy's outposts were driven in, and on the 27th they evacuated the fort. The enemy had 509 jazailchis, or musket-men, and were supported by several hundred Afridis. The British loss was 22 killed and 158 wounded. After this there was no further opposition."

Source: The Imperial Gazette of India. 1908. Vol. XV. Karachi to Kotayam p.299-303.
http://www.sanipanhwar.com/The%20Imperial%20Gazetteer%20of%20India%20Volume%20XV.pdf (Retrieved 27-6-2021).

Brutality and Religious Persecution by Invaders

Bitterness that lingers on till this day between the Hindus and the Mohammedans has its roots in the brutal forays and persecutions by Afghan, Persian, and Mughal invaders between 10th and 15th century AD. Brutality is a conscious or unconscious behaviour that is cruel and violent showing no humane feelings and guilt for others. Religious persecution is a deliberate act of aggression towards a single person or a group owing to their different beliefs in religion other than those of the persecutor. Raiders that came into India had both the traits of brutality and religious persecution. By the time the Mughal Empire went into decline with the demise of Aurangzeb, Mughals were ruling almost all of India (cf. Fig 1.5).

Historian Gupta (Gupta, 1984), based on a range of original sources, gives graphic accounts of the brutality and persecution of Hindus by invaders; destruction caused by raiders such as Timur (1398-99) included ruinous demolition of cities and mass execution of Hindus (executing in one instance 10,000 captive Hindu men, women, children). In Timur's own words we get an insight into his fanatic approach in the following passage from his memoirs (Timur, 1830, pp. 14-15):

> ".....Another of the proofs of Divine aid which I received, was this, Syed Mahmud Gesuderaz waited on me, and congratulated me that Amyr Syed Aly Hamdany (another Saint) had deputed him to tell me, that the Holy Prophet had taken in under his care and protection, in order that I might propagate the faith of Islam in the extensive region of India: on receipt of this message, I bound up my loins in the service of Amyr Syed Aly, because previous to this time while I was at Samerkand, he had used very harsh expressions towards me, which had very much affected me, but for which he afterwards apologized. I was however afraid that he was still incensed against me, till I received this message, when I was convinced that these people (the Saints) do not harbour malice, I therefore recovered my spirits."

> "Soon after this notice, I began to destroy the temples of India, and to give currency to the Muhammedan religion in that country; when I destroyed the temple of Kukel, which was one of the greatest in that region, I broke the images with my own hands, previous to which the Brahmans brought me several loads of gold, and requested me to spare their gods; I said to them, I will break your gods, to give them an opportunity of performing a miracle by healing themselves. "Amongst the images, was one the size of a man, which they begged

me not to break, and even threatened me with his vengeance, saying, "amongst the miracles, which the original of this performed, was, his getting sixteen hundred women with child in one night." I replied," the cursed Satan debauches several thousands of persons in a very short period; therefore, this miracle is of no weight." Another extraordinary circumstance was this; whenever I undertook anything, I cared not whether it was deemed a lucky or an unlucky hour, but placing my faith on God, I commenced it, yet the Astrologers always affirmed that whatever I had undertaken, the hour had been propitious for the event."

Not only soldiers were encouraged but effectively ordered to do so, failing which they themselves could be executed. During his campaign in India Timur describes the scene when his army conquered the Indian city of Delhi (Gupta, 1984, pp. 11-38):

"In a short space of time all the people in the [Delhi] fort were put to the sword, and in the course of one hour the heads of 10,000 infidels were cut off. The sword of Islam was washed in the blood of the infidels, and all the goods and effects, the treasure and the grain which for many a long year had been stored in the fort became the spoil of my soldiers." "They set fire to the houses and reduced them to ashes, and they razed the buildings and the fort to the ground....All these infidel Hindus were slain, their women and children, and their property and goods became the spoil of the victors. I proclaimed throughout the camp that every man who had infidel prisoners should put them to death and whoever neglected to do so should himself be executed and his property given to the informer. When this order became known to the ghazis of Islam, they drew their swords and put their prisoners to death." (Timur, 1830).

Koenraad Elst[26] the Belgian scholar has compared the execution and slavery of Hindus to the Holocaust:

> "Hindus too experienced this treatment at the hands of Islamic conquerors, e.g., when Mohammed bin Qasim conquered the lower Indus basin in 712 CE. Thus, in Multan, according to the Chach-Nama, "six thousand warriors were put to death, and all their relations and dependents were taken as slaves." This is why Rajput women committed mass suicide to save their honour in the face of the imminent entry of victorious Muslim armies, e.g., 8,000 women immolated themselves during Akbar's capture of Chittorgarh in 1568 (where this most enlightened ruler also killed 30,000 non-combatants). During the Partition pogroms and the East Bengali genocide, mass rape of Hindu women after the slaughter of their fathers and husbands was a frequent event."

William Durant[27] (Durant, 1935, pp. 694-699) drawing on a number of sources has devoted a section on the massacres, loot, and pillage in India in his book which is painfully illuminating and worth reproducing here (paragraphing and italics are this author's):

> *"The Mohammedan Conquest of India is probably the bloodiest story in history. It is a discouraging tale, for its evident moral is that civilization is a precarious thing, whose delicate complex of order and liberty, culture and peace may at any time be overthrown by barbarians invading from without or multiplying within."*

26https://www.raoulwallenberg.net/news/was-there-an-islamic-%E2%80%9Cgenocide%E2%80%9D-of-hindus/

[27] William Durant (1885-1981) a Pulitzer Prize, and Presidential Medal of Freedom winner, was an American historian and philosopher best known for his 11-volume work 'The Story of Civilisation' written in collaboration with his wife Ariel Durant.

"The Hindus had allowed their strength to be wasted in internal division and war; they had adopted religions like Buddhism and Jainism, which unnerved them for the tasks of life; they had failed to organize their forces for the protection of their frontiers and their capitals, their wealth and their freedom, from the hordes of Scythians, Huns, Afghans and Turks hovering about India's boundaries and waiting for national weakness to let them in."

"For four hundred years (600-1000 A.D.) India invited conquest; and at last it came. The first Moslem attack was a passing raid upon Multan, in the western Punjab (664 A.D.) Similar raids occurred at the convenience of the invaders during the next three centuries, with the result that the Moslems established themselves in the Indus valley about the same time that their Arab co-religionists in the West were fighting the battle of Tours (732 A.D.) for the mastery of Europe."

"But the real Moslem conquest of India did not come till the turn of the first millennium after Christ. In the year 997 a Turkish chieftain by the name of Mahmud became sultan of the little state of Ghazni, in eastern Afghanistan. Mahmud knew that his throne was young and poor, and saw that India, across the border, was old and rich; the conclusion was obvious. Pretending a holy zeal for destroying Hindu idolatry, he swept across the frontier with a force inspired by a pious aspiration for booty. *He met the unprepared Hindus at Bhimnagar, slaughtered them, pillaged their cities, destroyed their temples, and carried away the accumulated treasures of centuries.* Returning to Ghazni he astonished the ambassadors of foreign powers by displaying "jewels and unbored pearls and rubies shining like sparks, or like wine congealed with ice, and emeralds like fresh

(Contd. on p67)

Figure 1. 8 Mughal Empire in India

Timur (1336-1405)   Genghis Khan (c.1155-1227)

Umar Sheikh Mirza the **father of Babur** has lineage going back to Timur Gurkani a Turco-Mongol conqueror who founded Timurid empire in and around modern-day Afghanistan, Iran, and central Asia.	Qutlugh Khanum the **mother of Babur** has lineage back to Genghis Khan the founder and emperor of the Mongol empire

BABUR defeated Ibrahim Lodī in battle of Panipat in 1526 marking the beginning of Mughal Empire in India. Lived 1483-1530: Ruled 1526-1530:   04 years

	Lived		
HUMAYUN	1508-1556	Ruled 1530-40; 1555-56	11 years
AKBAR	1542-1605	Ruled 1556-1605	49 years
JAHANGĪR (b. Salim)	1569-1627	Ruled 1605-1627	22 years
SHAH JAHAN	1592-1666	Ruled 1628-1658	30 years
AURANGZEB	1618-1707	Ruled 1658-1707	49 years
		Total	165 years

Mughal Empire began with several emperors and chieftains, Muslim and non-Muslims taking control of various parts of the country. After the death of Aurangzeb, his son Bahadur Shah I took control. After his death in 1712 chaotic situation resulted in four emperors ascending the throne between 1712 and 1719. Empire started to break up during Muhammad Shah's reign (1719-1748), followed by Shah Alam II (1759-1806) who unsuccessfully tried to reverse the tide of decline. By 1857 considerable part of India was under The British East India Company passing on to the British crown in 1858.

If we count the smooth years of the Mughal Empire from Babur to Aurangzeb (1526-1707: 165 years) and chaotic control from 1707-1857 (150 years) then the total time India remained under Mughal rule/influence adds up to 315 years.

Source: Compiled from various sources including Encyclopaedia Britannica.
https://en.wikipedia.org/wiki/Mughal-Mongol_genealogy
Photo sources: Timur: Forensic facial reconstruction by M. Gerasimov 1941.
Genghis Khan: simple English Wikipedia, the free encyclopaedia.

Figure 1. 9 India at the end of Akbar and Aurangzeb's Reign

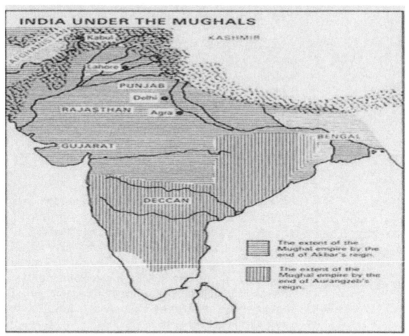

Source: http://www.vam.ac.uk/content/articles/a/the-age-of-the-mughals/ Retrieved 5-June-2021).

sprigs of myrtle, and diamonds in size and weight like pomegranates."

"Each winter Mahmud descended into India, filled his treasure chest with spoils, and amused his men with full freedom to pillage and kill; each spring he returned to his capital richer than before. At Mathura (on the Jumna) he took from the temple its statues of gold encrusted with precious stones, and emptied its coffers of a vast quantity of gold, silver and jewellery; he expressed his admiration for the architecture of the great shrine, judged that its duplication would cost one hundred million dinars and the labour of two hundred years, and then ordered it to be soaked with naphtha and burnt to the ground."

"Six years later he sacked another opulent city of northern India, Somnath, killed all its fifty thousand inhabitants, and dragged its wealth to Ghazni. In the end he became, perhaps, the richest king that history has ever known. Sometimes he spared the population of the ravaged cities, and took them home to be sold as slaves; but so great was the number of such captives that after some years no one could be found to offer more than a few shillings for a slave."

"Before every important engagement Mahmud knelt in prayer, and asked the blessing of God upon his arms. He reigned for a third of a century; and when he died, full of years and honours, Moslem historians ranked him as the greatest monarch of his time, and one of the greatest sovereigns of any age. Seeing the canonization that success had brought to this magnificent thief, other Moslem rulers profited by his example, though none succeeded in bettering his instruction."

"In 1186 the Ghuri, a Turkish tribe of Afghanistan, invaded India, captured the city of Delhi, destroyed its temples, confiscated its wealth, and settled down in its palaces to establish the Sultanate of Delhi - an alien despotism fastened upon northern India for three centuries, and checked only by assassination and revolt."

"The first of these bloody sultans, Kutb-d Din Aibak, was a normal specimen of his kind-fanatical, ferocious and merciless. His gifts, as the Mohammedan historian tells us, "were bestowed by hundreds of thousands, *and his slaughters likewise were by hundreds of thousands*." In one victory of this warrior (who had been purchased as a slave), "fifty thousand men came under the collar of slavery, and the plain became black as pitch with Hindus.""

"Another sultan, Balban, punished rebels and brigands by casting them under the feet of elephants, or removing their skins, stuffing these with straw, and hanging them from the gates of Delhi. When some Mongol inhabitants who had settled in Delhi, and had been converted to Islam, attempted a rising, Sultan Alau-d-din (the conquerer of Chitor) had all the males - from fifteen to thirty thousand of them - slaughtered in one day.""

"Sultan Muhammad bin Tughlak acquired the throne by murdering his father, became a great scholar and an elegant writer, dabbled in mathematics, physics and Greek philosophy, surpassed his predecessors in bloodshed and brutality, fed the flesh of a rebel nephew to the rebel's wife and children, ruined the country with reckless inflation, and laid it waste with pillage and murder till the inhabitants fled to the jungle. *He killed so many Hindus that, in the words of a Moslem historian, "there was constantly in front of his royal pavilion and his Civil Court a mound of dead bodies and a heap of corpses, while the sweepers and executioners were wearied out by their work of dragging"* the victims *"and putting them to death in crowds."*

"In order to find a new capital at Daulatabad he drove every inhabitant from Delhi and left it a desert; and hearing that a blind man had stayed behind in Delhi, he ordered him to be dragged from the old to the new

capital, so that only a leg remained of the wretch when
his last journey was finished."

"The Sultan complained that the people did not love
him, or recognize his undeviating justice. He ruled India
for a quarter of a century, and died in bed. *His
successor, Firoz Shah, invaded Bengal, offered a
reward for every Hindu head, paid for 180,000 of them,
raided Hindu villages for slaves*, and died at the ripe age
of eighty. Sultan Ahmad Shah feasted for three days
whenever the number of defenceless Hindus slain in his
territories in one day reached twenty thousand."

"These rulers were often men of ability, and their
followers were gifted with fierce courage and industry;
only so can we understand how they could have
maintained their rule among a hostile people so
overwhelmingly outnumbering them. All of them were
armed with a religion militaristic in operation, *but far
superior in its stoical monotheism to any of the popular
cults of India*; they concealed its attractiveness by
making the public exercise of the Hindu religions
illegal, and thereby driving them more deeply into the
Hindu soul."

"Some of these thirsty despots had culture as well as
ability; they patronized the arts, and engaged artists and
artisans - usually of Hindu origin - to build for them
magnificent mosques and tombs; some of them were
scholars, and delighted in converse with historians,
poets and scientists. One of the greatest scholars of
Asia, Alberuni, accompanied Mahmud of Ghazni to
India, and wrote a scientific survey of India comparable
to Pliny's Natural History and Humboldt's Cosmos."

"The Moslem historians were almost as numerous as the
generals, and yielded nothing to them in the enjoyment
of bloodshed and war. *The Sultans drew from the people
every rupee of tribute that could be exacted by the
ancient art of taxation, as well as by straightforward
robbery;* but they stayed in India, spent their spoils in

India, and thereby turned them back into India's economic life."

"*Nevertheless, their terrorism and exploitation advanced that weakening of Hindu physique and morale which had been begun by an exhausting climate, an inadequate diet, political disunity, and pessimistic religions.*"

"The usual policy of the Sultans was clearly sketched by Alau-d-din, who required his advisers to draw up "rules and regulations for grinding down the Hindus, and for depriving them of that wealth and property which fosters disaffection and rebellion." Half of the gross produce of the soil was collected by the government; native rulers had taken one-sixth. "No Hindu," says a Moslem historian, "*could hold up his head, and in their houses no sign of gold or silver . . . or of any superfluity was to be seen. . . . Blows, confinement in the stocks, imprisonment and chains, were all employed to enforce payment.*"

"When one of his own advisers protested against this policy, Alau-d-din answered: "Oh, Doctor, thou art a learned man, but thou hast no experience; I am an unlettered man, but I have a great deal. Be assured, then, that the Hindus will never become submissive and obedient till they are reduced to poverty. I have therefore given orders that just sufficient shall be left to them from year to year of corn, milk and curds, but that they shall not be allowed to accumulate hoards and property."

"This is the secret of the political history of modern India. *Weakened by division, it succumbed to invaders; impoverished by invaders, it lost all power of resistance, and took refuge in supernatural consolations; it argued that both mastery and slavery were superficial delusions, and concluded that freedom of the body or the nation was hardly worth defending in so brief a life.*"

"The bitter lesson that may be drawn from this tragedy is that eternal vigilance is the price of civilization. A nation must love peace, but keep its powder dry."

Similar sentiments have been expressed by Gautier (Gautier, 2003), Danielou (Daniélou, 2003), and Persian historian Tārīkh-i Waṣṣāf[28] and Emperor Babur himself (Thackston, 2002).

Indian historian Lal (Lal, 1973) estimates that the Hindu population in India decreased between 60-80 million between AD1000 and AD1525, an extermination unparalleled in World history[29]. This slaughter of millions of people occurred over regular periods during many centuries of Arab, Afghan, Turkish and Mughal rule in India. Poole (Lane-Poole, 1903, pp. 3-4) has described the overall impact of Muslim invaders poignantly as follows (italics are author's):

"The population of India in the present day is over three hundred millions, and every sixth man is a Muslim. *Nine hundred years ago there were no Mohammedans east of the Indus; where there are now more than fifty millions*......for six centuries the Hindus submitted to the sovereignty of Mohammedan kings. When we speak of the Mohammedans as foreigners, we mean of course the original conquerors. The present Muslim population is almost as native as the Hindus themselves. The invaders consisted of armies of men, very few of whom brought their women with them. They married Hindu wives, and the mixed race thus formed intermarried

---

28 Tazjiyat-ul-Amsar wa Tajriyat ul Asar (cf. Feldherr, Andrew et al., (2012), The Oxford History of Historical Writing: Volume 2: 400-1400, p. 269).
29
https://ia801602.us.archive.org/21/items/in.ernet.dli.2015.129758/2015.12975 8.Growth-Of-Muslim-Population-In-Medieval-India-ad-1000-1800_text.pdf (Accessed 7-2-2022). Although Lal's bold work and painstakingly assembled, estimates have been criticised as unrealistic, given the scale of massacre they do not seem to be far-fetched though to this author.

further with the natives, and each generation became more and more Indian, Beside the Muslims descended from the successive armies of invaders and their native wives, a very large proportion of the Indian Muslims were and are native converts from Hinduism. It has been estimated that about fifty thousand Hindus 'turn Turk' annually"

Disintegration of Mughal Empire Owing to Excessive Greed and Cruelty

Synonymous dictionary terms for cruelty, in successively higher stages, are ruthless rulers, vicious rulers, bloodthirsty rulers, evil rulers, and fiendish rulers. To some readers descriptions of the greed and cruelty of the invaders to India may seem extreme and to the cynical, perhaps, far-fetched. In real life, however, it was probably much worse than described in the available texts. It was this excessive greed and cruelty that became the nemesis of the Mughal rule in India. This started with the entry of Nader Shah (1698-1747) the Iranian Shah of Iran who idolized Genghis Khan and Timur, and in real life tried to emulate their military prowess and cruelty. Nader Shah overthrew the Safavid dynasty, which had ruled Iran for over 200 years, and become Shah himself in 1736. In 1738 Nader Shah invaded India, the governance of which had been weakened after the death of Aurangzeb in 1707.

Aurangzeb died after a 49-year reign without declaring a crown prince. When Nader Shah invaded India, Muhammad Shah, the fourth son of Bahadur Shah I was the emperor, who reigned from 1719 to 1748[30]. At the time of

[30] Aurangzeb had 5 sons; eldest Sultan died young; second son was Muazzam; third son was Azam; fourth son was Akbar who rebelled against his father, fled to Persia where he died in 1704; fifth and youngest son was Kam Bakhsh. Azam

Nader Shah's invasion, the once powerful Mughal empire had already become weak and was facing threats from Sikhs and Marathas who were gradually expanding their territories. The news of Nader Shah entry into India after its victories over Ghazni, Kabul, Peshawar, Sindh and Lahore sent waves of consternation. Muhammad Shah scrambled an army of 300,000 men to confront Nader Shah. The battle that was fought at Karnal (now in Haryana state) in 1739 and despite being outnumbered by six to one, Nader Shah crushed the Mughal army. Mohammad Shah was captured, and Nader Shah entered Delhi to begin the loot. Dalrymple describes the massacre and loot graphically as follows: (Dalrymple, 2020, p. 42):

> "On 29 March, a week after Nader Shah's forces had entered the Mughal capital, a news writer for the Dutch VOC[31] sent a report in which he described Nader Shah's bloody massacre of the people of Delhi: 'the Iranians have behaved like animals, 'he wrote. 'At least 100,000 people were killed. Nader Shah gave order to kill anyone who defended himself. As a result, it seemed as if it were raining blood, for the drains were streaming with it.[32]' Ghulam Hussain Khan recorded how, 'in an instant soldiers getting on tops of the houses commenced killing, slaughtering and plundering people's properties, and carrying away their wives and daughters. Numbers of houses were set on fire and ruined'[33]. "In addition to those killed, many Delhi

---

and Kam Bakhsh died during the struggle for succession. Second son Muazzam succeeded his father in 1707 under the title Bahadur Shah I; also known as Shah Alam.

[31] Stands for The Vereenigde Oostindische Compagnie (VOC), commonly known as the Dutch East India Company which was set up in 1602 with HQ in Amsterdam.

[32] Floor, 'New Facts on Nader Shah's Indian Campaign', p217 (as quoted in Dalrymple, 2020, p.419).

[33] Ghulam Hussain Khan, *Seir Mutaqherin,* vol I, pp315-17 (as quoted in Dalrymple, 2020, p.419).

women were enslaved. The entire quarter around the Jama Masjid was gutted."

" There was little armed resistance: 'The Persians laid violent hands on everything and everybody; cloths, jewels, dishes of gold and silver were all acceptable spoil,' wrote Anand Ram Mukhlis, who watched the destruction from his rooftop, 'resolving to fight to death if necessary…..For a long time after, the streets remained strewn with corpses, as the walks of a garden are with dead flowers and leaves. The town was reduced to ashes and had the appearance of plain consumed with fire. The ruins of its beautiful streets and buildings was such that the labour of the years could alone restore the city to its former state of grandeur'[34]. "The French Jesuits recorded that fires raged across the city for eight days and destroyed two of their churches. The massacre continued until Nizam went bareheaded, his hands tied with his turban, and begged Nader on his knees to spare the inhabitants and instead to take revenge on him. Nader Shah ordered his troops to stop the killings: they obeyed immediately. He did so, however, on the condition that the Nizam would give him 100 crores (1 billion rupees) before he would agree to leave Delhi. "The robbing, torture and plundering still continuous,' noted a Dutch observer, but not thankfully, the killings[35]."

Dalrymple describes further in vivid details how the already beleaguered populace were further forced to part with whatever valuables were left with them (Dalrymple, 2020, p. 43). "The military and the landed nobility of the Mughal state all contributed to the ransom money. Persians could not believe the riches that were offered to them in the days that followed – diamonds, gold, silver, pearls. Plunder

---

34 Mukhlis, Tazkira,' in Elliot and Dowson, *The History of India,* vol. VIII, p.87 (as quoted in Dalrymple, 2019, p.419).
35 Floor, 'New Facts on Nader Shah's Indian Campaign', p217 (as quoted in Dalrymple, 2020, p.419).

included the fabled Peacock Throne (which later served as a symbol of Iranian imperial might), troves of jewels, famous Koh-I-Noor diamond. The booty was loaded on 700 elephants, 4,000 camels, and 12,000 horses and taken back to Iran. "…in short the accumulated wealth of 348 years changed masters in a moment."

It is said that the plunder seized from India was so much that following his return Nader Shah stopped taxation in Iran for a period of three years. Nader also secured one of the Mughal emperor's daughters, Jahan Afruz Banu Begum, as a bride for his youngest son.

The impoverished Mughal Empire never fully recovered after the onslaught of Nader Shah and eventually succumbed to the British Raj via The East India Company. Tharoor has written a critical account of the British Raj in India (Tharoor, 2016). Sarkar (Sarkar, 1932-1938) in his 4-volume study 'Fall of Mughal Empire' written between 1932-1938 provides an angle of moral decadence and an insightful description of how the mighty Mughal Empire fell. Sarkar's following insight is worth noting[36]:

---

[36] The chaotic situation of the Mughal empire towards it ending years is also evident from a succession of rulers: Babur 1526–1530; Humayun (first reign)1530–1540; Humayun (second reign)1555–1556; Akbar 1556–1605; Jahāngīr1605–1627; Shahryar Mirza (de facto) 1627–1628; Shah Jahan 1628–1658; Alamgir I (Aurangzeb) 1658–1707; Muhammad Azam Shah 1707; Bahadur Shah I1 1707–1712; Jahandar Shah 1712–1713; Farrukhsiyar 1713–1719; Rafi ud-Darajat 1719; Shah Jahan II 1719; Muhammad Shah 1719–1748; Ahmad Shah Bahadur 1748–1754; Alamgir II 1754–1759; Shah Jahan III 1759–1760; Shah Alam II (first reign) 1760–1788; Shah Jahan IV 1788; Shah Alam II (second reign) 1788–1806; Akbar II 1806–1837; Bahadur Shah II 1837–1857 (source: Extracted from https://en.wikipedia.org/wiki/Humayun Accessed 10-2-2022).

"This book attempts to tell the full story of the actual fall of the Muslim empire which the Timurid prince Bābar had founded in India in 1526. The decline of that empire had, however, commenced nearly a century before the year 1738, from which this book starts. The first unperceived origin and the gradual spread of the moral decay has been studied by me in earlier works, to which the reader must turn if he wishes to learn how step by step the poison worked in the body politic of the Delhi empire. Outwardly the empire reached its zenith under Shāh Jahān (r. 1628–1658) but in this very reign its decline commenced (Sarkar, 1932-1938, p. 24)."

Legacy of Mughal Rule in India

As stated in box Figure 3.1, if we count the 'smooth years' of Mughal rule from Babur to Aurangzeb (1526-1707: 165 years) and 'chaotic control' (1707-1857: 150 years) then at a total of 315 years, the time India remained under Mughal rule and influence, adds up to about three and a quarter century. This is a lengthy period in which the Mughals left their mark on all aspects of Indian life - administration, education, language, cuisine, attire, etiquette, manners, theatre, art, infrastructure style of not only large monuments such as forts, palaces, parks, mausoleums, and mosques, but also the building designs of smaller and medium sized houses, many of which e.g., still have a dome shaped top. Mughal architecture made extensive use of red sandstone as a building material; 35km from Agra a city predominantly in red sandstone - Fatehpur Sikri built by Akbar[37]. Contribution of skilled Muslim

---

[37] The city was abandoned by Akbar in 1585. Reason for its abandonment is given as the failure of steady water supply. It has also been hypothesized that Akbar lost interest in it as it was built on his whim but when he was no longer resident there, he gradually lost interest in it (Petersen, 1999, p. 82).

craftsmen, artisans, and seamstresses (clothiers), continues till this day. No surprise therefore to find that the corner tailor shop in a locality is Muslim owned. A sizeable amount of international trade in arts and crafts have behind it the skills of Muslim craftsmen. A significant contribution of Muslim talent is in the Indian film industry where several well-known directors, actors, lyrists, musicians, script writers, and technicians have aided in providing seamless entertainment to the masses. Several well-known public figures and scholars have Muslim ancestry.

Possibly, the biggest of all influences, beginning with zero bases in mid-10th century AD, has been the formation of Islamic clusters - most visible of which was the erstwhile East Pakistan - now Bangladesh, and present-day state of Pakistan. The influence and communal harmony of these clusters touches all aspects of present day social, political, and economic aspects of India. It is sad to see hostilities between neighbours who have so much in common and some of the youngest and talented middle-class young work force whose energies can be harnessed for economic growth, and to alleviate the abject misery and poverty in both the countries. All that is required is to accept the past and move on. Atrocities meted by the invaders, and by both sides, during the partition of the country in 1947 are agonizing but can be understood in the context of their time. As Danish theologian and philosopher Soren Kierkegaard (1813-1855) has famously said 'life can only be understood backwards; but it must be lived forwards'.

Concluding the discussion in this section, it is challenging to measure in money terms the positive impact of such a vast volume of Mughal influence on Indian economy. It can only be imagined and conjectured. As an example, a monument such as the Taj Mahal with 6 million visitors a year generates a sizeable amount of employment and revenue. The forward and backward linkages of monuments scattered all over the country, giving boost to the tourism industry, can only be envisioned, and possibly, with some effort, calculated; 300,000 mosques in India also generate considerable employment. Then there are massive intangible contributions in the entertainment industry also colleges and universities which employ a mix of highly talented teachers. Armed forces now have the most loyal of recruits from both communities.

Lives of communities are so much intertwined owing to the revolution in telecommunications and social media, that with all the exposure to the outside world, it is challenging at an individual level not to be secular in thinking and approach. In this author's opinion, people, not only in this part of the world, but around the world as well, have had enough of the past miseries and are ready and willing to move on. No religion teaches bad - it is how we interpret the message in our holy scriptures, matters and is important.

Chapter Summary

This chapter was aimed at providing the reader with an overview of Indian and Punjab history. North-western part of India where Punjab is located had been in the firing line of invaders for centuries. These invasions have been especially brutal in their ferocity of loot, massacres, abduction, slavery, and all the ills that were meted out by the invading forces. The repeated invasions have left their mark on the culture, demography, language, cuisine, mentality, and physical make-up of the people owing to cross-breeding that increasingly occurred on a larger scale over the centuries of incursions than perhaps can be imagined.

Until the invasions began to take place from the mid AD 10th century onwards, India had been shielded by the sea in the south and mountains in the north, until a viable inlet in the *Khyber Passage* (from Afghanistan) was found and successfully exploited by the raiders. With the repeated incursions, India gradually became a melting hotpot of cross-culture mix, which happened partly by natural evolutionary process, but largely by coercion following the zeal of invaders to destroy sacred places of worship and conversion to Islam. It was only much later when the raiders settled and not return with their loot that the architectural monuments started to emerge, roads got built, and a taxation system put in place - i.e., some of the positives of incursions began to emerge. Cynics could argue that infrastructure, such as the roads which were put in place, were meant to facilitate the transportation process and forts were erected for security purposes; magnificent monuments and memorials such as the famous Taj Mahal were built to fulfil emperors' egos. Either way, a rich legacy has been left behind.

We shall see in the next chapter how the invasions had a deep and long-lasting impact on Sikh psyche and development of the Sikh religion. It is remarkable that the Sikh religion emerged as a peaceful religion out of this milieu, but a religion that also justifies the use of arms for righteous purposes.

Following summary lists further key points of this opening chapter.

1. The Indus valley civilisation which is among the oldest in the world prospered in the western flanks

of India around the river Indus. Erstwhile Punjab region was an integral part of this civilisation.

2. Punjab in its present form is among the prosperous states in India and owes its prosperity to the resourcefulness of its people who made good of the rich fertile land and irrigation facilitated by the snow-fed five rivers - Jhelum, Chenab, Ravi, Beas and Sutlej from which it also derives its name.

3. Presently, Punjab state in which Sikhs predominantly reside account for 20.9 million (1.72%) of India's population. Compared to all India figures, Punjab has a low fertility rate and higher death rate - a trend, if it continues, is bound to have an adverse impact on the demography of Punjab.

4. Being on the border of Afghanistan, Punjab bore the brunt of successive waves of Persian, Afghan, and Mughal invasions - 61 in total.

5. There were no Mohammedans in India prior to mid-AD 10th century. The Muslim population swelled *in Punjab* owing to forced conversions and cross marriages - so much so that in 1881 it had reached 47.6%, rising to 53.2% in 1941 (cf. Ch-2). In 2020, estimates put the Muslim population *in India* at 200 million (app. 15% of India's population). This is the world's third-largest cluster of Mohammedans (after Indonesia and Pakistan).

6. There are a few rough-terrain routes that invaders could have taken to enter India. Of these, one that was favoured by the raiders was the *Khyber Pass*

located in the northwest frontier. It is, in present times, a 33 miles long pass that connects Afghanistan and Pakistan.

7. In the beginning invaders came for the riches of India and were brutal in extracting these riches and also persecuting its people for their religious beliefs.

8. The brutality of looting and mass massacre executed by Persian king Nader Shah in 1738 surpassed all previous invasions and bankrupted the country laying the foundation of the decline of Mughal rule in India.

9. The beleaguered country after the loot and massacre left behind by Nader Shah resulted in a century of destabilisation in which rulers came and went paving the way for The East India Company (EIC) to make inroads into India and eventually its taking over by the British crown in 1858.

10. A painful past it may be owing to raiders meting out their brutality and the later partition of the country - he tangible and intangible contribution Mohammedans in almost all spheres of Indian society - political, economic, social is significant. It is high time for the Governments and people in both the countries to move on to a peaceful co-existence for the prosperity of the region. The massive defence budget of both the countries can be reduced and funds utilized for the welfare of people.

**

CHAPTER 2 EVOLUTION OF SIKHS UNDER 10 GURUS

Without a Guru none can cross
over to the other shore
(Guru Nanak)

Introduction

In order for us to understand and appreciate Sikh ethos, values, culture, and way of life dictated by their 10 Gurus and embodied in their holy Scripture, affectionately addressed by Sikhs as *Guru Granth Sahib*[38] it is essential to have, at least, an elementary grasp of Sikh history and the lives of Sikh's 10 Gurus, each of whom had his unique strengths and made a mark on the growth of the Sikh religion. This chapter focuses on these issues. The philosophy aspect of the Sikh religion is taken up in later chapters.

The Beginning

In chapter 1 we saw that Muslims had started to invade India from AD 712 onwards, with Babur in 1483 establishing an empire, with the intention to stay and rule over India. Muslim rulers were dislodged by the English when The East India Company established its hold on India

---

[38] As stated elsewhere, Granth is commonly understood as a hefty book of sacred writings; word 'Sahib' meaning 'Master' is added as a mark of respect,

in 1757. The beginning of Sikhs as a distinct community can be placed at year 1469 with the birth of their first Guru - Guru Nanak who began to instil a set of moral and ethical values in his devotees[39]. The separate identity in its purest form that Sikhs have today came much later, and was granted to them by their 10th Guru, Guru Gobind Singh in 1699- some 330 years later[40]. A distinct mark of this identity is the colourful *turbans* Sikhs wear; *untrimmed head and facial (moustache and beard) hairs*; a *dagger* which they are allowed to wear freely in their home state Punjab (in India); an iron or steel *bracelet*; a *long drawer* that reaches just below the knees; a small *comb* tucked in the turban behind knotted hair.

The logic behind the five identity features of Sikhs is as follows. Uncut hairs are in recognition of the nature that has created human beings as such; dagger signifies defence for self and the weak; bracelet signifies infiniteness of God's existence; long drawer implies chastity – this garment was also practical under the long-flowing top worn by warriors riding horses in olden times; use of comb is to help keep hairs tidy. Turbans are commonly worn by men in India in several states (in some states such as in Rajasthan) as a sign of regality. In the case of Sikhs, in addition to a regal feel, the turban keeps uncut knotted hairs on the head covered in a tidy fashion; turban also shield the head from extreme heat and cold. A devout Amritdhari Sikh follows this outfit, and also a written code of conduct (cf.

---

[39] Morality and ethics distinguish between 'good and bad' or 'right and wrong'. Morality is personal and normative i.e.it relates to a *standard* of behaviour of a person or a community. Ethics refers to *measures* of 'good and bad'. In day-to-day parlance, these terms are sometimes used interchangeably.

[40] Dhavan (Dhavan, 2011) describes the growth of Sikhs from their humble beginnings to Samurai like warriors they became – at one point establishing their own empire.

Ch-6 Appendix). No wonder Mountstuart Elphinstone (1779-1859), the Scottish statesman and historian who served in India on behalf of the British described Sikh religion in the following words "….the Sikhs have founded a sect involving such great innovations, that it may almost be regarded as a new religion (Elphinstone, 2014, p. 143)."

Sikh Population in Context

Table 2.1 represents the religious composition *of the Punjab* in ten-year intervals from 1881-1941. This table highlights some significant features. First, by the time of the 1881 census, the whole of Punjab could be neatly divided into four religious categories - Muslims, Hindus, Sikhs, and Christians. Second, the Muslim population *in Punjab* gradually increased from zero in 1027 to 47.6% of the total population in 1881, to a further 53.2% in 1941. In this period, the Hindu population declined from 43.8% to 29.1%. During this period, the growing popularity of Sikhs took their share in total population from 8.2% to 14.9% of the total; Christian population also gained momentum from being 0.1% of the total in 1881 to 1.5% of the total in 1941.

Some idea of Sikh population *at national level* in those times can be had from the following figures. To get a snapshot of real data, let us consider the data for the 1891 census when the total population of India was estimated to be 287,223,431. In this, people with Sikh faith had a share of 1,907,833 (0.66%); people with Islamic faith 57,321,164 (19.96%), those with Christian faith 2,284,380 (0.80%)[41]. Hence overall in 1891, the growth of people with Islamic faith, all over India (19.96%) along with Punjab, (in which

---

[41] Census on India https://www.jstor.org/stable/pdf/saoa.crl.25352813.pdf (Retrieved 12-1-2022).

they had 47.8% share) and where they were mostly domiciled, were doing well with their growth in India's total population.

In the 1941 census, Muslims had a share of 24.30% in the total population of India. In the 1947 partition of the country, the majority Muslim population became part of Pakistan Punjab, as a result of which, in the 1951 census their share in India's total population declined to 10.40%. This share steadily increased to 11.21% in 1971; 12.61% in 1991, and 14.23%. In the 2011 census, Islam came to be ranked as the second largest religion in India, with 172 million people or 14.2% of India's total population. The 2020 estimates are 213 million or 15.5% share, indicating a steady rise of people with Islamic faith in India, which is now home to about 11% of the world's Muslim population[42].

The decline in the Hindu population was owing to the conversion of mostly lower caste Hindus into Islam (Krishen[43]). The census data is a good indication of the rising influence of Islam, which had far-reaching implications in the partition of India in 1947, on the basis of religious divide. Two provinces that were sliced were the Muslim dominated eastern province (present day Bangladesh), and western province, the Punjab. Overall, such was the influence of Islam that within eighty years of the death of Prophet Muhammad (in AD 632) the entire population of Arabia, Iraq, Syria, Turkey, Egypt, Sudan, Libya, Tunis, Algeria, Morocco, had been converted to

---

[42] Data from various census sources and state publications.
[43]
https://punjab.global.ucsb.edu/sites/default/files/sitefiles/journals/volume11/n o1/6_krishan.pdf

Islam, with Afghanistan, Baluchistan, West Punjab, Sind, and Bangladesh following suit (Gupta, 1984, p. 12).

Cross Breeding of People of Punjab

*Good breeding consists in concealing
how much we think of ourselves and
how little we think of the other person*
(Mark Twain)

A generally accepted classification of people in India is that of four castes - Brahmins (priests, scholars, and teachers), Kshatriyas (warriors), Vaishyas (accountants/business-people), and Sudras (all other workers). There are numerous sub-castes/tribes within these four broad classifications. Cunningham (Cunningham, 1918, pp. 9-11) details the results of a survey of 1030 villages conducted in 1844 which lists following villages inhabited by the tribes (original wordings of Cunningham):

> Juts (443 villages), Rajpoots (194), Goojers (109), Syeds (17), Shekhs (25), Puthans (8), Moghuls (5), Brahmins (28), Khutrees (6), Araiens (47), Kumbos (19), Malees (12), Rors (33), Doghurs (Mahmoetans claiming Khshutrees origin) (28), Kulalls (5), Gosayen religionists (3), Bairaghee religionists (2), miscellaneous tribes (46)[44].

"With the onslaught of invasions came the cross-breeding as invaders, many of who settled down, took local women as their brides, as a result of which the blood of

---

44 Spelling as in original. Author of this source in preface of his book explains that he has chosen to write the name such that they are spelled correctly by native English speakers of England (Readers, e.g., read Khutrees as Kshatriyas, Mahmoetans as Mohmadans and similarly others).

many conquering races came to mingle and many alien languages - Arabic, Persian, Pushto, and Turkish - came to be spoken in the land. Thus, too, was the animism of the aboriginal subjected to Vedantic, Jain, and Buddhist religions of the Aryans, and to the Islamic faith of the Arabs, Turks, Mongols, Persians, and Afghans. Out of this mixture of blood and speech were born the Punjabi people and their language" (Singh K. , A History of the Sikhs: Vol 1 1469-1838, 2004, p. 13).

Table 2. 1 Percentage Religious Composition of
Population of Punjab 1881-1941

Census Year	Muslims	Hindus	Sikhs	Christians	Others	Row Total
1881	47.6	43.8	8.2	0.1	0.3	100%
1891	47.8	43.6	8.2	0.2	0.2	100
1901	49.6	41.3	8.6	0.3	0.2	100
1911	51.1	35.8	12.1	0.8	0.2	100
1921	51.1	35.1	12.4	1.3	0.1	100
1931	52.4	30.2	14.3	1.5	1.6	100
1941	53.2	29.1	14.9	1.5	1.3	100

Source: Census of India, 1931, Punjab, Part I p.69 and Census of India 1941;
as quoted in:
https://punjab.global.ucsb.edu/sites/default/files/sitefiles/journals/volume11/no1/6_krishan.pdf

Impact of Mughal Rule on Sikh Psyche and Culture

A convenient way to understand the impact Mughal rulers had on Sikh psyche and culture is to understand the Mughal emperor that was ruling at the time of the life of each of the 10 Sikh Gurus. Table 2.2 lists basic data on the dates of births and deaths of all 10 Sikh Gurus, followed by the period of their Guru-ship, ruler at the time of their Guru-ship, their key messages to disciples and their specific contributions to Sikhs and humanity in general. We begin with the first Guru - Guru Nanak.

Guru Nanak (1469-1539)

Guru Nanak was born in 1469 and died in 1539. In his lifetime Guru Nanak lived through the dictates of five Afghan and Mughal kings - Bahlūl Lodī (1451-1489), Sikandar Lodī (1489-1517), Ibrahim Lodī (1517-1526), Babur (1526-1530), and Humayun (1530-1554)[45]. As a result of Guru Nanak's presence in these rulers' time, he must have observed the working of various monarchs in the sphere of political and economic lives of the masses. There

---

[45] https://www.britannica.com/topic/Lodī -dynasty (Accessed 9-3-2022)

are, however, no records written by him of his observations, save for some indications in his hymns that throw light on the (cruelty) of some of the rulers. This is not surprising as most of his time was spent preaching the gospel of God to his followers. Guru Nanak also travelled far and wide to spread his message of universal love and brotherhood. Also, in his lifetime, the growth of Sikhs as a distinct community was in its infancy; the physical appearance and religious status, in which we see them today, came much later. In the following section we provide a brief account of Nanak's life.

A Sketch of Guru Nanak's Life[46]

About thirty miles south-west of the city of Lahore, the capital of the Panjab, and on the borders of the present civil districts of Gujranwala and Montgomery, stands the town of Talwandi, deep in a lonely forest. It is on the margin of the Bar or raised forest tract which occupies the centre of the Panjab. The town is still girdled by a broad expanse of arborescent vegetation, which, when not whitened by the sand blown by the winds of the desert, wears through all seasons a cheerful appearance. The Salvadora Persica[47] predominates, but there are also found the Acacia modesta and the Prosopis spicigera. The wild deer is seen occasionally to appear startled at the traveller who disturbs the solitude of its domain, and the hare and the partridge cower cautiously among the thickets,

---

[46] Data for ten Gurus in this chapter comes from various encyclopaedias including (Singh H. , 1992); and (Singh G. , n.d).

47 Salvadora Persica commonly known as the toots rush tree is a small evergreen tree native to the Middle East, Africa, and India. Acacia modesta now known as Senegalia modesta is a drought resistant plant commonly found in Pakistan, India, and Afghanistan. Prosopis cineraria is a species of flowering tree is native to arid portions of Western Asia and the Indian Subcontinent.

deprecating molestation. In this retreat was born Guru Nanak, the founder of the Sikh religion. His birth took place on the third day of the light half of the month of Baisakh (April-May) in the year 1469 (Macauliffe, 1909, p. 52). Nanak was born by a Muslim mid-wife Daulatan who, when quizzed by the astrologer who had come to make the child's horoscope, vouched that on birth she heard the voice as if it was the laughing voice of a wise man joining a social gathering (Ibid, p.1).

Nanak was born in an upper Hindu Kshatriya caste in a village known as Rai-Bhoi-Di-Talwandi taking its name from its founder Rai-Bhoi. Later it came to be addressed as Nankana Sahib (after Nanak's name). It is situated 76 km west of Lahore in the Punjab province of Pakistan, then under the Delhi sultanate[48]. In the present day, a small city of eighty thousand inhabitants, it has a large gurdwara commemorating the birthplace of the Guru. Nanak, whose father was a shopkeeper and village land record keeper, acquired the knowledge of arithmetic and accounts keeping from his father, and that of Arabic, Persian, and Devanagari (which uses ancient Brāhmī script akin to Hindi alphabets) from teachers. These skills must have come in handy when he worked as record keeper of a store where Delhi Sultanate's non-cash collections were kept. Nanak's only sister Nanki was five years older than him.

Nanak was married in 1475 and had two sons. Nanak led the life of a preacher. There is evidence that suggests that he travelled as far as Sikkim, Afghanistan, Iran, Iraq, present day Saudi Arabia, Bangladesh, Sri Lanka, where gurdwaras in his memory stand. Some

---

48 Pakistan is a federation of four provinces - Balochistan, Khyber Pakhtunkhwa (North-West Frontier Province), Punjab, and Sind.

sources also cite visits as far as Jerusalem, Azerbaijan, and Sudan (Singh & Singh, 1991) (Kohli, Travels of Guru Nanak, 1997). After leading the life as a preacher, Nanak settled in Kartarpur city in present day Pakistan Punjab and made his living as a farmer. Kartarpur is 137km from Lahore (in Pakistan) and 52km from Amritsar (border Indian town). The three important cities (Amritsar, Lahore, and Kartarpur) in Sikh history between them form a triangle. Guru Nanak died in 1539 at age 70.

As a child Nanak is said to have been a contemplative child not interested in the mundane day-to-day chores of life and lacked awareness of his father's shop-keeping business. He is said to have attained enlightenment in 1499 at age 30 after which he is said to have begun his travels within and outside India. There are stories of his generous, benevolent, and sometime miraculous temperament since childhood. These stories include how he spent his money his father gave him to buy merchandise for the shop on feeding the hungry, how he stunned his teacher with his knowledge in his first days in school, how he was shielded from the sun by a cobra's hood while fast asleep under a tree. Once he is said to have read the mind of a Muslim priest, who Nanak said, was busy trading horses while performing *namaz* (prayers of Muslims)[49].

A rare manuscript cAD1645, *The Dabistan*, (Mowbad, 2010) records the following incident related to

---

[49] Source of these tales is a collection, commonly known as an 'Janam Sakhis' (life stories), author(s) of which cannot be ascertained with certainty. The very first book of these tales is said to have been compiled on the initiative of second Guru Angad (1504-1552) from the eyewitness of Guru Nanak's life-long companion Bhai Bala (1466–1544). This author's source is *Puratan Janam Sakhi Sri Guru Nanak Dev Ji*, retrieved from the following source. Different versions of this text exist, but the contents are mostly similar.
http://www.panjabdigilib.org/webuser/searches/displayPage.jsp?ID=3330&page=1&CategoryID=1 (Retrieved 9-3-2022).

Nanak[50]. This incident happened when he was sent to live with his elder sister Nanki whose husband Jaya Rama was employed as keeper of the granary storage of Daulat Khan Lodī, a relation of the reigning emperor of Delhi. The author recorded the incident as follows:

> "...Nanac was a grain-factor of Daulat Khan Lodī, who ranked among the distinguished Umras of Ibrahim Khan, the sovereign of Hindostan. A darwish came to Nanc, having entered the granary, gave away, the property of Daulet-Khan, and his own, whatever, he found there and in his house,...Daulat Khan was stuck with astonishment at hearing this, but, recognising in Nanc the mark of a dervish, he withheld his hand from hurting him." (p.247-248)[51].

The final miraculous incident is said to have occurred on his death when both Hindu and Muslim disciples wanted, respectively, to cremate and bury him by their custom. Legend has it that a hermit suggested that both communities lay flowers on the body, and next morning whosoever's flowers had not withered would claim the body. Next morning both sets of flowers were found to be fresh, but Nanak's body had disappeared from under the sheets. The two communities then decided to divide the sheet between them to complete the rituals their way. It is his legacy that Nanak was held in such high esteem both by the Hindus and the Muslims that a decision to honour him with a university in his name in his birthplace is presently being considered by Pakistani authorities.

---

50 The Dabistan (Mollā Mowbad, vol. 2), (Paris: Asiatic Society, 1843 translation by David Shea and Anthony Troyer). Mollā Mowbad is now generally accepted as its author (cf. footnote at https://en.wikipedia.org/wiki/Dabestan-e_Mazaheb (Retrieved 22-12-2021).
51 Jay-Rama was put in prison imprisoned by Daulat Khan, on the charge of having dissipated his property, but was justified by Nanak's confessions (The Dabistan op.cit p248 footnote).

Contributions of Guru Nanak

Devout followers of Guru Nanak will vouch on the authenticity of mystical occurrences that came to be narrated during the lifetime of Nanak and written down by devotees posthumously[52]. Sceptics possibly would question the authenticity of some of these mystic tales. However, both the devout followers and the sceptics would unanimously agree that Nanak was much ahead of his time in his philosophical thoughts and discourse on the right path for individuals, family, and of the social responsibilities of human beings, and the righteous path all should choose on the *Road to Nirvana*. We shall briefly summarise Nanak's contribution that has since had a fundamental impact on Sikh psyche and philosophy of their lives. Nanak's teachings were further strengthened by the doctrines of subsequent Gurus; a key ethical trait was seen in the recent COVID pandemic in which Sikhs, notwithstanding risks to their own lives, offered themselves in the service of the community.

Possibly, the most profound of Nanak's thoughts and sermons to his followers was that *all human beings are created equal* and that there was no Hindu or Muslim, as was the demarcation line of communities in those times. Allied to this ethos was his sermon *that there is but one God* by whichever name you call him, and that, *he was present everywhere*. This is akin to what is in the present day known as 'universal brotherhood'. Nanak further discoursed that everyone *could find God* with good deeds, without taking recourse to priests or pundits. Secondly, he *condemned mistreatment of women* who in those times were cursed, e.g., for not bearing a male heir; and were brutalized during

---

52 Please confer footnote on previous page for details.

foreign invasions. Thirdly, Nanak vehemently opposed *flimsy rituals*. Coming from an upper Hindu caste family, this might have been the result of his first-hand observations of rituals at home, and in family and social life, by Brahmin pundits of his time[53]. Finally, he was a firm believer in *making an honest living* by dint of one's labour and sharing one's resources with others.

Nanak sought to instil a *sense of humility* in his disciples and lived by example. As a faqir, of course, he lived an austere life, his two disciples Bala and Mardana, who accompanied him in his travels were, respectively, Hindu and Muslim. After his return from his travels, he settled down to a farmer's life and made his living by dint of hard work on the farm till his death at age 70. In his lifetime Nanak also composed 947 hymns in 19 Rāgas (a melodic setup for improvisation in Indian classical music) which showed his poetic aptitude, abilities, and knowledge of intricate musical notes. Although there is no mention of Nanak taking tutoring in the world of Rāgas, at some stage in his youth he must have acquired intricate knowledge of Indian classical compositions based on Rāgas.

Ruler in Guru Nanak's Time

It can be argued that Saints and Gurus are born with embedded qualities not found in ordinary souls. This is also true of genius minds who with their skills and zeal also

---

53 Some of the rituals performed continue till this day. Rituals e.g., begin with the conception of the child and continue until his death. These include rituals on the birth of the child when homes are cleaned and worship performed, then there are rituals related to the naming ceremony, taking the child outdoors, when the child is put on solid food, shaving of head, piercing of ears, adding sacred thread on the body, wedding rituals, and elaborate rituals on the death and thereafter each year on the day when (called *Sharad)* pundits are fed – to name a few.

revolutionize social and physical engineering of the environment, and the way we live, think, and work. Many a times the cliché 'necessity is the mother of invention' applies in the case of environments and needs of the time. Classic instances of social engineering of ideas are the invention of communism in response to labour conditions of the time, and in the physical world, revolution in transportation and communications. In the case of Nanak, he lived through turbulent times when, within the fabric of society, domination of upper Brahmin class over the lower castes was total, and externally the rulers of the Lodī dynasty (1451-1526) and Mughal rulers (1526-1530) were dominant on *all* classes of society - lower or upper. These were not benevolent rulers. We have seen the brutality of Mughal invaders in chapter 1. Here we shall only briefly touch upon the times of the Lodī dynastic rulers during the life span of Nanak.

Lodī dynasty, which was an Afghan dynasty, was founded by Bahlūl Lodī , the fifth and final of the Delhi sultanate, and ruled from 1451 to 1526[54]. Sikandar Lodī (1489-1517) the second son of Bahlūl, succeeded him after his death in 1489 and took up the title Sikandar Shah. He founded Agra in 1504 and was instrumental in building mosques. On the positive, he abolished corn duties and was a patron of trade and commerce. He was also a poet of some repute. Ibrahim Lodī (1517-1526), the youngest son of Sikander Lodī, was the last Lodī Sultan of Delhi. Ibrahim Lodī was defeated in 1526 at the Battle of Panipat. This marked the end of the Lodī Dynasty and the rise of the Mughal Empire in India led by Babur (1526-1530).

---

[54] Sultanate means a state or country ruled by a sultan. Sultan is an Arabic word meaning authority or power.

The Muslim subjects of the Lodī's were required to pay the *Zakat tax*[55]; non-Muslim subjects were required to pay the *Jizya tax* for receiving state protection from Muslim rulers. In some parts of the Sultanate, Hindus also paid the *Pilgrimage Tax* levied on devotees visiting pilgrims. Sikandar Lodī inclined towards Sunni orthodoxy destroyed Hindu temples and was under pressure from the ulema (a body of Muslim scholars recognized as having specialist knowledge of Islamic sacred law and theology). As a result, Brahmins advocating Hinduism were executed. After the death of Ibrahim Lodī, Babur's (1526-1530) rule prevailed, the harshness of Babur's regime has been described in the previous chapter.

Nanak's thoughts would have been influenced by the environment in which he lived. He noticed, and did not approve, the ritualistic life led by the upper caste Hindus, and he must have been saddened by the plight of *all* Hindus (upper or lower caste) under Muslim rulers. There is some evidence in his hymns of his brief encounter with the regime and the atrocities that the regime was committing on the Hindu masses. Watching the discriminatory treatment of lower caste Hindus by the upper-class Brahmins, and the atrocities of the Muslim rulers over both the classes must have had an influence on his religious hymns through which he preached universal love and care of all. In chapters 3 and 4 we describe in some details the contributions of his hymns that urge all to adopt the path of benevolence.

---

[55] Zakat as tax used to be levied on Muslim population as part of five pillars of Islam (Shahada i.e., there is one God and Muhammad is the messenger of God; Prayer; Alms (Zakat); Fasting; and Pilgrimage. Purpose of Zakat is to help the needy.

Second Guru – Guru Angad Dev
(1504-1552)

One act of obedience is better than one hundred sermons (Dietrich Bonhoeffer).

Angad's Selection to Guru-ship

Guru Nanak chose his disciple Angad as his successor, sidestepping the claims of his two sons Sri Chand and Lakhmi Chand whom he did not consider to be the right choice for succession to Guru-ship. In modern management terms Nanak's choice can be termed as 'succession by merit', as he found Angad to be better educated and obedient and dedicated to the cause of righteous path begun by Nanak, and now followed by devotees. The eldest son who was bypassed to the throne in favour of Angad did cause difficulties for Angad in his smooth functioning of the Guru-ship. However, he was curtailed in his activities by Angad's popularity among the masses and also by the supreme humility Angad showed towards his adversaries. Guru Nanak was proved right in his choice when we look at the contributions made by Angad for the betterment and upliftment of the people. Before we enumerate Guru Angad's achievements we briefly sketch his life.

A Sketch of Guru Angad Dev's Life

Angad, whose father was a trader, was born in 1504 of Hindu parents of Khatri caste (considered higher than menial *Shudra* but lower than *Brahmin* - the priest caste). People of Khatri caste were judged to be suave and better skilled at administrative and finance matters. Angad at the time of his ascension to Guru-ship was married with two sons and a daughter. He was appointed second Guru at age 35. He lived and preached Sikhism from a small village, Khadur, 46km west of Amritsar. Now lovingly called Khadur Sahib, the village has expanded and has over 2000 families residing in it. Before becoming a devout and obedient follower of Nanak, Angad is said to be working as a teacher and a priest and was used to performing pooja for Goddess Durga, a major deity in Hinduism revered for the protection and combating evils that threaten peace and prosperity.

Angad in his duties as a teacher and a priest had a sizeable following of his own - another factor that played in his favour. Nanak chose to declare Angad the next Guru in a public gathering so that the message is openly relayed, spread and embedded in the minds of the masses. It needs to be mentioned here that till this day Sikhs have deep reverence to religious congregations and announcements made therein, especially, by the Gurus or those in the servitude of religious work. By announcing Angad to be the next Guru, Nanak, therefore, pre-empted any alternate claim to the dominion of Guru-ship, either from his own sons, or by anyone else. Guru Nanak's older of the two sons Sri Chand is said to be not interested in Guru-ship. Given his pious nature he had a following of his own; his followers though refused to accept Angad's succession to dominion. The matter, in due course was resolved by the intervention of elders.

Ruler in Guru Angad Dev's Time

During the time Angad was Guru i.e., 1539-1552, three monarchs ruled India. First was Babur's son Humayun (1530-1540); second was Sher Shah Suri (1542-1545); and third was Sher Shah Suri's son Islam Shah (1545-1553). In addition to being a warrior, Humayun also proved himself to be an able administrator. He introduced a measurement of the land for the assessment of the revenue and also introduced a silver currency. These measures provided a secure foundation for the Mughals, who later adopted them (Kulke & Rothermund, 2016, p. 154). He was also forgiving by nature (Lane-Poole, 1903).

Sher Shah Suri the founder of the Suri Empire was a commander in Babur's army. During Humayun's reign, and in his absence when Humayun was on an expedition, Sher Shar overran the state of Bengal and established the Suri dynasty. Sher Shah may have taken over the empire by deceit, but he proved to be an even better administrator than Humayun. Having worked his way up to be a commander in Babur's army he had an intimate knowledge of the functioning of military and administrative system of the Mughals. His key insight was that Mughal kings delegated too much of state work to subordinates who, under the influence of corruption, settled disputes and took decision not always in favour of the state[56].

In addition to being a gifted administrator and a general, Sher Shah also proved to be a great builder,

56 Abbas Khan: *Tarikh, p.330;* Ahmad: *Tabaqat,* vol.2, pp.150-52. As quoted in Fischer (2016), p.63.

creating a network of roads to facilitate trade and commerce, and build safe rest houses for travellers[57]. Sher Shah was also unforgiving to antisocial elements of the likes of thieves and robbers; this sternness transmitted a feeling of safety in people. Perhaps his greatest innovation was the strengthening of the land-owning system and revenues that it generated - which he made equitable depending on the land size and income it produced.

Sher Shah also patronised learned men. Sher Shah was mostly tolerant to Hindus, but he did not abolish the Jizya tax levied on Hindus. Sher Shah has also been accused of launching new cities in his name, on the ruins of old (Badā'ūnī, 1898); (Qanungo, 1965). Islam Shah – Sher Shar Suri's son continued the good work of his father. He codified the laws which made symmetric the handing of the justice. Like his father, Islam Shah also did not depend on *Ulema*[58]. Both father and son showed respect for peasants and the soldier class - the two pillars of an empire (Ibid). As a result of these policies during the lifespan of Islam Shah, a high degree of discipline and peace came to be maintained.

As would be obvious, there was little interaction of Mughals of the time with the Sikhs. There is, however, a legendary story of Humayun, who after losing a battle came to see Guru Angad but was asked to wait as Guru Angad was busy in discourse. Story has it that Humayun unsheathed his sword and threatened Guru Angad who then mocked him on his losing battle with the enemy, and now acting menacingly towards a holy man. It so happens, the

---

57 As it is still fondly remembered 'Sher Shah Suri Marg', he extended the Grand Trunk Road from Chittagong in the frontiers of the province of Bengal in northeast India, to the west in Kabul, Afghanistan.
58 The learned Islamic interpreters of religious knowledge and doctrine of law in Islam.

legend goes, Humayun apologised, upon which Guru Angad blessed him for his future successes.

Contributions of Guru Angad Dev

Guru Angad proved remarkably successful at the responsibilities entrusted to him by Guru Nanak. He soon realized that the hymns of Guru Nanak had not been compiled in a systematic manner. As was the traditional legacy of learning in those days, disciples learnt, and remembered by heart the slokas (a two-line verse usually religious) or hymns (a religious song or poem). Tale has it that Nanak was the initiator of alphabets of the Gurmukhi script that is in use today in the form of written language by Sikhs. A gurdwara by the name of '*Patti Likhi Sahib*' in Nankana Sahib (in Pakistan) has been built to commemorate the place where Nanak, in a contemplative trance, is said to have come up with 35 alphabets which he wrote down on a slate. The origin of these alphabets is the Laṇḍā scripts (from the term laṇḍā meaning 'without a tail). Laṇḍā script evolved from the Śārada during the 10th century[59].

It is not clear though in which language the utterances of Nanak were originally compiled. In this author's opinion, given that Nanak's two life-long companions were Hindu and Muslim, Nanak's utterances could have been in Devanagari or Urdu or even Persian or Arabic, as these languages were learnt and spoken in those days. Seeing Nanak's verses in diverse languages must have aroused a critical need for uniformity in Angad who

---

59 Sarada script writing system was used by educated Hindu minority in Kashmir and the surrounding valleys. Originating in the 8th century AD, Sarada descended from the Gupta script of North India, from which Devanāgarī also developed (Britannica encyclopaedia: Retrieved 22-6-21).

sat down to work to unify them. Angad borrowed from the 35 letters and came up with a complete Gurmukhi (meaning from the mouth of Guru) script which is still in use today by Sikhs as their written language. Guru Angad re-compiled all the 947 hymns of Nanak and distributed the copies to centres of learning.

The second key contribution of Angad was his foresight of looming confrontation with, the then, arch enemies of Sikhs - the Mughals. Although at the time of Guru Angad, the Sikh religion was still in its infancy, Guru Angad, given the past invasions, must have foreseen the oncoming confrontations - Punjab being the first in the line of fire when invaders crossed borders from the western frontier (Afghanistan). Angad held the view, possibly the first implicit signs of the fighting spirit of the Sikhs that, in the event of a battle with the enemy, it was the duty of the soldier to give battle, irrespective of the odds (Singh K. , A History of the Sikhs: Vol 1 1469-1838, 2004, p. 49).

With a view to raise able bodied men for the troops, Guru Angad began to emphasize on fitness by encouraging his disciples to engage in physical exercises, wrestling, games, and martial arts. Several such centres got started in the villages in and around Punjab. The implications of this move were far reaching, as till this day, the militant wing of the Khalsa, *Nihangs*, can be found engaged within the compound of their complexes (known as 'Deras') exercising, and ritual practicing with their weapons. Sikh youths in Punjab also emphasize on good health and well-built bodies - the overall fitness is admired throughout the region.

The third key contribution was that Angad institutionalized the concept of a langar (community kitchen) within the premises of the gurdwara[60]. Legend has it that the concept of feeding the needy has come about from Nanak who spent the money his trader father gave him to buy provisions for the store, on feeding the hungry sadhus Nanak happened to meet in the market during his shopping trip[61]. The concept of a free meal i.e., langar was not new as Hindu temples and Dharmshalas (inns) in those days often made the provision for such meals for the devotees or travellers (Singh P. , 1994), (Mandair, 2013). However, the concept and tradition of serving free meals begun by Nanak and regularized by Angad in his time did catch up in the imagination and psyche of future Sikh Gurus and the masses, who adopted it with zeal and fine-tuned the whole operation to perfection.

In present times the institution of langar has come to be embedded within the religious fabric of Sikhs who would find it very unusual, rather odd, not to see a kitchen and a langar hall attached to a gurdwara where people sit and eat together in rows, irrespective of caste and creed[62]. Alongside Sunday congregations, families also make provisions for meals on occasions such as children's' birth anniversaries or death anniversaries of elders. Devotees from both sex help prepare food which is always vegetarian.

A close look at langar tradition carried forward by Guru Angad reveals several merits associated with it. First, devotees who travelled from distant places were tired on

---

[60] Detailed discussion on Community Kitchen of the Sikhs can be found it (Singh P. , 1994).

61 Amount that Nanak spent in this manner is said to be Rs20 which in those days would be plenty.

62 Some Gurdwaras now provide a dual system of eating food either sitting on the floor, or eating standing, or sitting on a chair for older devotees for whom Gurdwaras now also provide sofa or chairs within the main congregation hall.

arrival and it made sense if they first ate and rested before joining the discourse in the congregation hall. Secondly, in this author's opinion, the practice of a community kitchen also works as a social club, especially for the women folk, who freed from the chores of the day, exchange family and social information - some also help out in the (community) kitchen. The now well-established institution of langar has also helped communities with food, in times of need such as floods and earthquakes. Some gurdwaras run a community kitchen on a daily basis.

Last but not the least, Guru Angad paid attention to education by opening schools and centres of learning which also disseminated religious knowledge to the masses. Confucius the Chinese philosopher (551BC-479BC) has famously remarked that 'if your plan is for 1 year, plant rice; if your plan is for 10 years, plant trees; if your plan is for 100 years, educate children.' The education system of Punjab that was started by the initiatives of the likes of Guru Angad was well advanced when the British inherited it with the occupation of Punjab in 1849. After occupation, the British went about to systematically destroy it. This sad historical fact has been candidly recorded by an English civil servant itself, G.W. Leitner (1840-1899)[63] in his book 'Indigenous Education in the Panjab since Annexation and

---

[63] Dr. G.W Leitner (1840-1899) was born to Jewish parents in Hungary. He was a linguist and was fluent in Arabic, Turkish, and several European languages. At 23 years of age, he was appointed Professor in Arabic and Muslim Law at King's College London. Later he also served as Principal of Government College University in Lahore and was instrumental in the formation of the University of Punjab in 1882. He founded schools, literary associations, public libraries, and academic journals and dedicated himself to the study of the cultures of the Indian subcontinent. Subsequently he also wrote two volumes on the history of Islam. (https://en.wikipedia.org/wiki/Gottlieb_Wilhelm_Leitner Accessed 24-3-2022).

in 1882' (Leitner, n.d). This is not the primary topic of discussion here but given its importance we quote following opening passages from Leitner's study (italics and paragraphing is by this author). These passages vividly describe the love for, and devotion to education by all strata of life in the then Punjab.

"I am about to relate - I hope without extenuation or malice - the history of the contact of a form of European with one of Asiatic civilisation; how, in spite of the best intentions, the most public-spirited officers, and a generous Government that had the benefit of the traditions of other provinces, the true education of the Panjab was crippled, checked, and is nearly destroyed; how opportunities for its healthy revival and development were either neglected or perverted; and how, far beyond the blame attaching to individuals, our system stands convicted of worse than official failure. Whether it is possible to rouse to renewed exertion, on behalf of its own education, *the most loyal population* that has ever been disappointed, is a question which the following pages will only partially attempt to answer. Much will, of course, depend on the wise adaptation of the noble principle just propounded – of "local self-government" - to a department of the Administration, - that of education, - in which, all others, it can be introduced with perfect safety and the greatest political advantage."

"Respect for learning has always been the redeeming feature of "the East." To this the Panjab has formed no exception. Torn by invasion and civil war, it ever preserved and added to educational endowments. The most unscrupulous chief, the avaricious money-lender, and even the freebooter, vied with the small landowner in making peace with his conscience by founding schools and rewarding the learned."

"There was not a mosque, a temple, a dharmsdla that had not a school attached to it, to which the youth flocked chiefly for religious education. There were few wealthy men who did not entertain a Maulvi, Pandit, or Guru to teach their sons, and along with them the sons of friends and dependents. There were also thousands of secular schools, frequented alike by Muhammaddans, Hindus and Sikhs, in which Persian or Lunde was taught. There were hundreds of learned men who gratuitously taught their co-religionists, and sometimes all-comers, for the sake of God - 'lilah' ."

"There was not a single villager who did not take a pride in devoting a portion of his produce to a respected teacher. In respectable Muhammadan families husbands taught their wives, and these their children; nor did the Sikhs prove in that respect to be unworthy of their appellation of learners and disciples. In short, the lowest computation gives us 330,000 pupils (against little more than 190,000 at present) in the schools of the various denominations who were acquainted with reading, writing, and some method of computation; whilst thousands of them belonged to Arabic and Sanskrit colleges, in which Oriental literature and systems of Oriental Law, Logic, Philosophy, and Medicine were taught to the highest standards. Tens of thousands also acquired a proficiency in Persian, which is now rarely reached in Government and aided schools or colleges. Through all schools there breathed a spirit of devotion to education for its own sake and for its influence on the character and on religious culture; whilst even the sons of Banyas who merely learnt what they absolutely required in order to gain a livelihood looked with respect, amounting to adoration, on their humble Pandhas, who had taught them the elements of *two* " r's *We have changed all this.*" (Leitner, n.d, p. 8).

Third Guru: Guru Amar Das (1479-1574)

Equality is the soul of liberty; there is, in fact, no liberty without it
(Frances Wright)

The second Guru Angad died in 1552 at age 48. Reasons of his demise are not clear. But it would not have been sudden as he had time to nominate his successor. Similar to his predecessor Nanak, Guru Angad chose his successor purely on merit, irrespective of the age, caste, creed, or any other consideration. Following in the footsteps of Nanak, and notwithstanding the fact that Guru Angad had two sons of his own, he chose Amar Das - a 73 old as his successor, who at the time of Guru-ship was married with four children. Amar Das for 12 years was in the dedicated service of Guru Angad, and it was his pious and saintly nature, coupled with the devotion and unflinching service that won him the love of Guru Angad, on whose choice, and upon his demise, Amar Das was elevated to Guru-ship (Singh H. , 1992).

Amar Das was born in 1479 to Hindu parents and was the eldest of four brothers, and followed Vaishnavism - a tradition in Hinduism that adheres to Lord Vishnu as their deity. Not much is known of Amar Das' life up to age 50 except that he was engaged in the family business of farming and some trading. What is known is that, as a devout Hindu, Amar Das took yearly pilgrimages in the Himalayas. Legend has it that until Amar Das met Guru Angad, he had been to pilgrimages 19 times, but after meeting Guru Angad and listening to his sermons, did no more pilgrimages (Sodi, 1995, p. 62). Tale has it that in a chance encounter, a Brahmin with the knowledge of astrology predicted that he will one day become a Guru; on another occasion another Brahmin refused alms from him prophesying that he would accept alms another day in a different form, as Amar Das was destined to become either a benevolent king or a famous Guru (Singh S. , Sri Guru Granth Sahib Darshan (In Gurmukhi), 1961, pp. 2-3).

Another narrative has it that in another meeting with a Sadhu who asked if Amar Das had a Guru and not hearing the answer in affirmative, turned away in disgust (Singh H. , 1992, p. 87). It was common in those days to have a living Guru, despite a plethora of Gods - one or more of whom, Hindus worshipped. The tradition of live 'Guru-following' originated in olden times when it was common for the young to leave home and live as a pupil for a few years in the company of a Guru, to acquire education - primarily of Vedas. After a few years of tutelage, bright pupils became Gurus in their own right. There is an ongoing craving till this day among Indians to join and venerate live Gurus[64]. However we interpret it, the encounter of Amar Das with the Sadhus proved a turning point. Based on his pious reputation, he was chosen by Angad to be the next Guru,

---

64 It is interesting to see that the tradition of craving to follow a live Guru is still so much alive in India. This is evident from several TV channels that devote generous time on self-proclaimed Gurus, dexterous at marketing themselves; some have become fabulously rich and have their own complexes known as 'Deras' which resemble little townships. Not all of them are clean though – some have been prosecuted for their shady conduct and embezzlement of funds to support their lavish decadent lifestyle.

following which, Guru Amar Das began dedicating his life to selfless service to the cause of Sikhism.

Guru Amar Das' unflinching dedication is often eulogised as a reason to his Guru-ship. However, when examined closely, it would transpire that Angad's decision, in addition to being influenced by the unyielding dedication of Amar Das, was based also on factual groundings – in management terminology, it was an informed decision. First, let it be remembered that Amar Das, when he approached Angad to be in his service, was 61 years of age - a mature, family person who would have seen life's ups and downs - but above all, similar to Angad, coming from a devout Hindu family he understood the strengths and weaknesses of the Hindu divine system of Gods and Goddesses. Angad must have realized that Amar Das had a wealth of worldly experience. It is said that Amar Das also had a sense of humour which he did not hesitate to apply in discourse with his disciples (Singh P. , 2019).

Bear in mind that Sikh religion at the time of Amar Das' induction into Guru-ship was very much at formative stages, open to threats from Muslim rulers as well as orthodox Hindus. It was owing to Guru Angad's great foresight that he anticipated these issues and decided that Amar Das would be the right choice for the dominion. Guru Angad was right in his judgement of new leader in Amar Das, for a fast-growing religious group that Sikhism was, and which later blossomed into a full-fledged religion that both Muslim and British had to come to terms with.

Contributions of Guru Amar Das

Building on Guru Angad's efforts to develop Gurmukhi script proved to be a boon for subsequent Gurus;

it standardised the written hymns in one language in which the collection of previous Gurus (Nanak and Angad) could be reproduced, to which Guru Amar Das also added hymns of selected saints of his time. He made all the compiled hymns available to his followers whose numbers swelled, as now they could understand Guru's message more simply than if it were in Sanskrit - a richer but difficult language to learn to speak, read, or write. Owing to the intricacies of Sanskrit language it had always been a monopoly of pundits who reigned supreme with captivating, almost mystic but hard to understand chants during ceremonies, which were plentiful in those days, and still continue in various forms till this day.

With the standardization of the readable, speakable, and understandable language, the number of devotees increased substantially. Another reason of the swell in devotees was that Guru Amar Das continued, with added vigour, the community kitchen ritual attached to the complex where devotees came to meet him. In fact, he directed that anyone coming to meet him must first eat and rest. This must have been a welcome move, particularly for devotees coming from distant places who must have been grateful not have to look for a place to eat and rest. Alongside convenience it must also have saved them cash - a welcome relief for poorer devotees in particular.

As devotee numbers swelled, organizationally it became harder to accommodate and serve them as Guru wished. This gave rise to what can be termed, in modern management parlance, 'decentralisation' process. Guru Amar Das created 22 new centres (dioceses) and trained selected devotees as his Deputies and put them in charge of these centres across the state[65]. The mandate of Deputies was to spread the teachings of Guru Nanak and instil religious discipline in devotees by observing a schedule of early rise, bathing, exercise, and worship before setting off to that day's work.

The duties and responsibilities of Deputies (known as '*Masands*[66]') included collections of donations from devotees, who were to donate 1/10th of their income in cash or kind for community causes - building and maintenance of gurdwaras, free kitchen (which is attached to all gurdwaras till this day), and also help solve civil disputes between the devotees. The decentralized system worked well, but in due course, Deputies became too powerful, corrupt, and arrogant, and problems ensued culminating in their removals and taking over of the centres to be run by committees formed by the devotee public.

One notable contribution of Guru Amar Das was the compilation of all the hymns available until then, to which he also added his own 869 hymns – the collected work which came to be known a 'Pothi Sahib' (Pothi meaning a small book) and which became the nucleus for '*Guru Granth Sahib*' (*GGS*) as we see it today. *GGS* is the Scripture venerated by Sikh's world over. One set of Guru Amar Das' hymns known as *Anand Sahib* is recited every day by Sikhs at the end of closing ceremony.

---

65 Known location of 16 is as follows: 5 were located in Amritsar and Lahore; 2 in Jalandar Doab; 2 in Kangra Hills; 1 in Kashmir Hills; 5 in the Malwa areas of Patiala, Ludhiana, Bhatinda; and 1 in Sind. The 22 managers or Masands as they were known came from different backgrounds; they were Pathan, Brahmins, pundits, Vaid (doctor) and Muslims; one was a female. https://www.sikhiwiki.org/index.php/Manji_System (Retrieved 26-6-2021).
66 From Arabic 'masnad' meaning a seat of honour.

We need to note one major shift here in Guru Amar Das' disposition after his elevation to Guru-ship. There is no record of Guru Amar Das having composed hymns prior to his Guru-ship; all 869 verses that came to be included in the Scripture were composed by Amar Das after he became the Guru. What is remarkable is that Guru Amar Das made use of Rāgas in the composition of his hymns. Acquiring knowledge of Rāgas is a time intensive and intricate process. At some stage in his career as a Guru, Amar Das seems to have acquired in-depth knowledge of Rāgas for him to be able to apply this knowledge with an exquisite charisma to his hymns. This transformation into a poet and a connoisseur of fine music, according to this author is remarkable - almost spiritual, as if there was a divine intervention in the intellect of Amar Das during the period he was serving the masses as a Guru.

Another prominent innovation of Guru Amar Das was that he fixed a day in late spring in Goindwal, a yearly meeting to celebrate the harvest[67]. Since it was not possible for him to cover vast distances to meet his Deputies individually, along with the celebrations, he used the occasion to meet his Deputies in person and catch up with the latest news and developments at the centres.

Other contributions of Guru Amar Das were in the spheres of social reforms and equality issues. Guru Amar Das sermoned against the veil system - much of which was in use among Hindu and Muslim females; he was also against the *Sati* system in which the wife of the dead person immolated herself on the funeral pyre of her husband. As a corollary to advocating abolition of *Sati* system, Guru Amar Das also encouraged re-marriage of widows. The *Sati*

[67] (Singh S. , Sri Guru Granth Sahib Darshan (In Gurmukhi), 1961, p. 48)

system was finally made illegal and abolished by law by the British in 1829. Guru Amar Das (similar to Guru Nanak) as a Guru turned out to be an embodiment of Equality.

Rulers in Guru Amar Das' Time

At the time of Amar Das' Guru-ship period, 1552-1574, Akbar was the emperor of India, when the relations between Hindus and the Muslim administrators were cordial. History has it that Akbar once visited Amar Das and met him as a commoner after he had had the langar as the tradition was. Pleased with his interface with the Guru, Akbar donated land where presently Harmandir Sahib stands (see below). Legend has it that on Guru's request Akbar also waived tax on Hindu pilgrims going to Haridwar. There is no mention in history of any unpleasantness of Hindus either with the emperor or the Muslim populace in general. Ironically, it is the Brahmins who began to feel threatened with the increasing popularity of the Guru and the populace, large chunks of whom began to renounce complicated rituals. The hegemony of pundits had started to be shaken and their influence and income from these rituals was beginning to get affected.

Fourth Guru: Guru Ram Das (1534-1581)

Being service to others is what brings true happiness
(Marie Osmond)

Guru Ram Das was born in 1534 in Chuna Mandi, Lahore to a trader Khatri family[68]. The area 'Chuna Mandi' which stands till this day is situated towards the north side of Lahore and has several stunning historic mansions (*Havelis* in Urdu) with magnificent architecture from the Mughal era. Situated in this area is also the gurdwara commemorating the birthplace of Guru Ram Das.

As a child Ram Das is said to have been handsome and cheery. Ram Das lost both his parents when he was a child. With parents expired and no source of income, Ram Das' education suffered, and he took to selling petite eatable items, sometimes giving them gratis to the hungry - this compassionate and generous nature is said to be akin to Nanak. With no source of livelihood, Ram Das' grandmother moved with him to her parental village Basarake Gillan (previously known as Basarake Tho) 13km from Amritsar. Third Guru Amar Das was also a resident of Basarake.

It was tradition in those days (it still is) that fellow villagers would visit and console the bereaved family and express their solidarity. Amar Das, who was residing in Lahore at the time would, whenever he visited Basarake, come and met Ram Das. As a result of his visits over the years the bond between the two grew stronger. Ram Das, whose parents were deeply religious, inherited similar traits early in his life and so found himself drawn to Guru Amar Das' pious company[69]. As he was growing up, he became increasingly fascinated and engrossed in Amar Das'

---

68 Guru Gobind Singh in his biography 'Bachitar Natak' (curious play) traces the lineage of Ram Das to lord Ramchander's son Lov (Padam, 2005).
69 (Singh S. , Guru Ram Das ank (in Gurmukhi), 1962), p.6 as quoted in (Sodi, 1995, p. 2).

sermons which he now regularly started to attend. During this time Ram Das also came in contact with Guru Angad when he visited Goindwal as a devotee and to contribute to the making of the langar. This was 1546 when Ram Das was 12 years old[70].

Dates in Table-2.1 tell us that Guru Ram Das lived between 1534-1581. Guru Nanak, Angad and Amar Das died respectively in the years 1539, 1552, and 1574. Hence in his lifetime he lived respectively 5, 18, and 40 years within the lifespan of three predecessor Gurus and saw first-hand the changing phases of Sikhism, especially during the time of Angad and Amar Das. Ram Das attended religious gatherings and learnt previous Guru's hymns. He selflessly participated and served in the langar (community kitchen) for about 28 years, all under the tutelage of previous Gurus, in particular Amar Das. It is this author's conjecture that during these long years Ram Das went through gradual but certain spiritual transformation which also ushered in him the poetic abilities which led him to write some of the most beautiful verses recorded in the scripture. Guru Ram Das got married to the younger daughter of Guru Amar Das, becoming his son-in-law in the process.

Similar to his predecessors, Amar Das chose the next Guru purely on merit, as a result of which, and despite the fact that he had two sons of his own, his preferred choice was Ram Das who was elevated to the position of Guru-

---

70 Goindwal, a religious city of Punjab is situated on the banks of river Beas towards the south- west direction and is about 50km from Basrake, as well as Amritsar. Story has it that Guru Angad had directed Amar Das to establish a new city which came to be called Goindwal - distorted from the name of a trusted devotee 'Gonde Khatri' who donated the land for the city. (Sodi, 1995, p. 3)

ship in 1574. Guru Ram Das served in this position for 7 years till his demise in 1581 at Goindwal.

Contributions of Guru Ram Das

Gur Ram Das made several notable contributions to Sikhism. He was instrumental in the construction (completed in 1604 after his demise) of what is globally known as *Harimandir Sahib* in Amritsar (previously Ramdaspur), the highest place of reverence and worship for the Sikhs. There is some controversy over how the land for the temple was acquired. Readers may find the following passage from 1888 excerpts of Amritsar Gazette that tell us that the land was obtained by Guru Ram Das from emperor Akbar, apparently owing to Guru Ram Das' good relations with the emperor who is said to have visited him (italics are this author's).

"Shortly after the middle of the 15th century, was born at the village of Talwandi, in the Lahore district, Nannk, the founder of the Sikh religion, and the first Sikh Guru. His history, however, is but little connected with that of this district. Nanak died in 1539 A.D. at a village on the opposite side of the Ravi to where now stands the town of Dehra Nanak, in Gurdaspur, founded by his descendants, and called after his name. His successor, Angad the second Guru, lived at the village of Khadur in the Taran *pargana,* a few miles from the Bias, and died there in 1552 A.D. Angad was succeeded by Amardas, the third Guru, who lived at the town of Govindwal on the Bias, some five miles from Khadur. He died in 1574 A.D. To him succeeded his son-in-law Ramdas, the fourth Guru, *who obtained from the emperor Akbar the grant of a piece of land on the spot where now stands the city of Amritsar, and dug the holy tank, and commenced the erection of a temple in its midst.* Ramdas died in 1581 A.D. His son and successor Arjan, the fifth Guru, completed the temple, and multiplied the buildings around it. Since then, Amritsar has ever remained the most sacred shrine of the Sikh people."

Source: Gazetter of the Amritsar District. 1883-4 Chap II p.9. https://dspace.gipe.ac.in/xmlui/bitstream/handle/10973/3663 5/GIPE-017907.pdf?sequence=3&isAllowed=y   (Retrieved 26-6-2021)

Guru Ram Das also strengthened the decentralisation process of the dominion of Sikh preaching as begun by Guru Amar Das who had initiated 22 centres and further sub-centres of excellence of teaching the principles of Sikhism. Such centres also collected donations from devotees for the community kitchen and allied services and kept them flowing to the central pool from where they were used for religious purposes. This organizational setup did help grow Sikhism in the years to come but ran into difficulties later owing to greed of the caretaker Deputies, as alluded to earlier.

Guru Ram Das composed 638 hymns, about ten percent of total hymns that are included in the Scripture. Guru Ram Das' grasp over the classical music is evident when we see that his work spans over 30 ancient Rāgas in Indian classical music. One of the enduring set of hymns is recognised by the law under 'Anand Marriage Act', if the wedding is conducted by the priest in the presence of the Scripture and with the chanting of 'wedding verses' from the Scripture[71]. Guru Ram Das also reinforced the move

---

71 In Hindu weddings with the chanting of salokas (short lyrical verses in Sanskrit – usually religious) couples slowly walk clockwise 7 times around fire; in Sikh weddings with the chanting of 4 lyrical hymns, couples slowly walk clockwise 4 times around the holy Scripture that is placed on higher ground from which are read the hymns by the priest in a slow and deliberate manner.

towards the abolition of Sati and the veil system among women.

Guru Ram Das had 3 sons. He chose the youngest son Arjan Dev as his successor instead of any of his two elder sons, despite considerable opposition and bickering by the eldest son. The choice of Arjan Dev as successor Guru was a massive feat and, as we shall see below, one that changed the face of Sikhism. From whichever angle we judge, the service provided by Guru Ram Das to Sikhism is invaluable - his biggest service to the community possibly was the nomination of righteous person Arjan Dev to Guru-ship. No records are available as to how he trained his son to be such a worthy successor, but a worthy successor he turned out to be, for, his feat of undertaking the task of unifying the whole of Sikh community with one holy Scripture worked, and still is working as an ever-lasting bonding for the Sikh community.

Ruler in Guru Ram Das' Time

Fortunately for Sikhs, the times of Guru Ram Das (1574-1581) were quiet. Emperor Akbar (1556-1605) was

---

In both, Hindu and Sikh weddings, the fire, and the holy Scripture are considered sacred, in whose presence, the wedding is conducted which is recognised by the law.

In a Sikh wedding, the first verse signifies the piousness of the marriage ceremony telling the bride and the groom to stay on the path of Dharma; the second verse tells the couple to put aside their egos and materialistic things in search of the true Guru; the third emphasizes the true love for God and advises the couple that their heart must always be filled with the divine love of the lord and the final verse explains that the couple has found the peace now that they have reached the God with great ease. With the final recitation, the wedding is declared complete.

on the throne at that time and being a diplomatic king, he left Hindus alone to their world of religion and worship. Akbar was on good terms with Guru Amar Das and is said to have visited him and as just explained, the land for the *Harimandir Sahib* was obtained with his patronage. The violent interaction of the Mughal emperors with Sikhs began in the reign of Jahāngīr which can be legitimately said to be a *tipping point for Sikhs in their future struggle and survival in their own state*. We take this up in the next section.

Fifth Guru : Guru Arjan Dev (1563-1606)

Loyalty and devotion lead to bravery.
Bravery leads to the spirit of self-sacrifice, the spirit
of self-sacrifice creates trust in the power of love.
(Morihei Ueshiba)

Arjan Dev was born in Goindwal and was the youngest of three sons of Amar Das, the fourth Guru. There is a gurdwara at his birthplace to commemorate the spot. Arjan Dev spent the first eleven years of his life there with the family. Upon the death of his father, at age 18 in 1581 he was appointed the next Guru. Arjan Dev, unlike his predecessors, did not dress plainly as a fakir; instead, he is said to have dressed himself in beautiful attire and sat on a decorated podium. Guru Arjan Dev was also fond of fine horses and elephants and lived in some splendour (Singh R. , 2015, pp. 40-41). In this author's opinion this must have been part deliberate as Hindus are used to seeing their Gods and Goddesses in some splendour. This would be evident from the posters of deities that we often see hung on the walls of the temples and in devotees' homes.

Arjan Dev took to his job of Guru-ship in all earnest. During his lifetime, Sikhism progressed at a steady pace with an increased number of converts. The fame of Arjan Dev and the increasing power he was amassing did not escape the attention of the then Mughal emperor, Jahāngīr[72]. Story has it that Jahāngīr's rebellious son Khusro had come to see Arjan Dev and sought his help to the throne; this irked, possibly alarmed Jahāngīr so much that he had Arjan Dev arrested and tortured to death. Jahāngīr's disdain, possibly after his son's meeting with Guru Arjan Dev, can be gauged from the following passage of his memoirs which also explain Arjan Dev's martyrdom. On p. 27b-28a he writes (Thackston, 2002, p. 59).

> "There was a Hindu named Arjan in Gobindwal on the banks of the Beas River. Pretending to be a spiritual guide, he had won over as devotees many simple-minded Indians and even some ignorant, stupid Muslims by broadcasting his claims to be a saint. They called him Guru. Many fools from all around had recourse to him and believed in him implicitly. For three or four generations they had been peddling this same stuff. For a long time I had been thinking that either this false trade should be eliminated or that he should be brought into the embrace of Islam. At length, when Khusraw [Jahāngīr's son] passed by there, this inconsequential little fellow wished to pay homage to Khusraw. When Khusraw stopped at his

---

[72] Jahāngīr was one of 11 children of Akbar; during succession, friction between brothers had broken out.

residence, [Arjan] came out and had an interview with [Khusraw]. Giving him some elementary spiritual precepts picked up here and there, he made a mark with saffron on his forehead, which is called qashqa in the idiom of the Hindus and which they consider lucky. When this was reported to me, I realized how perfectly false he was and ordered him brought to me. I awarded his houses and dwellings and those of his children to Murtaza Khan, and I ordered his possessions and goods confiscated and him executed."

Additionally, the following excerpt is worth noting.

"These days a cursed infidel of Gobindwal was very fortunately killed. It is a cause of great defeat for the reprobate Hindus. With whatever intention and purpose they are killed - the humiliation of infidels is for Muslims, life itself. Before this Kafir (Infidel) was killed, I had seen in a dream that the Emperor of the day had destroyed the crown of the head of Shirk or infidelity. It is true that this infidel [Guru Arjun] was the chief of the infidels and a leader of the Kafirs. The object of levying Jizya (tax on non-Muslims) on them is to humiliate and insult the Kafirs, and Jihad against them and hostility towards them are the necessities of the Mohammedan faith."

(Shaikh Ahmad Sirhindi, Letter to Murtaza Khan, On the execution of Guru Arjan).

There is controversy in literature over this narration which in fact, a respected personality Bhai Gurdas - the legendary poet, chronicler, and preacher (1506-1606) is said to have recorded from eyewitnesses account of the torture and death of Arjan Dev. Bhai Gurdas' account is also corroborated by a Spanish Jesuit missionary Jerome

Xavier (1549-1617) who was in Lahore at the time[73]. Jerome Xavier records that the Sikhs tried to get Jahāngīr to substitute the torture and death sentence with a fine, but this attempt failed as Arjan Dev refused to yield either to a fine or to public admission of any guilt. Another source also corroborates that, as a result of Arjan Dev's refusal, he was tortured to death[74]. Xavier, in appreciation of the courage of Guru Arjun, wrote back to Lisbon, that 'in that way their good Pope died, overwhelmed by the sufferings, torments and dishonours'[75]. Why this narration is plausible is because Jahāngīr at one place in his memoirs explicitly expresses disdain for Arjan Dev (see passage above). Paschaura Singh and Louise Fenech have examined specific and general aspects of martyrdom of Guru Arjan Dev[76]. (Singh P. , Understanding the Martyrdom of Guru Arjan Dev, 2022); (Fenech L. , 1997).

Guru Arjan Dev's Sacrifice for the Righteous Cause

The torture and death of Guru Arjan in 1606 is legendary in Sikh history and is etched in the memory of every Sikh. The martyrdom of Arjan Dev was the turning point that set events out of control for next 200 years until about 1800 when Ranjit Singh came to rule over Panjab. Legend has it that before he died, Arjan Dev urged his son Hargobind, who was to become the sixth Guru, to pick up arms for the righteous cause of the Sikh race.

---

73 Father Jerome to Father Gasper Fernandes, In (Madra, 2004, p. 7).
74 Mobad', Dabistan-i Mazahib, 1645-46, In (Grewal , Sikh History From Persian Sources, 2011, p. 67).
75 Jerome Xavier, Letter to Gasper Fernandes in Lisbon, On the execution of Guru Arjan, In (Barnes, 2011, pp. 242-246)
76 (Singh P. , Understanding the Martyrdom of Guru Arjan Dev, 2022).

Contributions of Guru Arjan Dev

Whereas the martyrdom of Guru Arjan Dev was a turning point in Sikh history, contributions made by Guru Arjan Dev towards the unification of Sikhs have also been a turning point within the Sikh world. Let us see how it happened.

Arjan Dev was a gifted and prolific poet of the highest order. In his short life he composed 2,218 hymns which formed the pillar of the Sikh scripture. The second mammoth task that he completed was the compilation of the Scripture - *Guru Granth Sahib* - the holy Scripture of the Sikhs. Guru Arjan Dev completed the construction of *Harimandir Sahib* or *Darbar Sahib* as it is known to Sikhs, where the first copy of the Scripture was installed in 1604. Darbar signifies something akin to the royal court; Sahib is added to it for respect - meaning a place where all Sikhs present themselves (in all humility). Arjan Dev also helped complete the sacred reservoir around *Harimandir Sahib* that all visitors see on entering the complex.

Guru Arjan Dev also strengthened the of teaching of Sikhism via the 22 centres in the state started by Guru Amar Das. These centres, as explained previously, performed valuable teaching and administrative services, including collection of donations for the betterment of the gurdwaras and the community, and also help sort civil disputes among devotees. It was Guru Arjan Dev who popularised the idea of devotees donating, in cash or kind, 1/10th of their earnings for the community purposes. The city of Amritsar also came to be developed in Guru Arjan Dev's regime. In due course, Amritsar and *Harimandir Sahib* came to be recognised as a central place for future

Sikh meetings and rallying points for actions for the betterment of the Sikh community.

For this author, the torture and death of Guru Arjan Dev at age just 43 snatched the most talented and versatile brain the Sikh community had amongst them. The reader will notice in chapter 3 the razor-sharp computer like brain Guru Arjan Dev had and which he put to use in the compilation *Guru Granth Sahib* - a gigantically complex task, by whichever angle we examine it. One wonders if Guru Arjan Dev was not put to death, what else he would have accomplished given his literary, music, and poetic abilities. Erma Bombeck's remark comes to mind when she said, "when I stand before God at the end of my life, I would hope that I would not have a single bit of talent left, and could say, 'I used everything you gave me.' Such a colossal waste, Guru Angad Dev never had the opportunity to fully blossom with his talents.

Ruler in Guru Arjan Dev's Time

During the times of Arjan Dev, Emperor Akbar was at the helm for 9 years (1556-1605) and Jahāngīr for 21 years (1605-1626). Akbar did not interfere in the religious affairs of Hindus and save for one incident when Guru Amar Das, father of Arjan Dev, had to clarify that there was nothing sinister about Muslims in the Scripture, Akbar's time, and interface with Sikhs was peaceful. The turning point came with the martyrdom of Arjan Dev, who before he was tortured and put to death by Jahāngīr, asked his son Hargobind to take up arms to protect the people and their religious beliefs.

Sixth Guru: Guru Hargobind (1595-1644)

Justice is the sum of all moral duty
(William Goodwin)

Guru Hargobind was born in 1595. In 1606 when he was just 11 years old, he was made Guru after the martyrdom of Guru Arjan Dev. Following on from his father's advice that he should take up arms in the cause of Sikhism, he publicly declared that Sikhs would bear two swords - one for the temporal (worldly) power and the second for the spiritual power - known to Sikhs as swords of *miri* and *piri*. In the Harimandir Sahib complex, then and now, the precinct where the Scripture is installed, is considered as the 'spiritual focal point' of Sikhs; a separate building (Akal Takht) is considered the focal point where 'worldly matters' are discussed, and decisions taken for any future course of action. Following his decision to take up arms, Guru Hargobind set out to build an army which he gradually equipped with arms and ammunitions - traditional and modern (canons), horses, and elephants. This shift in thinking and preparedness of army to meet any eventualities was the turning point in Sikh history, as no previous Guru had resorted to this degree of combat preparedness. Parallel to his army preparedness, Guru Hargobind also continued with the preaching of the principles of Sikhism in the plains and the hill areas around it.

With regard to Hargobind, fortunately there is a first-hand eyewitness account from Dabistan (c.1645) (Mowbad, 2010) that is worth reproducing here for the readers. This eyewitness account in summary form reproduced below (paragraphing is this author's) not only gives us the insight into the lives of the Guru but also gives us a glimpse of the history surrounding the Guru. Some clarifications are provided after the quote (spellings and all the rest as in original)

"Having recorded truly something of the Sikhs in general, I will now give an account of the chiefs of this tribes whom I have known myself. Hargovind was always attached to the stirrup of the victorious Jahāngīr. He became involved in many difficulties; one of them was that he appropriated to himself the pay due to the soldiers in advance…he kept beside many servants and was addicted to hunting."

"Jahāngīr, on account of the money due to the army, and of the mulct* imposed upon Arjuimmal sent Hargovind to the fort of Gwalior, where he remained imprisoned twelve years. He was not permitted to eat a good meal . During that time the deputies and other Sikhs used to come and bow before the walls of the fort. At last, moved by pity, the king granted him liberty."

"After Jahāngīr's death, Hargovind entered the service of his majesty Amír-ul Múnenîn Abu-ul-muzafer shahab ed-din Muhammed saheb Keran sani shah Jehan, the victorious king. When the Guru returned to Balnesh, which is a district of the Penjah, he attached himself to Yar Khan, the eunuch, who held the office of a Foujdar in the Nawabí of the Penjab, and whom he assisted in the administration."

"Hargovind returned to Rámadaspúr…..there he sustained an attack of the army which Shah Jehan, sent against him, and the Guru's property was then plundered. From thence he fled to Kartarpúr; there too war reached him, and on this occasion Mír Badherah, and Páindah Khan, the son of Fattah Khan Ganáida, found their death. Before and after this, he encountered great dangers of war, but with the aid of God he escaped unhurt, although he lost his property."

"It is related by one, Sadah by name, that in this war a man aimed a blow at the Guru, who parried it and struck him with his blade, saying: "Not in that manner, but so the "sword is used;" and with one blow he made an end of his foe. One of the companions of the Guru asked the author of this work: "What was the purport of the words by which the Guru accompanied his blow?" I said: "It was to give instruction, as it belongs to a Guru to teach also "how to strike a blow with a sword; for a Guru is called a teacher : he did not strike out of anger, which would have been blameable."

"At last he retired from the war of Kartarpúr to Bhagwarah, and because there, in the vicinity of Lahore, he met with difficulties, he betook himself from thence in haste to Geraitpúr, which lies in the mountainous district of the Penjab....The Guru Hargovind, in a letter to the author of this work, gave himself the title of Nânac, which was his right distinction. I saw him in the year 1053 of the Hejirah (A. D. 1643) in Kirtpúr."

*Fine or compulsory payment.

(Dabistan, (c.1645) op. cit; excerpts from pp. 272-277).

This quote describes how the increasing popularity of the Guru started to prove to be a threat, as a result of which he was imprisoned for 12 years and how his devotees still came and paid homage to him by bowing outside on the prison wall, and how he was released. It is said that some 52 hill chieftains were also in prison and who were good to Guru Hargobind and whom he refused to leave behind. As a compromise, the Guru was permitted to free anyone who could hold on to his arm. The story has it that a gown with 52 arms was made and Guru Hargobind freed the chieftains with him.

After the release, the Guru's relations with the emperor Jahāngīr improved and he also took up a post within the Mughal army setup, a mention of which is made in the excerpts. Gupta (Gupta, 1984) has hypothesized that the Guru did so to obtain insights into the functioning of the emperor's military machine. The second half of the above excerpts describe the combat skills and *samurai*-like behaviour of the Guru with his enemy. Slain Páindah Khan mentioned in the excerpt in one place he had worked with the Guru at one time as an ally. The Guru was equally ruthless with his enemies who betrayed him. One such was *Chandu Shah* who had grudges with the Guru after the Guru had spurned his daughter's wedding proposal. It was suspected that Chandu, holding a grudge against the Guru, had been feeding adverse information about the Guru to the emperor; the Guru also had reasons to believe that Chandu was instrumental in his father's (Arjan Dev) arrest, imprisonment, and torture leading to his death. After being on good terms with the emperor, Guru Hargobind obtained access to Chandu, had him tied and dragged through the streets of Amritsar, made him sit on hot slams (as his father reportedly was subjected to) resulting in his excruciating death[77].

Jahāngīr died in 1627 and was succeeded by his son Shahjahan and the troubles for the Guru started once again. Shahjahan, on coming to power, slew all his brothers and nephews and clearly was in no mood to tolerate any threat, small or large. Guru Hargobind fought five battles with the army of Shahjahan, often showing exemplary bravery even

---

[77] (Latif, 1891) as reported in (Gupta, 1984, p. 255).

when outnumbered in the battlefield. Guru Hargobind died peacefully in 1644 aged 49.

A Recapitulation of Key Contributions of Five Gurus Prior to Guru Hargobind

Up until the times of the sixth Guru Hargobind, the mission of five Gurus preceding him was preaching the gospel of God in a peaceful manner and not getting entangled with the rulers of their time; in modern parlance, they stayed away from the politics of the rulers and their administration - not that it did not affect them, or their disciples in some measure, but their approach to life and the Guru's teachings was peaceful. They did, however, undertake the task of building infrastructure surrounding the budding Sikh religion.

The first Guru, Guru Nanak, laid the foundation of moral and ethical values by the very first set of hymns emphasizing devotion in the name of God. The second Guru, Guru Amar Das, after discovering the written Gurmukhi script for the masses, took the initiative to extend education to the common man which made a dent on the monopoly of learning of the upper classes. The third Guru, Guru Amar Das, worked to reduce class prejudices and strengthened the growing concept of the free community kitchen - langar tradition, where all ate together sitting in a row; discouraged *Sati* tradition where the wife sacrificed herself on her husband's pyre; formalised the wedding ritual; initiated religious centres in the state and laid the foundation of Amritsar. Guru Arjan Dev compiled the Scripture, constructed the *Harimandir Sahib* and laid foundations of two cities - Taran Taran and Kartarpur. Thus, along with the preaching of the Sikh faith, for which predecessor Gurus exhorted disciples to focus, strengthen, and control their minds for daily meditations and devotion to God, they also helped build soft and hard infrastructure for the future of Sikhs.

Contributions of Guru Hargobind

The sixth Guru Hargobind was a turning point in how Sikhs started to view their personal and social life, for he taught Sikhs, and showed by personal example that it was not enough to strengthen the mind and be always peaceful. If need be, it was legitimate to take up arms to defend oneself and the vulnerable. His premise was that unchecked violence would only increase in intensity and further weaken the oppressed. This was probably the first time that a saint began to advocate the use of arms. Punjab, being the first crossing point for invaders, had started to witness the atrocities beginning in the mid-10th century, and it was the 17th century - that is, a gap of around 700 years that a saint had turned to the might of the sword to fight for injustice and dignity. The importance of this cannot be underestimated as Gurus that followed continued with this approach, culminating in the supreme sacrifice of the tenth Guru, Guru Gobind Singh to which we shall come to later.

Armed confrontation required physical fitness and training in martial arts. Guru Hargobind who understood this, was vocal in emphasizing this side of the combat. His concept of spiritual and worldly power was innovative in that spiritual power does strengthen the mind and part of this strength emanates from worldly power that one should also command - both *complement* each other. In simple language, what he advocated to his disciples was that 'people not always respect you because you are a good religious and spiritual person, they respect you also when they fear you'[78].

Sikh Gurus from Guru Hargobind onwards never advocated violence let alone intimidation. What they advocated was not to be silent in the wake of a threat or attack on themselves or on the weak. Reasoning was that with this signal people would refrain or think carefully before intimidating you. We will discuss this fact in some detail elsewhere in the book.

Guru Hargobind also eliminated the taboo of hunting and eating meat. (Burton, 2008, p. 51). This would have proved a boon for Sikh soldiers who often had guerrilla encounters with the Mughal soldiers following which they disappeared in the forests where animals could be hunted for a rich protein diet. Because in hunting, animals are killed swiftly, eating meat by killing an animal with the minimum of pain came to be an accepted method of eating meat. This method (called *jhatka* meaning swift) is in contrast to the Muslim way of preparing meat by Halal methods (in which animals are bled to death slowly with the utterance of prayers)[79]. Finally, we also notice from his act of brutal revenge on Chandu that he considered it legitimate to have your revenge on someone who has been sly and brutal to you or to your family. One would say that he had the streaks of a maverick Guru in him; possibly, this would be acceptable, but we ought to bear in mind that, along with all this, he never neglected his religious duties of preaching the tenets of Sikh religion. Guru Hargobind

---

[78] Author Carroll Bryant puts it rather bluntly: 'If they are not going to respect you, then they best damn well fear you'.
[79] There are elaborate rules as to how an animal should be slaughtered, in what manner, and which meat can be eaten (WHO, 1997)

had three wives from whom he had five sons and a
daughter.

Table 2. 2 Key Data related to 10 Sikh Gurus

Name, Date of Birth and Death, Age at Guru ship, Family	Period of Guru-ship and successor	Rulers in the lifetime of the Guru	Core message and contribution to Sikhism	Specific Contribution
Col-1	Col-2	Col-3	Col-4	Col-5
1. Guru Nanak (b. Nankana Sahib) 1469 – 1539. Lived 70 years. Considered Guru from an early age. 1 Sister: Nanki Married Mata Sulakhni. 2 Sons: Sri Chand Lakhmi Chand.	1469– 1539 70 years of Guru-ship Nominated Disciple Angad (born as Lehna) for succession	Bahlūl Lodī (1451-1489) Sikandar Lodī (1489-1517) Ibrahim Lodī (1517-1526) Babur (1526-1530) Humayun (1530-1540)	*Nirvana* through disciplined life and meditation on the divine name without superficial rituals and rites. Advocated earning livelihood by honest means. Inculcated sense of sharing. Preached against caste prejudices.	974 hymns included in the Scripture. Founded city of Kartarpur (meaning city of the Creator-now in Pakistan) – 40km on the right flank of river Ravi and 52km to the north of Indian border at Amritsar. Taught virtue of **HUMILITY**.
2. Guru Angad Dev (b. Matte di Sarai) 1504 – 1552.	1539– 1552 13 years of Guru-ship. Nominated devotee	Humayun (1530-1540) Sher Shah Suri	Selfless service to humanity. Against exhibitionist and	62 hymns included in the Scripture. Compiled first autobiographica l notes of Guru Nanak[80]

---

80 Popularly known as 'Bale wali Janam Sakhi' (autobiography by Bala).
Bala was one of two disciples of Guru Nanak who accompanied him most of
his life, as a result of which was eyewitness to events in Guru Nanak's life).
Note: The 1540 Battle of <u>Kannauj</u> was fought between Humayun and Sher

Lived 48 years. Guru-ship at age 35. Married Mata Khivi. 2 Sons: Baba Dassu; Baba Dattu. 2 Daughters: Bibi Amro Bibi Anokhi	Amar Das for succession	(1540-1545) Islam Shah (1545-1554) Humayun (1555-1556)	hypocritical lifestyles.	Formalized Gurmukhi, the written script for spoken Panjabi. Opened schools to teach it. Emphasised on physical fitness Instilled the virtue of **OBEDIENCE.**
3.Guru Amar Das (b. Khadur Sahib) 1479-1574 Lived 95 years. Guru-ship at age 73. Married Mansa Devi. 2 Sons: Bhai Mohan; Bhai Murari.	1552–1574 22 years of Guru ship Nominated son-in-law Ram Das for succession	Akbar (1556-1605)	Renewed vigour to community kitchen. Established 22 religious centres in the State, decentralising the administrative work of Sikh religious affairs.	907 hymns included in the Scripture. Four of these hymns are used to perform all Sikh weddings. Owing to good relations with Akbar had *Jazia tax* (annual per person tax on non-Muslims) abolished. Highlighted balance between asceticism and worldly duties. Advocated against *Sati* system. Emphasised virtue of

Shah Suri in which Humayun was defeated; Mughal empire was passed to Afghans (Suri Dynasty). Humayun spent 12 years in exile.

				EQUALITY.
2 Daughters Bibi Dani Bibi Bhani.				
4.Guru Ram Das (aka Bhāī Jeṭhā) (b. Lahore). 1534-1581 Lived 47 years. Guru-ship at age 40. Married Bibi Bhani (daughter of 3ʳᵈ Guru Amar Das). 3 sons: Prithi Chand; Mahan Dev; Arjan Dev	1574 – 1581 07 years of Guru-ship Nominated youngest of 3 sons, Arjan Dev for succession	Akbar (1556-1605)	Founded Rāmdāspur which later became Amritsar. Urged devotees to be true Sikhs by imbibing the name of God.	679 hymns included in the Scripture. Advocated virtues of SERVICE.
5.Guru Arjan Dev (b. Goindwal) 1563-1606 Lived 43 years. Guru ship at age 18. Married Mata Ganga. 1 son: Hargobind	1581– 1606 25 years of Guru-ship Nominated only son Hargobind as successor	Akbar (1556-1605) Jahāngīr (1605-1627)	Initiated and urged Sikhs to contribute 1/10ᵗʰ of earnings for community purposes. Showed the way to martyrdom for the rightcous cause.	2218 hymns included in the Scripture. Compiled Sikh Holy Scripture. Initiated in 1588 construction of what is now known as *Harimandir Sahib*. Showed the virtue of SELF SACRIFICE.
6.Guru Hargobind	1606 – 1644	Jahāngīr (1605-1627)	Preached that inaction against evil	Introduced the concept of early morning choirs

(b. Wadāli) (1595-1644). Lived 49 years. Guru ship at age 11. Only child of parents. Three wives: Damodri; Nanki; Marvahi. 5 sons: Gurditta Ani Rai Atal Rai Tegh Bahadur Suraj Mal. 1 daughter: Bibi Veero	38 years of Guru-ship. Nominated grandson Hari Rai as successor	Shahjahan (1628-1658)	encourages further evil. Gave Sikhs a warrior persona. Encouraged Sikhs to inculcate the spirit of sainthood as well as the worldly power, since former is dependent on latter.	where groups of devotees walk around their locality singing hymns. Within the complex of *Harimandir Sahib*, constructed a separate building '*Akal Takhat*' – the admin complex of temporal authority of Sikhs. Emphasised the virtue of **JUSTICE.**
7.Guru Har Rāī (b. Kiratpur Sahib) 1630-1661 Lived 31 years. Guru ship at age 14. Married Mata Krishen Devi. 2 sons Baba Ram Rai; Guru Hari Krishen	1644 – 1661 17 years of Guru-ship. Nominated younger son Hari Krishen as successor	Aurangzeb (1658-1707)	Added tradition of katha recitals to the Shabad Kirtan tradition. Love for animals.	Advocated benevolence towards animals and constructed 'Animal Care Homes'. Propagated the uses of Ayurvedic medicines. Advocated virtue of **MERCY.**

8.Guru Hari Krishan (b. Kartapur Sahib). 1656-1664 Lived 07 years. Guru ship at age 05. Not married.	1661 – 1664 03 years of Guru- ship. Nominate d Tegh Bahadur as his successor	Aurangze b (1658- 1707).	Service to sick and needy.	Died serving the sick in Delhi during smallpox epidemic. Emphasised the virtue of **PURITY** of thought and soul.
9.Guru Tegh Bahadur (b. Amritsar) 1621-1675 Lived 54 years. Guru ship at age 44. Married Mata Gujri. 1 son: Gobind Singh	1665 – 1675 10 years of Guru- ship Nominate d for succession only son Gobind Rai (Gobind Singh after Baptism).	Aurangze b (1658- 1707)	Belief in the right of freedom to follow one's religion	115 hymns included in the Scripture. Fought battles with the Mughals against forcible conversion to Islam. Gave the ultimate sacrifice for his cause (was publicly beheaded). Virtue of **CALMNESS** in adversity.
10.Guru Gobind Singh (b. Patna). 1666-1708 Lived 42 years. Guru-ship at age 09. Married Mata Jito; Mata Sundri; Mata	1675 – 1708 33 years of Guru- ship. Nominate d *Guru Granth Sahib* – Sikh's holy Scripture as future Guru,	Aurangze b (1658- 1707) Bahadur Shah-I (1707- 1712)	Never be afraid to adopt the right path and do the right thing.	(By choice) 1 hymn included in the Scripture. Gave Sikhs a distinct identity. Imbued in Sikhs the sense of courage, righteousness, and sacrifice. Discontinued the tradition of succession of Guru-ship, ending the

Sahib Devan. 4 sons: Ajit Singh; Jujhar Singh; Zorawar Singh; Fateh Singh.	ending succession line of living Gurus.			complexities of succession. Showed the virtue of **ROYAL COURAGE.**

Sources consulted: (Greenlees, 1952); (Singh & Fenech, The Oxford Handbook of Sikh Studies, 2014); (Singh & Singh, 2006); (Gupta, 1984); (Dhillon, 1988); (Singh S. , 2004); (Singh H. , 1992); (Singh H. , 1992)
https://www.worldatlas.com/articles/timeline-of-the-mughal-dynasty.html (Accessed intermittently, finally on 10-2-2022);
The Encyclopaedia of Sikhism (4 Vol 1992, 2011); Encyclopaedia: Britannica: https://www.britannica.com/; (Singh G. , n.d) Twarikh Guru Khalsa: various Gurus (In Gurmukhi);
https://www.britannica.com/summary/Mughal-Dynasty-Timeline(Accessed intermittently .

Ruler in Guru Hargobind's Time

Jahāngīr (1605-1627) and his son Shahjahan (1627-1658) were at the helm in the time of Guru Hargobind. As we have pointed out previously, Jahāngīr and Guru Hargobind started on a wrong footing but in due course their relations became smoother - most probably, owing to the exercising of some diplomatic skills by Guru Hargobind, who, as we saw, persuaded Jahāngīr to handover *Chandu* to him so he could exact his revenge on him. Shahjahan who came to power after slaying all his brothers and nephews, was a tough emperor to deal with, as a result of which Guru Hargobind fought several battles with his forces before smoothing terms with him. In the final analysis if we were to describe the character of Guru Hargobind, we could say that 'justice' was the hallmark of his operations. Sikh masses accordingly associate this trait with him.

Seventh Guru : Guru Har Rāī (1630-1661)

Teach me to feel another's woe; to hide the fault I see; that the mercy I show to others; that mercy also shows to me (Alexander Pope).

As stated, Guru Hargobind had five sons and a daughter. He, however, chose Har Rāī his grandson (from eldest son Gurditta), to be the next Guru, in preference to any of his own sons. To recapitulate, Guru Har Rāī was born into an upper Sodhi caste household. His father died while he was eight years old. Original sources on the life and times of Hargobind are scant. Oft-cited *Dabistan* (c.1645) (Mowbad, 2010) has very little to add to our knowledge, save for the following interesting incident in *Dabistan* leading to the Guru-ship of Har Rāī (paragraphing is this author's). Clarifications follow at the end of the excerpt.

> "The Guru Har-govind, in a letter to the author of this work, gave himself the title of Nânac, which was his right distinction. I saw him in the year 1053 of the Hejirah (A. D. 1643) in Kirtpúr."

> "The Guru Har-ráyi was the grandson of the said Guru. His father was Garuta (or Guru daitya), who is known under the name of Bábá Jév. The Guru Har-govind wished first to transmit his place to his son Garuta, or Bábá Jév but the Guru Nághura, one of the Sikhs,

brought his daughter to Bábá Jév. The Bábá wished to send her to his private apartments. His wife, the mother of Har-rayi, complained of it to Hargovind, her father-in-law, who, having heard her, said to Bábá Jév: "Having given to Nághura the name of my son, I own him as such, and his daughter cannot go to you, my son." Nághura refused to take back his daughter nor would Bábá Jév give her up. The Guru Har-govind then said: "May neither happiness nor success ever attend this husband and his wife!" Upon that, the same day, Bábá Jév threw away his nuptial dress and sent the daughter of the Guru Nághura untouched back to her house."

"In consequence of this event, Har-govind showed a more particular esteem for his grandson Har-rayi , the son of Bábá Jév. He gave him the name of his father, Bábá Jév, and appointed him his successor. Invested with this dignity, Har-rayi remained one year in Kirtpúr."

"When in the year of the Hejirah 1055 (A. D. 1645) Najábet Khan, the son of Sharogh Mirza, by order of the pádsháh Shah-jehan, invaded with an army the land of the rája Tarachand , and made the rája a prisoner, the Guru Har-ráyi betook himself to Thapal*, which the town is situated in the district of the rája Keramperkás, not far from Sirhind. The Sikhs call Har-rayi the seventh Guru. He was a great friend of the author of this work. I will therefore give an account of some among the principal chiefs whom I knew, as well as of some customs of this people. The Sikhs distinguish also the deputies of their Gurus by the name of Rámdais, "servants of God or of an idol.""

(*Dabistan c.1645 op. cit,* pp.281-82).
*Possibly Taksal - a village in the state of Himachal Pradesh in the foothills of the Himalayas.

The narration in the passage above is a little convoluted. Simplifying, it goes something like this. Guru Hargobind's eldest son is Gurditta (Garuta in the passage) who in turn has a son named Har Rāī. Guru Hargobind is father-in-law to Gurditta's (Gordita in the passage) wife (Bibi Nihal Kaur). A disciple whom Hargobind had given his name brought his daughter to Gurditta (possibly to be his second wife). Gurditta's wife complained to her father-in-law. It is not clear whether the objection was owing to Gurditta taking a second wife, or because there is a taboo marrying within the caste where family members are considered related. In either case, owing to the objection raised, Guru Hargobind declined the wedding proposal and conveyed his decision to Gurditta (his son) who must have been asked to send the girl back to her parents. Gurditta, it seems initially refused. The disobedience so annoyed Guru Hargobind that he chose not to pass over the Guru-ship to his son, even when the matter was resolved, and the girl was sent back untouched to her parent's house.

Sikhs reading this passage will possibly understand the intensity of this incident better. Hargobind, as a mark of respect, did not want to go against the wishes of his daughter-in-law. He had expected that his son would do the same when he asked him to return the girl. Gurditta's refusal must have infuriated Guru Hargobind. Gurditta possibly had to be persuaded that it was almost sacrilegious to go against the wishes of elders in those times - especially in conjugal matters which would affect the whole family. This incident may look minor but it most likely cost Gurditta his Guru-ship. The Guru-ship came to be passed to Hargobind's grandson Har Rāī (son of Gurditta). This author's impression is that the decision was based on the abilities of Har Rāī, closely observed by Guru Hargobind, but it is equally possible that the decision encompassed in it an affront to his son Gurditta for his disobedience. The move to make grandson Har Rāī the next Guru was also a clever one, since Gurditta, though may have been furious over the decision of him not getting the Guru-ship, could not harm or come in the way of his own son who was chosen to be the next Guru.

Contributions of Guru Har Rāī

Guru Har Rāī was more of a saint than a warrior. 'Mercy' is said to be his hallmark. He continued the work of previous Gurus by preaching the doctrine of Sikhism. His particular efforts in this direction in the state of Bihar where several Sikh centres by Har Rāī's messengers were established are worth noting (Gupta, 1984, p. 180). Guru Har Rāī did not like to hurt anyone let alone engage in bloody revenge and wars. He reared sick and injured animals in his private zoo in Kartarpur. Guru Har Rāī was also a propagator of Ayurvedic medicine[81]. His devotion to Sikhism can be gauged from the fact that he ex-communicated his son from the sect. The event goes something like this:

Aurangzeb, the then emperor, demanded to know if there was a profane sentence in the Scripture as he had heard that there was a hymn in which the word 'musselman' had been used in a derogatory manner. Guru Har Rāī sent his elder son Ram Rai to reason with the emperor the meaning of the verse in context of the hymn. Ram Rai who was aware of the fanatical nature of Aurangzeb towards Islam and given that he was in the pomp and show of the court and in the presence of the emperor and luminaries,

---

81 Both these passions can be said to be the forerunners of English charity 'The Royal Society for the Prevention of Cruelty to Animals (RSPCA)' and Ramdev's Patanjali Ayurved - a large set-up of Ayurveda based products at Haridwar, India. Here one cannot help being reminded of the following quote of Gandhi: 'the greatness of a nation and its moral progress can be judged by the way its animals are treated.'

buckled under fear and said that the word used was not 'musselman' but 'beimaan' (without honour). So incensed was Har Rāī with his son for lying and distorting the true meaning of the hymn in the holy Scripture that he ex-communicated him and changed his mind to make him the next Guru. Subsequently, nothing Ram Rai did would bring him back either in the community or face-to-face with his father who did not want to see him anymore (Macauliffe, 1909, pp. 309-310). Guru Har Rāī chose his younger son Harkrishan– then barely five years old to be the next Guru.

Ruler in Guru Har Rāī Time

Although Guru Har Rāī maintained an army of 2200 he was never engaged in a combat. He led a saintly life. This was probably also the reason that neither rulers - Shah Jahan or Aurangzeb saw him belligerent and had no military encounters with him, though there was an interface with him which is described below, but it was not bloody.

Aurangzeb (1658-1707) was at the helm at the time of Guru Har Rāī. In the passage cited above from *Dabistan* there is an indication that Guru Har Rāī retired for twelve years in the Taksal region in the hills. This was owing to Aurangzeb's father Shahjahan's drive in 1645 against expansion and taking chieftains prisoners of surrounding areas where Guru Har Rāī was also residing. As a precaution, Guru Har Rāī opted to move to the hills. In 1658 Guru Har Rāī returned to Kiratpur, which was also the year when Aurangzeb had defeated his rebellious brother Dara Shikoh who was close to their father Shah Jahan, and who was the preferred heir apparent to the throne.

Dara Shikoh fled and sought help and refuge with Guru Har Rāī. Keeping in with the ethos of Sikh values,

Har Rāī could not turn him (or anyone) away seeking protection. It is not clear how much help Guru Rai actually offered but the fact that Guru Har Rāī had entertained a meeting with Dara Shikoh (a renegade prince according to Aurangzeb), it was enough to arouse Aurangzeb's suspicion (Singh K. , A History of the Sikhs: Vol 1 1469-1838, 2004, p. 65). This was the time when Aurangzeb asked Har Rāī to justify the inclusion of what Aurangzeb thought was offensive reference to Islam in the Scripture and Har Rāī had sent his son to provide a rational explanation - this incident has been narrated above.

Aurangzeb had detained Guru Har Rāī's son Ram Rai, who with his sycophancy got himself in the good books of the emperor, who now wished Ram Rai to be the next Guru. Had this happened it would have been a silent coup by Aurangzeb and would have made it convenient for him to deal with Sikhs in the future. For, in Ram Rai as a Guru, he would have had a docile, reconciled, and amicable leader towards Islam. Aurangzeb, while he was the governor of Sind and Multan (1648-52) was aware of Guru's influence on Jat peasantry in Majha (north-west region) and Malwa (southern region) (Gupta, 1984, p. 181). Clearly, helping elevate Ram Rai to Guru-ship would have been in Islam's favour. This wish, however, did not materialise as Har Rāī died in 1707 at age 32 and nominated his younger son Hari Krishen as the next Guru.

Eighth Guru: Guru Hari Krishen (1656-1664)

Let us touch the dying, the poor, the lonely and the unwanted according to the graces we have received and let us not be ashamed or slow to do the humble work (Mother Teresa)

Guru Hari Krishen was born in 1656 and died in 1664 before reaching eight years of age. He was made Guru at a young age of five. However, it is so held that he showed maturity from a young age and was capable of holding himself in public meetings. He also sent missionaries to the farthest outposts of the region and conversed with confidence with those who came to see him (Greenlees, 1952, p. 68). By nature, he was devoted to serving people and famously is said to have helped the people of Delhi during the outbreak of smallpox and cholera, owing to which he himself contacted the disease and died of it. Aurangzeb was keen to install someone as Guru whom he could control, so he summoned Hari Krishen to Delhi where his elder brother Ram Rai was already staying as a state guest. Before any follow-up to the issue of Guru-ship could happen, Hari Krishen died. Before his death he conveyed to people around him that the next Guru would be found in the village of Bakala - it seems Hari Krishen muttered the words *Baba Bakale* before his death. Hari

Krishen's uncle Teg Bahadur was at that time living in that area, so it was deduced that Hari Krishen meant Tegh Bahadur to be the next Guru.

Contributions of Guru Hari Krishen

The principal contribution of Guru Hari Krishen is taken to be his trait of absolute purity of mind from a tender age. Children by nature are unspoilt anyway by the vagaries of social ills; Guru Hari Krishen is said to be totally benign and pure in his thoughts and soul and approach to the job he was handed over at such a young age.

Ruler in Guru Hari Krishen's Time

Aurangzeb was at the helm during the time of Guru Hari Krishen, but there is no meeting or record of his interaction with him or any of his emissaries. The closest that has been recorded is the following incident reported by (Greenlees, 1952, p. 68): "His father had warned the little Guru never to let Aurangzeb meet him, but as the Delhi Sikhs longed for his *darshan* (sight) he consented to visit the capital, but not to see the emperor. Raja Jai Singh of Amber, who had been sent to fetch him, agreed to these terms and the party set out:....when Har Krishen reached Delhi he was quite willing for Ramrai to take over all the political and organizing sides of the Guru-ship, but Ramrai was furious at the suggested compromise and demanded the integral Guru-ship for himself at once. While Hari Krishen was in Delhi, plague was raging in the city, and he healed many people of the dreaded disease by a few words or by the very sight of him. He again refused to meet the emperor in person but sent him a copy of one of Guru Nanak's hymns, which Aurangzeb is said to have approved." Soon after, Guru Hari Krishen contacted smallpox and succumbed to it.

Ninth Guru: Guru Tegh Bahadur (1621-1675)

The nearer a man comes to a calm mind, the closer he is to strength
(Marcus Aurelius)

Tegh Bahadur was born in 1621 and was residing in the village Bakala when dying Guru Hari Krishen announced him to be the successor, following which Sikhs set out to look for him. Tegh Bahadur was born within the Guru family lineage, so he was not difficult to trace but when Sikhs reached Bakala they found 21 rival claimants to the Guru-ship (Greenlees, 1952, p. 70); one of them even hired an assassin to eliminate him[82]! Paradoxically, Tegh Bahadur who had an ascetic, hermit like nature and preferred to be left alone, had retired to a quiet place (near Karatpur) away from the claimants' squabbles; he never lodged a claim for the Guru-ship of the sect. He was nevertheless urged and convinced by the devotees that it was the wish of the dying Guru Hari Krishen.

---

82 Memo: Tegh Bahadur was the youngest son of Guru Hargobind whose son was Gurditta and whose son was Har Kirshen.

Tegh Bahadur may have had a saintly temperament, but he was well trained in the art of combat by his father Guru Hargobind. Tegh Bahadur was born as Tyag Mal but was bestowed the name of Tegh Bahadur meaning 'mighty of the sword' by his father after he had shown exemplary courage in one of Hargobind's battles with Mughals when he was just 15 years of age. He had also acquired education in Gurmukhi, Hindi, and Sanskrit and in Hindu classics - Vedas, Upanishads, and the Puranas. There are tales surrounding his pious nature and mystical attributes. He is said to have forgiven the attackers who had made an attempt on his life, proclaiming that 'forgiveness is equal to ablutions at all places of pilgrimage' (Macauliffe, 1909, p. 334). He is also said to have read the mind of a devotee who had survived a sinking ship and had pledged 500 gold coins but offered just two to see if Guru could read his mind. Guru Tegh Bahadur was married but as yet had no children when he ascended to the throne of Guru-ship.

Contributions of Guru Tegh Bahadur

Not great many details are known of Guru Tegh Bahadur's time leading to Guru-ship in 1664 except that he spent most of his time ruminating in the memory of God. Following in Guru Nanak's footsteps, Guru Tegh Bahadur travelled to Eastern and Central India - in particular to Mathura, Agra, and Prayag (Allahabad). This author believes he chose travels to pilgrimage centres as he was likely to meet maximum God-fearing devotees in these religious clusters looking for salvation and *Nirvana*. Guru Tegh Bahadur might have been reluctant to succeed as a Guru but once he accepted the responsibility, he performed his duties to the point of sacrificing his life for it.

Guru Tegh Bahadur was aware that for the sect to survive it must increase its membership to a critical mass where it would have a momentum of its own. Although he never publicly declared this to be a critical issue, he seems to have well understood it, for as stated, he had already undertaken efforts to preach to the masses the newly formed religious doctrines of Guru Nanak. After he assumed the duties of Guru-ship he continued his journeys. He had lived in *Bakala* for over 20 years and was well entrenched in his comfort zone. He could have continued, and devotees would have visited him there. But he decided that it was essential to travel and meet people living in far off places.

By the time of Teg Bahadur, who was the ninth in succession, the fame of the sect had reasonably established owing to the good deeds and efforts of the previous eight Gurus, and it was critical that their good work be continued. In one of such journeys, Guru Tegh Bahadur is famously said to have mediated and avoided war between Aurangzeb's forces and Ahom tribe in Assam in eastern India. Guru Tegh Bahadur established, the now famous city of Anandpur (city of joy). Guru Tegh Bahadur also had literary skills and 115 of his hymns are included in the Scripture. The biggest contribution of Tegh Bahadur was his belief, (following on from Nanak) that all 'human beings are born equal' and that no one should subjugate anyone. So strong this belief was in him that, as we will see below, he gave his life for it.

Ruler in Guru Tegh Bahadur's Time

Aurangzeb was the emperor in the time of Guru Tegh Bahadur. Aurangzeb was well known for his orthodox beliefs in Islam, so much so that, in his opinion anyone who did not adhere to Islam was an infidel. Hindus, in his opinion, were the despicable infidels who should be converted to Islam by persuasion or by coercion. Pandits in Kashmir and Punjab, known to be pure Hindus, were in the direct firing line since persuasion method had not worked with them. In desperation, distraught Kashmiri pandits approached their Guru leader Tegh Bahadur for help, where upon Tegh Bahadur famously seemed to have told them to convey to Aurangzeb's messengers that if their leader converts to Islam, they will all convert with him.

As a result of the above declaration, Tegh Bahadur was summoned and he along with his five disciples had to present themselves to Aurangzeb. On their refusal to convert to Islam they were imprisoned and tortured. Tegh Bahadur was publicly beheaded[83]. He is famously known to have stayed very calm throughout the ordeal. His body and head were collected by devotees. In Delhi, respectively, Gurdwaras *Sis Ganj* and *Rakab Ganj* stand to mark the place where Tegh Bahadur was beheaded and where he was cremated. It has also been hypothesized in the literature that Guru Tegh Bahadur was executed for his tenacious religious beliefs but also for the fact that he was gaining rapid popularity among the masses in the north and central India and elsewhere. The incident described above, where he successfully mediated between imperial forces and Ahom king in Assam may have pleased Aurangzeb, but equally it could also have alarmed him since his deputies had repeatedly failed to win over the rebel king, either by persuasion or by force. After the martyrdom of Guru Tegh Bahadur, his son Gobind Das, then age 9, was elevated to Guru-ship by the devotees.

---

83 There are a number of explanations leading to the execution of Tegh Bahadur; Cf. e.g., (Macauliffe, 1909); (Gupta, 1984); (Singh S. , 2004)

Tenth Guru: Guru Gobind Singh (1666-1708)

Cowards die many times before their deaths; the valiant never taste of death but once...it seems to me most strange that men should fear; seeing that death, a necessary end, will come when it will come.
(*Julius Caesar, Act 2, Scene 2*)

Guru Gobind Singh was born in 1666 and died (assassinated) in 1708. In the 42 years of his life, he accorded Sikhism a distinct identity in appearance, enthused in Sikhs values of valour and honour *par excellence*, trained himself to be a skilled rider, archer and swordsman, trained his followers in the art of war, fought 20 small and large battles, built five forts as part of his combat measures, sacrificed himself and four of his sons in the defence of Sikh beliefs and terminated the Guru-ship model of Sikhism, declaring the holy Scripture (Guru *Granth Sahib*) the future spiritual Guru of Sikhs. A connoisseur of Indian classical music and a linguist scholar in Arabic, Persian, Sanskrit, Gurmukhi, Hindi, and other sister Indian languages, invigorated the literary side of Sikhs by giving them some of the finest enduring hymns found in Sikh literature. He went down battling for the identity of the Sikhs and their rights, ultimately making the supreme sacrifice of himself and his four sons in the process. By any measure he far surpassed the role of a Guru leader.

Gobind Singh, born as Govind Das in a Sodhi Khatri family in Patna, presently a sprawling city along the south bank of the river Ganges in Bihar state. His father was Guru Tegh Bahadur who was executed by Aurangzeb. His grandfather, Hargobind, was imprisoned by Aurangzeb for 12 years and his great-grandfather, Guru Arjan Dev, was also tortured to death by Aurangzeb. Along with these, several of his devout followers - in particular Mati Das, Sati Das and Dyal Das were also tortured to death by the emperor for refusal to convert to Islam[84]. These facts have to be born in mind as they might have had the deepest of influence on the conscious-subconscious mind of Gobind Singh. These facts, till this day, also carry the deepest of legacies in the Sikh psyche (wounds are still fresh in the mind and hearts of Sikhs) against Mughal rulers.

From his birthplace Patna, where Gobind Singh spent his early childhood, he was moved to Punjab. As the only son-heir of ninth Guru Tegh Bahadur, he was brought up well and acquired literary and combat skills mentioned previously. He was also said to be a fair complexioned and handsome person who liked to dress well and was fond of hunting. As was the tradition in those days he was married young at age eleven. He subsequently married twice more and had five sons from his first two marriages. A man of great honour and highest of disciplines, he was, as we shall see later in the section, not diplomatic or sly in his dealings. This was, perhaps, the reason that he never sought to build

---

84 It has been hypothesized in the literature that because Aurangzeb came to the throne after slaying his family which is anti-Islam, he wanted to prove that he was a devout Muslim, converting by any means, all Hindus to Islam. He became a zealot in his mission and as a result was particularly cruel to Hindus.

an empire with a desire to rule when he had the opportunity. As we shall see later, these lacunae may have cost him his life.

It was during his stay in Anandpur Sahib, where, as a young confident person, he began to assert himself and draw his own followers who would flock to him for devotional purposes and martial skills. As stated, the beheading of his father Tegh Bahadur and the torture meted on his family and followers by the Muslim machinery at the time must have had a profound impact on young Gobind, who from a young age began to train and assert himself in the art of warfare, realising that it would not be long before he might have to draw swords with the enemy. Ominously, this proved right. Anandpur Sahib, where Guru Govind Singh was based is located on the edges of Himachal Pradesh, a hilly state adjoining Punjab and inhabited by a number of chieftains. His proactive warlike preparations did not fail to attract the attention of chieftains whose feeling of insecurity first brought skirmishes and later a battle with one Bhim Chand when Gobind Singh was merely 16 years of age and again when he was 19 years of age[85].

To avoid further escalation and on the invitation of a friendly chieftain, Gobind Singh moved to a hilly location *Paonta Sahib* on the banks of River Yamuna - about 200km southeast of Anandpur Sahib. He made it a centre of learning and martial training. Gobind Singh lived there for just three years when he was drawn into a major battle with a consortium of chieftains who, alarmed by his growing popularity and power, banded together to take him out.

---

85 Gupta (1984, p.228: Original source: (Hutchison & Vogel, 1933).

However, the army raised by Gobind Singh did a heroic job and the syndicate of chieftains lost the battle.

In 1688 Guru Gobind Singh moved back to the plains in Anandpur Sahib. This was a strategic long-term move which served twin purposes of being in his known environment and culture and where he could fortify his position. Battles, either with the hill chieftains adjoining Punjab, or the emperor, or with both the enemies hand in hand did not stop coming. In total, Guru Gobind Singh fought twenty battles, nine before the formation of Khalsa and eleven afterwards (Gupta, 1984, p. 225). As part of his combat measures, Gobind Singh also built five forts (*Keshgarh, Lohgarh, Holgarh, Anandgarh, and Fatehgarh*) on the border of Anandpur Sahib with connected underground channels. These forts with gurdwaras attached to each of them stand till this day.

Formation of Sikhs as a separate identity

As stated, of the twenty major and minor battles fought by Gobind Singh, nine were fought prior to the formation of *Khalsa* - the pure race, in 1699 when Gobind Singh was 33 years of age. As stated, Gobind Singh fought his first battle in 1682 with hill chieftain Bhim Chand when he was a mere 16 years of age. By the time of forming the Khalsa at age 33, he had gained sufficient insight that in order to be a successful warrior, he had to raise an army where soldiers would have equal status - i.e., the army would be devoid of castes, prejudices, or biases of any nature. It would also have a distinct identity so that anyone fleeing the battlefield would be instantly recognised. Above all, soldiers of such an army would be courageous and fearless.

Two definitions correspond well with what Guru Gobind Singh must have had in mind for his band of fighters. Courage involves five factors: *candour* - speak and hear the truth, *purpose* - pursue lofty and audacious goals, *rigor* - invent disciplines and make them stick, *risk* - empower, trust, and invest in relationships, and *will* - inspire optimism, spirit, and promise (Klein, 2003). For Woodward (Woodard, 2004, p. 174). Courage is the ability to act for a meaningful noble, good, or practical cause, despite experiencing the fear associated with perceived threats exceeding the available resources. Let us see how Gobind Singh set about to achieve these aims.

Legend has it that on 30th March 1699 in a gathering of devotees Guru Gobind Singh addressed the need to raise an army of warriors who would stand up to the enemy against all odds in a tyrannical world. Humility and non-violence alone were insufficient to decide one's fate - in such situations, sword which is equivalent to God is required - for as God subdues, so does the sword[86]. With the scene set in this manner, Guru Gobind Singh demanded the heads of five bravest souls present in the congregation. After stunned silence, one-by-one five devotees did rise to the challenge. Story has it that each time Gobind Singh took the devotee inside the tent and returned with a naked sword laced in blood. Clearly, the idea was to identify the bravest. The sword could have been laced in non-human blood, but the display did the job of identifying the bravest from the congregation. The act was repeated five times after which Gobind Singh returned with all five devotees who appeared on stage with similar saffron and blue colour dresses and garlands.

---

[86] Chandi Charitar II. Chandi Charitar II is a heroic poetic composition, found in the 5th chapter of *Dasam Granth* of Guru Gobind Singh. (Singh G. , 1690)

These brave souls were then baptised and Gobind Singh in turn asked them to baptise him[87]. Since then, tradition has it that a baptised Sikh can baptise a fellow Sikh. In conducting this process, Gobind Singh must have had in his mind to create a new Sikh race with the bravest of the brave, and this, he thought would be the ideal way. Many devotees on seeing the blood-stained sword must have imagined that those who have offered themselves have been sacrificed. Some may have thought that Guru had lost his mind; some possibly fled from the congregation! Clearly, remaining devotees though did not come forward on the dais on Gobind Singh's invitation, did not lose faith in their Guru, so the belief goes, and came to be proved right in time.

The new identity that Gobind Singh gave had five emblems visible and invisible to the public. Uncut hair (knotted under the turban), a small comb behind the knotted hair, a steel bangle, a dagger, and knee-high shorts. In those days, also in present times, *Nihangs* wore a free-flowing long dress that comes down to their knees. Baptised Sikhs habitually began to have a turban, which in fact is a multi-purpose object; it takes the blow of a weapon and protects from extreme heat and cold. The whole attire was well tuned for riding and for combat. The original five attributes were followed up with directives from the Guru - incidentally, also five in total - not to cut hair, smoke, or eat Halal meat, not to wear the cap worn by Muslims, and not to worship at tombs. Sikhs were also decreed to follow five practices; pray before undertaking an enterprise, help each other and serve the *panth* (Sect), learn riding and use of arms, not to interfere in other's property and in conjugal

---

87 The five Sikhs were from a cross section of devotees from upper and lower castes: Daya Ram was a Khatri; Dharam Das was a Jat; Sahib Chand was a barber; Himmat Chand was a water carrier; and Mohkam Chand was a tailor.

relations. Sikh salutation includes four words in each of two lines (*WaheGuru ji ka Khalsa; WaheGuru ji ki Fatah;* meaning 'the pure belongs to the almighty'; 'victory to the almighty').

Critical Chamkaur Battle (1704)

Of all the battles fought, the battle of Chamkaur (located 50 km west of present-day Chandigarh, in the district of Rupnagar) proved to be the tipping point in the psyche of the Sikhs. This battle was fought over three cold days of 21-23 December in 1704 between the Sikhs, led by Guru Gobind Singh, and the coalition forces of the Mughals and Rajput hill chieftains.

The enemy's joint forces attacked Sikh forces who were tactically dispersed in different forts. Guru Gobind Singh with a small band of fighters, along with women and children of his family, was in one of the forts. Fierce battle ensued and the enemy, which despite a large contingent, could not gain victory and was forced to lay siege to the fort. The siege continued for seven months with the enemy facing intermittent losses whenever they attempted to invade the fort. Frustrated, to end the war, coalition forces' heads, swearing on Hindu and Muslim holy scriptures, reached an agreement for the safe passage for Guru Gobind Singh and his family in lieu of vacation of the fort. However, no sooner had Guru Gobind Singh come out of the fort, his contingent was followed and attacked on the banks of River Sirsa which was at a distance of 31km[88].

---

[88] Presently Sirsa river has been reduced to a drain carrying unchecked toxic industrial effluents of the Baddi-Barotiwala-Nalgarh Industrial hubs (in Himachal Pradesh where the river originates) which has more than 2000

River Sirsa originates in Shiwalik foothills of Himachal Pradesh, flows into Punjab, and joins River Satluj near Rupnagar at Taraf village (Figure 3.1). Sikhs, 400 strong, fought a valiant rear-guard battle helping Gobind Singh cross the river with his two elder sons (*Ajit Singh and Jujhar Singh*) but in the chaos of the battle two younger sons (*Zorawar Singh and Fateh Singh*) got separated (a gurdwara -'Parivar Vichora' now stands at this place). They, along with their grandmother, (Mata Gujri) were captured by the governor of Sarhind. Sons on the refusal to convert to Islam were bricked alive and when the wall reached shoulder height their heads were cut off. *Baba Zorawar Singh* as he has come to be remembered since then was 9 years old; *Baba Fateh Singh* as he has also come to be remembered since then was just 6 years old[89].

The Sikh contingent accompanying the Guru all perished in the battle. Gobind Singh, with a handful of remaining Sikhs, took refuge in a mansion in Chamkaur. Though utterly outnumbered, the Sikhs fought side by side with the two elder sons of Gobind Singh – *Ajit Singh and Jujhar Singh*. In the end, all perished in the battle. Ajit and Jujhar were 17 and 14 years of age at the time of their death[90]. This perhaps is the only example found in history where two young sons, not only volunteered, but insisted on joining the battle and died on the battlefield proving good the maxim, 'valiant never taste of death but once.' Meanwhile, invoking the power bestowed to the five Sikhs, in unison, they ordered the Guru Gobind Singh to escape in

---

industrial units. The health of villagers and cattle on the river has been greatly impacted.

[89] Baba as a noble title is reserved as a prefix (or suffix) as mark of highest respect for ascetics or persons of similar calibre.

[90] Both elder sons now also have the title Baba bestowed to their names by Sikh sangat.

the dead of the night and save his life and battle another day. Gobind Singh obliged and later with the help of Muslim and Hindu devotees reached a safer destination. Meanwhile, another Sikh stayed behind dressed as Gobind Singh providing cover for the Guru who, along with a handful of Sikhs who were still alive when Guru left, also perished fighting the enemy.

Figure 2. 1 Sirsa River Merging with Sutlej River near Taraf Village

Source
https://www.google.com/search?q=Taraf+village&oq=Taraf+village&aqs=chrome..69i57j33i160l2.
5083j0j15&sourceid=chrome&ie=UTF-8 (Retrieved 24-3-2022)

Implication of Chamkaur Battle

The battle of Chamkaur in 1704 brought home several learning points for the Sikhs. First, it proved that even the strongest of enemies was not invincible if you had the fighting spirit; second, it also dawned on them the unreliability of the Mughal and hill Chieftains' pledges even when they were taken on Holy Scriptures. Guru, who was used to honourable conduct even in a battle was so dismayed and rather appalled by this behaviour of

Aurangzeb's generals and hill Chieftains that he wrote an exquisite letter in Persian that contained 111 verses (known as *Zafarnama*), berating the false promises made despite Aurangzeb being a devout Musselman. Third, the martyrdom of 4 young sons of Gobind Singh instilled in Sikhs a spirit of valour and sacrifice unparalleled in Sikh history. Fourth, it strengthened their belief that force must be met with force, lest you be taken weak. Revenge was in the air for a long time and it did come with ferocity in the lead of Sikh warrior Banda Singh Bahadur when in 1710 in the battle of *Chappar Chiri* (a village outside Sarhind) with the Mughals, Sikhs killed the Governor of Sarhind and Dewan Suchanand, who were responsible for bricking alive the two sons of Guru Gobind Singh.

Final Showdown with Mughals

After having lost his family, the army and the forts, Guru Gobind Singh went through challenging times in the dense Lakhi Forest in the Ferozepur area (east side of the state). His close confidents and well-wishers did come and meet him whenever they could and extended as much assistance as they could. This did not escape the attention of the Mughal authorities, in particular Wazir Khan, the then Governor of Sarhind who had been after Gobind Singh for some time.

In 1705 Gobind Singh reached what is now known as *Muktsar* on the western flanks of Punjab (*Khidrana* in earlier times) which was to be the final showdown between Guru Gobind Singh and the Mughals. Such was the reputation of Guru Gobind Singh that he soon succeeded in assembling an army, the exact number of which is debated, but given the situation at the time, it could not have been a very large as opposed to the 10,000 strong under the command of Wazir Khan. The battle was fiercely fought and won by Gobind Singh. There is a legend connected with this battle.

Legend has it that during the seize of Anandpur fort, 40 Sikhs of the Majha region in the district of Amritsar deserted Gobind Singh, who accepted their desertion wish but asked the 40 deserters to give him in writing a disclaimer that they were no longer his Sikhs. The deserters did so and returned to their homes, hoping their wives would be happy to see them alive. However, the women, appalled at the cowardly act, refused to take them back declaring that they no longer needed such cowardly men and that they were capable of raising the family alone.

A woman by the name of *Mai Bhago* declared that she would go to battle as no men were left fit to battle with the Mughals. Unable to bear the burden of this eternal shame the 40 deserters joined the battle along with *Mai Bhago* and fought with such ferocity that Mai Bhago, lying wounded on the battlefield, narrated their story to Gobind Singh and told him how bravely they had fought for him[91]. All 40 perished in the battle - it is said that a dying Sikh by the name of Mahan Singh, whom Gobind Singh recognised, urged him to tear up the disclaimer. Gobind Singh complied with the wish of the last of dying Sikh leading to Mukti (salvation) of all 40; hence the name *Muktsar* came to be (sar is the shorter form of Sarovar - water reservoir). Till this day in all gurdwaras the 40 warriors are remembered in

---

[91] By all means Mai Bhago is not an isolated instance. Sikh history is replete with women who contributed on and off the battlefield for the honour and advancement of Sikhism. As a sampler, mention here can be made of Sada Kaur (for expeditions against Pathans of Hazara and Attock), Balbir Kaur (for fighting the British in 1797), Deep Kaur (single-handedly downed two and injured a third one to protect honour), Dalair Kaur (Anandpur fort seize fame).

prayers for their exemplary gesture of atonement with their lives.

Guru Gobind Singh stayed at Muktsar for a few months after the battle and then moved in 1706 to *Damdama Sahib* - about 80km southeast of Muktsar where he once again gradually began to assert his position. Meanwhile, Aurangzeb was occupied in wars with Marathas in Maharashtra state and with Rajputs in Rajasthan. It is suggested that around this time Aurangzeb deputed his principal officers to meet Gobind Singh and invite him for a parley[92]. There must be several reasons for this. First, belatedly, Aurangzeb might have realised that Gobind Singh was not seeking any new territory by engaging in war and that he simply wished to be left alone to pursue his religion. Second, the futility of revenge on Gobind Singh's sons may have weighed heavy on his mind now that he was growing old. Third, he had seen the fighting spirits of the Sikhs under Gobind Singh and if unchecked this could escalate beyond control. Finally, fighting wars with several sects (Sikhs, Marathas, Rajputs and others) must have had its damaging impact on the resources of the empire.

This author hypothesizes that being a devout Muslim, the letter (known as *Zafarnama*) that Guru Gobind Singh wrote berating Aurangzeb on breaking the promises made on the Holy Scripture for the exit passage in the last battle with Sikhs, could also have weighed on his mind. Whatever the reason may have been, it seems Guru Gobind Singh took the decision to meet Aurangzeb. This decision, given the past record of broken promises would not have been an easy one though. But the news of this meeting must

---

92 Singh, G, *Makhiz-e-Twarikh-e-Sikham, 74-75* As quoted in (Gupta, 1984, p. 312).

have spread among hill chieftains and also to Bahadur Shah, the eldest son of Aurangzeb. Before the meeting could take place Aurangzeb died on 20 February 1707. Gupta (Gupta, 1984, p. 315) opines that had the Guru then returned to Damdama Sahib he would have carved out a republic for the Sikhs. But this was not to be, and on the invitation of Shah Jahan Gobind Singh continued to be his guest where one day while at Nanded he was attacked and assassinated by two Pathans deputed by *Wazir Khan* whom the Guru had in mind to punish.

Ruler in Guru Gobind Singh's Time

Aurangzeb (1658-1707) and Bahadur Shah (1707-1708) were at the helm when Gobind Singh was elevated to Guru-ship. In the previous paragraphs we have described the intricate relationship Gobind Singh had with the emperors. More importantly perhaps, along with these two emperors, Gobind Singh had to face the onslaught of his zealot deputies such as Wazir Khan. The narrative of Gobind Singh's life and the Sikhs gets further complicated when we observe that alongside Mughal manoeuvrings, Sikhs also had to face the double dealings and treachery of hill chieftains who, in connivance with the Mughals, had operated to eliminate Gobind Singh. Gobind Singh thus had to face formidable enemies from all sides - enemies that would use any ruse to bar him from gaining popularity with the masses.

It can only be termed as short-sightedness of the hill chieftains who, instead of thinking strategically and engaging in a positive parley with the Guru to strengthen the hold of Hindus in Punjab and beyond, connived to work against him. Such a policy ended with a zero-sum game for all. Tragically this has been the bane of India that seldom rulers of smaller or larger states chose to bind together for a common cause of defeating the enemy. Their envy, petty egos, and short-termism have been ruthlessly exploited by invaders, resulting in India being a slave country for centuries.

Contributions of Guru Gobind Singh

Gobind Singh was the tenth Guru of the Sikhs and the last living one. One of his gigantic achievements was his foresight that the choice of any more living Gurus will only result in frictions and feuds between the families and devotees. This judgement of his must have been based on his observations of past succession stories which were not always smooth, with the result that splinter sects had surfaced - some, which arose in those times have since faded but some are present till this day in various degrees of strength in numbers, influence, and religious infrastructure[93]. Hence, he decreed that after him, *Granth Sahib* – the Holy Scripture would be the eternal guiding Guru for all Sikhs, a decree that Sikhs honour till this day.

Guru Gobind Singh's second masterly contribution had been the distinct appearance that he granted Sikhs with the formation of *Khalsa* (the pure) race. As described in the beginning of the chapter, he ordained five distinct identity features that all Sikhs were commanded to observe[94]. This distinct appearance bound together the newly formed Sikh race members who could now relate with each other. Once

---

93 Mention can be made of Udasis, Nirankaris, Namdharis, Radha Soamis, Ravidassias, Ramraiyas and Nanakpanthis. Some of these sects believe in a living guru, some are a hybrid between Sikhism and Hinduism and differ in dress codes (e.g., the way they tie their turbans).

94 To repeat, these were: *uncut hair*, a small *comb* that is tucked behind the knotted head hair; cast iron or *steel bangle*, a *dagger,* and a *longish drawer.*

baptised, the members of the group became a formidable fighting force. Baptism brought with it a code of strict discipline - e.g., of early rising, exercising, and reading passages from the Scripture before attending to daily duties. In modern parlance, by removing the cumbersome succession ritual and by standardising the physical and spiritual make up, Guru Gobind Singh brought to the mainstream a religion and gave it the universal name of *Khalsa* (the pure).

The third major contribution of Guru Gobind Singh was in the field of administrative shake-up of the working of the Sikh religious institutions. We have previously noted that fourth Guru Ram Das had initiated in Punjab 22 centres and further sub-centres of the teachings of principles of Sikhism. The managers of these centres, called *Masands,* also collected donations from devotees for community use. In due course the caretaker managers of these centres became powerful, corrupt, and arrogant - some even proclaiming themselves to be Gurus. All peaceful efforts to evict them from their posts had failed, some ending in the murders of devotees who were sent to reason with them. Clearly, *Masands* had started to pose a great threat to the future growth of Sikhism. It was the influence and efforts of Guru Gobind Singh that the centres came to be liberated from *Masands*. With a master stroke the management of these centres was changed from autocratic to democratic with the charge of centres entrusted to elected committees by the devotees.

The fourth significant contribution of Guru Gobind Singh was in the literary field. As stated, Guru Gobind Singh was a great linguist who had the intimate knowledge of several languages - Braj, Hindi, Sanskrit, Persian, Arabic and Gurmukhi among others. While he was stationed in

Paonta Sahib (a town in Himachal state) he had 52 bards in his royal assemblage who recited their works and the choicest works of renowned poets (Gupta, 1984, p. 335). Guru Gobind Singh also had an intimate knowledge of Indian classical Rāgas which comes alive in his hymns. Of his 16 major works (some are said to have been lost crossing swollen Sarsa river after leaving Anandpur and being pursued by the Mughal army). Several works are noteworthy - *Bachitra Natak* e.g., tells his life story in 471 poetic verses, *Chandi Charitra* based on the famous 'Markande Purana' which *eulogizes* the eternal power of shakti embodied in Goddess Chandi. *Zafarnama* is the epitome of finest application of *Persian,* written as a long poem containing 111 verses describing the greatness and the failings of Aurangzeb as a devout Musselman[95].

By this time the reader might have conjured the personality of Guru Gobind Singh who was a personification of rare courage, foresight, fairness, honour, valour, and literary genius. *The net result of his personality and works fundamentally changed the psyche of Sikhs forever. A large share of Sikhs' fearless nature, penchant for hard work to make a living, sense of sharing and fairness, can be traced back to this remarkable personality.*

How did the enemies view Gobind Singh? I believe they must have had a mixed feeling towards him. The following passages from (Machiavelli, 2021)[96] best

---

95 Known works of Guru Gobind Singh are as follows (number of verses in bracket) Akal Ustat (271 ½), Bachitra Natak (471), Chandi Charitra (first version 233; second version 262), Chandi di War (55), Chaubis Avtar (1201), Fatah Nama (23 ½), Gian Prabodh (336), Hikayat (756), Jap (199), Mir Mahndi (10), Pakhian Charitra (7569), Rama Avtar including Krishna Avtar (4370), Shabad Patshai Das (10), Shastar Nam Mala (1323), Swayyas (33), Zafar Nama (111), Misc (59) (Source: Various Encyclopaedias; (Gupta, 1984, p. 349).

96 Chapter XVII. Concerning Cruelty and Clemency, and Whether it is Better to Be Loved Than Feared.

describes how Gobind Singh must have left his impression on his enemies.

> "Upon this a question arises: whether it be better to be loved than feared or feared than loved? It may be answered that one should wish to be both, but, because it is difficult to unite them in one person, it is much safer to be feared than loved, when, of the two, either must be dispensed with."

> "Nevertheless, a prince ought to inspire fear in such a way that, if he does not win love, he avoids hatred; because he can endure very well being feared whilst he is not hated, which will always be as long as he abstains from the property of his citizens and subjects and from their women."

Chapter Summary

In this chapter we sketched the lives of 10 Sikh Gurus and their contributions in the growth of Sikh religion. We also commented upon the emperor in whose regime the 10 Gurus spent their lifetime. Depending on the nature and outlook of the emperor, they were either indifferent, were critical, or proved outright fatal. It is remarkable that the Sikh religion kept its steady growth pace despite enormous challenges it faced at times. Burton, writing in 1911 (Burton, 2008, p. 52) and borrowing partly from Cunningham (Cunningham, 1918), put the growth of the Sikh religion as follows:

> "....at the end of two centuries, had the Sikh faith become established as a prevailing sentiment and guiding principle to work its way in the world. Nanak disengaged his little society of worshippers from Hindu idolatry and Muhammadan superstition, and placed them free on a broad basis of religious

and moral purity; Amar Das preserved the infant community from declining into a sect of quietists or ascetics; Arjan gave his increasing followers a written rule of conduct and a civil organization; Har Govind added the use of arms and a military system and Govind Singh bestowed upon them a distinct political existence, and inspired them with the desire of being socially free and naturally independent. No further legislation was required; a firm persuasion had been elaborated, and a vague feeling had acquired consistence as an active principle."

The picture below brings together all 10 Gurus and the Holy Scripture which the 10th Guru Govind Singh declared to be the living Guru after him, thus ending the succession line of living Gurus.

Unique and Common Traits of 10 Gurus

An assessment of the lives of 10 Gurus in previous section tells us that 10 Gurus of the Sikhs had some distinctive features of their own, but they also shared some common traits. A discussion of these common and distinctive features would also serve as a summary for this chapter and act as a prelude to the next chapter in which we analyse, *inter alia,* the leadership qualities of 10 Gurus within the framework of theories of leadership.

Unique Traits of 10 Gurus

Guru Nanak was born with the temperament of a saint. He preached love and peace for mankind. We do not find anywhere that he advocated the use of force or violence. Nanak was the embodiment of humility par excellence. Guru Angad was an inventor - he gave shape to the written language of the Sikhs - Gurmukhi the seed of which was laid by Nanak, and which paved the way for the opening of the learning centres for the Sikhs. Angad was the initiator of *Langar* - the tradition of community kitchens for the devotees. Foreseeing the imminent confrontation with the Mughals he also stressed on physical well-being of his devotees. Amar Das may be considered an earliest management Guru of the Sikhs for implementing the idea of the decentralisation of the religious gatherings by opening 22 centres and putting in charge the manager priests authorised to collect the offerings of the devotees and imparting religious teaching and training. Guru Ram Das gave a *Sanctum Sanctorum* in the form of *Harimandir Sahib* – the centre of supreme worship of the Sikhs. Guru Arjan Dev showed the path of supreme sacrifice for the beliefs held.

Figure 2. 2 Photograph shows 10 Sikh Apostles with The Holy Scripture

The symbol and the writing in Gurmukhi are the basic chant or Mool Manter of Sikhs. Translated, it reads
(There is) One Universal Creator God. The Name is Truth. Creative Being Personified. No Fear. No Hatred. Image of the Undying, Beyond Birth, Self-Existent. By Guru's Grace[97]

Source: https://wallpapercave.com/sikh-guru-wallpaper-hd

---

97 Khalsa (na). Gurmukhi to English Translation of Sri GGS (p.1)

Guru Hargobind showed that it was not enough to strengthen the mind and be always peaceful. If need be, it was legitimate to take up arms to protect oneself and the vulnerable. Guru Har Rāī was probably unique in his display of love for the animals (much ahead of his time in fact) and his passion for indigenous Ayurvedic medicine. The child Guru Harikrishen, with all the purity of his mind, gave his life serving people suffering from the dreaded disease of smallpox. Guru Tegh Bahadur showed that peace in meditative life can be found and that hankering after power need not be the aim of life unless one was genuinely prepared to serve the people. Of the many contributions of Guru Gobind Singh, strategic long-term thinking and royal courage - sometimes against all odds, stand out.

Common Traits of 10 Gurus

With these distinctive features of the 10 Gurus, several uncanny common traits between them also stand out.

In this author's opinion, all Gurus were long-term thinkers and strategists. This is reflected in the decisions they took for the betterment of the budding Sikh community. Foremost of the strategic decision[98] was their total impartiality in choosing the right successor for the Guru-ship. This was a decision of paramount importance, and Gurus never failed to find the right successor, *purely on merit basis* - often ignoring their own offspring[99]. This

---

[98] A Strategic decision in management literature is defined as one the reversibility of which is costly in terms of time, effort, and money.

[99] A reviewer pointed out to me the choice of Gurus for succession was from within the acquaintances and family circles and no attempt was made to appoint a Guru from outside. The answer to this question is rather simple. Sikhism was a new religion and a close-knit circle of disciples and family members, who

was a crucial decision, and because it was taken right, Sikhs as a budding community continued to flourish with the growing number of devotees. The sense of impartiality and preference of innate qualities can be seen from the fact that half i.e., five of the 10 Gurus were age 18 and younger when elevated to Guru-ship with the belief that these youths had the sense of maturity which would soon flourish and work for the betterment of the masses.

The second key trait of Gurus was the linguistic skills, which coupled with their poetic bent of mind and intimate knowledge of the Indian classical music, gave birth to some of the enchanting hymns found in the Scripture and which are sung and listened to each day, every day, by millions of devotees worldwide.

The third common trait is that all Gurus, paid emphasis on learning, a disciplined life, and the maintaining of a healthy spiritual mind.

With the fourth, it has to be said that none of them buckled under pressure no matter how dire the situation was. They never wavered from the righteous path and never gave up their beliefs. Had Guru Tegh Bahadur e.g., caved under the spectre of torture and death and embraced Islam - Sikh history would be different. It was the Sikh Gurus' determination that despite being under severest of pressures they kept their faith in the Sikh religion going.

---

grew up within its bounds, understood intimately its functioning and ideal future growth trajectory. The appointment of someone from within was the logical and obvious choice, as the risk of a growing religion going astray would be higher under the leadership of an outsider Guru new to the religion. The succession system continued until the 10th Guru, Guru Gobind Singh, by which time the budding religion had largely stabilised. Guru Gobind Singh decreed the succession system to be discontinued proclaiming that from then on, the Sikh Holy Scripture would be the guiding Guru.

Corollary to above is the fact that all Gurus understood the wishes of the devotees well and took the decision to attend to it. The ritual of the community kitchen is one good example. Gurus soon realised that devotees coming from far off places needed rest and food before attending the congregation, since concentration is not possible for a tired and hungry body[100].

It is essential also to remember that although Gurus read the requirements of the devotees correctly and attended to it, they never made any attempt whatsoever to exploit it to their advantage - a quality *par excellence* that is missing in modern, self-proclaimed Gurus.

Last but possibly not least, an important common trait shared by all Gurus was that they never built any infrastructure - living quarters, working places, offices in modern parlance for their personal use. Whatever infrastructure was built was for the common good of all. This trait, again, is so much unlike modern self-professed Gurus - a plethora of whom can be found in modern India.

**

---

[100] Maslow's first requirement in his chronology of needs comes to mind (Maslow, 2014). Confer section on Rational Choice Theory.

CHAPTER 3   RISE OF SIKHISM, CULTURE SHIFT, AND LEADERSHIP

It is not the strongest of
the species that survive, nor the
most intelligent, but the one
most responsive to change
(Charles Darwin)

Introduction

As spiritual leaders, the 10 Sikh Gurus whose lives were sketched in the previous chapter, heralded a change, ushering an era that culminated in the emergence of a religion which is presently the fifth largest in the world (with 25-30 million followers). From the humble beginnings in 1469 with the birth of Nanak and the demise of Gobind Singh in 1708 Sikhs had the audacity to take on Mughals and battle with them to avenge the wrongdoings and win territories - at one time, for about 40 years (1799-1839) establishing their own empire with the centre at Lahore, the coveted epitome of Mughal power for centuries.

In this chapter we explore the elements that paved the way for the formation of the Sikh religion in the face of suppression, atrocities, and persecution, which at times were so intense that one wrong turn would have proved fatal and changed the course of Sikh history for ever. Envision, if Guru Tegh Bahadur, under torture, had succumbed to accepting Islam – the most likely outcome then would have been coming to halt, perhaps, irreversibly, the progress the Sikh religion had made till then. In the same vein, if Guru Gobind Singh was captured on leaving the Anandpur fort, he would certainly have been put to humiliation similar to one meted to Sambhaji, the son of Maratha warrior king Shivaji (1630-1680)[101]. This would have resulted in possibly irrevocable setback to the growth of Sikhism - not to mention the shameful dent on Sikh psyche which just falls short of worshipping their Gurus, and which possibly would never have recovered.

In order for us to understand how the Sikh religion survived against all odds and nurtured itself up to become a full-fledged religion, we take recourse to theories that explain how religions form, progress and survive as an institution. The emergence of the Sikh religion assumes particular importance in the wake of the fact that its seeds germinated leading to a fully blossomed tree at a time when there already existed several competing religions - Hinduism, Buddhism, Jainism, Christianity - not to mention several smaller indigenous, regional ones. Despite stiff competition, Sikhism not only attracted devotees from all sides but also survived against heavy odds. In the second section we discuss the issue of culture shift that made people migrate to the then newly forming Sikh religion. In the third section we invoke the theories of leadership to understand the successful governance style of 10 Gurus that helped shape the Sikh religion.

Emergence of Sikh Religion

---

101 Captured Sambhaji (1657-1689) was tortured - his eyes gouged out and subsequently humiliated by parading him wearing clown's clothes while Mughal soldiers hurled abuse at him. Coincidentally, this happened in Aurangzeb's reign (1658-1707) who was a year younger than Sambhaji.

The term religion has been defined in a variety of ways by classical and contemporary authors[102]. In fact, there is even a debate among academics if there is a need to define it. (Stausberg, Contemporary Theories of Religion: a critical companion, 2009); (Stausberg & Engler, The Oxford Handbook of the Study of Religion, 2018, pp. 9-32). The word 'religion' has its roots in the Latin word 'ligare' meaning to join or connect and is characteristically understood to mean the linking of humans with the divine. I believe scepticism towards having a definition arises because we all intuitively know what religion is and how members of a specific religious group behave within it. Since our purpose in this section is to outline the reasons behind the emergence of Sikhism, we shall make an attempt to define and understand, at least at an elementary level, what religion is and how does it grow in faith and size as a sect.

Defining Religion

For our purpose we draw on French sociologist Emile Durkheim's seminal work (Durkheim, 1915, pp. 23-47) whose definition of religion is described in the following passages.

> "Religion phenomena are naturally arranged in two fundamental categories: beliefs and rites. The first are states of opinion and consist in representations; the

---

102 Müller describes the difficulty in defining religion in following words "There seem to be almost as many definitions of religion as there are religions in the world, and there is almost the same hostility between those who maintain these different definitions of religion as there is between the believers in different religions....religion is something which has passed, and is still passing through an historical evolution, and all we can do is to follow it up to its origin, and then try to comprehend it in its later historical developments." (Mueller, 1878, p. 21).

second are determined modes of action. Between these two classes of facts there is all the difference which separates thought from action (p.36) ."

"All known religious beliefs, whether simple or complex, present one common characteristic: they presuppose a classification of all the things, real and ideal, of which men think, into two classes or opposed groups, generally designated by two distinct terms which are translated well enough by the words profane and sacred (profane, sacré). This division of the world into two domains, the one containing all that is sacred, the other all that is profane, is the distinctive trait of religious thought; the beliefs, myths, dogmas and legends are either representations or systems of representations which express the nature of sacred things, the virtues and powers which are attributed to them, or their relations with each other and with profane things (p.37)."

"A society whose members are united by the fact that they think in the same way in regard to the sacred world and its relations with the profane world, and by the fact that they translate these common ideas into common practices, is what is called a Church. In all history, we do not find a single religion without a Church (p.44)."

"Thus we arrive at the following definition: A religion is a unified system of beliefs and practices relative to sacred things, that is to say, things set apart and forbidden— beliefs and practices which unite into one single moral community called a Church, all those who adhere to them. The second element which thus finds a place in our definition is no less essential than the first; for by showing that the idea of religion is inseparable from that of the Church, it makes it clear that religion should be an eminently collective thing (p.47)."

In summary, what Durkheim tells us is that that religion is a set of beliefs and rites and that within the religion there are things that are uniformly considered sacred (ceremonies and symbols with holy meaning e.g.) or profane (everything mundane that makes up our daily lives - eating, sleeping, our job, commute to work etc.). Durkheim uses the term 'church' in the generic sense as an example but as a synonym for any religious institutions such as a temple for Hindus, gurdwara for Sikhs, synagogue for Jews, or a mosque for Muslims.

Characteristics of Religion

Religion practiced in whichever culture has some common characteristics. First, it worships some unseen world of Gurus, Gods, Goddesses, Spirits, Ancestors, and Demons or such form adopted as afterlife by someone who lived whom worshippers, or their predecessors have seen or invented in their lifetime, as the all-powerful figure worthy of reverence. Second, worshippers have over time developed a system of beliefs and rituals that surround the mystic figure they worship. These rituals they follow to seek peace and prosperity for themselves, their family, or the community they live in. Third, worshippers have created a sacred place where they meet and worship - churches, mosques, temples, synagogues, gurdwaras are examples. These sacred places have (trained) working hierarchy, e.g., bishops, priests, and deacons in a church who command respect and reverence from the worshippers and who conduct the ceremonies for the community. Fourth, all religions have an ethical and moral code of conduct and convictions about life after death, concept of heaven, hell, and in some religions such as Hinduism, reincarnation. The code of conduct may either be written in the sacred scriptures or carried over by traditions from the past or both.

Culture and Religion

Culture is defined as shared beliefs, norms, and values. Pioneering work in this field is that of Hofstede (Hofstede, Hofstede, & Minkov, 2010). The members of a religious group could be culturally uniform or culturally diverse in their day-to-day lives, but they are united in their common beliefs about rights and wrongs that a particular religion dictates. As an instance, Christians in the western world and in the African continent all consider the Bible as sacred and follow the ethical and moral values that Christianity teaches them[103]. Yet they may have different day-to-day (non-religious) lifestyles in whichever part of the African continent they live - lifestyles governed by tribal customs, traditions, values, ideals, principles, and beliefs.

The core shared 'non-religious' and 'religious' norms, values and beliefs held by the members of a religious group work as coalescing mechanism for the group, with members having a psychological contract with each other. This provides a strong bonding between the members. This bonding leads to social harmony within the group, whereby group members are willing and happy to provide emotional support to each other. The need for such a support arises during times of bereavement and such other mishaps in the family. In poorer densely populated countries where communities live cheek and jowl they often find such an emotional and financial support that comes with commonly shared religious beliefs immensely

---

[103] This is not to disregard sub-groups that also exist within religious groups - sometimes with different versions of religious practices. Examples are Shias and Sunnis in Muslims, Catholics and protestants in Christianity, different versions of Buddhism among the Japanese, the Tibetans, the Sri Lankans and the Thais.

helpful. Several Hindu and Sikh communities in India e.g., run free community kitchens where food is served on daily basis and where no questions are asked from the callers to such kitchens. In the section that follows we study how such close-knit religious groups are formed by gaining an insight into the theories of religion.

An Overview of Literature on Theories of Religion

The purpose of theory is understanding and prediction. A theory helps us understand a phenomenon and it predicts how this phenomenon would result in an empirical investigation - qualitative or quantitative. Thus, a theory can help us predict the empirical outcome of applied research, results of which may not all be according to specified hypotheses predicting the outcome, in which case, the theory is revised and becomes amenable to further research once again. Theories of religion is a much-studied area. Here we shall first provide an overview of research on the subject and then sketch an overview of core theories before devoting space to our preferred 'rational choice theory' and its applicability to the growth of the Sikh religion.

Pritchard (Evans-Pritchard, 1965) in one of the earliest works on traditional theories of religion covered the psychological and sociological dimensions of the theories; he devoted attention to Lévy-Bruhl's, the French philosopher cum-anthropologist's work who specialised in the study of primitive mentality. Kunin's (Kunin, 2006) volume is devoted to theories of religion ranging from classical to modern and cuts through the fields of anthropology, sociology, feminist, and psychological approaches. Stausberg's edited work (Stausberg, Contemporary Theories of Religion: a critical companion, 2009) is devoted to contemporary theories of religion and covers articles ranging from 1990-2007. A broader view of religion and theories within it can be obtained from Clarke's voluminous edited work (Clarke P. E., 2009) on the Sociology of Religion in which part I (pp.31-209) is devoted to theoretical side. A broader view on religion and social institutions can be obtained from Ebaugh's edited work (Ebaugh, 2005). Volume devoted totally to Rational Choice Theory is by (Young, 1997).

A Sketch of Selected Theories of Religion

Tylor (Tylor, 2016) an English anthropologist in *Primitive Culture* and *Anthropology* introduced the concept of Animism which refers to the belief that a supernatural power organizes and animates the plants and all inanimate objects in the universe. He believed that the residing spirits in plants and inanimate objects can harm, and it is essential to worship them to keep them appeased. Such type of worship led to polytheistic (belief in many Gods) religions of the ancient world[104]. This approach to understanding religion has come to be known as *Animistic Theory of Religion*. Related to this approach is the proposition of Anglican priest and anthropologist Henry Codrington (Codrington , 2005) who studied the Melanesian society and culture and put forward the concept of 'mana' - the supernatural power that belonged to the region of the

---

[104] A reviewer noted that many of the tribes in the east-central India, who believe in one almighty God (they call it 'Bonga' – a very abstract concept), but also believe that he has many forms, representative forces etc., in fact the entire natural world obeys Him/Her/ because of this belief that they are very ecologically conscious.

unseen and which God uses for good to reward people or punish the evil. Mention should also be made here of James Frazer (Frazer, 1890) the Scottish social anthropologist's contribution to, what is sometimes known as the *magic theory of religion*. Frazer argued that religion began when humans attempted to control nature with the help of magic and when that failed, they turned to religion and God worship and when that too failed, humans took recourse to science.

We have earlier cited the definition of religion by Durkheim. Following this definition, we can deduce Durkheim's views on religion as providing a set of moral values that form a collective conscience which helps social integration by binding people together. This collective conscience helps people do pious acts and puts the fear of God in their minds. Durkheim, who studied totemism in Australian aborigines, considered it to be the most basic form of religion where people gathered together to worship the totems[105].

In contrast to this, (Malinowski, 1979) considered death and times of crisis as the main drivers of religious beliefs. Religion acts as a psychological function helping people with emotional stress in uncertain situations. Building on the work of Durkheim and Malinowski, Talcott Parsons (Parsons & Clark, 1966) proposed that religion, in addition to helping people with unforeseen contingencies also helps in legitimising society's values and provides answer to question otherwise difficult to find answers to - e.g., why sometimes good people suffer or die early.

---

105 Totem is an object revered by a family or a group of people – such as a sacred wooden carving which are believed to possess magical qualities. It differs from animism which is the belief that all animate and inanimate entities possess a spiritual essence.

Neo-functionalist Bellah (Bellah, 1991) provided the answer to the question on how religion can unify a multi-faith society such as America. His answer lay in the 'civil religion' that multi-faith societies come to observe. This 'civil religion' consists of symbols they see, observe, and respect - symbols that also bind them. In the US, these symbols would include the Statue of Liberty, war hero cemeteries, holy sites and the Lincoln Memorial, sites that people visit and revere[106].

Max Müller (1823-1900), the German philologist and Orientalist, advanced *the nature worship theory*. Müller observed that primitive people, by observing the sun, moon, rain, and winds began to personify these elements and this personification led to their worshipping them. Müller, who studied Indian philosophical texts, held the view that the Vedic people represented a form of nature worship, an idea influenced by Romanticism. Müller shared many of the ideas associated with Romanticism, in particular his emphasis on the formative influence on early religion of emotional communion with natural forces[107]. He saw the Gods of the Rig-Veda as active forces of nature, only partly personified as imagined supernatural persons.

The next set of theories relate to the question as to *why people in the first place need to create a religious institution* and in search for this question, it emerged as what we can loosely term as *need-based theories of religion*. The first one in this line of thought was Ludwig Feuerbach, (Feuerbach, 2021) the German anthropologist and philosopher who maintained that in the face of challenges of life, people often find themselves powerless

---

[106] Possibly, this could be termed as supra-religious bonding.

107 Mittal, S, Thursby, G (2007), as quoted in
https://en.wikipedia.org/wiki/Max_M%C3%BCller (Retrieved 17-5-2022).

and seek divine intervention that might give them courage and strength to overcome difficulties. People e.g., remember Jesus as pious and helpful who steps in to help without any discrimination. However, Feuerbach also believed that as people become more knowledgeable and when technology starts to take over, religion becomes less important.

The second approach to the need-based theories of religion is summed up in the famous quote of Karl Marx (1818– 883) the German philosopher who proclaimed that religion stifles the oppression meted by the capitalist class on the working class; for the latter religion muffles the pain and the harsh realities of life; hence religion works as opium for the people. Many religions - Christianity, Hinduism, Jainism, and Sikhism paint a picture of life in heaven if one led a pious and peaceful life - a thought that leads to passive acceptance of the poor state of affairs people might be in.

Another psychological bend to the theories of religion is given by Sigmund Freud (1856-1939) the famous Austrian founder of psychoanalysis. As Freud puts it "….in a study of the origins of religion and morality of mankind which I published in 1913, under the title of Totem and Taboo, the idea was brought home to me that perhaps mankind as a whole has, at the beginning of its history, come by its consciousness of guilt, the final source of religion and morality, through the Oedipus-complex." Freud (Freud, 1920, pp. 195-196) Freud's psychoanalytic perspective viewed religion as the unconscious mind's wish for fulfilment. Because people need to feel secure and wish to liberate themselves of their guilt, Freud proposed that they choose to believe in God, who represented for them an all-powerful father-figure.

Finally, for the German Philosopher Kant (1781) religion is the product of limited empirical reason. Since there are phenomena which our five senses cannot fathom, religion is developed to fill in the gaps. To Kant, religious beliefs are unprovable; people are not religious due to their power of reason or their cognitive minds. Religion is an act of the moral will and not a product of reason (Kant, 2014). The work that looks into diverse aspects of sociology of religion is that of edited work of Peter Clarke (Clarke P. E., 2009).

Rational Choice Theory (RCT)[108]

Rational Choice Theory models have traditionally been used to understand and model economic behaviour. This approach, which has been a well-known paradigm in economics, has now made inroads into several disciplines [(Becker G. S., 1978), (Radnitzky & Bernholz, 1987); (Hogarth & Reder, 1987); (Swedberg , 2020); (Shapiro & Green, 1996)]. It has been successfully adopted in various forms in organisational psychology literature to understand and predict behavioural intentions with considerable success [(Ajzen & Fishbein , 1980); (Aijen, 2005); (Kolvereid, 1996); (Shapiro & Green, 1996); (Segal, Borgia, & Schoenfeld, 2005)].

RCT assume that individuals choose the best action according to stable preference functions and constraints. The underlying assumption is that, given a set

---

108 This section partly draws from author's following paper: Singh, Satwinder *et.al.* (2011). Motivation to become an entrepreneur: a study of Nigerian women's decisions. *African Journal of Economic and Management Studies*, 2, 202-219.

of choices and preferences, people try to maximise their benefits and minimise their costs by making rational choices. The rational choice model makes two further assumptions about an individual's preferences: completeness which signifies that all actions can be ranked in an order of preference and that the actions are transitive, i.e., if a_1 is preferred to a_2 and a_2 to a_3 then a_1 is preferred to a_3. For empirical testing of the model, it is further assumed that an individual has complete information about choices and that an individual has both the cognitive ability and time to weigh each choice against every other. Preferences are described by a utility function to which the individual assigns the ordinal numbers, such as $u(ai) > u(aj)$. The preferences then can be expressed as the relation between these ordinal assignments.

The starting premise in a rational choice model is that an agent or a group of agents aim to maximise utility i.e., choose the preferred alternative, given some constraints. Once a best solution to this constrained optimisation is found, a decision rule for future use is then set. This agent, or a group of them, is assumed to be representative of some larger group. Once the behaviour pattern is established, the researcher can proceed to examine how their choices interact to produce outcomes in general. An important element of rational choice model is the environment in which choices are made. The environment is usually taken to be a market in which agents make the choices. The role of constraints is important because constraints force agents to settle for trade-offs. These principles have been used to explore diverse behaviours outside mainstream economics such as church attendance (Azzi & Ehrenberg, 1975); suicide (Hamermesh & Soss, 1974); addiction (Becker & Murphy, 1988)], and entrepreneurial behaviour (Singh, Simpson, Mordi, &

Okafor, 2011). Each draw on notions of maximising behaviour and on factors that underpin utility or satisfaction.

Rational Choice Theory and the Emergence of Sikh Religion

Rational is when an act
is performed
based on logical grounds
(Duop Chak Wuol)

In order for us to understand how rational choice model applies to the emergence, growth and maturing of the Sikh religion between the birth of Nanak in 1469 and the demise of Gobind Singh, the 10th and the last of the Sikhs Gurus in 1708, a period of 239 years we have to cast our mind back first to Nanak's lifetime (1469-1539). We bear in mind that the seed of Sikhism was implanted in the society in 1469 and that prior to this date there were no Sikhs and hence no Sikhism. Nanak's were the times of staunch Hinduism and the successive Muslim rulers had made their mission to convert the Hindu 'infidels' to the only acceptable religion to them - the Islam.

Hindu society from the Vedic period had been classified into four castes - Brahmins (the upper cast - priesthood category), Vaishyas (business class), Kshatriyas (the warrior class), and Shudras (menial class). Members of Shudra caste are manual labourers, peasants, daily wage farm workers, artisans, blacksmiths - i.e., individuals working in occupations the other three classes considered low and would not normally engage in. There was, as yet a fifth extreme category - the 'untouchables,' who were engaged in the lowliest of low jobs considered 'unclean' by other castes - jobs such as manual scavenging, disposing of and skinning of dead animals for hide, cobblers, sewers and street cleaners and such. There is some overlapping of jobs between the last two categories.

The caste divisions in Nanak's times were nearly absolute. People lived and died as members of a particular caste. As if this was not enough in itself, each caste was further divided into several sub-castes, with members of sub-castes implicitly recognizing the ranking system within the caste they belonged to. Thus, both inter-caste and intra-caste distinction between classes existed - the hierarchy between which was recognised, accepted, and adhered to. The lower castes bearing little power always lived in fear of the wrath of the upper classes should there be a breach from their side in this tightly knit social caste-ridden hierarchical system, which to a great extent still exists to this day[109].

Stuck within the complex maze of the caste system were the women folk who had little voice within or outside the household. Married at a young age, within the family they were expected to attend to household chores and raise a family. In poorer households, women also went out to work, mostly on the farms, a backbreaking work carried out in the sweltering heat of the tropics. If the husband died before them, they were also expected to sit down on the husbands' pyre and perish with them[110].

---

109 The ferocity of the then caste system has still not subsided in India and is visible during elections and weddings which still take place within the castes of the bride and the bridegroom. This rigid system may have only slightly mellowed in the onslaught of the globalization process but is still deep-rooted in the elderly and in the countryside and also among the few so-called educated. 110 This brutal system was abolished by the British with help from social reformers of the time such as Raja Rammohan Roy.

Here it needs to be emphasized that in addition to Hinduism, sister religions - Jainism and Buddhism which existed side-by-side were also embedded in the caste system. It should be borne in mind that along with this built-in bias and discriminatory system of Indian religious communities, there also existed an elaborate labyrinth of rituals and rites - from birth to death of a person, observance of which was expected, often at the cost of time, efforts, and financial costs (Lee A. , 2020). As an instance, in Hinduism there are ceremonies prescribed for each of the following stages: intent to bear a child, nurturing of the foetus, childbirth, baby's first outing, initiation to solid food, first haircut, naming ceremony, earlobe piercing, commencement of education, engagement, elaborate (pre and post) wedding rituals, and often complex rituals on and after the demise of a person - just to name a few.

The entry of Mughal raiders into India from AD712 onwards superimposed yet another layer of suppression and exploitation on lower castes although raiders made no distinction between the classes and were indiscriminate in their plunder, pillage, rape, and abduction of women and in taking slaves whom they herded to their home destinations where they were sold, put to work, or enlisted in the army to fight for them (cf. Chapter-1). This was typical of the raiders who came to loot the riches with no intention of settling down. Later, when raiders settled down to rule India, the zeal to convert Hindus into Islam was equally ferocious - Aurangzeb's time was a classic period in which the enthusiasm to destroy Hindu temples and convert local populace to Islam was at its peak. Although no data is available to support this premise, statistically speaking there might also be a 'right' thinking section of the society who must have been sympathetic to the poverty ridden populace, irrespective of their castes. However sympathetic they might have been, given the rigidity of the system, they would not dare speak out openly in support of subjugated groups, so life carried on in *status quo.*

Entry of Guru Nanak on the Scene

We can conjure an approximate picture of life in Nanak's time. Here one could hypothesize that *possibly the caste-ridden social set up reeling also under the onslaught of raiders was ready for a change,* the seed of which got planted with the birth of Nanak in 1469. Not long after his birth, Nanak's fame started to grow, and he began to have a dedicated following of his own. Nanak's following included largely Hindus, but he also had Muslim followers as well. I believe by the time of Nanak's death, after about 70 years of his life, a large part of which was spent travelling and preaching the gospel of truth and worship, Nanak had built a critical mass of followers which subsequently swelled with the succession of each of the nine Gurus that followed. Several factors made Hindus and also members from sister religions and some atheists migrate to Sikh faith after Guru Nanak's demise. These are described below.

Sense of Equality

The first thing new devotees to Sikhism must have noticed would have been Nanak's core belief that he preached with zeal that *all human beings were born equal and were equal in society,* and that, no one should discriminate against anyone based on his caste or creed. A living proof of this was community kitchens where food was served to all as equals, and all ate sitting together on the floor next to each other irrespective of their status. This theory and practical side of Sikhism i.e., what was being preached was also practiced was a game changer since lower caste Hindus had never heard or experienced this phenomenon, and upper caste Hindus who came to the community kitchen must have had a sobering experience run through them - to put it rather mildly.

Another factor that is often ignored but one that is closely allied to the equality maxim is that during discourses in the congregation, male and female devotees were separated in attendance, but no distinction was made as to where devotees could or could not sit. An upper caste devotee was equally comfortable sitting next to a lower caste devotee and *vice versa*. Community kitchens and congregation halls must have been an oasis of calm for all castes where they could mingle as one.

A fundamental signal of equality that came a little later was in the formation of the sacred Scripture (*Granth Sahib*) that included the hymns of saints from all castes, states, and status in India. Hymns of Muslim saints were given equal status in the Scripture. The unification of the sacred teachings of all authors in one volume and not in different volumes is a triumph in unity.

Status of Women and Social Bonding

The second unifying factor was the equal status conferred to women whom Nanak held in high esteem - in fact in one hymn he questions why would one address degradingly a woman who gives birth to kings as well. Whether it is the congregation hall where religious proceedings took place, community kitchen, or admin posts within the gurdwara affairs, women were accorded equal rights and status. Nanak also condemned the *sati* tradition where a woman was expected to perish with her husband on his funeral pyre. Nanak who revered, respected, and held in high esteem the positive influence women could have on the family must have been horrified to see thousands of women wasted sacrificing themselves in the name of honour and tradition. The *Sati* system was finally outlawed by the British in 1829. Recently, 2014 Noble awardee, Malala Yousafzai has famously remarked that "there are two powers in the world: one is the sword, and the other is the pen. There is a third power stronger than both. That of women."

There is no data to support the following premise but this author conjectures that women must have played a big role in the conversion process to Sikhism[111]. The author's premise is based on some commonly observed, but often overlooked positives of Sikhism towards women folk. It is a common practice for food to be prepared and served in gurdwara kitchens by women during week-end congregations, and on occasions of anniversaries of Gurus, and when families celebrate their offspring's wedding, birthday etc. On days such as these, women folk are freed from cooking, cleaning and other chores associated with it. This brings great relief in their day-to-day schedules.

Corollary to above is also the fact that many women, who hitherto not regularly do so, also choose to help out in the community kitchen. This author has

---

[111] A related point that needs to be mentioned here is the soft power yielded by the Indian housewives. To the outside world, particularly the western world, the demure saree clad women, particularly in the rural areas, may look innocuous, whereas in reality they may be commanding sizeable soft power within the household. Most of them come trained by their mothers and married sisters and know how to play the (joint) family system.

observed how the environment in kitchen work is relaxed - often jovial, and how it works as a social club where a great deal of family and community information is exchanged with a minimum of, what economists call, *search cost*. Also, so often the surplus food that is not consumed by devotees is taken home by some families; this provides relief from kitchen work for an additional couple of days. This process is repeated when families organise any celebration at their home where food is invariably served to the attendees.

Food prepared is always vegetarian and hence amenable to easy storage for longer periods than non-vegetarian food. It should also be noted in passing that vegetarian food is easier to cook, has no pungent odour, and engages women folk - vegetarian or not, in cleaning, cutting, and preparing its ingredients - lentils, vegetables, dough, etc. - a chore in which all young and old (from both sexes) can contribute.

In addition to preparing food, serving it to devotees is another community virtue held in great esteem. In fact, it is quite a pleasant sight to see how food is managed and served in gurdwaras. Finally, the clearing-up process, including doing dishes, is another humbling chore held in great esteem by devotees, many of whom would also dust and polish footwear of fellow devotees left outside before entering the congregation hall[112]. Attending to these community chores also takes stress off from personal and family worries.

---

[112] A reviewer pointed out that such an act also breaks down the superiority complex of the wealthy and the upper caste people. Once you do the same work that the so called 'menial and lower caste' people do, you cannot look down on them anymore. Mahatma Gandhi used the same logic and almost forced everyone to sweep and clean toilets, so that 'Harijan's would not be denigrated.

Mental make-up and social bonding of children growing up in this environment is enriched and strengthened. By the time they grow up, all this has become part of their psyche and culture. I would also like to add that the relaxed attitude Sikhs have with regard to sharing food with guests (who sometimes drop in unannounced) can be traced back to gurdwara community kitchen culture[113]. The last but not the least point to be noted is the tremendous harmonious culture gurdwara and community kitchen culture enthuses in attendees who stay calm and connected, almost feeling virtuous, on the premises[114].

Language Development and Decentralization of Learning

Angela Carter, the English novelist, has famously remarked that language is power, life and the instrument of culture. It is, at the same time, the instrument of domination and liberation. In the case of the growth of the Sikh religion, the third essential factor appeared when the written language Gurmukhi was discovered and began to be taught in schools and learning centres where anyone could go and educate himself. At the same time the dissemination of preaching in 22 centres in the state made it convenient for the devotees to acquire knowledge about this newly

---

[113] This was the tradition in the early settlements and people in the American West also.

[114] Save for occasional discord between choice and functioning of committee members in charge of the gurdwara, this author has never seen disharmonious behaviour among devotees within the premises of the gurdwara, including the community kitchen. On the lighter side of life, I have heard that older women, sometimes, like to assert the right way a chore should be performed in the kitchen. This, I believe, is expected given that all women working in the kitchen are cooks in their own right. But the famous proverb about 'many cooks spoil the dish' does not apply as I have never seen a spoilt dish.

forming religion and its principles in locations near their place of residence. These centres gradually grew and had premises of their own where travelling devotees could spend the night in comfort as it provided board and lodging under one roof. Along with this infrastructure, larger complexes such as that in Amritsar and Kiratpur Sahib and Anandpur Sahib came up offering similar facilities on a larger scale.

Spiritual, Temporal, and Leadership Traits

As the Sikh religion progressed, prospective devotees must have noticed the secular nature of the Sikh religion which preached humility, courtesy, generosity, and forgiveness; a religion that sought the well-being of *all* and was willing and ready to serve *all* without discrimination. They must have also observed that although this newly forming religion never preached aggression, it will not hesitate to resort to arms to defend its people and those under its protection.

Alongside, new devotees must have also seen the unflinching personal and family sacrifices Sikh Gurus were making to protect the well-being of the masses (chapter 2). Devotees must also have recognised, for the first time, the emphasis the new religion was placing on physical fitness and readiness for all able-bodied males (it also welcomed female trainees), on acquiring arms training to protect themselves. The spiritual quality and physical fitness were something novel that, in this author's opinion, must have been very appealing and which was accepted with open arms by the younger devotees. They must have realised that by being physically fit and trained in the art of combat, they can, at least go down fighting with the enemy who repeatedly desecrated the places of worship and violated women folk.

The impartiality with which succession of Guru-ship took place, based purely on merit, must also have come to new devotees' attention. This was so much unlike succession of temple pandits where the son of the caretaker pandit took over father's job on his demise and where there was no proper accountability of the offerings. Sikh Gurus encouraged devotees to donate $1/10^{th}$ of their earnings - in cash or kind, for the betterment of the community and the donated funds were used as such for community purposes. Gurus never built edifices or businesses for their comfort and benefit and never used donated funds for their private or family purposes. This must have been striking for the prospective entrants to the new religion.

Applicability of Rational Choice Theory Assumptions

Rational Choice Theory's assumptions are adequately met when we apply them to the emergence of the Sikh religion.

For instance, RCT assumes that individuals choose the best action according to stable preference functions and constraints. Preference is precursor to a choice; first we prefer something then we choose it. To prefer is to express a bias in favour of something; to choose is to make an actual decision between alternatives. In this case, devotees, given the revolutionary changes they noticed in the new religion, preferred to migrate to it, and in due course did choose to adopt it. It clearly dawned on them that by choosing to be part of this emerging secular religion would enhance their benefits which came in the form of open-arm acceptance to the group with freedom to mingle and move with fellow followers, irrespective of their status and caste, not to mention the added protective feeling this new religion brought to them with minimum of costs and maximum of benefits. One way to minimise costs for prospective devotees was to have a minimum number of rituals and rites. Compared to complex Hindu rituals described earlier, the Sikh religion offered a simpler system of rituals between births and deaths.

The assumption of full information and completeness is also met, since given that the sister religions were Hinduism, Buddhism and Jainism, the broad principles of which devotees would be aware of, and the ranking of their preference function would be rather simple. If they preferred Sikhism to Hinduism then almost by default Hinduism was preferable to say Buddhism and Buddhism to Jainism, or other way round - but the preference function would be clear in each devotee's mind. This is because most of the shortcoming devotees felt about Hinduism were present in the latter two religions as well. Hence, an individual or group of devotees would have almost complete information about their available choices and the cognitive ability to weigh each choice against the other.

Rational Choice Theory emphasizes the role of constraints which is essential because constraints force agents to settle for trade-offs. The constraints devotees faced would have been the opposition from the family or community members but once this constraint was overcome, in selected households, it would provide momentum to others to join; the role of women in this has been highlighted in previous paragraphs.

Interestingly, an uncanny similarity is found here between the theory and practice. Theory tells us that once a best solution to this constrained optimisation is found, a decision rule for future use is then set. In due course in Punjab, an implicit understanding came to be popular under which, as a rule, the first-born son would become a Sikh and the rest can stay within the clan as Hindus.

One final element of the RCT model is the environment in which choices are made. The environment is usually taken to be a market in which agents make the choices. Here we define the market to be the market for religion within which agents i.e., the prospective new entrants made the choices.

Rational Choice Theory and Maslow

A hungry stomach cannot hear (Jean de La Fontaine)

The Rational Choice model explains *ex-ante* reasons for devotees to convert to Sikhism. Maslow's (Maslow, 2014) theory of motivation offers *ex-post* reasons of devotees' motivation to stay and offer their loyalty to Sikhism. Maslow proposed that for a person to be motivated, his requirements should be understood in a logical sequence. He suggested that on top of the list should be his physiological needs (food, clothing, shelter etc.) which have to be met first followed by safety needs (e.g., personal, family, and financial security). Once these have been met, attention could be paid to the extent of a person's belonging to the society (family, friends, and well-wishers). These parameters then would impact on, and attention then be paid to the degree of his self-esteem that all humans yearn for.

Once a base of all the aforesaid parameters has been built, cognitive needs (creativity e.g.) and aesthetic needs (attention to nature's beauty and splendour) can kick in. Once all these stages have been reached, the final stage of self-actualisation to a person's full potential can then occur. Although, Maslow's premises on motivation have been criticised and several variants have appeared on the scene (Ryan , 2019) Maslow's original premise would still make sense when applied to the times of our study. As can be seen, several of Maslow's requirements were met when devotees expressed their wish to join the growing Sikh sect. This was particularly so when a section of devotees also listed in the army service of the Gurus. Guru Gobind Singh e.g., encouraged the flourishing of one's mind in poetry and music once basic needs, as specified by Maslow, were met.

Speed of Shift to Sikhism

Culture as defined previously is shared values, beliefs, and norms which once established are sticky and not easy to shift. We do not have the data to analyse at what pace Sikh religion attracted devotees from adjoining religions such as Buddhism or Jainism to join them. I conjecture that this shift could have been in the shape of an elongated sigmoid function. A sigmoid function is a mathematical function which takes an elongated S shape. A common form for this function is the logistic function. A special case of sigmoid function is the Gompertz curve which could equally be applied to understand the growth pattern of Sikhism. Sigmoid functions have the domain of all real numbers, with response value commonly monotonically increasing.

Figure 3.1 shows a sigmoid function with three growth possibilities with varying speeds. The horizontal axis in the figure represents time and vertical axis growth; parameter c in the equation determines the steepness of the curve. In Figure 3.2 we have drawn such a function with data from Table 2.1, with time on the horizontal axis and growth on vertical axis.

Figure 3. 1 Sigmoid Function

(Horizontal Axis - Time: vertical Axis - Growth)

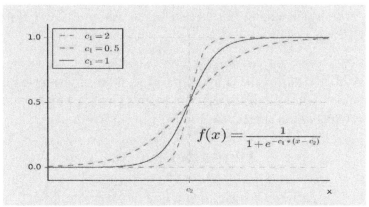

$$f(x) = \frac{1}{1 + e^{-c_1 * (x - c_2)}}$$

Source: Adopted from https://www.researchgate.net/figure/A-Basic-sigmoid-function-with-two-parameters-c1-and-c2-as-commonly-used-for-subitizing_fig2_325868989

Slope of the curve is hypothetical – in Figure 3.2 it could have been flatter or steeper during different regimes of Gurus.

I conjecture that the slope of the curve (the rate of growth of membership to Sikhism) could have been *steeper* during the time of the first and second Gurus, Guru Nanak and Guru Angad who between them shared 83 (70+13) years of Guru-ship (Table-2.1).

It could be *somewhat flatter* during the 29 years (22+7) regime of the third and fourth Gurus, Guru Amar Das and Guru Ram Das.

The curve could have been *steeper* during the 63 years (25+38) regime of the fifth and sixth Gurus, Guru Arjan Dev and Guru Hargobind, the martyrdom of Guru Arjan Dev, and declaration of readiness of war by Guru Hargobind.

The slope could have been somewhat *flatter* during a relatively shorter period of 20 years (17+3) regime of the seventh and eighth Gurus, Guru Har Rāī and Guru Hari Krishen.

The curve would have *peaked* and somewhat stabilized during the Guru-ship period of the ninth and tenth Gurus, Guru Tegh Bahadur and Guru Gobind Singh, who between them shared 43 (10+33) years of Guru-ship.

Gurus as Leaders

Earlier we stated that a key factor in the formation and subsequent advancement of the Sikh religion is the flawless ethical and moral code of conduct Gurus had. This was a necessary but not a sufficient condition for Gurus to have a sustained following which led to the formation of a totally new religion.

Figure 3. 2 Hypothetical Sigmoid Growth Curve of Sikhism

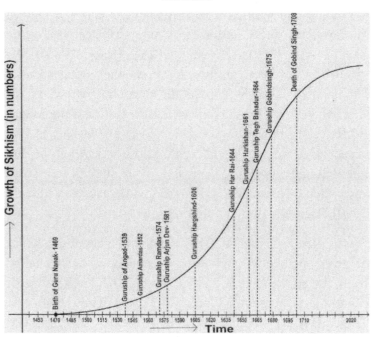

Source: Author

In the search for the answer to the question as to 'what led to the formation of the new religion, which has come to be known as 'Sikhism', we need to delve into the theories of leadership. This is because in the nascent stages of an institution's development, leaders play a vital role. Theories of leadership could help us understand the operational style of Gurus - style that made them popular, and the Sikh religion tick with the masses, resulting in a steady and sustained flow of converts to Sikhism.

In the process of delving into the theories of leadership we can also ascertain if *any theory in particular* is applicable to discern the leadership style of Sikh Gurus.

Leadership is a popular area of research with academics and practitioners, and several publications on the theory and applied side of the subject can be found in the literature [cf. (Cambridge University, 2017); (Nohria & Khurana, 2010); (Bryman, 2011); (Bass, 2009)]. An extensive applied study to find the cross-cultural dimensions of leadership in the corporate world is the GLOBE (Global Leadership and Organizational Behaviour Effectiveness) project[115]. Conducted in 162 countries, and based in 62 of the world's cultural clusters, it is a joint international work that, *inter alia,* is an attempt to discern and extend Hofstede's (Hofstede, Hofstede, & Minkov, 2010) original work on cultural dimensions.

Research in leadership is also linked with the theory of group behaviour and teams which have been studied from the management side and with the application of economic principles, including the use of game theory[116]. Topics that are studied within these fields include power, trust, delegation, accountability, rewards, co-operation, and conflicts. Our intention here though is rather humble. We wish to provide an overview of core leadership theories to see if any of the theories align with the behavioural pattern of the leadership of Sikh Gurus, and that what qualities Gurus had that distinguished them from the crowd.

---

115 Some details of 2020 GLOBE project can be had at
https://globe.bus.sfu.ca/about (Accessed 12-3-2022) and
 https://globeproject.com/study_2014 (Accessed 12-3-2022)
116 For a non-mathematical treatment of subject from the management side see (Brent & Dent, 2017). Pioneering work in the theory of games is that of (Neumann & Morgenstern, 1943) whose 1943 work *Theory of Games and Economic Behaviour* was published by Princeton University in 2007 as a 60th Anniversary Commemorative edition; it is now available on Kindle. Also, an early exposition involving economic principles is (Marschak & Radner, 1972).

Derivatives of core theories of leadership and empirical work in leadership studies are not discussed to keep the discussion streamlined. The interested reader can consult work cited earlier in the paragraph.

Core Leadership Theories

The first set of theories of leadership fall under the banner of 'behavioural leadership' that are: trait theories, contingency theories and power and influence theories. Allport, an American psychologist, is credited with the *Traits theory* (Allport, 1963) of leadership. He began by making a list of every term that could describe one's personality; this list he organised into three broad categories which he named cardinal traits, central traits, and secondary traits. Cardinal traits usually develop later in life and can come to dominate a person's personality so much so that his purpose, behaviour, and attitude comes to be described by them. Examples include Jesus Christ, Mother Teresa, and Hitler. Central traits which are more common among people can gradually develop to form a person's personality and character. Examples of such traits include honesty, penchant for hard work, generosity, and diligence. Secondary traits e.g., short-tempered nature, nervous dispossession under pressure, unpredictability at key decision times that a person may possess can reveal themselves under particular circumstances.

Traits' theory emphasizes that traits a person possesses dictate his leadership style. Research shows that traits such as honesty, intelligence, decisiveness, organisational capability, compassion, innovative and ambitious nature stand out[117]. Opposed to *traits theory* are the *contingencies theories* - also known as *situational theories*. Fiedler (Fiedler, 1978) is the main proponent of these theories which say that specific situations demanding a solution has a bearing on the behaviour of the leader i.e., how successfully or not so successfully a leader deals with the situation or the context of the problem of the situation in hand. Fiedler expounded that three elements are essential for the situational favourableness to solve a problem - how the leader's relations are with his subordinates, the power his position holds, and how the task is structured. An interaction of these three factors would determine the outcome of the situation.

Allied to contingency theories are the *transactional and transformational theories of leadership* which have emanated from the work of Burns (Burns, 1978) who first introduced these concepts. Transactional leadership is viewed as an exchange of rewards for compliance in which followers are motivated by appealing to their self-interest. Contrary to this, transformational leaders motivate their followers by inducing them to transcend their own self-interest for the sake of the good of the organization. I reckon that leaders in most Japanese organisations would fall into this category.

Transformation leadership is closely allied with the concept of *power, influence,* and *charismatic leadership* which states that to be successful leader, the leader should command trust and respect of his followers and the shared beliefs between the leader and the follower would then make latter put in their best for the organisation [(Yukl,

---

117 Pew Research Centre, (2015b), as quoted in the (Cambridge University, 2017, p. 6).

1989); (Bass, 2009); (French & Raven, 1959)]. Another allied theory falling within this category is the *Leader-Member Exchange* (LMX) theory which in essence is more of a paradigm than a theory *per se* [(Gottfredson, Wright, & Heaphy, 2020); (Gerstner & Day, 1997)].

The LMX paradigm is also closely aligned with the popular Principal-Agent model (P-A model) which is part of contract theory in economics (Laffont & Martimort, 2002). Within the LMX (and P-A model) the relationship between the leader and the followers is expected to function in a two-way mode. Since the spread of information is asymmetric between the leader (principal) and the follower (agent), the leader works such that a high level of trust is maintained between the two for the optimum performance and results from an individual or a team assignment (Dulebohn, Bommer, Liden, Brouer, & Ferris, 2011). A high degree of trust works as incentives and reduces monitoring costs allowing leaders to focus on more urgent issues.

Spirituality Dimensions and the Servant Leader (S-L) Paradigm

Serving others prepares you to lead others (Jim George)

The previous section contains the essence of core leadership theories found in the literature. In this section we shall discuss the theoretical framework of Servant-Leader theory which, (similar to the LMX model) is more of a paradigm and which we believe is relevant to the subject in hand. Before we do so we would devote some space to the understanding of spirituality which is the basis of the S-L paradigm. The Oxford dictionary meaning of spirituality is 'The quality of being concerned with the human spirit or soul as opposed to material or physical things.' Webster dictionary defines spirituality as 'the quality or state of being concerned with religion or religious matters: the quality or state of being spiritual.' Going by these definitions, a spiritual person would be God-fearing and less materialistic. By implication then such a person would be humble, church (or some equivalent institution) going, with certain ethical and moral standards. If such a spiritual person happened to be a leader, he would bring his personal value of humility and service in his work. This forms the basis of Greenleaf's (Greenleaf, 2002) concept of leadership.

In his 'Forward' written for Greenleaf (Greenleaf, 2002) Covey[118] puts the S-L paradigm eloquently as follows (paragraphing is this author's):

> "I believe that the essential quality that sets servant-leaders apart from others is that they live by their conscience - the inward moral sense of what is right and what is wrong. That one quality is the difference between leadership that works and leadership - like servant leadership - that endures. There is a mass of evidence that shows that this moral sense, this conscience, this inner light, is a universal phenomenon. The spiritual or moral nature of people is also independent of religion or of any particular religious approach, culture, geography, nationality, or race. Yet all of the enduring major religious traditions of the world are unified when it comes to certain basic underlying principles or values."

> "Immanuel Kant said, "I am constantly amazed by two things: the starry heavens above and the moral law within." Conscience is the moral law within. It is the

---

118 Covey,S.R (1991). *Foreward*. In Greenleaf (2002). P.4

overlapping of moral law and behaviour. Many believe, as do I, that it is the voice of God to his children. Others may not share this belief but still recognize that there is an innate sense of fairness and justice, an innate sense of right and wrong, of what is kind and what is unkind, of what contributes and what detracts, of what beautifies and what destroys, of what is true and what is false."

"Admittedly, culture translates this basic moral sense into different kinds of practices and words, but this translation does not negate the underlying sense of right and wrong. As I work in nations of different religions and different cultures, I have seen this universal conscience revealed time and again. There really is a set of values, a sense of fairness, honesty, respect, and contribution that transcends culture—something that is timeless that transcends the ages and that is also self-evident. It is as self-evident as the requirement of trustworthiness to produce trust."

This beautiful description signifies what a spiritual leader with a conscience, good ethical and moral values would stand for in a team, group, an institution, or even a nation. Greenleaf further clarified in his work essential attributes of a servant leader in the serving role to the people (Greenleaf, 2002, pp. 30-47). These are described below with brief explanations.

The first attribute is listening and understanding: this is the first of the attributes that has been emphasized to be of paramount importance so much so that the author ends up advising of not to be afraid of some silence between conversations; as the author puts it, that difficult it may be, but one should occasionally ask himsclf "In saying what I have in mind will I really improve on the silence?" (Ibid p.31). The second attribute is the emphasis put on language and imagination: as the author puts it "nothing is meaningful until it is related to the hearer's own experience." Every language has its nuances, and it is essential that the leader has the imagination to relate what he has to say to the hearer's experience related to the conversation on hand. The third attribute is the ability to withdraw from a conversation and find the time to think over and arrive at the optimum to the issue in hand.

The fourth element on which a leader could build is the ability to accept and empathize. Acceptance signifies acknowledging people's shortcomings and helping them improve. A servant leader accepts and empathises with his subordinate and does not reject but refuses to accept, if the performance is not good enough which is for the ultimate good of the subordinate. The fifth element is the ability of the leader to go beyond the conscious rationality. What it means is that given a leader's position and exposure he could have more information at hand which enables him to foresee the future events related to the issue being attended to by the subordinate. In such circumstances conscious rationality could dictate a certain approach whereas a leader could go beyond it balancing the desired outcome with what is achievable and what is not achievable. Clearly, respect and trust would kick in in a big way in such situations.

The sixth desirable trait of a leader is the presence of a better foresight. Foresight is the ability to judge the future events and base one's plans accordingly on the available knowledge and information about the situation. With a better foresight a leader is placed to deal with the situations seen and unforeseen. "Foresight is the "lead" that the leader has. Once leaders lose this lead and events start to force their hand, they are leaders in name only (Ibid p.39)."

The seventh trait emphasized by Greenleaf and the one that a leader should possess is the quality of awareness and perception. Awareness is a state of consciousness about a situation - mostly in the present tense. To have a perception or being perceptive of a situation is to go beyond the state of awareness and is usually applicable in the future sense. A leader who is both aware and able to perceive an impending situation(s) is in a position to lead and guide better.

Persuasion - sometimes one person at a time is the next feature that a leader ought to possess (p.42). The importance of the power of persuasion as a soft skill for leaders cannot be exaggerated. Persuasion is a substitute for coercion, bullying, and other forms that are often counter-productive for the completion of a job. Finally, the attribute of 'one action at a time - the way some great things get done' is emphasized as a quality leaders should possess (p.43). Tactically speaking this talent is *sine qua non* especially when a leader is directing a complex array of jobs. Identifying the suitability of each person for the jobs in hand helps to prioritise and lead it to completion under the supervision of the leader.

Sikh Gurus Within the Framework of Servant-Leader Paradigm

Greenleaf gives us the background leading to the development of the S-L paradigm. He says that he was influenced by the mythical book *Journey to the East* by German author Hermann Hesse. In this book, Hesse takes readers to a mythical journey with a group of travellers in which the central character is *Leo* who works as a servant for the group. One day *Leo* disappears living the group in disarray. The journey comes to a halt and is abandoned. Years later they find out that *Leo* who had all along served them as a servant was, in fact, a titular head of the order and a great noble leader. *Leo* had left the group to test the faith of group members if they could hold on their own - a test in which group members failed. Greenleaf says that "...to me, this story clearly says that *the great leader is seen as servant first,* and that simple fact is the key to greatness. Leo was actually the leader all of the time, but he was servant first because that was what he was, deep down inside. Leadership was bestowed upon a person who was by nature a servant. It was something given, or assumed, that could be taken away. His servant nature was the real man, not bestowed, not assumed, and not to be taken away. He was servant first." (Ibid p.21).

Characteristic features that define a S-L model *tailor fit* the lives of Sikh Gurus. Guru Nanak, the founder leader of the Sikh religion played the role of a prophet. His mission in life was to teach good for the betterment of the lives of the masses. He was a man of utmost humility with the welfare of all human beings in his heart. This comes out in his hymns and also in his personal life, towards the end of which he settled down to a farmer's life and worked on a field to make a living.

Following in the footsteps of Nanak was Guru Angad who was an inventor - and foreseeing the need for it, for the betterment of people, he gave shape to the written language which paved the way for centres of learning. Guru Angad also understood the need and long-term positives of the free community kitchen which he pursued for the benefit of his followers. Foreseeing the imminent confrontation with the Mughals, he also emphasised on physical well-being of the devotees.

Amar Das may be considered an earliest management Guru of the Sikhs who had the foresight of the decentralisation of the religious gatherings by opening 22 centres and putting in charge the manager priests authorised to impart religious training.

Guru Ram Das foresaw the need for infrastructure for the nascent Sikh religious institution to survive, and accordingly built the central place for gatherings and worship at *Harimandir Sahib*.

Guru Arjan Dev showed the path of supreme sacrifice that a leader would take for the beliefs he and his followers held.

Guru Hargobind told his followers that it was not enough to strengthen the mind and be always peaceful; if need be, it was legitimate to take up arms to protect oneself and the vulnerable.

Guru Har Rāī foresaw the focus required on the indigenous apothecary to treat the sick and emphasised the use of what was then available - the practice of Ayurvedic medicines.

The child Guru Harikrishen showed that it was not enough merely to preach but also to go out and serve the people as their servants. He died in the process of implementing his beliefs (treating the sick of smallpox).

Guru Tegh Bahadur showed that peace in solitary meditative life can be found and that hankering after power need not be the aim of life *unless one was genuinely prepared to serve the people.*

Of the many contributions of Guru Gobind Singh, strategic long-term thinking and royal courage, sometimes against all odds, stand out.

The ten Sikh Gurus each had a distinct quality described above. But all of them had in common the deepest of humility, highest of discipline, ethical and moral standards, with the best of conscience of right and wrong, which their followers sought to emulate. They never amassed wealth for themselves or their families - whatever they did was for the common good of the people. All the Gurus were also highly learned and possessed the knowledge of languages and classical literature and music theory. Although they were elevated to the position of Guru-ship, all of them considered themselves to be in the service of the people, and held the congregation which they held, in highest of esteem, and above themselves. One classic example of this is when Guru Gobind Singh, having baptised the chosen five Sikhs to kick-start the religion, asked the baptised five to baptise him in turn. The five Sikhs (not the same group) also ordered him to leave the Anandpur fort (and live to fight another day) when the battle was not going in the Sikhs' favour[119].

All the Gurus were fair in their choice of the ablest of person to be the next leader. As we notice from their contributions, all the Gurus had great foresight, were aware and listened to the need of their followers, empathised with them, and worked tirelessly for their betterment. They also never hesitated to point out the weaker spots which needed working individually and together as a community. The net result of all these positives was that, within the birth of the first Guru Nanak (1469) and the demise of the last and tenth

---

119 The thought behind this was that if the leader survives, he will be back for the battle another day.

Guru Gobind (1708) a formidable new religion with its own distinct identity, language, culture, scripture, and religious mentors had been established, with far reaching geographical, political, economic, and cultural significance.

Chapter Summary

The purpose of this chapter was to provide theoretical underpinnings to the growth of the Sikh religion. As a first step we defined religion which is a set of beliefs, values, moral code of conduct and rites specific to a group. Within each religion there are objects and matters that are uniformly considered sacred by its members - such as symbols and ceremonies. In each religion is worshipped some unseen world of Gods, Gurus, deity i.e., some powerful figure which is held in highest reverence. Rituals are held at a sacred place set aside (church, mosque, temple, synagogue, gurdwara) for prayers to seek peace, well-being, and prosperity.

There are several theories as to why and how religious communities are formed in the first place. These explanations range from the earliest observations of tribes and the aborigines worshipping of totems, nature, and mystic figures, to taking resort to magic failing, thus them taking recourse to religion. For scholars such as Karl Marx, religion is the recourse of the working class from the harsh realities of life.

For our purpose of explaining the formation and growth of the Sikh religion, we advanced the argument that *Rational Choice Theory* best explains the growth of the Sikh religion. Rational choice theory says that given a set of choices and preferences, people seek to maximise their benefits and minimise their costs by making rational choices. The gradual shift of people from other religions and those from lower castes (many of whom possibly were not aligned to any religion) to join Sikhism was a rational decision in the face of harshness and rigidity of the caste system versus the liberal approach the Sikh religion showed towards family and social rituals including the plight of women.

With regard to the speed of growth of the Sikh religion, we proposed that it took an elongated *S* shape with the rate of growth being steeper during the 83 years of Guru Nanak and Angad; somewhat flatter during the 29 years of Guru Amar Das and Ram Das; steeper in the times of Gurus Arjan Dev and Hargobind's regime of 63 years; flatter during in the reign of 20 years of Har Rāī and child Guru Hari Krishen; peaking and stabilizing during the Guru-ship period of the ninth and tenth Gurus who between them shared 43 years of Guru-ship.

Sikh Gurus showed remarkable leadership qualities which we also sought to study within the framework of leadership theories. Trait's theory of leadership postulates that traits possessed by leaders dictate their leadership style; according to contingencies theories leader behaviour is contingent on the situation; transactional and transformational leadership view the leader-follower relationship as an exchange of rewards for compliance in which followers are motivated by appealing to their self-interest. This approach is allied with the power, influence, and charismatic leadership theories. Leader-member exchange (LMX) paradigm sees the relationship between the leader and the followers as a two-way set-up in which a high level of trust reduces monitoring costs and enhances performance.

The theory that we postulate best explains the behaviour of Sikh leader Gurus is the *'servant-leader'* which says that the ideal relationship between the leader and follower is one in which a leader considers himself, in all humility, first as a servant of the followers, and does his best for them. Such a leader shall listen empathetically to the requirements of his followers and work towards fulfilling them.

The nature and behaviour of all 10 Sikh Gurus falls neatly within the *S-L paradigm*. Although all the Gurus had individual strengths, all of them had the deepest of humility, highest of discipline, ethical and moral standards with the best of conscience of right and wrong, which their followers sought to emulate. Sikh Gurus never amassed wealth for themselves or their clans - whatever they did was for the common good of the community. They were also highly learned with the knowledge of several languages and classical literature and music of the time. All the Gurus were entirely impartial in their choice of the ablest of person as their successor.

**

CHAPTER 4 FEATURES OF SIKH HOLY SCRIPTURE

The Holy Scriptures were not
given to us that we should enclose them
in books, but that we should engrave
them upon our hearts (John Chrysostom)

Introduction

In the preceding three chapters we presented a historical summary of the Punjab state and its people, followed by briefs on the lives of Sikh Gurus. This was then followed up with the discussion on the theories of religion and leadership and their applicability in the context of Sikhism. We now arrive at a core chapter of the book - the structure of the Sikh Holy Scripture, commonly addressed by Sikhs as *Guru Granth Sahib* (GGS) or sometimes by the name *Adi Granth* (AG) (the first book). This is not to be confused with *Dasam Granth* which is the name given to the collection of manuscripts of Guru Gobind Singh.

There is an academic controversy over the successive versions and alternations in the scripture, onto which we shall not dwell. The interested reader is directed to Singh P and Fenech L.E (Singh & Fenech, The Oxford Handbook of Sikh Studies, 2014, pp. Ch-9); (Singh P. , The Guru Granth Sahib: Canon, Meaning and Authority, 2003); (Mann G. S., 1993); (Mann G. S., 2001). Also details on how the scripture came about can be found in (Singh D. , 2004) and (Singh P. , Exploring Sikh Traditions and

Heritage, 2021)[120]. When we refer to *GGS, AG,* or Sikh Holy Scripture, or sometimes just the scripture in this book we refer to the final and approved version of the 1430 page scripture of the year 1864 ratified by the Singh Sabha reformers which is now the accepted version of the scripture (Singh & Fenech, The Oxford Handbook of Sikh Studies, 2014, p. 130) worldwide.

For the sake of brevity, sometimes the scripture is addressed as the *Holy Book.* Devout Sikhs find it incorrect to address the scripture in this way; they assert that it is much more than a holy book. It contains not only religious sermons but a whole lot of philosophical discourse on a number of diverse perspectives of life (discussed in the next chapter). We saw in chapter 2 that the fifth Guru Arjan Dev completed the scripture in 1604 and it was installed at *Harimandir Sahib* in the same year. In 1708, the tenth Guru, Guru Gobind Singh declared the scripture as the embodiment of the living Guru and decreed that from then on Sikhs would have no living Gurus, and that all Sikhs would follow the doctrines inscribed in the scripture. As a result of this decree, Sikhs in gurdwaras (and in their homes) install the scripture on a higher platform, decorated sometimes with a shiny canopy with a devotee fanning the scripture intermittently[121].

---

120 A key point of debate seems to be that the scripture evolved gradually culminating in the final shape given to it by Guru Arjan Dev. As we shall see, the coherence and accuracy of the scripture makes one wonder if such perfection would have been achieved if the scripture had passed through several hands, with alterations on the way in several time points. Assuming that the scripture did pass through several hands and evolved in some way over its journey to Guru Arjan Dev, he did a splendid job of turning it into a perfect timeless masterpiece that we have today.

121 This is to purify the air. In olden times when there was no AC or electric fans the handheld fan (called *Chaur Sahib*) would have also kept insects away.

Recall that in Indian history only kings and royals in a Darbar (court/council) received this treatment in their sitting arrangement on a decorated platform higher than the audience. Also, an attendant standing next to the royal, with a large fan (called pankha - from pankh, meaning feather) would intermittently fan the cool air onto the royal. The metaphor in Guru Gobind Singh declaring the scripture as the living embodiment of a Guru was that living Gurus come and go but the scripture, as living guiding Guru, will live and be revered *ad infinitum*.

One more clarification here is essential. Notice this author's address of *Harimandir Sahib,* which is also spelled by some as *Harmandar Sahib* or *Harmandir Sahib*. *Harimandir*, howsoever spelled, is made up of two words Hari+Mandir. Hari means someone or something supreme (equivalent to God) and Mandir means a sacred abode - a shrine. Sahib (sometimes written as Saheb) meaning master, is added for respect. *Harimandir Sahib* is also addressed as *Darbār Sahib* (sacred audience) as well as *Golden Temple* (mostly by non-Sikhs), owing to its gold coverings. *Harimandir Sahib*, or *Darbar Sahib*, is the correct address.

To keep discussion orderly, this chapter is divided in three sections. In section I we present the stylised facts about the scripture which summarises key elements related to its make-up and composition. In section II we explain the role of classical music in the scripture. In section III we explain, with the help of simple algebra, the complex task Guru Arjan Dev faced in the compilation of the scripture. This would show how formidable the task was which was manually completed by Guru Arjan Dev with just one assistant. In fact, the compilation task would be formidable even with the help of modern writing gadgets I am using, e.g., to write this book; and with recourse to programming language to put in right place a hymn according to its suitability in the overall scheme of the scripture.

Section - I Sikh Holy Scripture: Stylised Facts

Language of the Scripture

The scripture is written in Gurmukhi script as opposed to Sanskrit which had been the default norm language for religious scriptures in olden days. In the appendix of this chapter, we have reproduced 5 pages from the scripture - the reader can glance over it to get a visual of its style. The use of the Gurmukhi language must have been a deliberate choice so that the maximum number of devotees could read and understand the message conveyed in it by the Gurus. This is the literal meaning of Gurmukhi i.e., 'from the mouth of the Guru' which suits perfectly well for the scripture, since all the hymns in it have been penned by Gurus - both Sikh and non-Sikh. Gurmukhi script is also used to reproduce verses which were originally written in scripts other than Gurmukhi. Thus, for instance, verses which are in languages such as Lahnda (Western Punjabi), Braj (similar to Hindi), Sanskrit, Sindhi, and Persian were converted into Gurmukhi script for the purpose of their inclusion in the scripture, making it a coherent tome.

The language of the hymns chosen for inclusion in the scripture is simple and direct and drives home its intended message. Hymns in the scripture, when recited in Indian vocal and instrumental classical music measures, create an aura of spirituality. It is the opinion of this author that the scripture can be read and appreciated in its meaning, spiritual, and musical beauty, only in the language in which it is written i.e., Gurmukhi; it does not lend itself to translation into any other language, since the meaning and lyrical flow of the hymn is completely lost in the translation. Some noteworthy attempts though have been made in the translation of the scripture into the English language. See e.g., (Singh M. , 2009).

Hymns in the scripture are placed in a chronological order. Hymns of the first Guru (Guru Nanak) appear first, then of the second Guru, Guru Angad, and so on. 'Mahala' with associated numbers are identification codes that specify that this set of hymns belong to such and such Guru. 'Mahala 1' e.g., identifies that this set of hymns belong to Guru Nanak; 'Mahala 2' means the hymn belongs to the second Guru, Guru Angad, and so on.

Size of the Scripture

The scripture is printed two-sided, in landscape mode, with approximately 19 lines per page. It is a densely written scripture which is 1430 pages (or *Angs* in Gurmukhi) long. There are a total of 26,852 lines and 398697 words in it. A test by copying a page of the scripture on to an A3 landscape mode fitted on the page in 12 'Times New Roman' font with 1.5cm margins all round.

It takes 48-72 hours to read the scripture non-stop at a steady pace[122]. The scripture is quarter the size of the Indian epic *Mahabharata* (composed by Veda Vyasa[123]),

---

122 An approximate extrapolation shows that it would take 338 hours or 14 days to non-stop read the Mahabharata; 151 hours or 6 days to read the Holy Bible.

[123] Vyasa, the legendary sage in Hindu mythology is said to have categorized the Vedas into 4 volumes (Rigveda, Yajurveda, Samaveda, and Atharvaveda) making it easier to understand the divine knowledge in it.

which is the longest poem ever written and which has 1.8 million words; the scripture is about half the size of the *Holy Bible* which has 807,300 words[124]; it is five times the size of the *Holy Quran* which contains 77,437 words. A comparison with the academic publications is as follows.

The approximate length of a PhD thesis in social sciences and humanities is between 60-80,000 words. Taking the average at 70,000 words, the scripture is equivalent to about 6 PhD theses. A paper in an academic journal is between 8-10,000 words long. Taking the average to be 9,000 words the scripture is 44 journal papers. The scripture which can be construed as a long holy poem contains a total of 5882 hymns. Given the differing lengths of the hymns, it is not possible to accurately compare the scripture with other classics. As an approximate measure, *The Mahabharata* has over 200,000 verses. *The Ramayana*, another Indian epic, composed by Valmiki has 24,000 verses[125].

All copies of the scripture are printed strictly with the specifications described above and *all* are 1430 pages in length. Only the central managing committee of the Sikhs - Shiromani Gurdwara Parbandhak Committee (SGPC) (based at *Harimandir Sahib* complex in Amritsar) is authorised to print the official versions of the scripture. The standardised length helps to maintain a certain reading pace and the reciters are supposed to finish reciting in the

---

124 The Old Testament has 929 chapters and 23,214 verses which comprise roughly of 622,700 words. The New Testament consists of 260 chapters, and is divided into 7,959 verses, or roughly 184,600 words. This would give a typical Bible 1,189 chapters (929+260). These are made up of 31,173 verses: using a rough word count, this amounts to 807,300 words (622700+184600). https://wordcounter.net/blog/2016/02/21/101241_how-many-pages-are-there-in-the-bible.html (Accessed 18-Aug-2021).
125 Valmiki was the Sanskrit poet and scholar who is said to have composed Ramayana in 5BC.

expected time of around 48 hours. The text is read in whole, in time-bound fashion, on occasions such as celebrations of Gurus' birth and death anniversaries. Towards the end of the complete recitation, it is brought to a close, followed sometimes by sermons and a meal from the community kitchen.

The scripture is kept in gurdwaras in a special room adjacent to the congregation hall, and each morning with the chanting of hymns, is installed on a raised decorated platform on the opposite side of the entrance from where devotees enter the hall. The front of the platform is covered with colourful sheets. Devotees coming in, bow and pay their respect to the scripture before sitting down on the floor with the congregation. Sheets flowing down from the scripture above onto the ground below are often adorned with crossed swords and shields. Sikhs bow their head only to *AG*. Unlike the sitting arrangements in a church, devotees in the Sikh congregation sit on the floor covered, usually, with white sheets (nowadays carpets are laid under to provide a cushion). At the end of day, the scripture is put back to rest with a prayer. The scripture is sometimes ferried home by families wishing to have the complete scripture read on special occasions, such as to celebrate children's birthdays or events such on the passing away of a family member.

Authors in the Scripture

The Sikh scripture, a collection of 5882 hymns is penned by 42 authors from diverse backgrounds[126]. For our purpose, we have defined hymns to include all categories

---

126 Bhatt Satta & Balwand have eight pauris (stanzas) in one var (a verse form). If we take the count as eight, then the total = 5889.

of poetic verses - short or long, described in section III below. A cautionary note is required here. There is some discrepancy in the count of the total number of hymns in the scripture reported in the literature. For our purpose we have relied on (Kohli, Guru Granth Sahib: An analytical study, 1961), alongside the *AG*. Similarly, occasional discrepancy in the count of the total number of authors is also found in the literature. Here again we have relied on Kohli (1961)[127].

Let us first look at the number of authors. Of 42 authors, 13 are pre-Nanak (pre-AD1469) saints[128]. Seven Sikh Gurus whose hymns are included in the scripture are Guru Nanak, Angad, Amar Das, Ram Das, Arjan Dev (also the compiler of the scripture), Tegh Bahadur, and Gobind Singh. There are 22 saints and bards whose verses are also in the scripture[129].

The list of authors whose hymns Guru Arjan Dev included in the scripture reads like a 'who's who' of saints! As an example, Kabir, a weaver, born to a Brahmin mother, was raised by Muslim parents in Banaras; Namdev was a low-caste tailor from Maharashtra state; Ravidas from UP was born in a low-caste family; Sheikh Farid born in Punjab, also known as Bābā Farīd was a famous Muslim Sufi saint; Trilochan was a poet saint from Maharashtra; Dhanna from Rajasthan was a mystic poet; Shiekh Bhikan was a Muslim Sufi scholar from UP; Jaidev was poet of

---

127 Preference for Kohli (1961) stems from the fact that the book was the author's doctoral thesis. In its second edition there is no alteration to the original count.

128 In alphabetical order the 13 saints are: Beni, Dhanna, Jaidev, Kabir, Namdev, Parmanand, Pipa, Ramanand, Ravidas, Sadhna, Sain, Sheikh Farid, and Trilochan.

129 Bal, Bhal, Bhikha, Bhikhan, Das, Gayand, Harbans, Jal, Jalan, Jalap, Kal, Kasahar, Kirat, Mardana, Mathura, Nal, Sal, Satta & Balwand, Sewak, Sundar, Sur Das.

repute from Bengal; Surdas was a blind Brahmin poet from UP; Parmanand was a Brahmin poet from Maharashtra; Pipa was a Rajput King who abdicated the throne to became a saint; Ramanand, a Vaishnava was a devotional saint poet; Sadhna was originally a butcher by profession; Mardana was a Muslim Rebeck player and a long-time companion of Guru Nanak; Satta and Balvand are said to be brothers from a low-caste Mirasi[130] Muslim family who were mystic poet and Rebeck players; Sunder was the great - grandson of Guru Amar Das.

I believe this constellation of authors would have been a deliberate attempt by Guru Arjan Dev to make the scripture diverse across cultures, enriching it by including the hymns of saint poets from all strata of the social set-up. Guru Arjan Dev must also have taken into consideration the merit of the hymn as well for inclusion in the scripture. He did not let any other criterion such as the caste, creed or profession of the poet colour his opinion. The result is that Sikhs' have a scripture that is cross-culturally rich and democratic in its composition.

Distribution of Hymns Among Authors

The distribution of the 5882 hymns among the authors is as follows. The thirteen pre-Nanak saints' share in this is 794 (14%), and the Sikh Gurus' share is 4956 (84%), those of the saints and Bards at the time of Gurus is 132 (2%).

The largest share of hymns of saints from Pre-Nanak's time is that of Kabir (541) and Sheikh Farid (134),

---

[130] Traditional singers and dancers from low castes.

and Namdev (60) who between them have 735 hymns. With regard to Sikh Gurus, the distribution of hymns between them is as follows: Guru Nanak (974), Angad Dev (62), Amar Das (907), Ram Das (679), Arjan Dev (2218), Tegh Bahadur (115), Gobind Singh (1). Thus, seven of the ten Guru's hymns are included in the scripture - the largest number being that of Arjan Dev.

I presume Guru Arjan Dev in his effort to give the scripture a coherent read must have had to pen the hymns wherever required. Most Sikhs would believe this to be the reason behind him having the largest number of hymns in the scripture. Being a true Guru saint, full of humility, we cannot conceive of any other reason. I trust the Sikh community owe Guru Arjan Dev for fulfilling the task by filling in the gaps, wherever required, so admirably. This also shows his literary genius, not only in the editorial skills, but also his ingenuity as a literary poet.

With regard to the 132 hymns penned by saints and Bards at the time of Gurus, the distribution is as follows. Of the 22 poets that existed at the time of Gurus, 18 were poets in attendance in the courts of Gurus. The majority of the hymns, 124, are penned by these court poets[131].

What is not Included in the Scripture

It will be easier to understand the contents of the scripture if we first enumerate what is *not* included in it. First, there are no autobiographical notes or comments on

---

131 Their names in alphabetical order are: Bhal, Bhikha, Das, Gayand, Harbans, Jal, Jalan, Jalap, Kal, Kasahar, Kirat, Mathura, Nal, Sal, Satta & Balwand, and Sewak.

any celebrity person or otherwise, or of the authors whose hymns are included in the scripture. Second, the scripture does not contain stories, narrations, or any material of that nature. Third, there is no mention of historical dates or events such as battles fought by Sikhs, displacements, heroic acts, martyrdoms of Sikh Gurus or any phenomena of that nature. Fourth, there are no verses that depress, or are unusually provocative of any topic - family, social, or political. Finally, even the Rāgas suggestion to sing the hymns are moderate in nature - they are neither depressive nor overly buoyant in nature.

Layout and Contents of the Scripture

The Sikh scripture can be construed as a long poem of 1430 pages written with the built-in exquisite melodies. The scripture has the rigour of an underlying Hindustani classical music theory that runs as an undercurrent in all the hymns (save for a few that are meant to be recited). The tunes accompanying the hymns can be savoured and appreciated by anyone with the faintest interest in music – western or eastern.

In the first part of the scripture there are three compositions which are to be recited. These are *Japji* (morning prayers; p1-8), *Rehraas* (evening prayers; p.8-12), *Sohila*, (bedtime prayers; p12-13). These prayers occupy 13 pages out of 1430.

The second part (pages 14-1353 i.e., 1339 pages) occupy the bulk of the scripture and contain hymns. In the beginning of each hymn it is specified with which Rāga it is to be sung. Listed in the scripture are 31 main and 29 sub-Rāgas (of main Rāgas) (Table 4.1).

In the final section (1354-1430) are listed additional hymns of Gurus and saints. The section entitled *Mundavani* is the concluding section of the spiritual portion of the scripture. The end section called *Raagmala* is a list of Rāgas and their families.

One fact that has hitherto been not noted is that none of the pages in the scripture are part finished. All pages are filled with text till the end of the page; no space has been left blank. If, say, material in context has come to an end half or three-quarters of the way, additional hymn(s) have been skilfully added to it. An example can be found on p.1293 where 3 ½ lines of a hymn in Rāga *malar* are added at the tail-end of the page to make the page visually appealing and maintain symmetry with the rest of the scripture.

Layout of the Scripture Within 31 Rāgas

It will be helpful at this juncture to understand the different time slots of the day within which the 31 Rāgas specified which hymns are meant to be sung. An understanding of the demarcation of the day in different time slots is called *peher*. Traditionally, in India and also in Pakistan, people view the day composed of eight *pehers*, each *peher* consisting of 3 hours in the following sequence: early morning 3-6am; then 6-9am, 9-12pm, 12-3pm, 3-6pm, 6-9pm, 9-12pm, 12-3am.

In olden times when agriculture was the main occupation, an approximate description of work between these eight time slots can be described as follows: 3-6am (*Amrit vela* - 'nectar time' for Sikhs) is the time when people are supposed to have risen from sleep and after cleansing duties, recite morning prayers; in the countryside farmers also attend to early morning farming chores. The second and third *pehers* were then used to attend to one's profession. 12-3pm was the time for the mid-morning meal and rest; 3-6pm was again devoted to one's profession; it was also time for evening prayer - *Rehraas* recitation for Sikhs; 6pm onwards to 9pm for *pooja* (worship), evening meal and then getting ready to sleep to begin another day's cycle. People those days slept early and rose early to begin the day's work.

As can be imagined, our thoughts, emotions and aura are different in different *pehers* of the day. Taking this into account, music pandits have devised each Rāga (its tempo, rise, and fall of notes) to match the aura and mood of the day. Pandits of Hindustani classical music also advised that these Rāgas preferably be recited or played on instruments at the suggested time of the day for their optimal effect.

Table 4.1 presents in a succinct way the information on the 31 Rāgas accompanying the hymns in the scripture. These are listed in exact sequence in which they appear in the scripture. Table 4.1 has four columns.

Column-1 has three pieces of information – the name of the Rāga, time slot of the day for which that Rāga is the ideal recital time, and the actual time corresponding to that slot. For instance, in the first row, the listed information is: Siri Rāga–6 (6-9pm) - this corresponds to Sri Rāga which is meant for the 6th *peher* of the day, and the time corresponding to this slot is 6-9pm.

It should be noted that during recitals, the beginning ideal time of Rāgas may be followed, the ending time is not; hence a recital for a Rāga that is advised to be recited between say, 6-9 pm may begin at 6pm but go on longer depending on the mood of the reciter and the listeners. This author has observed this happening in person; when the reciters get into a semi-trance mood, they can often forget the time, along with the engrossed listeners; organisers also then prefer not to interrupt if they are not hard pressed for time.

Column-2 lists pages allocated to that particular Rāga.

Column-3 lists the page number in the scripture on which the Rāga appears.

Column-4 provides a brief description of the mood the particular Rāga evokes.

Recall that on pages 1-14 of the scripture are listed morning and evening prayers which are to be recited and not sung. From page 1352-1430 are hymns of Gurus and poets, and a list of Rāgas popular in those days, but not included in the scripture are listed. Beginning and end page numbers are added to keep the total number of pages to 1430, the length of the scripture.

Lock-Proof System of the Layout: An Example

While compiling the scripture, Guru Arjan Dev made sure that the layout of the scripture is such that nothing in it can be added, subtracted, or changed. The method he devised is ingenious and remarkable in its simplicity - the system is also praiseworthy in terms of ascertaining the ownership of the hymn and the sequential counting of the material in it.

For us to better understand how the lock-proof design has been put in place, we have reproduced from the scripture 5 pages of hymns in Rāga *Mali Gaura* on page 984-988 (these pages are appended with this chapter). Note the following highlights.

1. In the beginning of page 1/5, on the very top, the name of the Rāga and its authorship is stated. In this instance, the hymn is to be chanted in Rāga *Mali Gaura*, and this hymn is of the 4th Guru Ram Das. Similarly, the name of the Rāga and its author is described in the beginning of *all* the 31 Rāgas in the scripture.

2. The next two lines on the top (of page 1/5) are what Sikh's call '*Mool Mantar*' (basic chant). It includes the fundamental belief of Sikhs that there is but one God and that he is formless. These two lines of '*Mool Mantar*' appear before all the 31 Rāgas in the scripture.

3. The opening sentence of the main section (page 1/5) highlighted in italics and bold (for description only - <u>not</u> in the scripture) ends with the number 1 with two parallel bars on the left and right ‖1‖ followed by the word ਰਹਾਉ - *RAHAO* meaning pause. This instruction to momentarily pause appears in several places in the scripture and adds to the ambience of the hymn.

4. The next 4 lines are *chaupadas* - 4-line verses, each line of which is numbered at the end of the sentence (for Gurmukhi and English equivalent numbers see Glossary). For convenience, in this instance, this

author has added English numbers with Gurmukhi numerals.

5. On line 7 (page 1/5), the 4-line verse is completed, and this is indicated as ॥੪॥੧॥ ਮਾਲੀ ਗਉੜਾ ਮਹਲਾ ੪ ॥ (read as *Maali Gaura Mahla 4*) meaning the first set of the 4-line verses end here and that the reader is to continue in Rāga *Mali Gaura*.

6. At the end of the page, spilling over to next page (2/5), we see the symbol ॥੪॥੨॥ ਮਾਲੀ ਗਉੜਾ ਮਹਲਾ ੪ ॥ (read as *Maali Gaura Mahla 4*) meaning the second of the 4-line verses end here and that the reader is to continue in Rāga Mali Gaura.

7. The above pattern is repeated until we reach the middle of the third page (page 3/5). Here at the end of the sentence we find these symbols: ॥੪॥੬॥ ਛਕਾ ੧ ॥ - translated it reads as ॥4 ॥6॥ 6th 1 ॥ meaning 6x4 lines set verses of the 4th Guru end here as one set.

Similarly, the reader can find symbols interspersed all over the 5 pages reproduced here from the scripture. These symbols and digits identifying the internal structure of the hymns, with regard to the lines of the hymn, type of verse, Rāga in which the hymn is to be sung, its author, where it starts and ends, etc., makes it virtually impossible to tinker or alter any word - never mind a sentence. Everything that has been put in the *Guru Granth Sahib* has been sealed once and for all by its compiler the 5th Guru Arjan Dev and his assistant Bhai Gurdas. The Sikh scripture in other words is *Fort Knox*!!

Table 4. 1 Frequency Distribution of 31 Rāgas with Brief Description

Column-1	Colum	Colum	Column-	Column-5
Rāga Name, Time slot of the day, and preferred time of the day for its recitation. (Digits after the Rāga refer to 3-hour *peher/slot* of the day beginning with 1st at 3am-6am and last 8th at 12 midnight to 3 am)	Page Numbe rs in the Scriptu re	Total Pages Devote d in the Scriptu re	Cumulati ve Pages	Brief Description of Rāga
Morning, Evening, and Night-time Prayers	1-13	13	13	Jap, Sodar (Rāga-Asa), So Purakh (Rāga Asa), Sohila (Rāga Gauri Deepki).
1.Siri Rāga–6 (6-9pm)	14-93	80	93	An evening Rāga, its recital time is sunset. It creates ambience of devotion and dedication.

2.Maajh–5 (3pm-6pm)	94-150	57	150	An early evening Rāga, Rāga Maajh has its origins in folk music and evokes the feeling of yearning for one's beloved.
3.Gauri Guarariree– 5 (3pm-6pm)	151-346	196	346	Rāga Gauri, an early evening Rāga, espouses quiet determination in the listener towards his objectives without enhancing his ego.
4.Aasaa–1 (3am-6am)	347-487	141	487	An early morning tune, Rāga Aasaa inspires emotions of inspiration and courage to accomplish the task.
5.Gujri–3 (9am-12noon)	488-526	39	526	Rāga Gujari gently leads the listener to realise the importance of slipping time and his mortality, making the listener see for himself 'as he is' and making him search within himself for the truth and value of life.
6.Devgandh ari – 2 (6am-9m)	527-536	10	536	A morning Rāga, Devagandhari evokes the mood

				of reverence urging the listener to search for qualities to meet the Lord.
7.Bihagra–7 (9pm-12midnight)	537-556	20	556	A night melody, Rāga Bihagra evokes acute sadness which leads one to craving for truth and the meaning of life to find peace and fulfilment.
8.Vadhans–4 (12noon-3pm)	557-594	38	594	With its origins in folk music, this afternoon tune, Rāga Vadahans, evokes quiet and tender moods.
9.Sorath–7 (9pm-12midnight)	595-659	65	659	A night melody, Rāga Sorath conveys the feeling of strong belief in thoughts and its repeated recitation attracts the attention of listeners.
10.Dhanasiri–4 (12noon-3pm)	660-695	36	695	An early afternoon tune, Rāga Dhanashree evokes a cheerful, happy mood.
11.Jaitsiri–6 (6pm-9pm)	696-710	15	710	An early evening melody, Rāga Jaitsiri transmits the emotions of not being able to live

233

				without someone and anxiously seeking to reach one's beloved.
12.Todi–3 (9am-12noon)	711-718	08	718	Todi is a melodious morning Rāga and evokes a mood of playfulness.
13.Behrari–2 (6am-9am)	719-720	02	720	A morning Rāga, Behrari evokes the feeling as if the person is urged to continue with the task in hand to achieve higher heights in life.
14.Tilang–4 (12noon-3pm)	721-727	07	727	Rāga Tilang, a mid-day Rāga, evokes the feeling of ruminating and slight exhaustion (not anger) having failed to impress one you revere.
15.Suhi–3 (9am-12noon)	728-794	67	794	Suhi, a morning melody, evokes for the listener the feeling of proximity and love.
16.Bilawal–3 (9am-12noon)	795-858	64	858	Bilawal, a morning Rāga evokes the feeling of devotion in listeners.

17.Gond–7 (9 pm-12midnight)	859-875	16	875	A night Rāga, Gond arouses the feeling of enthusiasm in the singer and listener's longing for the creator.
18.Ramkali –1 (3am-6am)	876-974	99	974	Ramkali, an early morning Rāga is full of compassion and evokes similar feelings in both the singer and the listener.
19.Nat Narayan–7 (9pm-12midnight)	975-983	09	983	A delicate midnight Rāga – not easy to recite, it expresses the feeling of slight impetuosity/impati ence but at the same time retaining self-control by the singer.
20.Mali Gaura–6 (6pm-9pm)	984-988	05	988	An evening Rāga, recited at sunset time, it is a complex Rāga and conveys mixed feelings of happiness and urges control over vices such as anger, greed, self-indulgence.

21.Maru–4 (12noon–3pm)	989–1106	118	1106	Maru, a midday Rāga, usually recited at the time of death evokes twin emotions of sad bereavement and an urge to move on in life (e.g., in battles, times of war).
22.Tukhari–5 (3pm–6pm)	1107–1117	11	1117	Tukhari, an afternoon Rāga, paints the picture of a meditator silently revelling in separation of his beloved.
23.Kedar–6 (6pm-9pm)	1118–1124	07	1124	An evening to night-time melody, Kedar Rāga creates an ambience of peace - its playful note mix creates moods of joy and elation.
24.Bhairav–2 (6am–9am)	1125–1167	43	1167	A morning melody, Rāga Bhairav evokes introspection, devotion, and peacefulness.
25.Basant–6 (6pm–9pm)	1168–1196	29	1196	Rāga Basant ('spring') evokes freshness as on the oncoming of spring, encouraging listeners to brush

				away complication in their minds, generating hope for a fresh start.
26.Sarang– 3 (9am- 12noon)	1197- 1253	57	1253	Recited late morning to early afternoon, Sarang Rāga has the connotation of mythological events in Hindu religion e.g., love between Krishna and Radha.
27.Malhaar –7 (9pm- 12midnight)	1254- 1293	40	1293	A night-time joyous Rāga has the legend attached to it that it can cause rains!
28.Kaanara –7 (9pm- 12midnight)	1294- 1318	25	1318	A serious night-time melody, Kaanara can evoke strong emotions leading to moods of stillness and grandeur.
29.Kalyan– 6 (6pm- 9pm)	1319- 1326	08	1326	An evening Rāga, Kalyan (meaning good luck) is considered to be a blessing-seeking and a soothing melody.
30.Prabhati –1 (3am- 6am)	1327- 1351	25	1351	An early morning Rāga, it conveys the emotions of extreme devotion and love.

31.Jaijawan ti–8 (12midnigh t-3am)	1352 (2.5 lines end on) pp.1353	01	1352	This Rāga can simultaneously express feelings of joy of achievement and grief of losing someone – a duality of emotions that bars one from being over - joyous (e.g., post-battle feelings).
	1353 –	78	1430	Hymns

Note: Some of the 31 main Rāgas also have sub- Rāgas. There are 29 such sub-Rāgas that takes the total number of Rāgas in the scripture to 60. In the description below, **31 Rāgas are in bold** with their sub- Rāgas (non-bold). Corresponding page numbers of these Rāgas in the scripture are also given.

1. Asa - 10; 2. Gauri Deepaki - 12; 3. Dhanasri - 13; 4. Gauri Poorabi - 13 (these Rāgas up to p.13 belong to *Rehraas* (evening prayer), and *Sohila* (night-time prayers) ; 5. **Sri - 14;** 6. **Maj - 94;** 7. **Gauri Guarairee - 151;** 8. Gauri Dakhani - 152; 9. Gauri Chaitee - 154; 10. Gauri Bairagan - 156; 11. Gauri Poorabi Deepaki - 157; 12. Gauri Majh - 172; 13. Gauri Malva - 214; 14. Gauri Mala - 214; 15. Gauri Sorath - 330; 16. **Asa - 347;** 17. Asavari - 369; 18. Asa Asavari - 409; 19. **Gujari 489;** 20. **Devgandhari - 527;** 21. **Bihagra - 537;** 22. **Vadhans - 557;** 23. Vadhans Dakhani - 580; 24. **Sorath - 595;** 25. **Dhanashri - 660;** 26. **Jaitsri - 696;** 27. **Todi - 711;** 28. **Bairarri - 719;** 29. **Tilang - 721;** 30. Tilang Kafi - 726; 31. **Suhee - 728;** 32. Suhee Kafi - 751; 33. Suhee Lalit - 793; 34. **Bilaval - 795;** 35. Bilaval Dakhani - 843; 36. **Gound - 859;** 37. Bilaval Gound - 874; 38. **Ramkali - 876;** 39. Ramkali Dakhani - 907; 40. **Nut Narayan - 975;** 41. Nut - 975; 42. **Mali Gaura - 984;** 43. **Maru - 989;** 44. Maru Kafi - 1014; 45. Maru Dakhani - 1033; 46. **Tukhari - 1107;** 47. **Kedara - 1118;** 48. **Bhairo - 1125;** 49. **Basant - 1168;** 50. Basant Hindol - 1170; 51. **Sarang - 1197;** 52. **Malar - 1254;** 53. **Kanra - 1294;** 54. **Kaliyan - 1319; 55.** Kaliyan Bhopali - 1321; 56. **Parbhati - 1327; 57.** Parbhati Bibhas - 1327; 58. Parbhati Dakhani - 1344; 59. Bibhas Parbhati - 1347; 60. **Jaijavanti - 1352. (Total = 60** Rāgas).

Source for the Table and notes: The Sikh Holy Scripture; (Vasant, 1990); (Wickramanayaka , 2020); (Mone, 2021); (Singh S. , Sri Guru Granth Sahib Darshan (In Gurmukhi), 1961); (Singh S. , About Compilation of Sri Guru Granth Sahib, 1996).

Highlights of Table 4.1

Table 4.1 has several highlights.

First let us look at the space (pages) allocated to hymns for different time slots of the day. A count from column 3 tells us that the maximum space (265 pages 19% of total space in the scripture) has been allocated to early morning (3-6am) hymns, closely followed by early afternoon (3-6pm) slot which has 264 pages allocated to it; third place is occupied by late morning slot (9-12noon 235 pages); afternoon slot (12-3pm – 199 pages); night time (9-12midnight 175); late evening (6-9pm 144 pages); morning (6-9am 55 pages); and 2 pages for dead of the night (12midnight to 3am).

The allocation of space to hymns for different time slots of the day as described above becomes much clearer when we juxtapose it with the nature of the tunes assigned to accompany the hymn by their allocated slot. Once we do so, the following broad scheme of arrangement starts to emerge.

The tunes accompanying morning hymns (e.g., Asa, Ramkali) evoke the feeling of much compassion, devotion, and emotions.

When we move to the next part of the day (6-9am) the tunes accompanying the hymns (e.g., Behrari, Bhairav), gets less intense.

Next *peher* (9-12noon) tunes (e.g., Sarang, Suhi) accompanying the hymns get more playful in nature.

Midday (12-3pm) is time to take a break from work for meals and afternoon rest from work (in olden times agriculture work reigned supreme) as a result, tunes (e.g., Tilang, Maru) accompanying the hymns get contemplative in nature. Midday is also the time to attend to rituals after cremations, and tunes accordingly reflect the feelings.

The fifth *peher* (3-6pm) is the time before finishing work and tunes accompanying the hymns (e.g., Tukhari, Gauri) reflect a mix of silent revel into meditation and also determination towards listeners' objectives in life.

The sixth *peher* (6-9pm) is the time when the sun is setting and tunes (e.g., Kedar, Kalyan) accompanying the hymns reflect the appropriate ambience for listeners, reminding them of the blessings of God and prompting them to eschew greed, anger, and other vices.

The penultimate seventh *peher* (9-12 mid-night) is to prepare for another day in life with reinforcement of good beliefs, penchant for devotion and the quiet joy of life, and tunes (such as Sorath, Kanara) accordingly reflect this.

The final eighth *peher* (12mid-night; mid-night- to 3am) tune (Jaijaiwanti) is sombre and does not let devotees be over-joyous or buoyant.

Section – II   Role of Indian Vocal Classical Music in Sikh Scripture

Elements of Indian Classical Music

Music is a higher revelation than all
wisdom and philosophy (Beethoven)

Before we discuss the role classical music plays in the lives of Indians and Sikhs in particular, as a background it will be of help to have a brief overview of the origin and nature of Indian classical music. This will help us put contents of this section into context.

Indian classical or Hindustani music (from north India) and Carnatic music (from south India) have their origins in the over 3000 years old Indian classic Samveda (Pandey, 2018). Samveda is one of four Vedas (the other three being Rigveda, Yajurveda and Atharva veda). A branch of Samved is 'Gandhar Veda' which is the study of all art forms - music, dance, and poetry. This Vedic text contains rules on how to practice music and links it with the wellbeing of body and soul and its relationship with the divine. The text describes the suitability of a Rāga for particular times of the day.

Until the entry of Islamic invaders in the mid-10th century AD, reaching its peak in Akbar's reign (1542-1605 (Akbar famously had nine jewels of varying talent in his court, Tansen, the musical genius being one of them) there was only one form of classical music - Indian classical music.

The bifurcation into Hindustani and Carnatic music began when the Muslims brought with them their style - mostly Persian and Arabic, into India. Because Islamic invaders called northern India as Hindustan, the music that existed and which came to be influenced by them, also came to be known as Hindustani music.

South Indian music, largely from Karnataka region, remained by and large unaffected by Islamic influence and the music that came with it. Music from Karnataka state kept its momentum on traditional lines and came to be known as Carnatic music, which, as a result of relative isolation, stayed rigorous on its underlying theory and rendition than Hindustani music.

The Hindustani music came to be influenced by Sufi (devotional) music of Islam. The common element between north and south music is that both are Rāga based and have pre-defined rules of recitation. Improvisation during performances in both kinds is encouraged and does happen. This is in contrast of Western orchestral music which strictly follows written notations. One will rarely see an Indian vocal classical reciter looking into his/her notes while reciting on the stage. Decades of everyday practice etches the complicated notes in the memory of the reciter.

Whichever form of music we listen to, it follows basic rules of notes. Sounds that are sweet and travel at regular intervals and which are used to produce music are called '*notes*' – or '*svar*' in Indian music. There are seven natural or *shudh* notes - Sa, Re, Ga, Ma, Pa, Dha, and Ni. Their western equivalent is: Do Re Mi Fa So La Ti.

A Rāga is a composition of notes - *shudh*, sharp (*tivra*), or komal (*flat*). The meaning of the word Rāga is something that colours our mind with pleasing effect. Each

Rāga has its own set of *svars* which have to be obeyed while reciting that Rāga.

The three elements of Hindustani music are the sound (explained above), time, and composition. Time can be maintained through beats and beats occurring in a certain cyclical style become *taal*. *Bandish* or composition binds the sound and time together, acting as a road map to be followed in a Rāga.

In one of the earliest classifications of Rāgas, six Rāgas (Bhairav, Malkauns, Hindol, Deepak, Megh and Shree) were considered male Rāgas with each of these having five female Rāgas (called Raagnis) making the original total of Rāgas 36 - though scores of variants are also found.

An approximate count of the myriad of variants of Rāgas puts the total number of Rāgas around 1071[132]. A fairly detailed discussion of Hindustani and Carnatic list of Rāgas can be found in Srivastav (Srivastav, 1980) and Vasant (Vasant, 1990).

As described earlier, different times of the day evoke different moods; Rāgas are meant to suit this mood. For instance, morning is akin to enthusiasm and readiness for the day; afternoons are hot, and brightness is the norm; evenings can be contemplative and can evoke pensive mood; dusk can be reflective and yearning for retirement

---

132 The exact number of all classical Indian Raags is not known. The number cited here is a count from the following site:
https://en.wikipedia.org/wiki/List_of_Rāgas_in_Hindustani_classical_music (Accessed 14-3-2022).

for the night's rest; and calmness of night can evoke notion of erotic romanticism[133].

Spell Binding Properties of Indian Classical Music

What passion cannot music raise and quell
(John Dryden)

If anyone, in particularly a non-Sikh has had the opportunity to visit or pass by a gurdwara, he/she may have heard gentle melodious tunes floating in the atmosphere. Music attracts and holds our attention - we all have preferences for different genres of music but can be tolerant to music that is gentle.

Sikhs and those who can understand the spoken Punjabi language will agree that listening to musical hymns in a gurdwara can be a spiritual experience. Although presently some performers have begun to experiment with guitar, sitar, and other instruments, hymns in most gurdwaras are still recited with the help of just two instruments - a set of *Tabla* (drums) and a *harmonium*. Because hymns have an underlying metrical beat and follow a pattern, listening to them is a soothing experience. Often devotees, particularly elderly, play religious tunes at home in the background while going about their chores.

---

[133] Ravi Shankar, the sitar maestro, puts it as follows "There are thousands of ragas and they are all connected with different times of the day, like sunrise or night or sunset. It is all based on 72 of what we call 'mela' or scales. And we have principally nine moods, ranging from peacefulness to praying, or the feeling of emptiness you get by sitting by the ocean." (https://www.greatsayings.net/sayings-about-ragas/ (Accessed 4-2-2022).

With modern technology, several gurdwaras in India and overseas relay daily prayer and *kirtan* (recitation with musical instruments) online. There is great demand for talented performers who can sing and play the hymns in tunes specified in the scripture. Their recorded performances have graduated from humble audio cassettes to CDS, DVDs, memory sticks, and now several command millions of hits on YouTube. The result of institutionalizing the application of music by way of its uses in the hymns sung and played on musical instruments in gurdwaras world-over has the bonding effect on Sikhs. No wonder most have great musical sense, and a great number can also sing and play instruments.

If Gurus, in particular Guru Arjan Dev, who compiled the scripture had the foresight of tapping into the power of music to bind the community, then he certainly has succeeded.

Section – III   Compilation of Holy Scripture

Passion is the Genesis of Genius
(Galileo Galilei)

Scripture and the Sikh Masses

Since its installation in *Harimandir Sahib* in 1604, the scripture has become the sacred *alma mater* of the Sikh world. Parts of it are recited in hundreds of thousands of homes and gurdwaras each day; conferences have been organised around it, doctoral studies have been conducted on its contents; academic papers and books have been written and scores of people have made a career out of it in the colleges and universities around the world, not to mention the jobs the scripture has created for *Granthis* as readers of the scripture in gurdwaras and as teachers of the scripture.

The astonishing, rather extraordinary fact to note is that, despite its repeated exposure for over 400 years under the watchful and microscopic analysis of millions of people, not one slip or mismatch of any kind has been found in it. Since its inception, no errors in its composition or contents have been reported and as a result, none have been corrected. At the same time, as described above, the layout of the scripture is so exact that it is not amenable to any alteration without completely messing up the section in which the change would be attempted.

In short, from whichever angle we examine it, the completed scripture by Guru Arjan Dev is nothing short of a masterpiece in its class - a rare piece of originality in compilation at each individual level – in four words it is the 'work of a genius.' The sweat, the time, the unflinching devotion of Guru Arjan Dev in assembling it paid off in a timeless work of art, which will be viewed in awe, read, and studied by future generations *ad infinitum*.

As stated, the scripture is read every day in thousands of gurdwaras in India and overseas and has become a bonding mechanism for Sikhs. I wonder if Guru Arjan Dev had not taken the initiative to compile the scripture which way the Sikh religion would have gone. This is a disturbing thought, as without a shared scripture it is likely the newly emerging religion would have withered away. The scripture is a powerful medium which has kept the community together.

It is the gurdwara where people gather on Sundays and on occasions such as the birth and death anniversaries of Gurus, social and family events, and rejoice and reinforce shared beliefs of one God, truthful living, humility, living by honest means and other positives the scripture teaches. Conservative estimates put the number of gurdwaras worldwide at 32000[134]. The simple economics of these large number of gurdwaras can be gauged in its generation of direct and indirect employment via supply chains. The gurdwaras have become the institutional symbol of Sikhs worldwide with the scripture as its focal point.

Programming the Scripture – The Theory

The features of the scripture, as described above, in stylised facts show that a compilation of a scripture of this size was an immensely complex task. In this section we shall attempt to explain the enormity of the task that faced Guru Arjan Dev and Bhai Gurdas who assisted him. We shall explain the process in steps, at the end of which, the reader will realise that the task Guru Arjan Dev completed would be a formidable one, even with the help of writing gadgets and software the likes of the one I am using to write this book and the programming help that I can draw upon.

The problem Guru Arjan Dev faced and resolved is akin to a linear programming problem which is a method used for obtaining an optimal solution for a problem with given constraints. Optimisation is finding optimal points (maxima, minima) in a system and uses a set of algorithms

---

134 Estimated with the help of the following site and online search.
https://www.sikhiwiki.org/index.php/Number_of_Gurdwaras_around_the_wo rld (Accessed 7-9-2021)

to a mathematical model to find the best design. An optimisation problem can be written as:

$$\max f(x) \; ; \quad subject\ to \quad LB \leq x \leq UB \; ;$$
$$g(x) = 0; \; h(x) \leq 0.$$
$$x$$

where *x are the decision variables in a vector* $x = [x_1\ x_2\ x_3\dots\dots]$; $LB \leq x \leq UB$ are the constraints on decision variables; $g(x) = 0$ is the equality constraints; $h(x) \leq 0$ is *inequality* constraints. There are various forms of optimisation problems - linear, quadratic, non-linear, mixed integer programs, which in turn can be linear or non-linear.

Constrained optimization models have three major components: decision variables, objective function, and constraints.

Programming the Scripture – The Practice

Skill Set Required for the Compilation

Guru Arjan Dev was a prodigy who was elevated to Guru-ship at age 18. Let us consider the skills he would have had to have at his disposal to compile the scripture. Here is a selected list.

First, he had to have a complete knowledge of the hymns penned by preceding Gurus.

Second, he would require the knowledge of hymns of non-Sikh Gurus existing prior to and at the time of compiling the scripture.

Third, he would require an intimate knowledge of Hindustani classical music to be able to make the right choice in choosing the appropriate tune for a hymn and its placement in the scripture.

Fourth, he would have to have an in-depth knowledge and imagination as to (a) which Rāga was suitable for which hymn, (a) of which Guru, as out of respect he wanted to maintain the hierarchy (chronology) while positioning the hymns in the scripture. He wanted hymns of the first Guru to appear first, then of the second, and so on.

Fifthly, there must have been a timeframe in his mind within which he wanted to accomplish the task (The scripture is said to have taken five years to complete).

Goals and Objectives

Goals

The goal Guru Arjan Dev had was to compile a scripture that would serve devotees with a moral and ethical code of conduct at the community, family, and personal level.

Secondly, such a code of conduct would stand the test of time i.e., the compiled scripture would be a focal point for guidance in all walks of life *ad infinitum*.

Thirdly, the scripture would be laid out in a format that was watertight with no alterations of any kind possible.

Objectives

The primary objective would have been to *optimise* i.e., to get the most out of available material at his disposal.

This material was in the form of previous hymns of Sikh and non-Sikh Gurus.

The second objective would have been to make the reading of the hymns in the scripture spiritually lyrical yielding maximum recitation and hearing pleasure. This would be possible only with the use of the appropriate Rāga for each of the hymns.

The third objective would be to make sure that the scripture contained appropriate hymns for all major events of a devotee's life, such as those required for conjugal and funeral rites.

Allied to the third objective was the fourth objective that hymns to suit all the eight *pehers*, or time slots of the day (described earlier) were to be included.

The fifth objective would have been to make the scripture accessible to a wider audience by compiling it in an accessible language. In response to this objective, Guru Arjan Dev continued with the use of the Gurmukhi language, converting the hymns which were in non-Gurmukhi language into Gurmukhi.

Constraints

Guru Arjan Dev must have faced multiple constraints in the compilation of the scripture. Before we list these constraints, let's have a subjective overview of the constraints.

Subjective Constraints

In present times we have at our disposal modern gadgets - laptops, printers, plentiful supply of paper and also appropriate software; we are also networked with co-authors, publishers, and reviewers around the world. With all these facilities around us, when academics handle a multi-party research project, they have a written plan (based on which sometimes funding from private and public institutions is sought), flow charts and tables are drawn, feedback from meetings with the colleagues and staff seminars is sought and research plans are revised and modified.

Often on research projects, research assistants at senior or junior levels are hired, equipment and software bought, and secretarial assistance made use of. When the work progresses, drafts of academic papers are written, presented, and discussed and the feedback taken before they are sent off for publications in journals or as research monographs. The publication process is lengthy - particularly for journal papers for which referee comments and feedback has to be considered in the revision process (the classic RR situation - revise and re-submit). When the project is completed, a detailed report is sought and submitted to a funding agency or to the head of the school if funding obtained was internal. Often samples of completed research projects are made available for future use[135].

In the case of the compilation of the scripture, the only information we have is that Guru Arjun Dev was handed the hymns of previous Gurus and that he had deputed his disciples to collect the hymns of saints and that he had access to Bhai Gurdas (in modern terminology his

135 ESRC -The Economic and Social Science Research Council in the UK provides on its website samples of some of the completed research projects.

research associate[136]) to work with him and to whom he dictated the version of the scripture which we see in present form. Beyond this, there is no other record of his work plans.

The story has it that Guru Arjan Dev did not want to work within the complex of *Harimandir Sahib* owing to a constant stream of devotees. To overcome this constraint, Guru Arjan Dev and Bhai Gurdas, in their search for a quieter place came across a peaceful location which had clusters of vegetation and banyan trees with plenty of shade within it. This place which Guru Arjan Dev and Bhai Gurdas chose for the job of compiling the scripture now has a gurdwara built on the site. *Gurdwara Ramsar* (named after Guru Ram Das) as it has come to be known, is 1.2km to the south-east side of the *Harimandir Sahib*. Appropriately located on this site are also printing facilities for the scripture which commemorates the site where the first (hand-written) edition of the scripture was completed.

It is not clear how long the duo, Guru Arjan Dev and Bhai Gurdas took to complete the task. All we know is that Guru Arjan Dev completed the scripture in 1604 dictating the entire manuscript to Bhai Gurdas. We do not know how many drafts scripture went through, or working how many hours a day the scripture was completed. But it would be very many as early rising was the norm in those days. This author's take is that, working throughout the day, the duo would have worked all day along, with breaks for morning and mid-day meals and some rest. Working with

---

[136] I have used the term assistant or associate for Bhai Gurdas, and not amanuensis (someone who writes from dictation or copies manuscript) since I believe a scholar of the highest order in his own right, Bhai Gurdas was more than an amanuensis to Guru Arjan Dev. It is not possible or likely to work with someone of Bhai Gurdas' calibre and not consult or discuss scripture matters with him.

this gruelling routine, it took Guru Arjan Dev and Bhai Gurdas five years (1599-1604) to complete the holy scripture (Singh S. , 2005, p. 28).

Additional Constraints

a. Guru Arjan Dev was handed a copy of hymns of previous Gurus to be included in the scripture. The sanctity of Rāga in which Gurus specified their hymns had to be maintained. This may have helped but it also reduced degrees of freedom to choose the Rāga for the hymn.

b. The chronology of the Gurus hymns was to be maintained - Guru Nanak's hymns were to come first, followed by the second Guru Angad, then Guru Amar Das, Guru Ram Das, Guru Arjan Dev and then Guru Tegh Bahadur. No one dictated this order to Guru Arjan Dev, but he must have decided to follow the chronology out of respect and reverence.

c. With constraint (b) above met, the next constraint would have been to find a method by which the reader would readily identify the hymn back to its author. I believe this was an important constraint to be met to avoid confusion and controversy over authorships.

d. The hymns of 15 non-Sikh saints were to be included at appropriate places in the scripture. It is highly probable that Guru Arjan Dev initially may have considered inclusion of hymns of more than 15 non-Sikh saints. If this was so, then the background work carried out by Guru Arjan Dev would have been more complex.

e. Guru Arjan Dev also decided to show same respect to non-Sikh saints, similar to what he displayed for Sikh

Gurus, by including their hymns in a chronological order which was necessarily subjective. Table 3 in the appendix maps out this chronology which Saint Kabir leads.

f. Out of a total number of 5882 hymns in the scripture, the contribution of Guru Arjan Dev is 2218 hymns (38%). These hymns fill in an important gap wherever required. Guru Arjan Dev must have been faced with a massive challenge to pen these hymns, to the point of excellence, where they became worthy of inclusion at the right place in the right order.

g. Permutation and combination: The reader with an elementary knowledge of statistics will appreciate the combination topic: $nCr = n! / r! * (n - r)!$, where n represents the number of items and r represents the number of items being chosen at a time.

Guru Arjan Dev must have been faced with a similar sort of situation given the number of Rāgas available at his disposal. For the sake of simplicity let us assume he had 200 Rāgas to choose from. The Rāgas he chose to apply were 60 (31primary + 29 secondary).

If we assume that half the hymns handed to him came with pre-defined Rāgas with which to recite hymns to, he would still be left with choosing appropriate Rāgas for the remaining hymns i.e., about 3000. In addition, he would also have had to worry about the suitability of Rāgas to the time of the day. Furthermore, the lengths of hymns were another important consideration to be considered.

To recapitulate: the total number of hymns in the scriptures is 5,882, the number of authors is 43

(13 pre-Nanak's time - i.e., pre-1469; 7 Sikh Gurus; 23 saints and bards during the times of Gurus). There are *dupadas* (2 verses - 608 in number), *Tripades* (3 verses - 73), *Chaupadas* (4 verses - 1255), *Panchpadas* (5 verses - 0), Chhepedas (6 verses - 11), *Ashtpadian* (8 verses - 311), *Sohilas* (16 verses - 62).

Variables such as these must have made the task a complex and mammoth one to manage. As stated previously, the task was made further complicated as selected previous Gurus who wrote the hymns had specified with which Rāga it should be sung. Although this must have been helpful, such specification also added a constraint since a hymn can be sung with the aid of more than one Rāga. It would have been easier for Guru Arjan if he had a clean slate to work with which would have given him more degrees of freedom to choose a Rāga for the hymn.

Completion and Untimely Death of Guru Arjan

Guru Arjan Dev completed the task of the compilation of the Sikh scripture and died soon after in 1606 at age 43 at the hands of the Mughal regime that tortured him to death. It is a colossal pity that the regime felt threatened from a saint-scholar of the calibre of Guru Arjan Dev. Guru Arjan Dev's death is rightly regarded and remembered as martyrdom in Sikh history and psyche; it should equally be remembered as a day when a Guru with such ingenious qualities was wasted by the Mughal regime. The loss of Guru Arjan Dev was the loss of a literary genius of the calibre rarely seen again in Sikh history.

The scripture was installed in *Harimandir Sahib* in 1604. The tenth Guru, Guru Gobind Singh, added selected hymns of the ninth Guru Tegh Bahadur and one of his own in it and proclaimed in 1708 that the sacred scripture would be the future Guru of the Sikhs, thus ending the succession line of living Gurus.

Chapter Summary

The Sikh scripture was compiled by the fifth Guru Arjan Dev. It was completed in 1604 and installed in the *Harimandir Sahib* in the same year and has since become the spiritual guide of the Sikhs.

The scripture is 1430 pages long and contains 5882 hymns penned by 43 Gurus, saints and bards from all walks of life. The scripture has morning and evening prayers and hymns to attend to occasions in life such as weddings and funerals. The scripture is laid out in a sequence of 31 Rāgas and 29 sub Rāgas. Hymns have been recorded in order of chronology with hymns of the first guru recorded first, followed by the second guru and so on; there is also a (subjective) chronology followed in the recording of the hymns of non-Sikh Guru authors. Saint Kabir heads this list.

Given the number of hymns, their suitability for the time of the day, number of authors, length of the hymn, and a myriad of other constraints, the compilation of the scripture was a highly complex task, akin to Linear Programming in operations research, where optimisation to a situation is sought given the constraints.

It is truly a remarkable feat that Guru Arjan Dev, with his literary genius, gave Sikhs a holy scripture that is so perfect, not only in its compilation, but also in its imparting of the code of moral and ethical conduct to help Sikhs lead a life of contentment and fulfilment. In the next chapter we shall study the contents of the scripture.

**

Appendix Table 4. 1 Pages 984-988 of the Scripture

ਰਾਗੁ ਮਾਲੀ ਗਉੜਾ ਮਹਲਾ ੪

Rāga Mali Gaura Mahla 4
(This is the name of Rāga; and hymn is by 4th Guru Ram Das)

This is 'Mool Mantar' – (basic chant) → ੧ਓਂ ਸਤਿ ਨਾਮੁ ਕਰਤਾ ਪੁਰਖੁ ਨਿਰਭਉ
ਨਿਰਵੈਰੁ ਅਕਾਲ ਮੂਰਤਿ ਅਜੂਨੀ ਸੈਭੰ ਗੁਰ ਪ੍ਰਸਾਦਿ ॥
'Mool Mantar' in English →Ek Onkar Satnam Karta Purakh Nirpau
Nirwair Akal Murat Ajuni Sabhang Gur Prasad
Meaning: (There is) One Universal Creator God. The Name Is Truth.
Creative Being Personified. No Fear.
No Hatred. Image Of the Undying, Beyond Birth, Self-Existent.
By Guru's Grace[137]

ਅਨਿਕ ਜਤਨ ਕਰਿ ਰਹੇ ਹਰਿ ਅੰਤੁ ਨਾਹੀ ਪਾਇਆ ॥ ਹਰਿ ਅਗਮ
ਅਗਾਧਿ ਬੋਧਿ ਆਦੇਸੁ ਹਰਿ ਪ੍ਰਭ
ਰਾਇਆ ॥੧॥ਰਹਾਉ॥RAHAO ਕਾਮੁ ਕ੍ਰੋਧੁ ਲੋਭੁ ਮੋਹੁ ਨਿਤ ਝਗਰਤੇ
ਝਗਰਾਇਆ ॥ ਹਮ ਰਾਖੁ ਦੀਨ ਤੇਰੇ ਹਰਿ
ਸਰਨਿ ਹਰਿ ਪ੍ਰਭ ਆਇਆ ੧॥੧॥ ਸਰਣਾਗਤੀ ਪ੍ਰਭ ਪਾਲਤੇ ਹਰਿ
ਭਗਤਿ ਵਛਲੁ ਨਾਇਆ ॥ ਪ੍ਰਹਿਲਾਦੁ
ਜਨੁ ਹਰਨਾਖਿ ਪਕਰਿਆ ਹਰਿ ਰਾਖਿ ਲੀਓ ਤਰਾਇਆ ੨॥੨॥ ਹਰਿ
ਚੇਤਿ ਰੇ ਮਨ ਮਹਲੁ ਪਾਵਣ ਸਭ ਦੂਖ
ਭੰਜਨੁ ਰਾਇਆ ॥ ਭਉ ਜਨਮ ਮਰਨ ਨਿਵਰਿ ਠਾਕੁਰ ਹਰਿ ਗੁਰਮਤੀ
ਪ੍ਰਭ ਪਾਇਆ ੩॥੩॥ ਹਰਿ ਪਤਿਤ
ਪਾਵਨ ਨਾਮੁ ਸੁਆਮੀ ਭਉ ਭਗਤ ਭੰਜਨੁ ਗਾਇਆ ॥ ਹਰਿ ਹਾਰੁ ਹਰਿ
ਉਰਿ ਧਾਰਿਓ ਜਨ ਨਾਨਕ ਨਾਮਿ
ਸਮਾਇਆ ੪॥੪॥੧॥ ਮਾਲੀ ਗਉੜਾ ਮਹਲਾ ੪ ॥ ਜਪਿ ਮਨ ਰਾਮ
ਨਾਮੁ ਸੁਖਦਾਤਾ ॥ ਸਤਸੰਗਤਿ ਮਿਲਿ ਹਰਿ

---

137 Khalsa (na). Gurmukhi to English Translation of Sri GGS (p.1)

ਸਾਧੂ ਆਇਆ ਗੁਰਮੁਖਿ ਬ੍ਰਹਮੁ ਪਛਾਤਾ ॥੧॥ ਰਹਾਉ ॥ ਵਡਭਾਗੀ ਗੁਰ ਦਰਸਨੁ ਪਾਇਆ ਗੁਰਿ ਮਿਲਿਐ ਹਰਿ ਪ੍ਰਭ ਜਾਤਾ ॥ ਦੁਰਮਤਿ ਮੈਲੁ ਗਈ ਸਭ ਨੀਕਰਿ ਹਰਿ ਅੰਮ੍ਰਿਤਿ ਹਰਿ ਸਰਿ ਨਾਤਾ ॥੧॥ ਧਨੁ ਧਨੁ ਸਾਧ ਜਿਨ੍ਹੀ ਹਰਿ ਪ੍ਰਭੁ ਪਾਇਆ ਤਿਨੑ ਪੂਛਉ ਹਰਿ ਕੀ ਬਾਤਾ ॥ ਪਾਇ ਲਗਉ ਨਿਤ ਕਰਉ ਜੁਦਰੀਆ ਹਰਿ ਮੇਲਹੁ ਕਰਮਿ ਬਿਧਾਤਾ ॥੨॥ ਲਿਲਾਟ ਲਿਖੇ ਪਾਇਆ ਗੁਰੁ ਸਾਧੂ ਗੁਰ ਬਚਨੀ ਮਨੁ ਤਨੁ ਰਾਤਾ ॥ ਹਰਿ ਪ੍ਰਭ ਆਇ ਮਿਲੇ ਸੁਖੁ ਪਾਇਆ ਸਭ ਕਿਲਵਿਖ ਪਾਪ ਗਵਾਤਾ ॥੩॥ ਰਾਮ ਰਸਾਇਣੁ ਜਿਨ੍ਹ ਗੁਰਮਤਿ ਪਾਇਆ ਤਿਨੑ ਕੀ ਊਤਮ ਬਾਤਾ ॥ ਤਿਨ ਕੀ ਪੰਕ ਪਾਈਐ ਵਡਭਾਗੀ ਜਨ ਨਾਨਕੁ ਚਰਨਿ ਪਰਾਤਾ ॥੪॥੨॥

ਮਾਲੀ ਗਉੜਾ ਮਹਲਾ ੪ ॥ ਸਭਿ ਸਿਧ ਸਾਧਿਕ ਮੁਨਿ ਜਨਾ ਮਨਿ ਭਾਵਨੀ ਹਰਿ ਧਿਆਇਓ ॥ ਅਪਰੰਪਰੋ ਪਾਰਬ੍ਰਹਮੁ ਸੁਆਮੀ ਹਰਿ ਅਲਖੁ ਗੁਰੂ ਲਖਾਇਓ ॥੧॥ ਰਹਾਉ ॥ ਹਮ ਨੀਚ ਮਧਿਮ ਕਰਮ ਕੀਏ ਨਹੀ ਚੇਤਿਓ ਹਰਿ ਰਾਇਓ ॥ ਹਰਿ ਆਨਿ ਮੇਲਿਓ ਸਤਿਗੁਰੂ ਖਿਨੁ ਬੰਧ ਮੁਕਤਿ ਕਰਾਇਓ ॥੧॥ ਪ੍ਰਭਿ ਮਸਤਕੇ ਧੁਰਿ ਲੀਖਿਆ ਗੁਰਮਤੀ ਹਰਿ ਲਿਵ ਲਾਇਓ ॥ ਪੰਚ ਸਬਦ ਦਰਗਹ ਬਾਜਿਆ ਹਰਿ ਮਿਲਿਓ ਮੰਗਲੁ ਗਾਇਓ ॥੨॥ ਪਤਿਤ ਪਾਵਨੁ ਨਾਮੁ ਨਰਹਰਿ ਮੰਦਭਾਗੀਆਂ ਨਹੀ ਭਾਇਓ ॥ ਤੇ ਗਰਭ ਜੋਨੀ ਗਾਲੀਅਹਿ ਜਿਉ ਲੋਣੁ ਜਲਹਿ ਗਲਾਇਓ ॥੩॥ ਮਤਿ ਦੇਹਿ ਹਰਿ ਪ੍ਰਭ ਅਗਮ ਠਾਕੁਰ ਗੁਹ ਚਰਨ ਮਨਿ ਮੈ ਲਾਇਓ ॥ ਹਰਿ ਰਾਮ ਨਾਮੈ ਰਹਉ ਲਾਗੋ ਜਨ ਨਾਨਕ ਨਾਮਿ

ਸਮਾਇਓ ॥੪॥੩॥ ਮਾਲੀ ਗਉੜਾ ਮਹਲਾ ੪ ॥ ਮੇਰਾ ਮਨੁ ਰਾਮ ਨਾਮਿ ਰਸਿ ਲਾਗਾ ॥ ਕਮਲ ਪ੍ਰਗਾਸੁ ਭਇਆ ਗੁਰੁ ਪਾਇਆ ਹਰਿ ਜਪਿਓ ਭ੍ਰਮੁ ਭਉ ਭਾਗਾ ॥੧॥ ਰਹਾਉ ॥ ਭੈ ਭਾਇ ਭਗਤਿ ਲਾਗੋ ਮੇਰਾ ਹੀਅਰਾ ਮਨੁ ਸੋਇਓ ਗੁਰਮਤਿ ਜਾਗਾ ॥ ਕਿਲਬਿਖ ਖੀਨ ਭਏ ਸਾਂਤਿ ਆਈ ਹਰਿ ਉਰ ਧਾਰਿਓ ਵਡਭਾਗਾ ॥੧॥ ਮਨਮੁਖ ਰੰਗੁ ਕਸੁੰਭੁ ਹੈ ਕਚੂਆ ਜਿਉ ਕੁਸਮ ਚਾਰਿ ਦਿਨ ਚਾਗਾ ॥ ਖਿਨ ਮਹਿ ਬਿਨਸਿ ਜਾਇ ਪਰਤਾਪੈ ਡੰਡੁ ਧਰਮ ਰਾਇ ਕਾ ਲਾਗਾ ॥੨॥ ਸਤਸੰਗਤਿ ਪ੍ਰੀਤਿ ਸਾਧ ਅਤਿ ਗੂੜੀ ਜਿਉ ਰੰਗੁ ਮਜੀਠ ਬਹੁ ਲਾਗਾ ॥ ਕਾਇਆ ਕਾਪਰੁ ਚੀਰ ਬਹੁ ਫਾਰੇ ਹਰਿ ਰੰਗੁ ਨ ਲਹੈ ਸਭਾਗਾ ॥੩॥ ਹਰਿ ਚਾਰਿਓ ਰੰਗੁ ਮਿਲੈ ਗੁਰ ਸੋਭਾ ਹਰਿ ਰੰਗਿ ਚਲੂਲੈ ਰਾਂਗਾ ॥ ਜਨ ਨਾਨਕੁ ਤਿਨ ਕੇ ਚਰਨ ਪਖਾਰੈ ਜੋ ਹਰਿ ਚਰਨੀ ਜਨੁ ਲਾਗਾ ॥੪॥੪॥ ਮਾਲੀ ਗਉੜਾ ਮਹਲਾ ੪ ॥ ਮੇਰੇ ਮਨ ਭਜੁ ਹਰਿ ਹਰਿ ਨਾਮੁ ਗੁਪਾਲਾ ॥ ਮੇਰਾ ਮਨੁ ਤਨੁ ਲੀਨੁ ਭਇਆ ਰਾਮ ਨਾਮੈ ਮਤਿ ਗੁਰਮਤਿ ਰਾਮ ਰਸਾਲਾ ॥੧॥ ਰਹਾਉ ॥ ਗੁਰਮਤਿ ਨਾਮੁ ਧਿਆਈਐ ਹਰਿ ਹਰਿ ਮਨਿ ਜਪੀਐ ਹਰਿ ਜਪਮਾਲਾ ॥ ਜਿਨ੍ਹ ਕੈ ਮਸਤਕਿ ਲੀਖਿਆ ਹਰਿ ਮਿਲਿਆ ਹਰਿ ਬਨਮਾਲਾ ॥੧॥ ਜਿਨ੍ਹ ਹਰਿ ਨਾਮੁ ਧਿਆਇਆ ਤਿਨ੍ਹ ਚੁਕੇ ਸਰਬ ਜੰਜਾਲਾ ॥ ਤਿਨ੍ਹ ਜਮੁ ਨੇੜਿ ਨ ਆਵਈ ਗੁਰਿ ਰਾਖੇ ਹਰਿ ਰਖਵਾਲਾ ॥੨॥ ਹਮ ਬਾਰਿਕ ਕਿਛੁ ਨ ਜਾਣਹੂ ਹਰਿ ਮਾਤ ਪਿਤਾ ਪ੍ਰਤਿਪਾਲਾ ॥ ਕਰੁ ਮਾਇਆ ਅਗਨਿ ਨਿਤ ਮੇਲਤੇ ਗੁਰਿ ਰਾਖੇ ਦੀਨ ਦਇਆਲਾ ॥੩॥ ਬਹੁ ਮੈਲੇ ਨਿਰਮਲ ਹੋਇਆ ਸਭ ਕਿਲਬਿਖ ਹਰਿ ਜਸਿ ਜਾਲਾ ॥ ਮਨਿ ਅਨਦੁ ਭਇਆ ਗੁਰੁ ਪਾਇਆ ਜਨ ਨਾਨਕ ਸਬਦਿ ਨਿਹਾਲਾ

॥੪॥੫॥ ਮਾਲੀ ਗਉੜਾ ਮਹਲਾ ੪ ॥

ਮੇਰੇ ਮਨ ਹਰਿ ਭਜੁ ਸਭ ਕਿਲਬਿਖ ਕਾਟ ॥ ਹਰਿ ਹਰਿ ਉਰ ਧਾਰਿਓ ਗੁਰਿ ਪੂਰੈ ਮੇਰਾ ਸੀਸੁ ਕੀਜੈ ਗੁਰ ਵਾਟ ॥੧॥ ਰਹਾਉ ॥ ਮੇਰੇ ਹਰਿ ਪ੍ਰਭ ਕੀ ਮੈ ਬਾਤ ਸੁਨਾਵੈ ਤਿਸੁ ਮਨੁ ਦੇਵਉ ਕਟਿ ਕਾਟ ॥ ਹਰਿ ਸਾਜਨੁ ਮੇਲਿਓ ਗੁਰਿ ਪੂਰੈ ਗੁਰ ਬਚਨਿ ਬਿਕਾਨੋ ਹਟਿ ਹਾਟ ॥੧॥ ਮਕਰ ਪ੍ਰਾਗਿ ਦਾਨੁ ਬਹੁ ਕੀਆ ਸਰੀਰੁ ਦੀਓ ਅਧ ਕਾਟਿ ॥ ਬਿਨੁ ਹਰਿ ਨਾਮ ਕੋ ਮੁਕਤਿ ਨ ਪਾਵੈ ਬਹੁ ਕੰਚਨੁ ਦੀਜੈ ਕਟਿ ਕਾਟ ॥੨॥ ਹਰਿ ਕੀਰਤਿ ਗੁਰਮਤਿ ਜਸੁ ਗਾਇਓ ਮਨਿ ਉਘਰੇ ਕਪਟ ਕਪਾਟ ॥ ਤ੍ਰਿਕੁਟੀ ਫੋਰਿ ਭਰਮੁ ਭਉ ਭਾਗਾ ਲਜ ਭਾਨੀ ਮਟੁਕੀ ਮਾਟ ॥੩॥ ਕਲਜੁਗਿ ਗੁਰੁ ਪੂਰਾ ਤਿਨ ਪਾਇਆ ਜਿਨ ਧੁਰਿ ਮਸਤਕਿ ਲਿਖੇ ਲਿਲਾਟ ॥ ਜਨ ਨਾਨਕ ਰਸੁ ਅੰਮ੍ਰਿਤੁ ਪੀਆ ਸਭ ਲਾਥੀ ਭੁਖ ਤਿਖਾਟ ॥੪॥੬॥ ਛਕਾ ੧ ॥ ॥੪॥੬॥ ਛਕਾ 1 ॥

ਮਾਲੀ ਗਉੜਾ ਮਹਲਾ ੫

ੴ ਸਤਿਗੁਰ ਪ੍ਰਸਾਦਿ ॥ ਰੇ ਮਨ ਟਹਲ ਹਰਿ ਸੁਖ ਸਾਰ ॥ ਅਵਰ ਟਹਲਾ ਝੂਠੀਆ ਨਿਤ ਕਰੇ ਜਮੁ ਸਿਰਿ ਮਾਰ ॥੧॥ ਰਹਾਉ ॥ ਜਿਨਾ ਮਸਤਕਿ ਲੀਖਿਆ ਤੇ ਮਿਲੇ ਸੰਗਾਰ ॥ ਸੰਸਾਰੁ ਭਉਜਲੁ ਤਾਰਿਆ ਹਰਿ ਸੰਤ ਪੁਰਖ ਅਪਾਰ ॥੧॥ ਨਿਤ ਚਰਨ ਸੇਵਹੁ ਸਾਧ ਕੇ ਤਜਿ ਲੋਭ ਮੋਹ ਬਿਕਾਰ ॥ ਸਭ ਤਜਹੁ ਦੂਜੀ ਆਸੜੀ ਰਖੁ ਆਸ ਇਕ ਨਿਰੰਕਾਰ ॥੨॥ ਇਕਿ ਭਰਮਿ ਭੂਲੇ ਸਾਕਤਾ ਬਿਨੁ ਗੁਰ ਅੰਧ ਅੰਧਾਰ ॥ ਧੁਰਿ ਹੋਵਨਾ ਸੁ ਹੋਇਆ ਕੋ ਨ ਮੇਟਣਹਾਰ ॥੩॥ ਅਗਮ ਰੂਪੁ ਗੋਬਿੰਦ ਕਾ ਅਨਿਕ ਨਾਮ ਅਪਾਰ ॥ ਧਨੁ ਧੰਨੁ ਤੇ ਜਨ ਨਾਨਕਾ ਜਿਨ ਹਰਿ ਨਾਮਾ ਉਰਿ ਧਾਰ ॥੪॥੧॥

ਮਾਲੀ ਗਉੜਾ ਮਹਲਾ ੫ ॥ ਰਾਮ ਨਾਮ ਕਉ ਨਮਸਕਾਰ ॥ ਜਾਸੁ ਜਪਤ ਹੋਵਤ ਉਧਾਰ ॥੧॥ ਰਹਾਉ ॥ ਜਾ ਕੈ ਸਿਮਰਨਿ ਮਿਟਹਿ ਧੰਧ ॥ ਜਾ ਕੈ ਸਿਮਰਨਿ ਛੂਟਹਿ ਬੰਧ ॥ ਜਾ ਕੈ ਸਿਮਰਨਿ ਮੂਰਖ ਚਤੁਰ ॥ ਜਾ ਕੈ ਸਿਮਰਨਿ ਕੁਲਹ ਉਧਰ ॥੧॥ ਜਾ ਕੈ ਸਿਮਰਨਿ ਭਉ ਦੁਖ ਹਰੈ ॥ ਜਾ ਕੈ ਸਿਮਰਨਿ ਅਪਦਾ ਟਰੈ ॥ ਜਾ ਕੈ ਸਿਮਰਨਿ ਮੁਚਤ ਪਾਪ ॥ ਜਾ ਕੈ ਸਿਮਰਨਿ ਨਹੀ ਸੰਤਾਪ ॥੨॥ ਜਾ ਕੈ ਸਿਮਰਨਿ ਰਿਦ ਬਿਗਾਸ ॥ ਜਾ ਕੈ ਸਿਮਰਨਿ ਕਵਲਾ ਦਾਸਿ ॥ ਜਾ ਕੈ ਸਿਮਰਨਿ ਨਿਧਿ ਨਿਧਾਨ ॥ ਜਾ ਕੈ ਸਿਮਰਨਿ ਤਰੇ ਨਿਦਾਨ ॥੩॥ ਪਤਿਤ ਪਾਵਨੁ ਨਾਮੁ ਹਰੀ ॥ ਕੋਟਿ ਭਗਤ ਉਧਾਰੁ ਕਰੀ ॥ ਹਰਿ ਦਾਸ ਦਾਸਾ ਦੀਨੁ ਸਰਨ ॥ ਨਾਨਕ ਮਾਥਾ ਸੰਤ ਚਰਨ ॥੪॥੨॥ ਮਾਲੀ ਗਉੜਾ ਮਹਲਾ ੫ ॥ ਐਸੋ ਸਹਾਈ ਹਰਿ ਕੋ ਨਾਮ ॥ ਸਾਧਸੰਗਤਿ ਭਜੁ ਪੂਰਨ ਕਾਮ ॥੧॥ ਰਹਾਉ ॥ ਬੂਡਤ ਕਉ ਜੈਸੇ ਬੇੜੀ

_____

ਮਿਲਤ ॥ ਬੂਝਤ ਦੀਪਕ ਮਿਲਤ ਤਿਲਤ ॥ ਜਲਤ ਅਗਨੀ ਮਿਲਤ ਨੀਰ ॥ ਜੈਸੇ ਬਾਰਿਕ ਮੁਖਹਿ ਖੀਰ ॥੧॥ ਜੈਸੇ ਰਣ ਮਹਿ ਸਖਾ ਭ੍ਰਾਤ ॥ ਜੈਸੇ ਭੁਖੇ ਭੋਜਨ ਮਾਤ ॥ ਜੈਸੇ ਕਿਰਖਹਿ ਬਰਸ ਮੇਘ ॥ ਜੈਸੇ ਪਾਲਨ ਸਰਨਿ ਸੇਂਘ ॥੨॥ ਗਰੁੜ ਮੁਖਿ ਨਹੀ ਸਰਪ ਤ੍ਰਾਸ ॥ ਸੂਆ ਪਿੰਜਰਿ ਨਹੀ ਖਾਇ ਬਿਲਾਸੁ ॥ ਜੈਸੇ ਆਂਡੇ ਹਿਰਦੇ ਮਾਹਿ ॥ ਜੈਸੇ ਦਾਨੇ ਚਕੀ ਦਰਹਿ ॥੩॥ ਬਹੁਤ ਓਪਮਾ ਥੋਰ ਕਹੀ ॥ ਹਰਿ ਅਗਮ ਅਗਮ ਅਗਾਧਿ ਤੁਹੀ ॥ ਊਚ ਮੂਚੌ ਬਹੁ ਅਪਾਰ ॥ ਸਿਮਰਤ ਨਾਨਕ ਤਰੇ ਸਾਰ ॥੪॥੩॥ ਮਾਲੀ ਗਉੜਾ ਮਹਲਾ ੫ ॥ ਇਹੀ ਹਮਾਰੈ ਸਫਲ ਕਾਜ ॥ ਅਪੁਨੇ ਦਾਸ

ਕਉ ਲੇਹੁ ਨਿਵਾਜਿ ॥੧॥ ਰਹਾਉ ॥ ਚਰਨ ਸੰਤਹ ਮਾਥ ਮੋਰ ॥ ਨੈਨਿ ਦਰਸੁ ਪੇਖਉ ਨਿਸਿ ਭੋਰ ॥ ਹਸਤ ਹਮਰੇ ਸੰਤ ਟਹਲ ॥ ਪ੍ਰਾਨ ਮਨੁ ਧਨੁ ਸੰਤ ਬਹਲ ॥੧॥ ਸੰਤਸੰਗਿ ਮੇਰੇ ਮਨ ਕੀ ਪ੍ਰੀਤਿ ॥ ਸੰਤ ਗੁਨ ਬਸਹਿ ਮੇਰੈ ਚੀਤਿ ॥ ਸੰਤ ਆਗਿਆ ਮਨਹਿ ਮੀਠ ॥ ਮੇਰਾ ਕਮਲੁ ਬਿਗਸੈ ਸੰਤ ਡੀਠ ॥੨॥ ਸੰਤਸੰਗਿ ਮੇਰਾ ਹੋਇ ਨਿਵਾਸੁ ॥ ਸੰਤਨ ਕੀ ਮੋਹਿ ਬਹੁਤੁ ਪਿਆਸ ॥ ਸੰਤ ਬਚਨ ਮੇਰੇ ਮਨਹਿ ਮੰਤ ॥ ਸੰਤ ਪ੍ਰਸਾਦਿ ਮੇਰੇ ਬਿਖੈ ਹੰਤ ॥੩॥ ਮੁਕਤਿ ਜੁਗਤਿ ਏਹਾ ਨਿਧਾਨ ॥ ਪ੍ਰਭ ਦਇਆਲ ਮੋਹਿ ਦੇਵਹੁ ਦਾਨ ॥ ਨਾਨਕ ਕਉ ਪ੍ਰਭ ਦਇਆ ਧਾਰਿ ॥ ਚਰਨ ਸੰਤਨ ਕੇ ਮੇਰੇ ਰਿਦੇ ਮਝਾਰਿ ॥੪॥੪॥ ਮਾਲੀ ਗਉੜਾ ਮਹਲਾ ੫ ॥ ਸਭ ਕੈ ਸੰਗੀ ਨਾਹੀ ਦੂਰਿ ॥ ਕਰਨ ਕਰਾਵਨ ਹਾਜਰਾ ਹਜੂਰਿ ॥੧॥ ਰਹਾਉ ॥ ਸੁਨਤ ਜੀਓ ਜਾਸੁ ਨਾਮੁ ॥ ਦੁਖ ਬਿਨਸੇ ਸੁਖ ਕੀਓ ਬਿਸ੍ਰਾਮੁ ॥ ਸਗਲ ਨਿਧਿ ਹਰਿ ਹਰਿ ਹਰੇ ॥ ਮੁਨਿ ਜਨ ਤਾ ਕੀ ਸੇਵ ਕਰੇ ॥੧॥ ਜਾ ਕੈ ਘਰਿ ਸਗਲੇ ਸਮਾਹਿ ॥ ਜਿਸ ਤੇ ਬਿਰਥਾ ਕੋਇ ਨਾਹਿ ॥ ਜੀਅ ਜੰਤੁ ਕਰੇ ਪ੍ਰਤਿਪਾਲ ॥ ਸਦਾ ਸਦਾ ਸੇਵਹੁ ਕਿਰਪਾਲ ॥੨॥ ਸਦਾ ਧਰਮੁ ਜਾ ਕੈ ਦੀਬਾਣਿ ॥ ਬੇਮੁਹਤਾਜ ਨਹੀ ਕਿਛੁ ਕਾਣਿ ॥ ਸਭ ਕਿਛੁ ਕਰਨਾ ਆਪਨ ਆਪਿ ॥ ਰੇ ਮਨ ਮੇਰੇ ਤੂ ਤਾ ਕਉ ਜਾਪਿ ॥੩॥ ਸਾਧਸੰਗਤਿ ਕਉ ਹਉ ਬਲਿਹਾਰ ॥ ਜਾਸੁ ਮਿਲਿ ਹੋਵੈ ਉਧਾਰੁ ॥ ਨਾਮ ਸੰਗਿ ਮਨ ਤਨਹਿ ਰਾਤ ॥ ਨਾਨਕ ਕਉ ਪ੍ਰਭਿ ਕਰੀ ਦਾਤਿ ॥੪॥੫॥

ਮਾਲੀ ਗਉੜਾ ਮਹਲਾ ੫ ਦੁਪਦੇ

ੴ ਸਤਿਗੁਰ ਪ੍ਰਸਾਦਿ ॥ ਹਰਿ ਸਮਰਥ ਕੀ ਸਰਨਾ ॥ ਜੀਉ ਪਿੰਡੁ ਧਨੁ ਰਾਸਿ ਮੇਰੀ ਪ੍ਰਭ ਏਕ ਕਾਰਨ ਕਰਨਾ ॥੧॥

ਰਹਾਉ ॥ ਸਿਮਰਿ ਸਿਮਰਿ ਸਦਾ ਸੁਖੁ ਪਾਈਐ ਜੀਵਣੈ ਕਾ ਮੂਲੁ ॥ ਰਵਿ ਰਹਿਆ ਸਰਬਤ ਠਾਈ ਸੂਖਮੋ ਅਸਥੂਲ

॥੧॥ ਆਲ ਜਾਲ ਬਿਕਾਰ ਤਜਿ ਸਭਿ ਹਰਿ ਗੁਨਾ ਨਿਤਿ ਗਾਉ ॥ ਕਰ ਜੋੜਿ ਨਾਨਕੁ ਦਾਨੁ ਮਾਂਗੈ ਦੇਹੁ ਅਪਨਾ ਨਾਉ ॥੨॥੧॥੬॥ ਮਾਲੀ ਗਉੜਾ ਮਹਲਾ ੫ ॥ ਪ੍ਰਭ ਸਮਰਥ ਦੇਵ ਅਪਾਰ ॥ ਕਉਨੁ ਜਾਨੈ ਚਲਿਤ ਤੇਰੇ ਕਿਛੁ ਅੰਤੁ ਨਾਹੀ ਪਾਰ ॥੧॥ ਰਹਾਉ ॥ ਇਕ ਖਿਨਹਿ ਥਾਪਿ ਉਥਾਪਦਾ ਘੜਿ ਭੰਨਿ ਕਰਨੈਹਾਰੁ ॥ ਜੇਤ ਕੀਨ ਉਪਾਰਜਨਾ ਪ੍ਰਭੁ ਦਾਨੁ ਦੇਇ ਦਾਤਾਰ ॥੧॥ ਹਰਿ ਸਰਨਿ ਆਇਓ ਦਾਸੁ ਤੇਰਾ ਪ੍ਰਭ ਊਚ ਅਗਮ ਮੁਰਾਰ ॥ ਕਢਿ ਲੇਹੁ ਭਉਜਲ ਬਿਖਮ ਤੇ ਜਨੁ ਨਾਨਕੁ ਸਦ ਬਲਿਹਾਰ ॥੨॥੨॥੭॥ ਮਾਲੀ ਗਉੜਾ ਮਹਲਾ ੫ ॥ ਮਨਿ ਤਨਿ ਬਸਿ ਰਹੇ ਗੋਪਾਲ ॥ ਦੀਨ ਬਾਂਧਵ ਭਗਤਿ ਵਛਲ ਸਦਾ ਸਦਾ ਕ੍ਰਿਪਾਲ ॥੧॥ ਰਹਾਉ ॥ ਆਦਿ ਅੰਤੇ ਮਧਿ ਤੂਹੈ ਪ੍ਰਭ ਬਿਨਾ ਨਾਹੀ ਕੋਇ ॥ ਪੂਰਿ ਰਹਿਆ ਸਗਲ ਮੰਡਲ ਏਕੁ ਸੁਆਮੀ ਸੋਇ ॥੧॥ ਕਰਨਿ ਹਰਿ ਜਸੁ ਨੇਤ੍ਰ ਦਰਸਨ ਰਸਨਿ ਹਰਿ ਗੁਨ ਗਾਉ ॥ ਬਲਿਹਾਰਿ ਜਾਏ ਸਦਾ ਨਾਨਕੁ ਦੇਹੁ ਅਪਣਾ ਨਾਉ ॥੨॥੩॥੮॥੬॥੧੪॥

ਮਾਲੀ ਗਉੜਾ ਬਾਣੀ ਭਗਤ ਨਾਮਦੇਵ ਜੀ ਕੀ   ੴ ਸਤਿਗੁਰ ਪ੍ਰਸਾਦਿ ॥

ਧਨਿ ਧੰਨਿ ਓ ਰਾਮ ਬੇਨੁ ਬਾਜੈ ॥ ਮਧੁਰ ਮਧੁਰ ਧੁਨਿ ਅਨਹਤ ਗਾਜੈ ॥੧॥ ਰਹਾਉ ॥ ਧਨਿ ਧਨਿ ਮੇਘਾ ਰੋਮਾਵਲੀ ॥ ਧਨਿ ਧਨਿ ਕ੍ਰਿਸਨ ਓਢੈ ਕਾਂਬਲੀ ॥੧॥ ਧਨਿ ਧਨਿ ਤੂ ਮਾਤਾ ਦੇਵਕੀ ॥ ਜਿਹ ਗ੍ਰਿਹ ਰਮਈਆ

ਕਵਲਾਪਤੀ ॥੨॥ ਧਨਿ ਧਨਿ ਬਨ ਖੰਡ ਬਿੰਦ੍ਰਾਬਨਾ ॥ ਜਹ ਖੇਲੈ ਸ੍ਰੀ ਨਾਰਾਇਨਾ ॥੩॥ ਬੇਨੁ ਬਜਾਵੈ ਗੋਧਨ ਚਰੈ ॥ ਨਾਮੇ ਕਾ ਸੁਆਮੀ ਆਨਦ ਕਰੈ ॥੪॥੧॥ ਮੇਰੋ ਬਾਪੁ ਮਾਧਉ ਤੂ ਧਨੁ ਕੇਸੌ ਸਾਂਵਲੀਓ ਬੀਠੁਲਾਇ ॥੧॥ ਰਹਾਉ ॥ ਕਰ ਧਰੇ ਚਕ੍ਰ ਬੈਕੁੰਠ ਤੇ ਆਏ ਗਜ ਹਸਤੀ ਕੇ ਪ੍ਰਾਨ ਉਧਾਰੀਅਲੇ ॥ ਦੁਹਸਾਸਨ ਕੀ ਸਭਾ ਦ੍ਰੋਪਤੀ ਅੰਬਰ ਲੇਤ ਉਬਾਰੀਅਲੇ ॥੧॥ ਗੋਤਮ ਨਾਰਿ ਅਹਲਿਆ ਤਾਰੀ ਪਾਵਨ ਕੇਤਕ ਤਾਰੀਅਲੇ ॥ ਐਸਾ ਅਧਮੁ ਅਜਾਤਿ ਨਾਮਦੇਉ ਤਉ ਸਰਨਾਗਤਿ ਆਈਅਲੇ ॥੨॥੨॥ ਸਭੈ ਘਟ ਰਾਮੁ ਬੋਲੈ ਰਾਮਾ ਬੋਲੈ ॥ ਰਾਮ ਬਿਨਾ ਕੋ ਬੋਲੈ ਰੇ ॥੧॥ ਰਹਾਉ ॥ ਏਕਲ ਮਾਟੀ ਕੁੰਜਰ ਚੀਟੀ ਭਾਜਨ ਹੈਂ ਬਹੁ ਨਾਨਾ ਰੇ ॥ ਅਸਥਾਵਰ ਜੰਗਮ ਕੀਟ ਪਤੰਗਮ ਘਟਿ ਘਟਿ ਰਾਮੁ ਸਮਾਨਾ ਰੇ ॥੧॥ ਏਕਲ ਚਿੰਤਾ ਰਾਖੁ ਅਨੰਤਾ ਅਉਰ ਤਜਹੁ ਸਭ ਆਸਾ ਰੇ ॥ ਪ੍ਰਣਵੈ ਨਾਮਾ ਭਏ ਨਿਹਕਾਮਾ ਕੋ ਠਾਕੁਰੁ ਕੋ ਦਾਸਾ ਰੇ ॥੨॥੩

Appendix Table 4. 2 Authors in Sikh Scripture

Col-1	Col-2	Col-3	Col-4
PRE-NANAK SAINTS	**HYMS**	**SHLOKS**	**SWAYYAS**
Jaidev	2	0	
Sheikh Farid	4	130	
Namdev	60	0	
Trilochan	4	0	
Parmanand	1	0	
Sadhna	1	0	
Beni	3	0	
Ramanand	1	0	
Dhanna	4	0	
Pipa	1	0	
Sain	1	0	
Kabir	292 Including pauris of *Bawan* Akhri, Thittin and var sat.	249	
Ravidas	41	0	
SIKH GURUS			
Nanak	974 Including pauris & sloks		
Angad	0	62	
Amar Das	907 Including pauris & sloks		
Ram Das	679		

	Including pauris & sloks		
Arjan Dev	2218 Including pauris & sloks		
Tegh Bahadur	59	56	
Gobind Singh		1 In the sloks of Tegh Bahadur	
SAINTS & BARDS OF THE TIMES OF THE GURUS			
Bhikhan	2		
Sur Das	2		
Sundar	1 poem with six pauris		
Mardana		3	
Bhatts/poets in the court of Gurus			
Kal			49 (46 swayyas & 3 Sorathhas)
Kasahar			4
Tal			1
Jalap			4
Jal			1
Kirat			8
Sal			3
Bhal			1
Nal			6
Bhikha			2
Jalan			1
Das			14

			(7 swayyas, 3 Rad, & 4 Jholnay)
Gayand			5
Sewak			7
Mathura			10
Bal			5
Harbans			2
Satta & Balwand			1 var containing 8 pauris
TOTAL 5882	5257	501	124

Source: (Kohli, Guru Granth Sahib: An analytical study, 1961)

Appendix Table 4. 3 Sequence of Hymns by Saints, following Gurus' Hymns

Note: please confer Table 4.1 for details.

1.Siri Rāga	Ka bir	Triloch an	Kabir	Beni	Ravi das	x	x
2.Maajh	x	x	x	x	x	x	x
3.Gauri Guarari	Ka bir	Namde o	Ravida s			x	x
4.Aasa	Ka bir	Namde o	Ravida s	Dhann a	Sheik h Farid	x	x
5.Gujri	Ka bir	Namde o	Ravida s	Triloc han	Jaide v	x	x
6.Devgan dhari	x	x	x	x	x	x	x
7.Bihagra	x	x	x	x	x	x	x
8.Vadhan s	x	x	x	x	x	x	x
9.Sorath	Ka bir	Namde o	Ravida s	Bhika n	x	x	x
10.Dhana siri	Ka bir	Namde o	Ravida s	Triloc han	Sain	Pippa	Dhan na
11.Jaitsiri	x	x	Ravida s	x	x	x	x
12.Todi	x	Namde o	x	x	x	x	x
13.Behrar i	x	x	x	x	x	x	x

14.Tilang	Ka bir	Namde o	x	x	x	x	x
15.Suhi	Ka bir	x	Ravida s	x	Sheik h Farid	x	x
16.Bilawa l	Ka bir	Namde o	Ravida s	Sadhn a	x	x	x
17.Gond	Ka bir	Namde o	Ravida s	x	x	x	x
18.Ramka li	Ka bir	Namde o	Ravida s	Beni			
19.Nat Narayan	x	x	x	x	x	x	x
20.Mali Gaura	x	Namde o	x	x	x	x	x
21.Maru	Ka bir	Namde o	Kabir	Jaidev	Kabir	Ravi das	x
22.Tukhar i	x	x	x	x	x	x	x
23.Kedar	Ka bir	x	Ravida s	x	x	x	x
24.Bhaira v	Ka bir	Namde o	Ravida s	Namd eo	x	x	x
25.Basant	Ka bir	Raman and	Namde o	Ravid as	Kabir	x	x
26.Sarang	Ka bir	Namde o	Parman and	Surdas	Kabir	x	x
27.Malha ar	x	Namde o	Ravida s	x	x	x	x
28.Kaanar a	x	Namde o	x	x	x	x	x
29.Kalyan	x	x	x	x	x	x	x
30.Prabha ti	Ka bir	Namde o	Beni	x	x	x	x
31.Jaijaw anti	Ka bir	Sheikh Farid					
1352 – 1430 Hymns							

Source: The Scripture.

CHAPTER-5 SIKH SCRIPTURE AND THE ARISTOTELIAN MODEL OF MORAL PHILOSOPHY

Moral values and a culture and a religion maintaining these values are better than laws and regulations
(Sivananda)

Introduction

The purpose of this chapter is two-fold. First to summarise the principles of moral philosophy enumerated in the Sikh scripture, and second, to analyse these principles vis-à-vis the Aristotelian model of moral philosophy as sketched out in his famous work *Nicomachaen Ethics*. Moral philosophy, a branch of philosophy contemplates *what is right and wrong*. It explores the nature of morality and analyses how people should live their lives in relation to others.

We begin by explaining the procedure adopted to summarise the key Sikh moral principles found in the Sikh scripture and then list, in summary form, these principles in the Appendix Table 5.1 at the end of this chapter. We then describe the relevance of the Sikh scripture in the present-day world, followed by the definition and research on the concept of 'happiness' - the ultimate goal of human beings. This is followed with a discussion on Aristotle's model of moral philosophy detailed in his classic work *Nicomachean Ethics*. Subsequent sections describe the commonalities and difference between the 'Sikh model' and the

'Aristotelian model', and discuss the value added by the former to the latter, and to the potential happiness of mankind.

Methodology Adopted for this Chapter

In the previous chapter the layout, contents, and the complex task of compiling the scripture was described. As a follow up, in this chapter, we enlist and explain the key (morality related) messages that the Sikh scripture conveys to its readers. This is a job though easier said than done. There are several reasons for this. First is the language itself which is not always easy to comprehend. The written language of the scripture is Gurmukhi, but hymns often have words from sister languages - Hindi, Brij, Kauravi, Sanskrit, Sindhi, Persian, Urdu, and Arabic. Second, the meaning of the hymns can be interpreted in more than one way. Considering that the scripture is laid out in 1430 single space, large, landscaped pages, the task is formidable. Despite this author's best efforts, scholars who have spent a lifetime studying the scripture may find the coverage not adequate. My only defence to this criticism is rather simplistic. My focus was to seek out the key messages that shape and guide the virtuous living of an individual, a group, or a community, and not to delve into the philosophical interpretation of the verses, several volumes of which are already available (cf. e.g., (Singh G. , 1960); (Singh M. , 2009); (Singh S. , Sri Guru Granth Darpan (in Gurmukhi), 1972))[138] and which is also a project beyond the scope of this book.

---

[138] Sahib Singh's (Singh S. , Sri Guru Granth Darpan (in Gurmukhi), 1972) monumental work on the translation and meaning of the contents of the Sikh scripture, completed in 30+ years, is the most comprehensive, rather astonishing piece of scholarship that runs into 6288 pages! A team of dedicated

In my reading of the scripture, I stayed focused on the *guidance* that I thought was being imparted to the reader to lead a morally rich, happy, and contented life. Table 5.1 contains, what are according to this author, observations, discourses, advice, sermons, cautions, do's and don'ts, collectively termed for the purpose of this chapter as 'messages', imparted to the reader of the scripture. For simplicity's sake, the table has only two columns - the page number on which the message was found and the message itself in summary form - mostly in one or two lines. The table does not contain any other information e.g., which Guru or saint wrote the hymn, or the philosophical interpretation of the hymn. Furthermore, while interpreting the message, I do not pass any value in judgement. I interpret it as I see it.

Key Messages in the Scripture

Veneration of the Lord's Name

As an approximate guess, about fifty percent of the scripture, in beautifully written hymns, urges the reader to be always in commemoration of God and seek his blessings by way of prayers, meditation, and devotion of the highest order that comes from being a person of purest of mind and conduct. Hymns in the scripture recognise that this is not an easy job, given that a person's priority is to make a living and meet the demands of job, family, and community life - the pull and push pressures of which can pollute the (intended) virtuous living of a person. The scripture does

---

Sikhs have digitised the work of Sahib Singh and made it available free of cost on the net: cf. https://www.srigranth.org/guru_granth_sahib.html (Accessed 4 April 2022).

not put out a plan for us on how we can balance our work, family and social life and still be passionately reminiscing the Lord's name (which the scripture repeatedly urges us to do). However, by the time we reach the end, we are able to piece together the model of ideal living based on a set of moral principles.

In addition to the scripture, to arrive at the model of virtuous living, we can draw upon two additional sources.

First is the written code of conduct (CoC) approved by the central committee of the Sikhs - SGPC. Appendix 5.2 has in summary form this CoC, translated from Gurmukhi by this author.

Second, Guru Gobind Singh, in the final years of his life at Nanded (Maharashtra) gave 52 edicts (or commandments) for Sikhs to follow in order for them to live a virtuous life. Appendix 5.3 has a summary of these edicts, also translated from Gurmukhi by this author.

Most edicts in these two sources have their origin in the scripture. The 52 decrees of Guru Gobind Singh are clearly stated in a matter of fact, easy to understand, style. There is some overlapping between Guru Gobind Singh's list which is dated 1708 and SGPC's original list which was drawn much more recently in 1945. Hence, we can safely conjecture that the SGPC list of CoC draws on both the scripture and Guru Gobind Singh's list. For our purpose of drawing up a model of a virtuous Sikh, we have drawn on the scripture but have also consulted the two sources mentioned since both are also an integral part of a Sikh's CoC.

A Note on Guru Gobind Singh's list of 52 edicts

Before we proceed further it will be instructive to make some observations on Guru Gobind Singh's list of edicts which is an eclectic mix of personal and social discourse to Sikhs of the time. Several edicts, however, seem to be tailor-made for the present day as well.

Edict # 16 e.g., says 'do not rebuke your spouse in a violent way.' It may come as a surprise to some readers, that it was common in those days (almost accepted) that a husband would occasionally hit his spouse. It could be part of the husband's domination strategy in the clan or to keep his 'face' in his circle of male associates. Whatever the reason, this edict explicitly bars a man from this act. Similarly, the edict # 37 that asks to abstain from drinking and offering liquor to anyone was meant to protect from the vice, as drinking costs money (hard earned those days from farming) and can also result in domestic violence. Edict # 50 bars standing as a false witness. Courts in those days were not prevalent, and in a litigation, one man's word against the other (e.g., in a village council) was legible as a witness statement This edict explicitly bars false witness statements. The importance of this edict is also all important in present day judicial system in all the countries. Edict # 43 on honouring one's (true) word is allied to this.

Edicts # 27, 28, 29, 31 encourage a Sikh to have an open and free-thinking mind, and also study the art of diplomacy/politics, which Guru Gobind Singh must have observed was lacking in Sikhs and felt essential that this art should be mastered. In fact, this advice for Sikhs was never so valid as it is in the present day, given that Sikhs are constantly losing face, land, property, power, and dignity and are often left to trail behind events at state and national level. Edict # 29 says that '....if all fails, battle is a justified act of *Dharma'*, a situation in which Sikhs often have been pushed. Allied to this is also # 26 that cautions believing someone who swears to convince you of anything. To be read in conjunction with # 26 is # 48 that says, 'abstain from theft, pseudo-friendship, thuggery, deception, and trickery.' On the lighter side of life, this author finds # 13 insightful into the psychology of the congregation when it says, 'so long *Prasad* is being distributed, the congregation stays quiet.' Bemused, this author has often observed congregations getting restless as soon as proceedings are over, and *Prasad* begins to get distributed.

Digression: Macauliffe's Summary of Teachings of the Sikh Religion

Max Arthur Macauliffe (1838-1913) an English civil servant had a degree in modern languages and served as Deputy Commissioner, and later as Divisional Judge in Punjab. With his Sikh associates, he studied in-depth the Sikh religion and conducted detailed research on the Sikh scripture and published six volumes on its meaning and interpretation. So enamoured was he by the Sikh religion that he converted to Sikhism in 1860. As one of a few earliest exponents of the Sikh religion he summarised its teachings in the following words (Macauliffe, 1909, p. location 259):

> "To sum up some of the moral and political merits of the Sikh religion: It prohibits idolatry, hypocrisy, caste exclusiveness, the concremation[139] of widows, the immurement[140] of women, the use of wine and other intoxicants, tobacco-smoking, infanticide, slander,

---

[139] The tradition in olden times in India where a widow self-immolated on her husband's funeral pyre.
[140] Imprisonment.

pilgrimages to the sacred rivers and tanks of the Hindus; and it inculcates loyalty, gratitude for all favours received, philanthropy, justice, impartiality, truth, honesty, and all the moral and domestic virtues known to the holiest citizens of any country."

This summary by Macauliffe succinctly lays bare the essentials of Sikh moral behaviour. Macauliffe arrived at this summary conclusion after an in-depth study of the scripture - six volumes of which he produced.

Threats to a Virtuous Life Specified in the Scripture

Though he did not explicitly describe it that way, Macauliffe in his summary of key moral principles from the Sikh scripture does lay bare the caveats to a virtuous life. In this section we shall examine in some detail the key messages in the scripture based on *our* summary of reading the scripture. The following passages draw from the summary appendix table to this chapter.

1. The greatest threat to our well-being, which the scripture points out, is the blind following of an undisciplined mind (uncontrolled mind). This, the scripture points out, is the root cause of our problems.

2. Second, the threat to our peace, harmony and growth in life comes from five Vikars or vices named as: Kam (lust/sexual desires), Krodh (anger), Lobh (greed), Moh (attachment), and Ahankar (ego/extreme pride).

3. The third threat comes from the unchecked control of our 5 *Inderiyans*. *Inderiyan* refer to the medium by which we interface with the outside world which is vision, hearing, smell, taste, and touch (skin).

In addition to these three caveats, the mention of some of which occur multiple times in the scripture, the following key conclusions about life are also observed - some stated multiple times in various contexts.

Key Lessons from the Scripture

1. A repeated message that comes up on reading the scripture is to inculcate in us good virtues for us to become a virtuous person. An ideal life a person can lead is that of contemplative devotion to the Lord's name. Such a life, when led in a disciplined fashion, would bring peace, honour and eternal happiness.

   Good virtues that come up in the scripture include abstinence (from vices), charity (to community), contentment (self), devotion (to duty and the Lord's name), compassion (for fellow human beings, and animals), forgiveness, generosity (in physical and material help), honesty (to self and community), supreme humility (self), self-control (on vices), kindness (to others), love and well-being (for all), mercy (for all including defeated foes), patience (self), righteousness (of moral principles), self-discipline (with daily routines and in work), service (to humanity), spirituality, temperance (including food and drink), truth and trust.

2. The cycle of life and death is mentioned at several places. You will recall that an essential part of the state of *Nirvana* is to break this cycle and reach the state of bliss once and for all. According to the scripture there are 8.4 million cycles of life and death (that include all living beings in the human and animal kingdom) into which we keep cycling with repeated births and deaths.

3. To break the cycles of life and death, the scripture urges us to lead a virtuous life, which according to the tenets of the scripture can be defined as a life of high moral principles led by an honest living made by dint of our hard work.

4. The scripture counsels us that to lead a virtuous life we need not don saffron cloths and go off to mountains or forests to live in solitude the life of an ascetic and meditate. The scripture firmly recommends that a virtuous life can be had by staying at home within the community and by faithfully attending to the duties of family and social life, and reminiscing the Lord's name and by doing good deeds to others.

The definition of a virtuous life, in addition to reminiscing the Lord's name each day include simplicity. The recommended simplistic life measures include not observing complicated rituals such as shaving our heads on special occasions (recommended in Hinduism), rubbing sandalwood on foreheads, donning a

Juneau (sacred cotton thread worn around body), execute complex birth, death, and other rituals, conducting *Yagnas* (ritual done in front of a fire with mantras), worshipping idols, and going to pilgrimages.

The definition further includes abstinence from slanders (especially of saintly persons), jealousy, back-biting, not casting a bad eye on other's property and woman i.e., observing a certain moral code of conduct.

The scripture specifies that the fear of ailments, old age, and death do not perturb a true devotee.

5. The scripture reminds the reader of the fundamental nature of the perishability of our bodies. As a result, it cautions us to abstain from excessive love for animate and inanimate objects. The former includes parents, spouse, brothers, sisters, relatives, and friends. The latter includes wealth, liquidity (cash, jewellery etc.) or immovable property. The perishability nature of our existence implies that all near and dear ones perish one day and that nothing travels with us in our next life. The journey has to be done alone.

6. The scripture counsels us that we have arrived at this life after lengthy cycles of re-births and that the life that has been given to us is precious which we should not waste but put to good use by reminiscing the Lord's name and by doing good to fellow human beings. Life, the holy scripture says, is akin to a dream in which we almost sleepwalk the world - implying that in a

world that is surreal we should not fall in love with it or its surroundings.

7. Distractions to our mind come from all sides. In order to neutralise the distractions, the company of pious people 'Satsang' is repeatedly recommended. Satsang, as described, is the congregation of saintly people. A common form of Satsang is the daily or weekly congregations in holy places - for Sikhs - gurdwaras. Not all people attending congregations are saintly or pious, however, the theory is that once we are in the presence of *'Guru Granth Sahib'* - the holy scripture, and in the company of fellow devotees, an atmosphere of calmness descends as devotees sit in silence and listen to discourse and melodious Kirtan which has a soothing influence on our mind. The scripture specifies that the company of virtuous people in a Satsang has a dissipating effect on 5 Vikars (KKLMA) described in the beginning in #2.

On the lighter side of life, the scripture specifically warns us not to entangle ourselves with fools and sycophants who can wear us down with their gibberish talk. Contrary to this, the scripture is all praise of learned persons (*Brahm Gyanis*) whose company should be sought.

8. There is specific advice to women folk on being devotional to the Lord's name and faithful to spouses. As homemakers, the importance of their role is explicitly acknowledged with such sermons. We comment on this and other points later in the chapter.

9. The life journey is divided into 10 stages with a brief description given for each stage - at the end of the 10th stage we return to the dust and ashes from which we were born. Our body is made up of food grown from the earth to which we return when our life comes to an end.

10. The connection with Hinduism comes alive in the scripture multiple times and can be noticed with the mention of the following - sometimes in more than one place: Lord Brahma, Vishnu, Shiva, (the trinity), Krishna, Rama, and Inder. Mention is also made of Vedas, Puranas, and Shastras. Devaki, in one hymn, is eulogised as the mother of Krishna. In one place, 4 Yugas (Satya Yuga, Treta Yuga, Dvapar Yuga, and Kali Yuga) are mentioned[141]. According to Hindu mythology, the four Yugas (or lifetimes) rank in descending order in terms of the virtuous living of people. We are presently in Kali Yuga.

---

141 According to Hindu mythology there are four long cycles:

Satya Yuga (the 'age of truth' - the 'Hindu golden age' (beginning c.11,501 BC and lasting 4,800 years) is the first and considered the best yuga - has no crime, and human beings are youthful, learned, and virtuous and have a long life.

Treta Yuga (beginning c.6701 BC and lasting 3,600 years) is the second yuga in the cycle - it has three quarters virtue and one quarter sinfulness. In this age, virtue begins to diminish. It is said that in this age, emperors rise and dominate the world, wars become frequent, and weather begins to change to extremes.

Dvapara Yuga the third yuga (beginning c.3101 BC and lasting 2400 years) has two quarters virtue and two quarters sinfulness and people are not so virtuous. Discontent has descended and humans fight with each other.

Kali Yuga (present Yuga) the last in the cycle (beginning c.701 BC and lasting 1200 years) has one quarter virtue and three quarters sinfulness; it is the age of darkness and ignorance. People do not follow Dharma and cease to be virtuous and become slaves to their passions and are not healthy.

Source: Varied sources. See https://en.wikipedia.org/wiki/Yuga_Cycle (Accessed 6-12-2021).

11. The scripture treats Hindus and Muslims alike in its advice. The scripture e.g., states that a good Muslim is one who is engaged in *Tariqas* - the Muslim path towards direct knowledge of God; a good Brahmin is one who is engaged in the study of Vedas and Puranas. Instead of arguing with each other, the scripture says, both should recognize that they have descended from the same God.

Sikh Scripture and the Modern World

The origin of scriptures can be traced back to 1469 with the birth of the first Guru, Guru Nanak, who wrote some of the enduring hymns that Sikhs all over the world recite till this day. Beginning with Guru Nanak's contributory hymns, successive Gurus added their hymns, to which the fifth Guru Arjan Dev also added the hymns of holy persons (from across India), with the final completed version of the scripture taking its place in *Harimandir* (popularly known as 'Golden Temple') in 1604. The scripture is thus over 500 years old. The question is, are the messages found in the scripture valid in today's modern fast-moving world? Putting it differently, can the Sikh's sacred scripture add value to our life - day-to-day or long term until the time of our demise and beyond for those who would come after us? For us to answer this question we shall first dwell on the state of the present day.

World we Live in Today

(Rostow, 2017) in a celebrated work characterized the growth process of nations in five stages. In its first stage a society is traditional in nature and after it has made some minimum progress it creates preconditions for it to take off. In the third stage the society takes off on its path to growth. It then gradually drives itself to a state of maturity. In the final fifth phase, the society reaches a stage of mass consumption. Presently this phase is prominent in several countries in the western world, but emerging economies are fast catching up[142].

The revolution in digital technology, ushered in the 1970s, has fuelled the growth and unified the world through the internet, bringing the far-flung corners of the world together, via a plethora of social media platforms[143]. Globalization of the world, as we see today, is the increasing inter-dependence of nations brought together by international trade and investment and the growing movement of people around the world working for multinational enterprises and its affiliates and via tourism. Great advances in technology and telecommunications have facilitated this increasing interdependence, and in some cases inter-locking of nations, by making them dependent on each other via trade, investment and geo-political concerns[144]. Cross-cultural interactions have greatly impacted on the value system of erstwhile conservative nations whose citizens are now demanding freedom of speech, attire, food, and other amenities which until recently were the prerogative of the west.

---

142 Emerging economies are broadly defined to include all developing economies who have a lower per capita income and low state help for its citizens.
143 Prominent of these, with over a billion users are: Facebook, YouTube, WhatsApp, Messenger, WeChat, and Instagram.
144 As I write this, the Russian invasion of Ukraine is on. This war, news of which is reaching the world, almost minute-by-minute, has also rung alarm bells, particularly, in the western world.

This newfound freedom, however, is not without cost. Divorce rates have increased and the escalating relational problems between couples have led them to co-habit without a legal contract of marriage. This shifting dynamics of social fabric in modern societies greatly masks the toxic effect of freedom brought by increased choices. Immediate visible costs of broken homes or dysfunctional conjugal relationships are delayed decisions to raise a family leading sometimes to complicated child births, smooth and happy growth of children (society's future), a couple's own happiness, care of aging parents (sometimes relatives too) especially in emerging economies, not to mention the shame and stigma of broken relationships in conservative societies.

Western societies have long gradually worked towards developing a social care and support system in income supplements, medical facilities, and a myriad of help lines. These processes are gradually being replicated in emerging economies, though seriously skewed income distribution, lack of management finesse, distributional bottlenecks of food grains [(Sen A. , 1990), (Sen & Foster, 1997)] and corruption hinder the move towards smooth setting up and functioning of physical and emotional support for the masses. As a result, the gap between what this author calls the 'ideal happiness index' and 'actual happiness index' is wide; it is wider in emerging economies than developed economies[145].

Research on Happiness

The net result of our briefly described state of modern world is the impact it has created on our happiness.

---

145 I would say, any index below 5 on a 10-point scale is low and not ideal.

No wonder, therefore, the theoretical and applied studies in happiness abound. These studies attempt to define and understand happiness via several routes - psychological, philosophical and spiritual. An extensive review of literature on the subject can be found in (David, Boniwell, & Ayers, 2013) which is a collection of 79 chapters covering practically every research aspect on happiness. Annas (Annas, 1993) work provides a philosophical approach to the morality of happiness beginning with Aristotle. Cahn and Vitrano (Cahn & Vitrano, 2008) provide a condensed summary of key historical sources on happiness, along with contemporary theoretical approaches. Several works that can be accessed by non-academics and some prescriptive handbook type material is also available [(cf. e.g., (Bloomfield, 2014); (Haidt, 2006); (Levenson & Dwoskin, 2020); (Solomon, 1999)]. Russell provides an interesting personal approach to happiness and God (Russell B. , The Conquest of Happiness (First published, 1930), 1993) (Russell B. , The Problems of Philosophy (First published 1912), 2022)

A branch of 'Happiness Economics' has sprung up and applied work is being undertaken with the help of survey instruments on global happiness index. Prominent among these are the World Happiness Report[146], Our World in Data[147]. The United Nations has declared 20th of March

---

146 https://worldhappiness.report/ (Accessed 24-11-2021).
A survey of happiness on a 10-point scale for 2018-20 put the following 20 countries on top of the list: 1. Finland (7.842) 2. Denmark (7.620) 3. Switzerland (7.571) 4. Iceland (7.554) 5. Netherlands (7.464) 6. Norway (7.392) 7. Sweden (7.363) 8. Luxembourg (7.324) 9. New Zealand (7.277) 10. Austria (7.268) 11. Australia (7.183) 12. Israel (7.157) 13. Germany (7.155) 14. Canada (7.103) 15. Ireland (7.085) 16. Costa Rica (7.069) 17. United Kingdom (7.064) 18. Czech Republic (6.965) 19. United States (6.951) 20. Belgium (6.834). (Source: Figure 7, p.21 of the Report).
147 https://ourworldindata.org/ (Accessed 24-11-2021).

as the 'International Day of Happiness', recognizing the significance of happiness and well-being as universal goals and aspirations in the lives of human beings around the world[148]. In brief, an industry on the study of happiness has sprung around us.

Interestingly, Bhutan, a small deeply Buddhist country, though ranked at 95 (2019 data) in the world has won the admiration of the world owing to its holistic approach to, what has come to be known as, 'gross happiness index' that lays emphasis on sustainable and equitable socio-economic development; environmental conservation; preservation and promotion of culture; and good governance. One of the earliest, interesting, and a little cynical account that gives a philosophical account in support of existentialism, dealing with such topics as consciousness, self-deception, and the existence of 'nothingness' is that of Sartre (Sartre, 2003).

Defining Happiness

The dictionary definitions of happiness are 'a state of well-being and contentment'; 'the state of pleasurable contentment of the mind'; 'deep pleasure in or contentment with one's circumstances.' Clearly, these are a simplistic way of putting a matter which is a highly complex construct. Despite extensive theoretical and applied work that has been undertaken, the definition of happiness is still a controversial subject (Uchida, Ogihara , & Fukus, 2015). There is as yet, no one universally accepted definition of

---

148 https://www.un.org/en/observances/happiness-day (Accessed 24-11-2021).

happiness (Flavel at. al., 2016). Intuitively though, readers would understand what happiness means *in their* context. If all of us know what happiness means to us, then in theory, there could be as many definitions of happiness as there are people! We shall touch here only briefly on the general definitional aspect of happiness before moving on to next stage of discussion, *en route* to the discussion on *Nirvana.*

We all understand when we are happy and realise that 'it is a mental and emotional state of being so.' Such a state of well-being could be of a stable nature for hermits or people with saintly traits. Such a state could happen a few times a day for some or sparsely only, depending e.g., on financial situations, conjugal relations, family connections, interface with colleagues at work, or with our line manager. A feeling of happiness could also be influenced by or depend on our genetic makeup, training, childhood and past memories. The job of defining happiness gets further complicated when we begin to consider cross-cultural differences between nations - sometimes even between regions within a nation. At macro level, happiness could also depend on political, social, economic, technical and legal environment of the country we live in. India, as an instance, though considered as a spiritual hub was ranked 139, not far away from Afghanistan, ranked last at 149 in the list of happiness index 2018-20[149]!

'Happiness' thus is a complex construct with several mini constructs embedded within it. Formally, some definitions can be quoted though. Lyubomirsky (Lyubomirsky, 2010) e.g., defines happiness as "the

---

149 https://happiness-report.s3.amazonaws.com/2021/Appendix1WHR2021C2.pdf (Figure-7 p.23: (Retrieved 25-11-2021)

experience of joy, contentment, or positive well-being, combined with a sense that one's life is good, meaningful, and worthwhile." Daniel Kahneman a 2002 Noble Laureate in Economics observes that "experienced happiness refers to your feelings, to how happy you are as you live your life. In contrast, the satisfaction of the remembering self refers to your feelings when you think about your life."[150].

Happiness in Moral Philosophy

The greatest happiness of the greatest number is the foundation of morals and legislation
(Jeremy Bentham)

The happiness construct is intimately linked with the world of moral philosophy which draws distinction between right and wrong or good and bad behaviour. One branch of moral philosophy - *meta-ethics* examines questions such as: what is morality, justice, and perceptions of truth. A second branch - *normative ethics* addresses the question 'what we ought to do' and provides us with guidelines on *deontology* (nature of duty and obligations), *utilitarianism* (relating to utility or usefulness), *virtue ethics* (virtue or moral character of the person carrying out an action). The third branch is *applied ethics* which addresses morality related decisions such as: should we help our relatives go to war with another nation.

A discussion related to moral philosophy can be found in the writings of eastern and western philosophers and spiritual leaders. A comprehensive but lucid overview of philosophy is provided by Bertrand Russell, British

---

150 https://www.azquotes.com/quote/152289 (Retrieved 25-11-2021).

philosopher, mathematician and social critic's classic text (Russell B. , 2004). For our purpose we shall focus on the model of moral philosophy put forward by Aristotle (384-322 BC). We shall then examine the framework put forward by Aristotle with a discussion on the principles of moral philosophy found in the Sikh scripture (AD1604) and provide extensions and value additions found in the latter.

Aristotelian Model of Moral Philosophy

Only morality in our actions can give
beauty and dignity to life
(Albert Einstein)

Socrates (c.470BC-399BC) the Greek philosopher is considered to be the father of western philosophy. Socrates was teacher to Plato (c.428-424BC) who in turn was teacher to Aristotle (384BC-322BC). The trio, SPA - given the breadth and depth of their works are considered to be the giants of philosophy, so much so that, well known British mathematician and philosopher Whitehead once famously put Plato's contributions as follows.

"The safest general characterization of the European philosophical tradition is that it consists of a series of footnotes to Plato. I do not mean the systematic scheme of thought which scholars have doubtfully extracted from his writings. I allude to the wealth of general ideas scattered through them. His personal endowments, his wide opportunities for experience at a great period of civilization, his inheritance of an intellectual tradition not yet stiffened by excessive systematization, have made his writings an inexhaustible mine of suggestion" (Whitehead, 1979, pp. 39-40).

Aristotle, a titan of western philosophy and teacher to 'Alexander the Great' (356BC-323BC) was a prolific writer who wrote on such diverse subjects as literature, politics, philosophy, physics, meteorology, and economics. His best-known work *'Nicomachean Ethics'* (written c.340BC) lays bare the principles of ethical behaviour. The book is about 175 pages long, consists of ten books-Bk (chapters). The Human Good (Bk-1), Moral Virtues (Bk 2,3,4), Justice (Bk 5), Intellectual Virtue (Bk-6), Continence and Incontinence (Bk-7), Friendship (Bk 8,9) Pleasure, Friendship (Bk 10)[151]. Aristotle has another book 'The Eudemian Ethics', (Kenny, 2011) chapters of which overlap with 'Nicomachean Ethics' (Aristotle, The Nicomachean Ethics, 2009). In our discussion we have relied on material from *Nicomachean Ethics*. Both books are lessons in applied ethics[152].

Aristotle's Concept of Eudaimonia

The book opens highlighting the fact that the highest aim or good for all humans is *eudaimonia*. Eudaimonia consists of two Greek words - *Eu*: Good and *Daimon*: soul. Hence the end result of what humans do should be aimed at becoming a good soul.

A good soul consists of a bundle of virtues - the highest of which is the virtue of happiness. A virtuous person lives a good life with reason in thought and speech.

The focus of Aristotelian ethics is about what makes a 'virtuous person'? To arrive at a virtuous character, a series of steps are required. The actions of the person

---

151 (Aristotle, The Nicomachean Ethics, 2009)
[152] For a discussion on theories of ethics in their classical and modern form see (MacKinnon & Fiala , 2017), (Graham , 2010), and (Foot P. , 1967).

should be righteous, he should have just habits (learnt under good teachers) to help him in the development of a good character.

The formation of a good stable character, which, Aristotle says, should be maintained with some effort, involves conscious choices. All efforts involving good choices help nourish and develop a good soul.

Aristotle lists four specific virtues that embed in them all other virtues: a person with a 'great soul' who deserves praise from all; virtue of fairness and justice of a good ruler; practical judgement shown by good leaders; and finally, virtue of being a truly good friend.

With this summary, going through the chapters of the book we can summarise Aristotle's thoughts on ethics - forming his model of ethics as follows[153].

A Virtuous Character

Moral virtues are acquired by the repetition of the resultant acts i.e., they are habit forming and cannot be prescribed exactly. They should, however, avoid excesses. If a person is engaged in virtuous acts, it is a sign that he has acquired the disposition of a virtuous person. Virtue and vices are within the power and control of a person. Aristotle suggests that ethics is not an exact science like mathematics and hence it is unreasonable to expect exact results - a subjective mean (balance) of virtuous traits - courage, temperance, generosity etc. would be acceptable. The aim

---

[153] For a discussion on theories of ethics in their classical and modern form see (MacKinnon & Fiala , 2017), (Graham , 2010), and (Foot P. , 1967).

of a good soul should be to live well and (think and) do well for others.

Three types of lives are distinguished: *one of slavish pleasure* which is commonly understood by people as happiness; *refined and active way of politics which aims at honour* (doing good for others); and thirdly, *life as a way of contemplation*.

Possessing virtues but remaining inactive despite suffering evils, misfortunes, and hardships would not be considered virtuous. Also, life engaged in money making pursuits would not be considered virtuous. Happiness in life includes virtues and self-sufficiency - but not in the sense of a hermit but someone *with* a family, friends, and community which make life more fulfilling. Aristotle also emphasises the *importance of a healthy and energetic life to lead a virtuous life of happiness over a lifetime.*

How do we know that someone has acquired virtuous disposition? We know this *when the person feels pleasure in doing virtuous acts*. Moral virtue, according to Aristotle should not be fleeting or fickle; it should become a part and parcel of a person's character and should not be a passing phase. A virtuous act should be performed for the good of the receiver voluntarily with full knowledge of the circumstances and without being forced into it.

Courage and Temperance

In Book III Aristotle describes 'courage' as the balance or mean between 'courage' and 'fear.' By this he meant that a brave person would be aware and thoughtful of the situation and not rash or foolhardy (i.e., he would not be blindly over-confident). The extreme side of courage is cowardice which displays an inadequate state of confidence. An angry person acting bravely in anger can become blind to dangers. A truly courageous person, even when he is not certain of victory does not entertain fear. Aristotle also chides a person who is overconfident owing to ignorance - such a person will be the first to run at the first signs of things not going his way.

Here he also explains the concept of 'temperance' as the soundness of mind and moderation, which is the mean with regard to pleasure and pain; excesses, Aristotle explains, mostly occur with regard to pleasure, which he divides into bodily pleasures and pleasure of the soul. A self-indulgent man is similar to a spoilt child. A temperate, that is a balanced person is not led to endure pain, but an intemperate person does, even with his pleasures, owing to his excessive longings. As he puts it:

> "Plainly, then, excess with regard to pleasures is self-indulgence and is culpable; with regard to pains one is not, as in the case of courage, called temperate for facing them or self-indulgent for not doing so, but the self-indulgent man is so called because he is pained more than he ought at not getting pleasant things (even his pain being caused by pleasure), and the temperate man is so called because he is not pained at the absence of what is pleasant and at his abstinence from it"
> (Aristotle, The Nicomachean Ethics, 2009, p. 57).

Aristotle praises a temperate person who desires things that are not impediments to health, or contrary to beauty, and are within one's resources - such a person makes judgements based on right reasons. He also warns that vices come from bad habits and clamouring for wrong things. He advises that the desirous part of the human soul should be kept in harmony with the rational part - unchecked desires can impair reason. Ignorance or being ill-informed about the consequences of vices, he says, is no excuse. Aristotle does not agree that people have innate visions of what is good (Aristotle could have been hinting that they have to be cultivated/learnt).

Generosity, Honour, Anger, Honesty

In Book IV continuing with moral virtues, Aristotle emphasizes on getting the balance of one's behaviour right in the social and political settings. Here he begins with a discussion on virtues concerned with money and specifies that two extreme un-virtuous traits linked with money are, wastefulness and meanness. A wasteful person who will have vices may be ruined by his own doings. A virtuous person with money is one who gives his money in the right amount to the right people and at the right time. Aristotle puts this in his style of words as follows:

> "And gratitude is felt towards him who gives, not towards him who does not take, and praise also is bestowed more on him. It is easier, also, not to take than to give; for men are apter to give away their own too little than to take what is another's. Givers, too, are called liberal; but those who do not take are not praised for liberality but rather for justice; while those who take are hardly praised at all. And the liberal are almost the most loved of all virtuous characters, since they are useful; and this depends on their giving. Now virtuous actions are noble and done for the sake of the noble. Therefore, the liberal man, like other virtuous men, will give for the sake of the noble, and rightly; for he will give to the right people, the right amounts, and at the right time, with all the other qualifications that accompany right giving; and that too with pleasure or without pain; for that which is virtuous is pleasant or free from pain-least of all will it be painful." (Aristotle, The Nicomachean Ethics, 2009, p. 60).

Such a person Aristotle says, creates beautiful things and earns the accolade. Aristotle also describes magnificence as a virtue going beyond generosity when a person shares a large amount of his wealth with others - this, he said, should be done without any show of impropriety. At some length in this book is also discussed the *virtues of honour which he says is the greatest of all honours* possessed by 'great souled people' who have in them the following traits: they can take large risks without regard to safety to their lives; are calm and not swayed by popular fascinations; lead a modest life, do not speak ill of others, are generous in helping others but coy in receiving favours; are kind to people below them but stern to ones above; express their opinions without fear or malice and speak steadily.

Aristotle's analysis of anger is insightful. He does not disagree with the right amount used against the right person in the right circumstances. He points out that a person with uncontrollable anger would be unfair in his responses, and a person with zero anger would not be able to defend himself. His advice would be to channel the anger to productive purposes which would be virtuous. His observations on 'honesty' are equally insightful. Aristotle poses the question that how much of comparison with others is ideal and how honest and frank one should be when talking about one's qualities? Here one could be boastful or reticent. Aristotle suggests that a virtuous person states his qualities without exaggeration or understating them. It would be pardonable if a person with qualities occasionally exaggerated them for the purpose of glory or honour and not for money. On the lighter side of life, Aristotle finds it acceptable to be witty and charming when in leisure mode. He does not consider a sense of shame to be a virtue but just a trait caused by fear and adds that an honest person would not do anything shameful.

Justice and Fairness

In Book V Aristotle talks about justice and fairness. With justice attributes he applies similar approach of finding or settling at *Mean*. Types of justices he discusses are lawful, i.e., the justice that follows the rule of the law. When law is playing its role well and institutions are functioning properly and there is overall sense of well-being i.e., when we are in an ideal state of happiness in the society then we can say that justice is virtuous (we all are virtuous towards each other).

Aristotle suggests that the justice that is meted out should be fair and equal i.e., it is distributive and rectificatory i.e., it is fair for what it has been granted and it is also reformatory (corrective in its nature). In the broader non-legal sense, distributive justice also means that there is equal or proportional share and recourse to resources of the economy - e.g., state help with regard to medical facilities, jobs, etc. When this does not happen, corrective justice could kick in.

There should also be reciprocity in justice which is also akin to fairness. In simple terms, when someone is good to us, we should be good to them. In the broader sense, let us say if the state provides us with clean streets then as citizens it is our duty to maintain cleanliness by not throwing rubbish around. Finally, justice should also carry in it the element of discretion, even when it may look unfair to some. As an instance, a judge may use his discretion to rule in favour of harsher punishments in case of heinous crimes; however, in events when justice is to be meted, we ought to know what the aim of the justice is.

Intellectual Virtues

Book VI has in it the discussion on intellectual virtues: theoretical wisdom, knowledge of science, intuitive understanding, practical wisdom, philosophic wisdom (union of intuitive reason and science), relation between practical wisdom and science, and craft expertise (knowledge of how to make things). Aristotle also outlines some minor intellectual virtues concerned with conduct e.g., goodness in deliberations and their relation to practical wisdom and understanding. Aristotle also raises and discusses the question 'what is the use of philosophic and practical wisdom and its relation between practical wisdom to natural virtue, moral virtue, and correct reason'. What he is implying is that practical ethics that embodies good character in it also requires variety of knowledge and thought. He divides intellect into *contemplative and calculative.* "The object of the contemplation is truth; that of calculation is truth corresponding with right desire." (Aristotle, The Nicomachean Ethics, 2009, p. 102)

For intellectual virtues Aristotle is not discussing mean - on the contrary he is implying that *'more' here is better than 'less.'* The happiest life, he says, is that of a philosopher who over a longer period of time exercises the virtues of theoretical wisdom. It is pertinent to note the difference between moral virtues and intellectual virtues.

Moral virtues include courage, kindness, generosity, respect, humility, patience, and such other attributes; intellectual virtues on the other hand are art, knowledge, practical wisdom, philosophic wisdom, and intuitive reasoning.

Whereas the aim of moral virtues is to make us feel good, the aim of intellectual virtues is to search for 'truth'. For moral virtues the standard is the middle ground - the mean; for intellectual virtues more truth is better than less truth. As an instance, for art and crafts, there is no end to learning and one finished product can always be improved upon. A similar analogy applies to other intellectual virtues - scientific knowledge, or philosophical knowledge e.g., for which more is better than less. The route to more truth is via learning additional techniques in art; knowledge (for scientific knowledge), prudence (for practical wisdom), wisdom (for philosophic wisdom), and intellect (for intuitive reasoning).

Obstacles to Moral Virtues

Book VII entitled 'Continence and Incontinence: Pleasure,' discusses obstacles to virtues. The dictionary meaning of continence is 'self-restraint, with regard to desires, indulgence, sex or such traits'[154]. Incontinence is opposite to self-restraint. A continent person deliberates and follows reason and logic to his actions as opposed to incontinent person who acts more on impulses - he knows that an action is wrong but still pursues it. A subtle difference between an incontinent person and temperate person should be noted. A temperate person believes that a decision is right for him to pursue as it would bring him pleasure. Lovers of gourmet food is an example, excess of which is sometimes consumed. Unlike true vices,

---

154 Commonly it is interpreted as 'the ability to control movements of the bowels and bladder.'

incontinences are more like weaknesses where one can passively follow one's urges rather than making an active or deliberate choice for it. Incontinence contrasted with 'true vices' (we could call them 'hard core vices') are more of a weakness.

The second concept that is discussed in the chapter is 'bestiality' i.e., beast-like behaviour which is the opposite of something human. According to Aristotle, terms 'God-like' or 'beast-like' are more applicable to humans because they would not have virtues or vices. Bear in mind that Aristotle is writing prior to Christ's time so the concept of God, if any, he had in his mind could have been linked to powers of nature.

Aristotle's suggestion to a virtuous person is to avoid three particularly negative traits: continence, bestiality, and vice (opposite to virtue). If a person has continence and observes it, then he has knowledge that something is considered as universally good and pursue it - examples could include abstinence from drugs and violence.

A key point that comes around is that unchecked vices can make us lose mastery over ourselves in two principal ways: first through impulsiveness, when we do not wait for reason, but are led by our imagination - being unprepared for the consequences; in the second scenario, a weak person who may have thought through but is swayed by his passion to take actions which lead to undesired consequences.

Towards the last part of the chapter Aristotle also discusses the concept of pleasure and as pointed out previously, he is not averse to the idea of pleasure, but it should be *a* good and not *the* good[155]. This is a profound statement that says that pleasures have to be kept in check - in particular, bodily pleasures.

Friendship

Friendship is the relationship between two people or a group of people who are similar to each other on some value traits and enjoy each other's company. Another way to define friendship will be to say that it is 'bonding' between people. Depending on how strong or weak this bonding is determines the lifespan of the friendship i.e., how long it would last.

In Book VIII and IX Aristotle provides a taxonomy of friendship and their characteristics that is valid till this date - so much so that they could form the PowerPoint lessons for a class on the topic. In the explanations of the taxonomy, Aristotle explains the underlying reasons of three different categories of friendship - reasons which determine the strength or weakness of the bonding; this in turn determines the lifespan of the friendship.

First in the category is the friendship based on utility or usefulness; in the second category is friendship based on mutual pleasure; the third and the last category is the friendship based on the pursuit of some common good between the parties.

The first type happens when people come together covertly or overtly expecting to gain something from each other - examples would be working relations formed in businesses - on the face of it very cordial and friendly but with underlying reasons of expected gains. This type of

---

155 Stanford Encyclopaedia of Philosophy (p.11)

friendship also happens between people who run into each other and choose to network for future gains. Such friendships do not last a long time.

The second type of friendship happens when people come together for mutual pleasure. Common examples would be friends made at college and social networks on which offers of friendship or casual relationships abound. Such friendships also do not last a long time.

The third category of friendship happens when people come together because they have common virtues and mutual appreciation and have respect for each other and wish to be in each other's company for some common good. A friendship based on these traits would last.

Repeat interactions with good intentions cements the bonding, leading to mutual trust and results in better payoffs (mostly abstract in nature) that happen between friends[156]. The payoffs usually occur in the form of mutual exchange of ideas, learning from each other, community help, and in similar ways.

If we could form a virtuous index - it would be highest for the third category of friendship which lasts a long time. It is possible though that accidental meetings with people and friendships, the basis for which is mutual gain and pleasure may occasionally also last a long time, but, because the virtuous index is weak such likelihood is not common.

---

156 Game theory economists analyse such co-operations under 'infinitely repeated games scenario' in which players cooperate and play a socially optimum strategy. There are several theorems which deal with how to achieve and maintain a socially optima equilibrium in repeated games.

Aristotle's premise is that while truth and friends are both loved - truth stands on higher grounds than friends.

Pleasure, Happiness, Contemplation, Education

Aristotle ruminates towards the end:

> "After these matters we ought perhaps next to discuss pleasure. For it is thought to be most intimately connected with our human nature, which is the reason why in educating the young we steer them by the rudders of pleasure and pain; it is thought, too, that to enjoy the things we ought and to hate the things we ought has the greatest bearing on virtue of character." (Aristotle, The Nicomachean Ethics, 2009, p. 183).

In Book X Aristotle lays bare his thoughts on pleasure, happiness, contemplation, and up-bringing. A focused discussion whether pleasure is good or bad and if it is *the* chief good is given in Book VII (1152b-1154b)[157] as well; overall Aristotle approves of pursuing pleasure for its own sake if it is not *The Good*. As he puts it:

> "....the pleasures that do not involve pains do not admit of excess; and these are among the things pleasant by nature and not incidentally. By things pleasant incidentally I mean those that act as cures (for because as a result people are cured, through some action of the part that remains healthy, for this reason the process is thought pleasant); by things naturally pleasant I mean those that stimulate the action of the healthy nature." (Aristotle, The Nicomachean Ethics, 2009, p. 140)

---

157 (Aristotle, The Nicomachean Ethics, 2009)

Intuitively, we all know what pleasure is - when we are in 'pleasure mode' bodily or non-bodily, we momentarily forget all our concerns. Aristotle put it formally as saying that pleasure is 'static' in nature and not dynamic. That is, it begins and ends with no elements of permanence in it. As an instance, we derive pleasure from a sense of taste and touch. Some pleasures are preferable to others - Aristotle ranks them as follows in terms of the happiness they generate: *highest is the pleasure that results from thinking*, followed by sight, hearing and smell and taste. This takes us to the discussion of happiness.

Aristotle does not believe that play or bodily pleasure is happiness; according to him, the highest form of happiness is divine in nature and emanates from intellect. More precisely, *he rates contemplation as the highest form of sustainable activity that generates genuine happiness.* This is an activity of purest joy. As he puts it:

> "This is indicated, too, by the fact that the other animals have no share in happiness, being completely deprived of such activity. For while the whole life of the gods is blessed, and that of men too in so far as some likeness of such activity belongs to them, none of the other animals is happy, since they in no way share in contemplation. Happiness extends, then, just so far as contemplation does, and those to whom contemplation more fully belongs are more truly happy, not as a mere concomitant but in virtue of the contemplation; for this is in itself precious. *Happiness, therefore, must be some form of contemplation.*" (Aristotle, The Nicomachean Ethics, 2009, p. 197) (Italics are this author's).

A key point Aristotle makes on education is that, in addition to formal education, family and community can provide invaluable education to children. Activities in which we find pleasure we keep repeating and get better at them. That is, the activities and their outcomes have the property of reinforcing each other. A simple example could be a hobby we pursue, get good at it, and happily keep doing it over and over. This is applicable to both positive and negative habits. A crucial point that he makes is that listening to discourse only does not improve our mental health and make us a better human being - good habits and practice do not lead to nurturing and fostering good virtues.

A core point that Aristotle makes is that to nurture ethical traits, education and cultivation of the mind should be the prerogative of the state; the state can promulgate appropriate laws; a good dose of state efforts can then be supplemented by parental efforts. In a remarkable feat of foresight Aristotle thus provides us with the blueprints of raising virtuous souls.

Commonalities Between Aristotelean Model and Sikh Model of Virtuous Living

In the preceding sections we presented two models of virtuous living written about 2000 years apart. Aristotle wrote 'Nicomachean Ethics' around 340 BC; the Sikh Holy Scripture was compiled and then installed in completed form in *Harimandir Sahib* in AD1604. However, one is astounded by the uncanny similarities between the two.

As we described in the previous chapters, how the Sikh scripture began to take shape with the hymns of the first Guru, Guru Nanak (b.1469) to which additional hymns of successive Gurus were added, with the scripture gaining its present shape in the hands of the fifth Guru Arjan and its installation in *Harimandir Sahib* in AD1604.

Communication channels as we have them today were non-existent in those days and translations of Aristotle's book were not available and Sikh Gurus, dexterous though they were in several languages, Greek was not one of them. Still, it seems as if Aristotle provided blueprints of moral philosophy and about 2000 years later Sikh Gurus implemented them with a zeal in laying the foundations of a new religion. Let us briefly enumerate the similarities between the two approaches. For an orderly discussion we shall adopt the same headings as in the previous section.

Eudaimonia: Aristotle's proposition that the highest aim for humans should be to attain eudaimonia i.e., to become a good soul, gels perfectly well with the Sikh ethos and teachings that says that we should all aim and work towards having the purest of souls so that we can reach *Nirvana*. The route for Sikhs to be in the perpetual state of bliss and eternal happiness is by being in the company of virtuous people (Satsang) and by reminiscing God's name.

Virtuous Character: There is near total conformity on this attribute between what Aristotle had proposed and what the Sikh Holy Scripture repeats at several places i.e., moral virtues (and vices) are within a man's control and that they are acquired by repeat virtuous (or dis-virtuous) acts which then become part of us.

Both sets of thoughts (Aristotle's and Sikh Scripture's) do not consider life engaged just in money-making to be a virtuous one; more importantly both sets of thoughts are in total harmony when they say that happiness and a virtuous life can be had by being with family and community and that a healthy and energetic life is essential to lead a virtuous life of happiness.

Aristotle's suggestion of finding a mean (balance) in ethical traits (generosity, temperance, etc.) corresponds to the idea of 'moderation' in Sikh teachings. Another fine point on which there is perfect harmony between the two sets of thoughts is that virtuous acts should become part of us (our character) and that such acts should impart us happiness.

Courage: Here again we find harmony between two schools of thought; a courageous person is also a thoughtful person and not impulsive or rash, however, the best of all statements Aristotle made, and with which all Sikhs will happily agree is that *'a truly courageous person, even when he is not certain of victory does not entertain fear*[158].' Both school of thought are in total agreement when they say that source of vices are bad habits and clamouring for wrong things. Again, here too, there is total harmony between the two schools when they say that moderation in most things is *sine qua non* for a virtuous life.

Generosity, Honour, Anger, Honesty: There is agreement here too on finding the balance with regard to virtue of generosity and wastefulness. Sikhs regularly donate funds to charitable causes staying within the bounds of their earnings, however, for bigger projects they are also generous (Aristotle does allude to this as a virtue in his book). There is total agreement between the two schools when they say that 'virtue of honour' is the greatest of all virtues. Sikhs will vouch for this, especially with regard to

---

158 Guru Gobind Singh has immortalised this virtue in the following verse that is close to all Sikh's hearts:
Deh shiva bar mohe eh hai; Shubh karman te kabho na taron; Kabho na taron; Na daro arr so jab jaaye laro; Nischay kar apni jeet karo. (a warrior is seeking Shiva's blessing of never to be fearful of battle but win it with determination, no matter what the odds).

their given word and in a battle[159]. With regard to anger too there is total agreement on its control and regulation.

Justice and Fairness: Justice is considered to be a big virtue in Sikh ethos and philosophy. Whatever we have explained with regard to theoretical treatment of the subject by Aristotle is applicable almost *in toto* in the Sikh world of ethos and moral character. So much so that a Sikh will often not only fight for justice and fairness for himself but also for others. Sikh history is evidence to this (cf. Ch-2).

Intellectual Virtues: Again, we find almost complete congruence between the two schools of thought on inculcating intellectual virtues. This was amply evident in the 40 years reign of Punjab by Sikh emperor Ranjit Singh (1801-1839) who made learning and education accessible to all by making it compulsory for a school to be attached to every gurdwara[160]. Both schools of thought are also in total agreement when they say that the ultimate aim of intellectual virtues is the search for truth.

Obstacles to Moral Virtues: Here too Aristotle's enumerated obstacles to moral virtues are in near total conformity with Sikh explanations. In fact, at several places, the Sikh scripture clearly warns us to be conscious and weary of giving in to our impulses and vices which have the capacity to make us behave like animals.

Friendship: Again, the teachings of the Sikh Holy Scripture are in total agreement with Aristotle's premise that an ideal and best long-lasting friendship happens with

---

[159] The following adage applies to Sikhs and Pathans: 'ye jabaan pe marten hain aur jabaan pe marte hain' (they 'die on their word and kill on their word').

160 Punjab was the last state to be conquered by the British, who after its take-over 1849, systematically dessimated the then education system of Punjab as a long-term policy to weaken the state to rule over it (Cf. Ch-1).

like-minded people. The scripture repeatedly urges us to be in the company of virtuous people who can be found in holy congregations (Satsang)[161].

Pleasure, Happiness, Contemplation, and Education: The central point of utmost importance and agreement between the two schools of thought is that the highest form of pleasure is that of contemplation. The Sikh scripture is more precise on this when it suggests that this contemplation, *inter alia,* should be in the memory of God and that we all should pray for good virtues and patience for us to be able to do good for *all.* However, both schools of thought are not averse to moderate pleasure (or for that matter some banter and fun) - again though the sense and suggestion of exercising moderation exists in both schools.

Extensions in Sikh Scripture

The mind is everything; what you think you become (Socrates)

Reality is created by the mind; we can change our reality by changing our mind (Plato)

The energy of the mind is the essence of life (Aristotle)

Win over the mind; win over the world (Guru Nanak)

There is a great deal of similarity between the theoretical Aristotelean model of moral philosophy and the

---

161 Readers would bear in mind that in those days this was the common forum of meeting.

applied one which Sikh's observe. However, there are some subtle differences, owing mostly to different times when the two sets of thoughts came into being.

Aristotle wrote his work when Greece was in the midst of in-fighting between states. In 323BC when the hostilities toward Macedonians in Athens increased, Aristotle is said to have escaped to the island of Euboea (40 miles north-east of capital Athens), where he lived and died in 324BC. The times when the Sikh scripture was taking shape, Mughals were ruling India and although there was hostility and in-fighting between the states, Sikh Gurus observed the atrocities of the rulers and the rigidities of the Hindu religion to which their families also belonged. The mention of both - the atrocities of Mughals and the rigidities of the Hindu religion are found in the scripture.

The emphasis the scripture puts on is to do away with hollow rituals and immerse ourselves in reminiscing the name of God, in whose name 'true happiness' is to be found, by cleansing our souls with virtuous thoughts and pious deeds. To achieve this aim, the scripture provided a triangular approach of control on three sets of attributes - the apex entity 'mind' that directs everything; the control over 5 embedded vulnerabilities of human beings that make them digress from the path of virtuous living and thirdly, the control over 5 *Inderiyan*.

We can represent the three sets with an isosceles triangle with the vertex angle 120^0 and two base angles at 60^0 each. An isosceles triangle nicely represents the triangularity - the largest vertex angle represents 'mind' that dictates everything to us. The Sikh scripture accords the highest importance to 'mind' which, it says, is the source of all our vices and virtues. Diagrammatically, we can represent the idea as follows.

Two base angles of 60^0 each representing the 5-Vikars and 5-Inderiyans are accorded the same weight. Two one-way arrows from 'mind' to the Vikars and Inderiyans show a one-way causation; two-way arrows between Vikars and Inderiyans show a two-way causation between them - i.e., attributes within both sets influence each other[162].

Aristotle does refer to 'Mind,' 'Vikars,' and 'Inderiyans,' in his book however, Sikh scripture explicitly states them and puts a great deal of emphasis on them. Aristotle also has another book 'De Anima' (On the Soul) in which he discusses the kinds of souls possessed by living beings and the plant kingdom and argues that only humans have Mind and that the rational soul is immortal and can exist without the body (Lawson, 1986)[163]. There is no specific discussion on 'mind' and the role it can play in a virtuous life.

---

162 In Hinduism there is the concept of 5 *Karmendriyas* meaning organs of action. These are Vāk - speech; Pāṇi - hands; Pāda - feet; Pāyu - excretory organ; Upastha - organ of reproduction. Also, there is the concept of 5 Jnanendriya, described here, i.e., the sensory organs. These are nose (ghrana), eyes (caksu), tongue (rasana), skin (tvak) and ears (srotra). Jnanendriya, are supposed to increase the reach of mind for the purpose of knowledge seeking. They should not be allowed to rule our behaviour without the pros and cons being assessed by the mind.
163 In Chapter-3. As stated elsewhere, in both of Aristotle's books the chapters are referred to as Books.

Figure 5. 1 An Isosceles Triangle Describing Mind,
Vikars, and Inderiyans

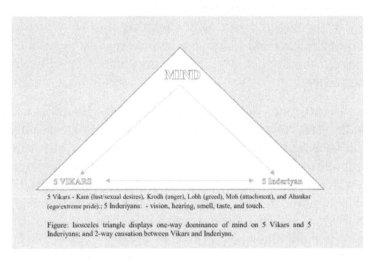

5 Vikars - Kam (lust/sexual desires), Krodh (anger), Lobh (greed), Moh (attachment), and Ahankar (ego/extreme pride).; 5 Inderiyans: - vision, hearing, smell, taste, and touch.

Figure: Isosceles triangle displays one-way dominance of mind on 5 Vikars and 5 Inderiyans; and 2-way causation between Vikars and Inderiyan.

Additional issues on which the scripture comes out strongly relates to the cycles of life-death; rituals of Hindus; constant reminder of our perishability and futility of excessive love for material wealth and extreme love for our near and dear ones; specific advice for women folk to be devoted in God's memory and service to their spouse. There are also numerous references to Hindu Gods.

Throughout the scripture there is mention that our souls can be cleansed in the veneration of God's name; no such mention is found in Aristotle. It is not that Aristotle was anti-God - in fact in one of his works he explicitly acknowledges God's existence[164]. Sfekas lucidly explains Aristotle's God (Aristotle, The Metaphysics [Kindle edition 2004], c.335-323BC) as follows[165]: "Aristotle

---

164 (Aristotle, The Metaphysics [Kindle edition 2004], c.335-323BC)
165 Sfekas, Stanley. Aristotle's Concept of God.
https://heptapolis.com/aristotles-concept-god (Accessed 8-12-2021).

conceived of God as outside of the world, as the final cause of all motion in Nature, as Prime Mover and Unmoved Mover of the universe. He was the crowning objective of all dynamic development in the cosmos from matter to form and from potentiality to actuality. He stood outside the Great Chain of Being, yet was the source of all motion and development. Aristotle did not attribute mercy, love, sympathy and providence to God, but rather eternal self-contemplation." The Sikh definition of God (cf. Entries in Appendix table) is similar to Aristotle's.

Aristotle's concept of God was enthusiastically adopted by Christian theologians, most prominently by St. Thomas Aquinas (1225–1274) the Italian philosopher and Catholic priest who combined the studies of theology and philosophy and greatly influenced western thought. He also wrote extensively. His most widely recognised scholarly work (though unfinished) is *Summa Theologica* (Aquinas, 2018) in which he advances five reasons for the existence of God; and *Disputed Questions on Truth* (Mulligan, 1952) in which he delves into the study of the human soul, the virtues and spiritual substances.

Aristotle gave the world via 'Nicomachean Ethics' a solid theoretical grounding in the principles of moral philosophy which can be used as a benchmark to test the applied side of religions. No religion teaches bad and similarities in their moral sermon to their devotees can be found embedded in the ethical principles laid by Aristotle in 340BC. Remarkably, a totally new religion that Sikhism is and that began taking shape in 1469AD - over 1800 years later, found several of its founding moral principles embedded in the Aristotelian model of moral philosophy[166].

---

[166] A reviewer with a philosophic bent of mind, playing devil's advocate, argued that this is not very surprising, because Aristotle did not go into difficult

What remains to be seen is how the duo of Aristotle's theory and practice of Sikh ethos can direct us the to the *Road to Nirvana*. Which is the focus of our final chapter.

Chapter Summary

The purpose of this chapter was to summarize key guiding messages in Sikh scripture on how to live a virtuous life. A read through the scripture yielded a wealth of information which we presented in sequential steps. The scripture grants supreme importance to 'control over the mind' that drives and steers us into doing all that we do in our lives. A controlled, composed mind, full of virtuous traits can put us on the path of a virtuous life.

Threats to the composure of the mind come from five adversaries – lust, anger, greed, excessive attachment to worldly entities, and ego. These in turn are impacted by what we see, hear, smell, taste, and touch.

For a person seeking path to a virtuous life, search begins with keeping in check the adversaries affecting the mind so that the mind takes virtuous decisions. To keep these adversaries in check and for us to lead a life so pious that it will free us from repeated cycles of births and deaths,

---

issues of moral philosophy on which religions may differ. His treatise provides the minimum common denominator of most philosophies. The more ambivalent issues like 'does the good of many justify harm to a few?', or 'is any form of persuasion – including, but not limited to violence – justified to modify someone else's beliefs, were not touched by him. Good and bad are relative terms and depend on the 'environment', including the society one is in. We may be shocked by cannibalism, but for the tribes that practised it, it was not 'bad' but normal. Our philosophies cannot transcend our value systems that are in turn conditioned by our 'environmental factors'. Basically, after reaching a certain stage of civilization, value systems that develop are very similar across societies, the moral philosophy that arises from it is also similar, and therefore the basic commonalities.

the scripture advises us to seek and be in the company of righteous persons and embrace the habit of being compassionate and charitable, practicing at the same time humility, self-control, kindness, mercy, patience, self-discipline, truth, trust and service to humanity.

The scripture tells us that the virtuous traits can be practiced by being in a family and part of the community without taking recourse to solitude or complicated rituals. The scripture reminds us of the nature of perishability in all mortal objects and urges us to make good use of our lives. The positive role of women in family and social life is explicitly acknowledged and encouraged. The scripture is rich in its reference to Hindu mythological past (Vedas, Puranas, Gods, and Goddesses) and is universal in its message for people from all caste and creeds.

The end result of leading a virtuous life is the innate happiness it can generate. 'Happiness' which we all intuitively understand, is an elusive construct that has been extensively researched. There are volumes written and theoretical and applied studies done on all angles of happiness - psychological, sociological, philosophical, and spiritual.

The momentum in happiness studies in the recent past is part owing to seismic changes ushered in by the revolution in telecommunications that has laid bare aspects of good, bad and the worse aspects of life in all corners of the globe. The exposure has shaken the family harmony and impacted on people's conjugal relations. The unprecedented changes coupled with lack of adherence to principals of a virtuous life is leading us to a state of unhappiness - so the Sikh scripture would explicitly argue today, if it could.

Around 1800 years prior to the Sikh scripture taking shape, Aristotle wrote a classic on the principles of moral philosophy, unknowing that one day his principles would come to be absorbed in a new religion. There are uncanny similarities in Aristotle's theoretical work and applied moral principles of Sikhs' daily lives.

Both schools of thought believe that, with the goal of true happiness in mind, the primary aim of a human being should be to nurture a soul full of good virtues. A person should keep his vices e.g., love for bodily pleasures under check. Both schools also profess that a virtuous person would also be courageous, believe in justice and fairness, and will be charitable, and will make all attempts to harness intellectual virtues. Both schools believe that the highest form of virtue should be the pleasure of contemplation i.e., a truly contemplative person would be on (constant) guard of virtuous and non-virtuous acts in life.

The Sikh scripture additionally extends the road map of happiness, leading to *Nirvana*, by urging devotees to be early risers, observe a disciplined life, make an honest living by dint of one's hard work, and reminisce in God's name, and always keep God's memory in mind.

**

Appendix Table 5. 1 Key Themes in Sikh Scripture

Page numbers in the scripture	Key Themes
1-13	Pages 1-13 of the scripture contain basic chant, morning, evening, and night-time recitals. These are the contributions of the first Sikh Guru, Guru Nanak.
	Basic chant has only the following words in it: *Ik-oa'nkār sat nām kartā purakh nirbhao nirvair akāl mūrat ajūnī saibha'n gur parsād Jap*. The following words are not part of the basic chant but are added here for us to understand the Sikh definition of God (see below): Āad sach jugād sach Hai bhī sach Nānak hosī bhī sach.
	The morning recital is known as *Japuji* (p.1-8); Pages 8-14 contain the evening recitals *Sodar and Sopurakh* - together commonly known as '*Rehraas*'; The night-time recital is known as *Sohila*.
	From p.15 onwards the scripture contains hymns in classical *Rāga*s.
	Basic chant as outlined above leads to the Sikh definition of 'God' as follows:
	There is one universal creator God of us all. He is self-existent and is beyond the cycles of births and deaths; he is devoid of fear or hatred towards anyone; he is present everywhere. This has been the truth and will be so for all times to come.

In addition to the basic chant and recitals, the following core messages are to be found on the first 13 pages of the scripture.

Key messages in first 13 pages:

The opening part of the scripture eulogises the creator for his creation. It subsequently lays bare the fact that the mind cannot be cleansed by visiting pilgrimages and superficially cleaning the body each day - instead focus should be on the virtuosity of the mind which we should not fill with bad deeds as, unlike the washing away the dirty linen, accumulated impact of bad deeds (in the mind) is hardest to wash away. The advice here is that our character builds on our daily deeds - hence we should be on guard as to what and how we perform our everyday duties as we reap what we sow. Excessive love for wealth can lead us to negative acts and drive us beyond the memory of God.

(Memo - Sikhism is a monotheistic religion (belief that there is only one God).

There is explicit mention of creator God Brahma, and an appeal is made to him to grant us the goodness like him. There is also the mention of Vedas, Shiva, Inder, Krishna, and Gopis in various contexts.

Two key messages are given in hymns 27 and 28 (p.6). First is the suggestion that one who loves all as equal has achieved the highest order of achievement in the world of universal brotherhood. Second, one who wins over his mind (i.e., controls his mind) wins the world. This is one of several places where the importance of the mind, its role and control is urged.

	Merits of Satsang is emphasized (p.12). Similar to the mind, mention of the merits of Satsang occurs at numerous places in the scripture.
19	Sermon for married woman not to be attracted to outwardly pleasures and neglect her spouse - such an act would lead to moral decay, and she would never appeal to her spouse despite all outwardly cosmetic make-up. Instead, she would better devote her time in the memory of God.
30	Specific sermon on the renouncing of back-biting (slandering), 'haume' (ego), and 'ahankaar'(pride).
31	Caution against following one's mind blindly; virtues of Satsang highlighted.
39	Detailed discourse on the negatives of 'haume' which is hard to get rid of just by visiting pilgrimages. Accumulation of wealth, knowledge, doing charitable works with no humility, breeds 'haume', which has to be won over by being a determined and pure devotee.
44	Virtues of Satsang highlighted.
58	Discourse to women folk to be devotional to God and to her spouse.
60-62	Caution against excessive love for worldly attractions.
64	Reminder that we all live in a world which is not only fickle but also fleeting.
71	Advice on staying home and worshipping (i.e., not to go to forests/mountains for it).
72	Importance of dealing with *Ahankar* is highlighted.
73	Selfless sacrifice of oneself in the reverence of God.
76	Old age and death - should be a stark reminder to us all.
77-78	4 parts or *pehers* of a life cycle - 'childhood', 'youth', 'old age' and 'death' highlighted.
82, 84	Wealth - advice on shunning excessive love for material goods - emphasis on good deeds in life, for this, and the next life.
82	Highlighted is the fact that the purpose of life is: 'Devotion to God'.
84	Puranas are mentioned.

85,86	Warning that the cycle of life and death does not end for non-worshippers - i.e., they never achieve *Nirvana*. Advice on the control of one's *Inderiyans* and *mind*.
87	Merge and make yourself as 'Hari' (another name for lord Vishnu); a worshipper always has glow on his face.
88	There are 84 lakh (8.4 million) birth-death cycles - to achieve *Nirvana* is to free oneself from the cycle of births and deaths.
89	A person who always follows his mind is compared to a woman of dubious character who is never satisfied in her endeavours.
91	Advice on restraining from back-biting, anger.
91	Virtues of Satsang emphasized.
92	Advice against excessive love for life, family, and money. Reminder of a person's mortality.
95,96	Virtues of Satsang highlighted.
99	Grief happens when one forgets God.
103, 108	Virtues of Satsang emphasized.
109	Sermon against making unreasonable demands to God such as for liquor, drugs!
114-15	Advice on using one's mind as a mirror to see and judge oneself.
116	Mention of 8.4 million cycles of life and death.
129	Caution against excessive love for money.
133	Emphasized that life would be barren without the memory of God.
133	12 months of a year described
137, 138	10 stages of life are described as follows: stage-1: a child is aware of suckling her mother's breast for milk; stage-2: child begins to recognise his father and mother; stage-3: he is aware of his brothers and sisters; stage-4: child is engrossed with his playing; stage-5: he gets fond of eating and drinking; stage-6: his (strong - rather blind) sexual desires are aroused; stage-7: he establishes his house; stage-8: the anger element in him is aroused which can be the cause of his decay; stage-9: his hairs turn grey and health issues pick up; stage-10: he dies and is turned into ashes.

140	Sermon against cheating (suggesting that if you cheat someone you are cheating yourself).
140	An address to Muslim devotees is made here who are advised to make benevolence, their mosque; honest earnings; their holy Quran; staying away from bad deeds is an act equivalence to 'Sunat'; be of the highest character which is equivalent to 'Kaba'; be the same person inside and out which is equivalent to being a 'peer' (a Sufi spiritual guide); let pious deeds be 'Namaz'; do whatever is acceptable to God, who then in turn is always on the side of such a pious Muslim. On the same page, advice continues for both Muslim and Hindus with this sermon: grabbing others right is an act equivalent to being a pig and a cow; angels are on your side only if you are righteous in your character and acts. Taking a cue from 5 times 'Namaz' of Muslims, it is suggested that our first time Namaz should be adherence to truth; rightful (halal) earnings the second time Namaz; asking well-being of all from God the third Namaz; keeping intentions and the mind clean the fourth Namaz; praising God the fifth time Namaz. With the help of these 5 'Namazs' we can build the highest of character and become a true Muslim.
142	Caution not to get stuck with worldly pleasures.
143	There is an incisive hymn, on this page, on the characteristic of a foolish person - no matter how much you counsel him, whenever he speaks it would cause loss to someone (there is a direct hint here to shun the foolish and not waste one's energy on them).
145	True belief and devotion in God can calm our minds and help us find our way in life.
146	Virtues of early rising and praying emphasized.
149	Caution against sinning; advise on looking inside ourselves (to find answers).

154	Cycle of life-death is an unending game - in order to achieve a state of *Nirvana* one has to immerse in the memory of God and become like him.
155-156	Sermon on controlling one's vices.
165	Passionate appeal to Lord Rama as 'Malik', 'Hari' asking to keep the earnestly appealing devotee in his (God's) fold - pleading that the 'devotee's goodwill is also the Lord's goodwill'.
170, 71,73,74,78	Mention of Lord Rama, Hari, and Gobind in various contexts of worship.
201	Negative mention of Bhoj (feasts offered to and accepted) by Brahmins.
206	Sermon on how a person has come bare in this world and will depart bare.
210	Advice against excessive love for worldly belongings - family - filial, spouse love.
211	8.4 million cycles of birth-death mentioned.
213	Caution against excessive love for money, sex.
217	Lord Ram and prayers to him mentioned several times.
219	Caution against excessive love for money, worldly pleasures, filial love.
220	Advice to put to good use one's life - lest it be equal to losing life in gambling.
222	Caution against excessive love for money, worldly possessions. Advice to fight one's inner demons before fighting external demons.
224	Specific mention of *Ahankar* with examples including those of Ravana.
225	Specific mention of Duryodhana in connection with *Ahankar*.
237	Positives of worshipping God's name enumerated.
238	Once advice on p.237 is observed, all will look friendly, brotherly
242,44,45	Advice to married women to be a religiously devotional spouse.
251, 252	Caution on excessive love for money repeated.
254	Vedas mentioned - all Vedas support worshipping of God as the only way to salvation.

255	Emphasis on early rising and venerating God to cleanse the mind.
256	Virtues of Satsang emphasised.
258	Victory over the mind stands above all else in our life.
259	Relentless pressure of greed lies around us (of which we should safeguard).
260	Passages on the negatives of haume (ego), and the need to keep the mind under check.
262, 263	Emphasis on venerating God's name (Prabu Simran).
265	Merits of Satsang emphasized - only fortunate ones reap benefits from it.
266	*Ahankar* (excess pride) vanishes in the company of pious Sangat (congregation).
266-267	Good deeds of Lord Rama mentioned. An interesting parable with a donkey who washes out all dirt from his body - not knowing good and bad dirt.
271	Virtues of Satsang and the goodness of the company of a *Gurmukh* (God like person) stated. This is followed by the praise of a Brahmgyani - a highly learned and pious person (see below).
272-273	Virtuous qualities of a Brahmgyani who is beyond the attractions of the material world and is an erudite person stated with the advice that his company should be highly sought after.
274	A virtuous person is defined as follows: he does not lie; has the desire to meet the Almighty; does not caste a bad eye on other's woman; seeks the company of persons with saintly traits; does not hear the back-biting of others; does not consider himself superior to others; is not impacted by material goods; does not let sexual thoughts pollute him; keeps his *Inderiyans* under check. 'Such a person, who would be one in a million, can be said to be 'pure' (*Paras* in Gurmukhi).
278	Destiny of an ill-intentioned person is described here as follows: a person who craves to rule is destined to be reborn as a 'dog'; one who considers himself beautiful is an insect in dirt; one who

	considers himself as a doer of good deeds is stuck in the cycles of rebirths; one who considers ruling this earth is a 'fool' and a 'crude' person. A person who is full of humility is shielded from bad deeds in this world and finds peace in the next world as well.
279-80	Caution against criticising a virtuous person.
297	Sermon on too much love for money which can give rise of 5 Vikars – Kam, Krodh, Lobh, Moh, Ahankar (KKLMA).
301	Haughtiness following excessive love for riches works as poison - following it blindly would lead to losses.
304	Caution against being dominated by one's unchecked mind.
305	Merits of early rising and worshipping.
309	This body (and mind) given to us is pious and full of Dharma (religious and moral law governing individual conduct) to be exploited for good ends.
312	Negatives of 'Haume' highlighted.
313	One-liner on a heart dominated by money.
318	Satsang - its importance is highlighted - God is in all of us.
324	By living naked, shaving one's head does not help in attaining God.
327	Sermon on virtuous woman who devotes herself to her husband.
328	World is a burning desire propelling us to go forward.
332	On negatives of 'shrads' (ceremony to honour the elders, *inter alia*, with feast offered to Brahmins) which do not reach parents; negatives of idol worship; blessings of God - Guru emphasised.
333	World is a market - we are all businesspeople - carrying our *Trishna* (thirst, greed, craving for something) over and over again. Note: connection with philosopher Schopenhauer, (Schopenhauer , 2010, p. 23)
334	Prayers essential for all to stay humble - Raag Gauri on positives of the dedication to God.

334-335	Meaning of a real Jogi stated: one that stays at home in family life and faces the world; sermon against hollow rituals.
336	Fruitlessness of *Tiraths* (pilgrimages) after living a futile life.
338	Sermon against going to forests for worship, idol worship, pilgrims, preaching others, going in samadhis (a state of absorptive contemplation of the Absolute), show of wealth. *Road to Nirvana* is via venerating the name of God.
339	Urge to remove *haume* (ego) in us.
340	A good Muslim is defined as one who is engaged in Tarīqah which is the Muslim path toward direct knowledge of God or Reality. A good Brahmin is defined as one who is engaged in the study of Vedas and Puranas.
341	Appeal to us all to search for the presence of God in us.
343	Sermon against the company of people who have anger and have sexual demeanours.
345	So long as one is excessively attracted towards worldly pleasures and material wealth he/she cannot become a good devotee. A devotee who remains in constant meditation develops a deep love for God and is purified. Appeal in all earnest to Lord Rama and to Ravidas to keep the praying devotees in their folds for blessings.
346	In a long passage here, an address is made to Pandits that they have been unable to show a way to *Nirvana*. The role of pilgrimages is emphasized, but by ablutions in holy waters, only outside body is cleansed - so this cannot be the way to it - neither would be a way by way of alms, *Yagnas* (worship, and offerings to any ritual done in front of a sacred fire, often with mantras) idol worship, or worship of incarnated Gods and Goddesses. It is suggested that the ideal way is to be *genuinely immersed* in God's name without razzmatazz; it is the ideal way forward to achieving *Nirvana*.

352	Clear suggestion here that controlling one's mind is equivalent to the knowledge of 6 shastras.
352	Satsang - importance of it mentioned in strongest terms.
355	Advice to Brahmins about the futility of idol worships and *Janeu* the sacred thread.
356	Sermon on coming off from excessive love for the world by repelling one's oscillations, to focus on the mind. Sermons against begging for alms (Sikh religion does not permit or condone begging as a way of life).
363	Caution against excessive love for money with examples.
364	Reference to past life and positive God's grace on virtuous souls.
372	Mention of 8.4 million (84 lacs) cycles of life-death.
372	Futility of a Brahmin's way of life.
377	True pilgrimage is a journey in God's name only.
379	Merits of Satsang extolled.
379-80	Futility of worldly possessions in God's house.
380-81	Advice against mean talk about saints.
386	Mention of Govind (one of many names of Krishna).
390	Negatives of excessive (craving for) wealth.
391	Advice for women on merits of Satsang.
394	Discourse on the negatives of excessive obsessions with maya (money).
398	Discourse on caution to the mind to be aware of excessive love for material things.
400	Caution to the mind to be aware of excessive love for material things surrounding it.
402-3	Caution against 5 Vikars (vices) – KKLMA - if one is addicted to these, he is stuck in the 8.4 million cycles of life and death.
404, 408	Merits of Satsang emphasized.
416	Names of Lords Ram, Hari, and Gopal mentioned.
423,25	Mention of the mind made in the first person on the Vikars.
429	Caution against too much 'I' and 'Mine'.

430	Sermon for women to be good natured, devoted to God - such women live happily with their husbands.
431	Murari (another name for Lord Krishna) mentioned.
432	Sermon on the mind.
439-440	Advice to women to be devoted to God and husband.
445	Sermon on control over one's *Inderiyans;* Treta Yuga mentioned.
447	Mention of life-death cycle; road to *Nirvana* via Guru only.
455	Advice that Guru can be obtained in Satsang which is alternative to going to forests for meditation, doing pilgrimages, and other rituals. Earnest appeal to Lord Shiva for blessings.
461	Caution against cheating fellow human beings.
464	Talk of judgement day - good deeds will help - non-materialistic people live happy.
470	'Yuga' is a period in history. On this page in the scripture, with the help from Vedas it is described as follows. Sam Veda says that in 'Sat Yuga' people were virtuous and truthful; Rig Veda says in 'Treta Yuga' Lord Ram's name was so pure that just by uttering it could cleanse our sins; Yajur Veda says that in 'Dvapar Yuga' Lord Krishna and his cohort Gopis brought love and peace in Vrindavan (place in UP state where Lord Krishna spent his childhood). And now in Kaliyuga, the name of 'Khuda' and 'Allah' is all powerful, Turks and Pathans are supreme (reference to atrocities of invaders – cf, contents of Ch-1). Whatever the Yuga was, people have always found peace and happiness by being immersed in almighty God's name.
470-71	Sermon against pandits - reading Granths, worshipping idols, etc. not required - simply remember God's name.
473	Passage on appreciation of women's contribution to the family, society and community - beginning with her giving birth to looking after a family; it is women through whom family relations get built.

	Short but powerful passage recognizing women's role in Indian society at highly conservative times.
477	In this passage there is an appeal to Hindu and Muslims that instead of heated arguments they should recognise the fact that both have descended from the same God. Simply by being a Muslim one does not go to *Bahist* (heaven); and being a Hindu one does not go to *Dozakh* (hell).
	Sunnat is the way of life prescribed as normative for Muslims on the basis of the teachings and practices of the Prophet Muhammad and interpretations of the Koran.
	Sunnah are the traditions and practices of the Prophet Muhammad, which constitute a model for Muslims to follow.
	Scripture says that if this is the way to be a good Muslim then women cannot achieve Sunnat - i.e., be a good Muslim.
486	Merits of Satsang reinforced.
495	Talk about 'Shastras', 'Vedas', 'Smritians', world tours vs name of God is the true route to *Nirvana*.
499	Brother, mother, father, friend, relatives, and wealth - all these are weak relations - the name of Guru is ever lasting.
502	Strongest words against 5 Vikars - KKLMA.
504-5	Caution against criticising Guru's disciples. Appeal to search and find God within you.
512	Hymns berate persons who follow their mind blindly - our God could be anyone - The scripture urges us to be devoted followers of our chosen God.
516	Brahma and Shiva also remembered as God's names - is there God above them? - question asked.
526	Rebirth happens in many forms depending on what one is thinking at the time of his death. Think of money - reborn as a snake; think of women – reborn as prostitute; think of sons reborn as pig,
536	Mother, father, brother, sons, relatives, wife - all relations are good when alive - when dead, nobody wants to keep you home. All are with you for their own benefits - end time, no one is with you. Interesting dialogue here in 1st person with Mind.

538	Dialogue in 1ˢᵗ person with Mind - counselling the mind not to fall in love with wealth and guard against distractions.
544	Discourse on women - importance for them of spouse, Satsang, and God.
548	#11 in the passage states Satsang as a 'Pathshala' (place of learning/school).
549	Shortcomings of people who follow their mind only - such people are full of conceit.
550	Fool's heart is always full of conceit; if one is obsessed with Lobh, Moh, Ahankar - there is no *Road to Nirvana* for him; he is stuck in the cycles of re-births.
558, 560, 564, 565	1ˢᵗ person counselling to the mind - to be away from negative thoughts.
579-80	On death - speaking ill on death prohibited - live well and die good - get yourself accepted to God while alive by always remembering him. Advice not to weep over someone's death.
585	#4 in the passage is on merits of Satsang - attending Satsang takes you to the path of veneration.
595	Four sources of income mentioned - farming, shop keeping, business, jobs; rightful income is God's name - remembering it.
598	Merits of Satsang emphasized.
601	First person dialogue with the mind - counselling that for a virtuous person, in the end, 'God will stand by him'.
601-602	Accept God's creed and stay with it.
602	Repeated advice not to follow whatever your mind says. Importance of Guru emphasised.
606	Direct reference to Krishna as an embodiment of living God.
607	Advice against not following one's mind blindly.
609	Dialogue on the mind in first person. Emphasis on making us understand that body is perishable - decays into dust - never consider yourself immortal in a mortal body.
610	Emphasis on Satsang which helps us get rid of negative thoughts.

611-12	Emphasis on devotion to Guru and his name. Emphasis on early rising, bathing, and meditation. Advice on shedding *Ahankar* (ego).
613	Merits of mental and emotional links with Guru emphasised.
614	With total devotion to God, fear of 'Yamraj' (God of death) disappears, and internal peace is achieved.
616	Caution that God is watching all our moves. Emphasis on Simran (reminisce - continuous remembrance of God). A true devotee seeks elimination of hollow pride from within him.
617	Reminder that God is omnipresent.
622	Fear disappears if one is truly devoted to God.
623	Merits of praying with Sangat. Singing praise of God keeps the mind calm.
624	A restless wife can find peace in Guru's meditation.
627	Merits of praying in Sangat.
631	Spouse, son, vehicles, all assets are perishable - name of God is the real companion. We have got this human body after several re-births - we should make good of it to be one with God.
632	Abstain from speaking ill of others, casting a bad eye on someone's woman, and back-biting - instead be immersed in the meditation of God's name.
633	Passage on this page is a direct sermon to humans on the following lines: make no mistake - the world around us is perishable - it does not take long for it to perish - comparison here is made with walls made of sand that collapse in no time. There is no one in this world who will go all the way with us. People are with us in happiness, but few will stand by us in grief. Human nature and the mind are compared with a dog's tale that does not get straightened easily; appeal to God that 'I am trying hard - do help me'. In whose heart does God reside? One who is not afraid of hardship and griefs; one who does not fall in love with comforts; one who is fearless; one who considers gold as equivalent to sand i.e., not swayed by material things.

634	World walks with you only in good times and leaves you in bad times - even a beloved wife on the demise of her husband distances herself immediately saying 'he is dead' - in the end only the name of God remains with you.
635	Long passage on advice not to follow blindly one's mind.
635-36	Caution to Pandits against excessive pilgrimages (which are not productive).
639-40	Admiration for women who pray and live within the bounds of their husband's wishes. Merits of Satsang emphasized.
641	Caution against the company of atheists and following one's mind blindly.
641-42	Advice against blindly believing in one's 'Kundli' (horoscope) - blind belief in the (predicted) goodness of it can lead us to conceit. Giving alms alone will not take us to the path of meeting God - good deeds are also required. No correlation between love for money and meditation; way to reach God is via the company of virtuous persons.
642	God cannot be achieved by idol worship; lengthy 'namaskar-am' (greetings/praying with folded hands), 'Dandot' (praying lying face down), by acquiring knowledge; Yoga asanas; or by giving alms. 84 Yoga asanas alone can lengthen our lives but cannot help us meet God. Indulgence in women folk; craving for kingships (titles); rubbing sandalwood on our body are futile - company of Satsang and being in the praise of Lord is the way forward. 'Sorath' raag is considered sweet if women use it to sing the praise of God.
644	Sitting in lotus position, acquiring knowledge, is of only small help in controlling the mind. Real devotion to God's name is essential. 68 'Tiraths' (pilgrimages), can be ineffective in controlling one's mind.
646	Luxury attire and exotic food is of no use if the Lord's name is forgotten.

647	Caution to Pandits against hollow preaching after reading of Vedas.
650	Erudite persons may have acquired knowledge by reading books and by discussions; still might have hearts devoid of the Lord's name.
651-52	Caution to women who do not adore their spouses - cannot be pious women.
652-53	A person who is always obsessed with money is self-centred - and, in reality no one is close to him. Advice to such persons is to start focusing on the Guru's name to find internal peace.
654	Excessive love for money is the road to death of the soul.
655	Dialogue with the mind in first person to stay focused on the name of God.
656	Passage here points towards the basic requirements of a person. In first person narration, a true devotee is asking God for the following: some food to survive, a cot to sleep, and a quilt to cover himself. Once these basic needs are fulfilled, he can be immersed unhindered in his name.
658	Appeal to genuinely believe and focus on the memory of God and not to fall in excessive love for material wealth.
659-60	Human life is similar to a bird in her nest who flies out in the morning. Such is the truth of our lives as well; then why are we being so arrogant? Excessive love for your own body can only lead to gradual self-destruction.
662	You reap what you sow. A thief before a judge cannot prove innocence by arguments - no one vouches for the goodness of a thief. Hence no matter what you attempt - the reality is never hidden from the world (no one stands with a person of dubious character - hence caution against getting into bad deeds).
663	A wise person is one who truly toils towards cleaning his mind of negative thoughts. He is a true Muslim who cleanses his mind of the dirt; he who is a scholar understands the true path of life - such person(s) is accepted in God's court.

664	Sermon to women to be devoted to the Lord's name which will help to be a good wife.
665	Repeated urge to listen to Gurbani - the word of God.
671	Merits of Satsang which help us shed negatives of life.
676	Appeal / urge to put one's life to good use.
678	Sermon in first person to follow the Guru's name.
679	One in whose heart God resides - *Ahankar* does not enter.
686	Sermon to people who worship statues, do pilgrimages, reside in forests (to meditate). All such people can cleanse their mind by truthfully following and remembering the Lord's name.
687	Merits of Satsang emphasized.
687-88	Having God's name in your heart is equivalent to be in a pilgrimage.
689	Reincarnation and its legacy are paid in this life i.e., all good or bad deeds get accounted for in this life itself. Good *Karma* is way to emancipation.
691	Mention of 4 Vedas, 18 Smiritians, and 18 Puranas. All these holy books directly-indirectly sermon us to remember the Lord's name.
692	Reminder that we are inching towards death each minute - so be mindful and engage in the Lord's chants. Water when mixed with water becomes one - so a true devotee when immersed in the Guru becomes like him. Sermon on lonely life on this earth as family or our assets, none travel with us.
692-93	Sermon again on the perishability of this body - instances of Kauravas, Pandavas, (characters from epic *Mahabharta*) and Ravna (character from epic *Ramayna*) cited -several celebrated entities have died in disgrace owing to their *Ahankar.*
693	Commitment to God can help us have control over our *Inderiyans*.
697-98	Dialogue in first person on the merits of 'Naam' (recitation of the Lord's name).

700	Who is a real pal? Answer is given as the person on whom God is merciful. Mother, father, son, relatives, brothers, friends, all are with us, owing to our connection with them in the past life. However, no one is going with us, except the Lord's name recited in Satsang.
705	Sermon to refrain from excessive love for material things - forgetting God in the process is the route to repeated wanderings in re-births.
708	Question mark on accumulating excessive wealth that does not travel with us.
709-10	Satsang and company of saints mentioned as the route to reach God.
711	Fear of ailments, old age, sufferings do not enter a true devotee's mind.
718	Interesting hymn mentioning the holy place Gokul (childhood place near Mathura in UP state in India where Lord Krishna spent part of his childhood).
722-23	Saidpur massacre mentioned. Saidpur, now Eimanabad, is the city where Guru Nanak was present when Babur captured the city. Guru Nanak is said to have witnessed the atrocities and was imprisoned there and made to work in a stone mill.
726	Berating of the mind in first person to be good and not be attracted to world's distractions.
730	Advice that you do not meet God by going around as an ascetic with a stick in hand, head shaved, playing a musical instrument (we still find such ascetics on the streets of India). Way to meet God is to reduce your love for material goods and devote yourself to his name.
733	Heart eventually turns barren if one always blindly follows it.
740	*Gyaninderiyans* (senses used to acquire knowledge) mentioned. We are reminded that this world is akin to a dream which a person is watching in sleep - and falls in love with surreal happenings.
747	Advice that Vedas, Puranas, Smritians, Quran - reading of religious scriptures would not lead us to

	a state of *Nirvana*. True belief and devotion to divinity will.
750	Hymn devoted to Lord Rama to grant peace and well-being.
754	In the hymn on Gods mention is made of Brahma, Vishnu, Mahesh, and Shiva.
773-74	Gratitude to Lord Rama for his benevolence. These pages contain 4 hymns recited during Sikh weddings; in all four hymns blessings of Lord Rama are sought.
785	Sermon for married women who should always be devoted to the glory of God.
787	A devoted spouse to her husband is also as pious as a Sati (ritual in which a wife self-immolated herself on the pyre of her husband).
788	A person who carries the fear of God in his mind will have no other fear.
790	Thieves, prostitutes, thugs, and other anti-social elements work hand in hand with each other with devilish thoughts in them - such people cannot be purified even by rubbing sandalwood on them. Remark about people who eat and fatten up with no trace of God's name in them.
802-03	Merits of Satsang emphasized.
815	Dialogue with the mind in the first person saying it cannot be trusted - following it blindly would only get us in trouble.
823	Advice against criticising and back-biting. People engaged in this fail in all measures of ethical and moral values.
835	Renouncing one's family and living naked in a forest - one might still be haunted by (all sorts of) thoughts. It is much better to simply follow the path of devotion to God.
838	Interesting suggestion on how to be devoted to the divine: observe the devotion of young woman to her husband; miserly to money; how milk takes to water; hungry for food; mother to child; insect to fire; thief to thievery; elephant to sexual urge; and a man to an addiction. So should be a devotee's focus on his devotion to divine.

843	Advice to married women to be devotional to God and spouse.
851	Caution against following one's mind blindly - such a habit can lead to perpetual unhappiness.
855	God pardons previous ill deeds - so long as one is earnest in his repentance.
856-57	Hymn urges devotees to move further from yoga practice and pranayama (basic breathing exercises in yoga). Advice against running after wealth creation all the time.
858	Appeal to Lord Rama asking him to be in our protection and guidance.
865	Five Vikars (KKLMA) exist in this world, but they become slave to a Guru's devotee.
870	'Body dies but soul lives on' a devotee says in this hymn that he is beginning to believe in this premise.
874	You become the person you worship - if you worship a demon, you will become a demon; if you worship a saintly person you will become like a saintly person.
884	Hymn describes how the almighty has staged a huge drama on this earth and is now quietly watching it.
914-15	As is fire with cold - so is the company of a sinner with a saint (i.e., it is soothing).
915	5 Vikars (KKLMA) and a habit of slandering can be overcome by choosing the path of devotion to the almighty.
922	Hindu rituals on death are described in some detail.
923	In this hymn there is a description on how during the last hours of his life, Guru Amardas called family members and urged them not to weep over his death but to remain cheerful and recite katha (religious tale) and kirtan (singing religious hymns). The tradition of katha and kirtan continue till this day.
932	As chemicals erode gold, so do Kam, Krodh which can turn a man weak. Acknowledged on this page in a hymn is the fact that there does exist excessive love of human beings for wealth until he dies.

950	Caution against blindly following one's mind filled with 5 Vikars.
951	Hymn on this page describes the shallow values of holy men, inconsiderate spouses, pseudo-Brahmins, Kazis (Muslim priests), Hindu leaders following Turkish masters' orders, Yogis with long hair and ashes on their bodies. This is Kalyuga, the hymn says - in which a self-centred man masters himself and praises his own acts.
952	Keep body and mind clean and pious for God to reside in it. There is clear message on this page as to what will not lead you to *Nirvana*: meditating in forests, standing on water, shaving one's head, tying iron chains around oneself; eating leaves and forest foods, - all are no help *en-route* to *Nirvana*.
953	One's body is 'Hari Mandir' - in which God resides. There is no need to search for God outside - God is within us. However, people who always follow their mind never find it.
953-54	Legendary tale of love and devotion of Lord Rama and Sita stated.
954	Real blind are those who are away from the Lord's name.
956	Advice to be always humble - you may be in your most beautiful attire riding a horse - still you may fall from it with head down.
966	People who have a healthy mind and body are filled with pious memories of God's love and benevolence that make them happy.
970	Advice to be a good devotee by staying within the bounds of family (and attending to its duties).
973	Dialogue in first person with Mind to be a good devotee.
974	Hymn here clearly states that 5 Vikars (KKLMA) have defuncted spirituality many a person's lives.
988	Ram, Krishna, Dewaki, explicitly mentioned along with the flute of Krishna and greatness of his mother (Devaki) who gave birth to such a great soul.
992	Eulogy of Brahma, Inder, Vishnu, Shiva.

999	Questions put to a person in this hymn: where have you come from? how much you have travelled to be here? Why are you so proud of yourself? Be humble and do the good - remembering that world is perishable and so are you.
1009-1010	God is pleased only with the purity of one's heart. One who has won over his Ahankar (ego) has won over (broken) the chains of life.
1015	Way to find Guru is through Satsang - always remember that all relatives, including parents part company one day - only the divine name stays with us forever.
1036-37	A body in which resides service, contentment, highest character, patience, and such virtues finds God and remains in the memory of God.
1059-60	One who conquers his anger has purified his heart.
1065	Hymn on this page urges reader to make good use of this life which has been obtained after so much hardship.
1084	A Muslim who carries a soft heart, cleanses it from the negativities, stays away from the glitter of this world is as pure as silk.
1097	Similar to a fly who dives in jaggery and gets stuck in it and dies - so is the person who gets stuck in the greed of gathering money. Only the virtuous can rise above it.
1100	Destroyers, rich people, Khans, estate owners, poor, people with high authority, spiritual leaders, - all 8.4 million animals, mammals, and insects are destined to perish one day and leave this world and are doomed to the cycles of rebirths. Only 'Khuda ke bande' (Allah's people), the hymn says, would escape the cycle of rebirths. All are perishable except the lord and his devotees - they escape the cycle of rebirths (and reach Nirvana).
1102-03	Pandits who in 'Yagnas' sacrifice animals are derided in this hymn - they prohibit eating meat and yet consent to animal sacrifice (present day the ritual of 'Bali' in which live animals are sacrificed

	to please Gods and Goddesses still continues in some parts of India and Nepal).
1110	All of us eventually pay for our good and bad deeds.
1124	Hymn dictates that it is idiotic to fall in love with this body which is nothing but sand and dust.
1151	5 Vikars dissipate in the company of saints and Satsang - it is, however, acknowledged in the hymn that it is not always easy to find such a virtuous company.
1177	People who only follow their mind gradually inch towards spiritual death.
1186	Clear advice here to stay away from sycophants and ignore criticism.
1190-91	Clear mention of Muslim led domination of life in those days (cf. Ch-1,2).
1216	One gains respect by being in Satsang.
1219	All the three 'Lokas' (abodes) in Hindu mythology i.e., Shiv Lok, Braham Lok, Indra Lok are recognised in hymn on this page. Mention is also made of the fact that worship brings peace - a fact which is also mentioned in Vedas, Puranas, and Smritis. Yogis and saints have all recognised this truth.
1229	18 Puranas and 6 Shastras mentioned in this hymn.
1237	Man's mind is a room with a lock on it - Lord's name is required to open it.
1251	Excessive love and attachment to wealth, family, relatives, is self-defeating as nothing lasts forever nor does it travel with us.
1261	Sermon to Pandits to think beyond the reading of Vedas and Puranas and delve earnestly in the glory of God.
1265	Caution against following one's mind blindly as doing so could lead to eternal shame.
1279	Acknowledged here is the fact that as rains impact people in different walks of life differently (e.g., brings joy for farmers, and hardship for travellers) so does the discourse on divine impact differently on different people. Implication is that despite all good intentions and coaxing, in the end, the divine discourse *impacts* differently on different people.

1288	Advice here for atheists - it is good to remain silent - a better option when one has no faith in God's name. Kingship (power), wealth, beauty (yearning for sex), higher castes, and youth are 5 thugs who have looted this world - whosoever has followed them blindly has lost respect.
1303-04	Kam, Krodh, Lobh are the root cause of repeated cycles of rebirths.
1312, 22, 35	Satsang is God's Pathshala (school) through which Godly hymns teach us good - as God resides in Satsang.
1346	The world itself is 'Hari Mandir' but is barren without God's name in it.
1348	By donning saffron colour outfit, piercing ears, begging for food, does not lead one to Gurudom, in fact doing so could make one more unhappy. By going silent does not kill your inner vices; doing so a person might in fact remain stuck in the cycle of rebirths.
1352	Simplicity without any razzmatazz is recommended in worship.
1353	Hymn here specifies that a Pandit's job is to acquire knowledge; Brahmin's job is to ponder over Vedas; Khatris job is to be warriors; Shudara's job is to serve. However, the prime focus for all should be to remember God and reminisce in his name. By doing so, in all earnest, one become God like (i.e., inherits his qualities).
1364	Clear mention of Lord Rama's name which brings peace and tranquillity.
1365	Directive over not to weep over the death of a saint who has found an abode from which no one will drive him out. We could cry over the death of non-saintly (who are stuck in the cycles of rebirths).
1369	Instead of shaving one's head, one should shave off bad deeds from one's mind.
1371	Caution against the worshipping of idols to reach God's kingdom.
1372	Clear advice that in order to make the best out of your 'diamond' like life, there is no need to

	renounce family and community life (God can be found by living and serving the community).
1373	God's name is 'Diamond'; A true devotee is similar to a trader of diamonds as he trades/spreads the gospel of God in the Satsang. A sandalwood tree never leaves its cool fragrance despite being surrounded by snakes who coil around it for its fragrance and cooling. So is a true saint who does not renounce his good character despite surrounded by millions of non-believers and people of dubious characters.
1374	As it happens with the make-up of cities, this body too (is made of 5 elements - air, water, fire, earth, and space) and returns as dust and ashes to the ground.
1376	An incisive hymn on this page that reminds us of the futility of earnings by shady means after elaborate worship rituals. It is equivalent to losing one's finely ground grain in mud (i.e., illicit earnings are not good).
1377	Hymn on this page asserts that if you are a person with a family and do perform your family duties well and also do not drown yourself in chasing the money then you are doing well; but if you are engaged in chasing money most of the time then it is unfortunate, and you also belong to nowhere. Another hymn eloquently explains that the time of our death is fixed even before we are born.
1378	If someone inflicts grief, you do not reciprocate by giving back grief - instead stay calm and do not lose your demeanour. Respect clay as you will return to it one day.
1379	A famous hymn on this page advises us to be happy with a simple meal and not to be jealous watching someone eat an elaborate meal.
1381	If one does not read Namaz five times a day and never visits a mosque (for Satsang) his life cannot be commended. Hymn directs that we wake up (early) do 'wudu' (wash our face, arms, wipe the head and wash the feet) and perform Namaz.

	A head that does not bow before God (Allah) is worthless and can be incinerated as dry wood.
1382	Hymn here says that we do good to people, even to those who do not do good to us - this way (i.e., by adopting this pious way) our body will stay healthy.
1383-84	If you rise early and do not pray then early rising is only a partial success.
1390	Guru Nanak's lineage traced back to Krishna, Guru Angad, and Guru Amardas.
1403	Hymn here says that our body, our dwelling, spouse's affection, this world - all these are mind games.
1413	Message in this hymn says that if one totally forgets Guru's name, he is doomed to do bad acts such as kill a Brahmin, a cow, or even his own daughter - such people earn wrath of the Lord and the people.
1417	Interesting hymn on this page - hymn advises us to refrain from trusting a greedy person. In the end, however, a greedy person comes to be deceived himself as no one would help him; such a person always earns a bad name.
1419	Caution against excessive love for money - people obsessed with money are doomed to cycles of rebirths (anti-thesis to achieving *Nirvana*).
1424	An atheist may always be conceited - in his conceit ('haume') he often ends up choosing the wrong path.
1427	Reaching last few pages of the scripture, message here in first person is that we should all try and renounce 5 Vikars – KKLMA - and choose the right path of 'Vairaag' (salvation).
1429	In this penultimate page of the scripture, truth about the certainty of death is repeated - when old age descends, head starts to shake, we straddle while walking, eyesight wanes, - still too often we are attached to material goods. O 'Nanak', Lord Rama departed from this world - so did Ravna - this world is similar to a dream - all shall depart (and dream would break) one day - so we should shed our unending love for money and remember God.

Source: (a) Sikh Sacred Scripture, *Guru Granth Sahib*, (b) (Singh M. , 2009); (c) Sri Guru Granth Darpan http://www.gurugranthdarpan.net/darpan.html; (Accessed intermittently on various dates) (d) (Singh G. , 1960). (Singh S. , Sri Guru Granth Darpan (in Gurmukhi), 1972).

Appendix Table 5. 2 SGPC Approved Written Sikh Code of Conduct

Code of Conduct (CoC) are guidelines specifying the norms (or rules) of behaviour for an individual, group, or an organisation. In the context of religion, such norms can be found embedded in the sacred scripture of the religion and in the code of behaviour based on mutual beliefs that come to be expected by its members.

In the case of Sikhs, in the previous chapter we highlighted the norms in the scripture and dictated by self-example by Sikh Gurus. In addition, the central committee of the Sikhs - the SGPC (Shiromani Gurdwara Parbandhak Committee) has published a written CoC (SGPC, 2019). This CoC has in it the key norms of behaviour specified in the scripture, plus additional rules of conduct agreed by the central committee.

To get a holistic view of the CoC of Sikhs i.e., the one found in the scripture and in the SGPC ratified document, this author has culled relevant portions applicable to an individual.

SGPC Approved Code of Conduct[167]

The CoC - '*Sikh Rahit Maryada*' is available on the website of the SGPC[168]. It is a 34-page document that has laid out the expected individual, family, and social guidelines Sikhs are to follow. The work on this CoC was started by the SGPC in 1936 and completed in 1945 after extensive consultations (SGPC, 2019, pp. 1-8) and has been hailed by the Committee as one of its major achievements. It should be noted that, prior to this final

---

[167] Translated from Gurmukhi by the author.
168. http://sgpc.net/?page_id=653   In Gurmukhi (Retrieved 20-9-2021).

approved version of CoC by the SGPC, several versions of CoCs existed. McLeod (McLeod W. H., 2003) has provided a summary of these codes of conduct[169].

The SGPC ratified CoC is thorough and includes sections on the daily routine of prayers, etiquettes to be observed in a gurdwara, rules governing *Kirtan,* (recitation of religious hymns with musical instruments), reading of the scripture, preparation of *Prasad,* and food prepared in the community kitchen, guidelines related to celebrations at birth, wedding, death, and community service[170].

What follows is a summary of CoC for individuals culled from the SGPC ratified CoC and translated from original which is in Gurmukhi.

Appendix Table 5. 3 Summary of SGPC Code of Conduct for an Individual

1. A Sikh wakes up early in the morning in the first *peher* (3-6am; cf. Ch-2,3) of the day, bathes, and recites morning prayers *Japuji.* In addition, as a daily routine he also recites evening prayers, *So Dar Rehraas,* during sunset- and night-time prayers, *Sohila,* before going to sleep. He is also supposed to recite a full-length prayer, *Ardas,* after morning and evening recitation of prayers.

---

169 Rahit-namas summarised include, *Prahilad Rai Rahit-nama, Sakhi Rahit Ki* (by Nandlal), *Desa Singh Rahit-nama, Daya Singh Rahit-nama.* McLeod's list includes 21 complete *Rahit-namas,* and excerpts from publications that include reference to CoCs.

170 Prasad is an offering - sweets, fruit, or food, for devotees - either brought by devotees or prepared on the premises. In Sikh gurdwaras, it is mostly taken to be a semi-solid sweet prepared with three ingredients - flour, sugar, and ghee (clarified butter). In Hindu as well as Sikh religion, food (always vegetarian) is ceremonially prepared as an offering to the divine and is considered holy and blessed and is always accepted when offered.

The CoC provides additional stanzas which should be recited as part of the morning and evening prayers and also provides a full script of the *Ardas*. No alterations are permitted in this; some additions such as asking for the blessing for the newly born, newlywed, and peace for the departed soul can be added by the prayer reader.

2. It is advised that an individual gains most by being in the company of fellow devotees (Satsang); hence he should make the attempt to read and recite the hymns in Satsang.

3. An individual should leave his shoes outside and make sure the feet are clean (several gurdwaras provide water tubs to walk through before entering a gurdwara. The devotee should not be carrying any intoxicants on him, and his head should be covered. Once inside in the presence of the scripture (which is placed on a higher platform) he should sit on the (lower) ground at an available place next to anyone, irrespective of the caste, colour, and creed of the person.

4. A Sikh is encouraged to install in his home a copy of the scripture in a separate room designated for it. He is also advised to encourage his children to learn to read Gurmukhi script for him to be able to read the scripture. Preferably, each morning before the morning meal he should open the scripture to read an excerpt from it and contemplate over its meaning. He is also encouraged to read the scripture at whatever pace he can and make an effort to complete the reading in his time.

5. A Sikh is to believe in one God and should have total devotion in the 10 Gurus of the Sikhs. It is believed that after Guru Nanak, successive Gurus were only his embodiment - so in essence, all 10 Gurus are in fact one Guru.

- A Sikh should not worship statues of Gods/Goddesses and abstain from hollow rituals e.g., those related to certain days, nights, life cycle (saṃskāra), death and ancestor worships, or worship by way of yajñas (ritual performed in front of a sacred fire with the chanting of mantras).

- A Sikh is free to read Vedas and other classics for knowledge purposes.
- A Sikh may be deeply religious, but he should never hurt a non-believer.
- A Sikh should always pray before beginning a new job.
- A Sikh should gain knowledge of Sikhism and also educate his children in it.
- A Sikh should keep his hairs and should not pierce his ears or nose. He should abstain from intoxicants.
- Female infanticide is forbidden.
- A Sikh should not steal or gamble; he should earn his living by dint of his labour and help the poor.
- A Sikh should respect all women and should not indulge in adultery; similarly, a woman should be loyal to her spouse and household.
- Face coverings are forbidden.
- Salutation for both male and females when they meet is the same (*Wahe Guru ji ka Khalsa; Wahe Guru ji ki Fatah* (Khalsa belong to the Almighty; victory be to the Almighty).
- Beyond turbans and long boxer style shorts there is no restriction on clothing for both sexes; a turban is optional for females.
- A Sikh should not demand a dowry while wedding his son.

NOTE: Service to the community and for the mankind in general occupy a central place in Sikh conduct. This takes many forms - donations and work in community kitchens, assistance during epidemics, assistance in educational institutions, clinics, hospitals, cash, or kind help with weddings of couples from poorer households.

Appendix Table 5. 4 52 Edicts of Guru Gobind Singh
(Translated from Gurmukhi by the author)

1. Make a living by honest means.
2. Donate 1/10th earnings.
3. Learn by heart all *Gurbani* (hymns in Sikh scripture).
4. Rise early in the morning.
5. Serve a fellow Sikh with reverence.
6. Know the meaning of *Gurbani* from the learned.
7. Maintain 5 symbols of Sikhs with determination.
8. Practice hymns (in the scripture).
9. Stay focused on venerating the true God.
10. Recognize the scripture as a true Guru.
11. Pray before the start of a job.
12. At births, deaths, weddings, recite *Japuji*, prepare food and after reciting *Anand Sahib,* serve (food) first to 5 pious Sikhs and the *Granthi* (reader of the scripture) and then to congregation.
13. So long as *Prasad* is being served the congregation stays quiet.
14. Abstain from physical relations without marriage.
15. Consider non-related females either your sister, daughter, or mother.
16. Do not rebuke your spouse in a violent way.
17. Renounce the vices of tobacco and slander.
18. Seek company of devout dedicated Sikhs.
19. Do not be lethargic towards jobs that *you* need to complete.
20. Listen to *Gurbani* and religious discourse each day.
21. Abstain from slander, back-biting, and envy.
22. Do not pride in your wealth, youth, ancestry, or caste.
23. Keep thoughts pious and virtuous.
24. Keep yourself engaged in devout works.
25. Accept that God is the reason of our intellectual strength.

26. Do not trust people who swear (to convince you of anything).
27. Cultivate strength of free thinking.
28. Do study politics too.
29. Deal with the enemy with the right tact and diplomacy; if all fails battle is a justified act of *dharma*.
30. Learn the art of weaponry and horse riding.
31. Study classics of other religions but maintain faith in the scripture.
32. Follow teachings of the Guru.
33. After reciting *Rehraas* (evening prayer) do the prayer (*Ardaas*) standing up.
34. Recite *Sohila* (bed-time prayer) before going to sleep.
35. Keep (head) hairs covered.
36. Address a Sikh by his complete name.
37. Abstain from drinking and offering liquor to others.
38. Do not give your daughter to a clean-shaven person; give her to a pious Sikh household.
39. Accomplish tasks according to guidelines in the scripture.
40. Do not spoil anyone's work by back-biting.
41. Do not hurt anyone with harsh words.
42. Do pilgrimages of gurdwaras only.
43. Honour your said word.
44. Help and serve guests, strangers, the needy, persons in grief and a handicapped person.
45. Consider daughter's earnings as poison for you (i.e., refrain from living on it).
46. Refrain from becoming only a showbiz Sikh.
47. Respect and protect your hairs.
48. Abstain from theft, pseudo-friendship, thuggery, deception, and trickery.
49. Trust a Gursikh.
50. Abstain from false witness statements.
51. Do not lic.
52. Practice equality in serving *langar* (community kitchen food).

**

CHAPTER 6 ROAD TO NIRVANA:THE SIKH WAY

ਜਗੁ ਸੁਪਨਾ ਬਾਜੀ ਬਨੀ ਖਿਨ ਮਹਿ ਖੇਲੁ ਖੇਲਾਇ ॥

The world is a drama, staged in a dream.
In a moment, the play is played out.

Guru Nanak Dev ji

https://twitter.com/Supriya23bh/status/926535325962321920/photo/1

Knowing yourself is the beginning of all wisdom
(Aristotle)

Introduction

We arrive at this chapter after acquainting ourselves with the Sikh history and the moral principles of the Sikhs originating in the teachings of Sikh Gurus and the Sikh holy scripture. Both, the teachings of Sikh Gurus and the scripture, carry within them the blueprints of the *Road to Nirvana*.

Recall from chapter-1 that the word 'Sikh' has its origin in the Sanskrit word śiṣya, meaning a 'disciple' whose job it is to learn as a pupil from his Guru. We broaden this definition of a Sikh as 'a disciple whose job it is to be a life-long learner and practitioner of moral principles of his Gurus and his Gurus' scripture', so well that one day, the Guru's Sikh, and whosoever is following in the footsteps of Gurus and the scripture's teachings attains *Nirvana.*

To recapitulate, *Nirvana* is a state of ultimate bliss - a transcendent state in which a person has been released from the effects of *Karma* and the cycles of re-births. In common parlance, the term is understood as an apex state of peace and happiness.

The ultimate aim of life in Sikhism and its sister religions - Hinduism, Buddhism and Jainism is to free oneself from the cycles of rebirths by attaining a state of *Nirvana.* The state of *Nirvana* can be reached by good *Karma*[171]. *Karma* is the sum total of a person's actions in *this* and *previous* lives, which together, decide his future. Good *Karmas* are desired as they help liberate a person from the repeat cycles of rebirths - it is believed that bad *Karmas* could keep us forever in this cycle, with no certainty that we will be reborn as humans - with bad *Karmas* we could be reborn and stuck in the animal and mammal kingdom for ever - so the theory goes[172].

The purpose of Sikh moral philosophy is to teach us how we can be virtuous and do good deeds i.e., good *Karmas,* for us to lead a virtuous life and free ourselves and attain *Mukti* i.e., liberation from the cycles of re-births.

---

[171] Karma is sometimes wrongly interpreted by some writers as fate. It is actually a short form of '*Karmaphala'*, the outcome of one's actions.
[172] One is reminded of Marcus Aurelius' sermon of finding one's place in the universe and understanding that everything came from nature, and so everything shall return to it in due course; Marcus Aurelius also advised staying focused and to be without distraction all the while maintaining strong ethical principles such as "being a good man" (Chrystal, 1902).

It needs to be pointed out here that there is no separate or specific mention of happiness in the Sikh scripture. The concept of happiness is embedded in the moral principles of Sikh philosophy. The principles presume that if one strives to be a virtuous person, he would be intrinsically happy most of the time. Striving to inculcate and strengthen personal, family and community virtues (Figure 6.1) woud keep a person occupied with pious ways of life and keep him engaged and happy. Alongside, one can always pursue chosen hobbies and passions which could supplement a person's happiness index.

An engrossed lifestyle of working to make a living, pursuing one's pastime and passions, and striving to be a virtuous person at the same time would not leave room for negative thoughts or boredom in life. As Guru Nanak has so rightly pointed out (pic above) 'the world is a drama staged in a dream; in a moment the play is played out.' This simple but profound statement tells us that all of us have limited time; we should make the best of this time for us, our family, and for the world in general. Alongside making ourselves happy, if we can make others happy as well, we have played out our time well[173].

Two terms - 'Virtuous person and 'Spiritual person' are sometimes used as synonymous. There is a difference though. A Virtuous person is an ethical and moral person with a sense of right and wrong. Such a person e.g., would be honest, benevolent, forgiving, courageous, and kind. Virtues, some of which may be innate i.e., we may be born

[173] Here we could invoke the concept of Italian economist Vilfredo Pareto's 'efficiency criteria' in which social welfare is maximized such that re-allocation of resources would not make anyone better off without making someone worse off. Our goal in life could be to move ourselves to a Pareto efficient state.

with them (they are in our DNA), mostly need to be cultivated for us to become a virtuous person. 'Spiritual' means relating to religion or religious beliefs. A spiritual person believes in some supreme authority, usually God, who is above him, and in whom he believes. For a *truly* spiritual person, it is a *necessary condition* to be a virtuous person first, as it encompasses within it the foundations to become a truly spiritual person.

In this author's opinion, even if we disregard, as a sceptic, the concept of the *next* life - a case for a virtuous living can still be made to keep us happy and contented in *this* lifetime, notwithstanding what happens to us in the next life. If we lead a virtuous life and are reborn in the human kingdom in our next life, we have at least the opportunity to try even harder to reach *Nirvana* in the life after. Let us see how we can do this the Sikh way in this lifetime.

Sikh Road to *Nirvana*

In 340BC Aristotle decreed to the world a model of moral philosophy, not knowing that in future there could be an application of his ideas in the form a brand-new religion. The Sikh holy scripture has in it the ideas of Gurus and Aristotle's principles which together give us the blueprints of the *Road to Nirvana*. Sikh Gurus, as we have described in the previous chapter, added value to 'Aristotle's Model' enriching it in many ways. In order for us to lay the tarmac for the *Road to Nirvana*, let us list the essential ingredients of it. We shall first list them and then explain their importance, one at a time.

Based on Sikh Gurus' teachings and the wisdom in the scripture, we have put together the essential ingredients of the *Road to Nirvana* in Figure 6-1. This figure has four sets of virtues presented in the top four boxes – the first box of Set-1 virtues consists of 'personal virtues' expected of a Sikh; the second box of Set-2 virtues consist of 'ten specific virtues of ten Gurus', which Sikhs are expected to inculcate in themselves; the third box consists of family virtues, a Sikh is expected to internalise and impart to his family; the fourth box consists of 'community virtues' that a Sikh is expected to imbibe in himself.

Rectangular boxes beneath the square boxes list the virtues. The two-way arrows between the four sets of virtues tell us that the virtues in four square boxes *interact and impact on each other*. For instance, a person's robust personal virtues would influence virtues listed in other boxes and *vice versa*. Before we proceed further credit is due to Greenlees (Greenlees, 1952) who for the first time succinctly summed up ten specific virtues of ten Sikh Gurus (listed in set 2 virtues in Figure 6.1) that we have adopted in this book.

The ingredients presented in modular form in this Figure 6.1 may look restrictive in the first instance as they are directed towards a devout Sikh who follows the dictum of Gurus and the scripture *in toto* for him to lead a virtuous life of peace and contentment. However, if we look closely at the figure, we realise that barring the routine of prayers prescribed for the Sikhs, the elements of the model are very much applicable to anyone who can direct himself to the path to *Nirvana* by following these elements. The virtue of prayers, much emphasized in Sikh moral philosophy, also comes handy in this journey. In fact, prayers are an integral part of all religions anyway.

Taking a cue from Rostow's (Rostow, 2017) stages of economic growth described in chapter 5, virtues in Set-A are 'pre-requisite virtues' for us to be in a ***pre-take-off*** stage towards reaching *Nirvana*; once this stage has been reached, Set-B virtues should be won over to move us further to the **take-off** stage. After the successful take-off stage has been accomplished, Set-C virtues should be won over to propel us to the **maturity stage.** The overlap between acquisition and practice of virtues is possible and should be encouraged.

Set-A Personal Virtues – *Pre-take-off Stage to Nirvana* (5 goals to achieve)

1. The basic working premise of the *Road to Nirvana* is that, unless there is an inhibiting condition (e.g., an ailment) anyone wishing to achieve *Nirvana* should work towards habiting his soul **in a healthy body and healthy mind. This is Goal #1.**

2. Once condition #1 is met, a conscious effort should be made to inculcate the following virtues shown by example by 10 Sikh Gurus: virtue of humility, obedience, equity, service, self-sacrifice, justice, mercy, purity of service, calmness, and courage. **This is Goal #2.**

3. To help achieve #2, the company of virtuous persons should be sought e.g., in religious congregations (church, gurdwara, shrine, synagogue and the like), and in social circles as well. **This is Goal #3.**

4. The end goal of #1, #2, and #3 should be to gradually work towards controlling the following 5 human weaknesses -

unwarranted sexual urges, anger, greed, excessive attachment to family and the world and one's ego. **This is Goal #4.**

5. To assist in #1-4, a check on the following 5 sources of our interface with the world should be kept - vision, hearing, smell, taste, and touch (skin). **This is Goal #5.**

Set-B Family Virtues – *Take-off Stage to Nirvana* (3 goals to achieve)

1. Teach children, among all else, religious virtues. **This is Goal #6.**
2. Retain loyalty to spouse. **This is Goal #7.**
3. Care for family elders. **This is Goal #8.**

Set-C Community Virtues – *Drive to Maturity Stage* (4 goals to achieve)

1. Donate, keep aside part of earnings for just causes ($1/10^{th}$ recommended in Sikhism). **This is Goal #9.**
2. Extend help in community works. **This is Goal #10.**
3. Help out in times of crisis e.g., epidemics. **This is Goal #11.**
4. Do not discriminate anyone on the basis of caste, creed, or colour. **This is Goal #12.**

Rationale of Set-A Personal Virtues

Virtue of Good Health and Sound Mind

Personal virtues Set-A says that we should all pursue and inhabit a healthy body and mind, both of which are very much related[174]. This is sound advice with far reaching implications. There is an ever-greater emphasis placed on controlling one's mind which is considered to be the root cause of all that we do. So much so that in one place the scripture says in just 3 words *'Mann Jite Jagjeet'* (*'Mind is won'; 'world is won'*).

Succinctly put, we need to keep a tight control on our wants and desires. Western thought recognizes that 'wants are unlimited', but Eastern philosophies would want a tight control on wants. A key tenet of Sikhism (also in Buddhism) is that much of our grief originates in unfulfilled desires. Ergo, if we want to be happy, we should learn to keep a tight leash on our wants. Less of one's wants and desires, less is one's unhappiness. Once this control is achieved, it is easier to move to the next stage of controlling one's mind - that of concentrating and directing it into 'good' thoughts and objectives, and eventually into a contemplative bliss.

To have a mind to whom *we* want to do, what *we* want it to do, we also have to have, as a pre-requisite, a healthy body in which our (healthy) mind can inhibit. Good

---

[174] Importance of this connection can be gauged from the fact that a Google search with the key words 'mind-body connection research' yielded nearly 300 million hits. The legacy, however, is carrying on from previous works. See e.g., https://www.ncbi.nlm.nih.gov/pmc/articles/PMC1456909/ (Accessed 12-1-2022). This is the year 2006 article in *European Molecular Biology Organization* by Howard Wolinsky doi:10.1038/sj.embor.7400670.

health is a pre-requisite anyway to successfully attend to and enjoy all the chores in life (even money-making!). Ill-health can keep a person in a perpetual cycle of unhappiness, depression, and can be a cause of suicidal thoughts and in extreme cases – suicides.

There can be several reasons for bad health - most, however, are man-made. A recent study (Ohrnberger, Fichera , & Sutt, 2017) confirmed life-style choices, diet, smoking, drinking, stress, and cognitive skills to be the major inhibiting causes contributing to physical and mental health. Even if we disregard scientific studies, commonsense dictates that the lack of a sensible daily routine, unhealthy food, a mind that is bereft of virtuous thoughts, can all lead to the deterioration of physical, and in turn, mental health. Deterioration of physical health usually begins with obesity, a curse, which is fast becoming a global trend; sadly, even in countries which have a tradition of simple, healthy home-cooked food, are falling prey to junk food popularised by multinational enterprises (MNEs) chains and domestic food chains mimicking the success of MNE food joints with larger, invariably greasy portions. In 2021, the global market for weight loss products and services was a staggering $255 billion which is projected to grow to $377 billion by 2026[175].

---

[175] https://www.globenewswire.com/news-release/2021/08/03/2273363/28124/en/Key-Trends-and-Opportunities-in-the-Global-Weight-Loss-Products-and-Services-Market-to-2026.html (Accessed 31-7-2022).

Figure 6. 1 A Virtuous Model of Sikh Life

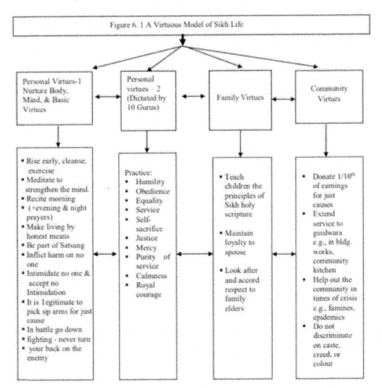

The impact of poor mental and physical health on family, social, and work life can be profound, resulting in strained relations, fall in work productivity, in worst cases loss of job and livelihood. No wonder, therefore, that good health had always been considered a factor of prime importance by Sikh Gurus in Sikhism. The Sikh way urges an early rise as a first step to a healthy life[176]. In modern working life, where travel to work may be involved, we may have to leave home early for work, for which we have to be organized - the process of which should begin with an early rise. One does not have to have a detailed routine of exercises (which can be left to weekends e.g.) - a simple stretch, free-hand and breathing exercises requiring concentration can calm the mind and contribute positively to health. Equally important is what we eat. Along with a healthy diet, the amount we consume should also be controlled - particularly for evening meals (ideally consumed early) and drinks need to be kept in check, especially if we are aiming to rise early to a healthy start the next day[177].

Ten Core Virtues

The second set of virtues that the Sikh way of life urges us to inculcate is the ten virtues in our character - the virtues of Humility, Obedience, Equality, Service, Self-sacrifice, Justice, Mercy, Purity of service, Calmness and Courage. Personal and professional executive development programmes in the corporate world have now started to pay

---

[176] Experience shows that with enough sleep, when we wake up early, we not only feel alert all day, but we also control time instead of time controlling us with a late-rising up routine.
[177] Increasing trend of working from home owing to COVID can be a blessing if used judiciously,

attention to several of these virtues in their training programs. For instance, the Servant-Leader model described in chapter-3 has in it several traits embedded from this set of ten virtues. Let us analyse why these virtues are so important to be inculcated in our character.

Let us take **'Humility'** first. Humility is not meekness, submissiveness, timidity, lack of confidence, or pride. True humility is the absence of aggressiveness and unwarranted assertiveness in character. For instance, at the workplace, to make a point we can be humble and still be quietly confident. The same approach can be applied in social settings.

Similarly, **'Obedience'** does not mean being subservient, tame, docile, or slavish; what it means is amenable, obliging, and yielding for what is rightly asked for.

'Equality' refers to just and fair treatment to anyone we come across (in one-off or repeat interactions) in our social or professional life. By keeping our behavioural pattern this way, we play a fair game which can yield a feeling of satisfaction and happiness - such an approach can also yield goodwill for us.

'Service': we provide service when we offer help in cash or kind to people in need. Such an act encompasses within it benevolence, grace, kindness and similar other traits. Services can be provided at personal or community level and goes a long way in bonding social ties. Studies have shown that the act of giving back to the community enhances our happiness, health, and sense of well-being.

'Self-sacrifice' goes a step further than 'Service' as, self-sacrifice means we give up our own interests to help others - an act that displays our selflessness and sense of caring and compassion - we deny comforts to ourselves to help others. Such an act can yield immense intrinsic happiness and enrich our spiritual lives.

'**Justice**' refers to fairness in the way people are dealt with e.g., in the court of law with regard to the crimes committed and punishment given. In day-to-day life, a person who has in him the virtue of justice believes that all have equal rights and that all opportunities should be treated in fairness to all. In day-to-day life, people with power over subordinates e.g., in the workplace or in social settings, can derive a great deal of satisfaction and happiness with their belief and practice of this virtue. A key point in Plato's Republic is that justice is a right action and good in itself and that it should be pursued even when it does not seem to confer immediate advantage (Lee D. , 2007).

'**Mercy**' refers to compassionate treatment to someone over whom we have the power to punish. History has examples where winning kings in battle have spared the lives of prisoners. Mercy treatment comprises in it the act of forgiveness and kindness. In whatever situation we are in our daily lives, if we have the 'mercy' virtue in us we shall have the ability to show it at one time or the other. A common situation in which it can arise is when we hire someone to work for us.

'**Purity of service**' refers to a service provided with deep affection that is devoid of any malice or prejudice. A recent example from COVID pandemics is Sikh volunteers proffering their services to help, treat and cremate infected dead bodies when people, in some cases even families, were reluctant - rather petrified to come forward for the funeral, the proper methodological completion of which is such an integral part of Indian culture and religion.

The **'Calmness'** virtue refers to a composed state of mind, particularly in difficult situations. The virtue of calmness has in it the strength and courage to assess a situation calmly and act accordingly. Our workplaces are abound with situations that require a calm approach to deal with a situation. People with this virtue can recall how they have had a difficult situation diffused when, if it was not handled with a certain calm, could have gone seriously wrong.

'Courage' is a broad construct which may mean different things in different situations e.g., in battlefields, street fights, standing for one's rights, courage to say the right thing at right time, reacting to injustice meted to someone, and such other situations. In Sikh psyche it is generally taken to mean holding fearlessly in combat even when the odds are against you. Sikh history is replete with examples of this - not long ago a motion picture on such an act of valour was made (Saragarhi[178]). The Sikh scripture is very clear on this virtue - at one place it says that 'once you hold someone's arm to help, you should never leave it - no matter what the cost (or situation) is. In modern social parlance, the virtue of courage means not showing cowardice when courage is required - in what proportion and how it should be exercised will depend on the situation.

Virtue of Pious Company (Satsang)

The Sikh scripture repeatedly urges us to seek the company of pious people. The scripture was compiled over 400 years ago and accordingly the concept of pious

---

178 https://en.wikipedia.org/wiki/Battle_of_Saragarhi (Accessed 12-1-2022). In 1897 in the Battle of Saragarhi (a village in the border district of Kohat, in present-day Pakistan) 21 Sikh soldiers refused to vacate their posts and fought to their last man against 10,000 Afghans.

company or *Satsang* has the connotation of older times when it was mostly sought in religious congregations which are held in present times as well. The pace of modern life has led to the standardisation of these congregations which are now held mostly on weekends. Secondly, the nature and mode of conduct has also altered, e.g., sometime before the proceedings of the day come to a close, attendees are appraised of gurdwara accounts and forthcoming programs. However, the core consisting of sermons and *Kirtan* is the same. Kirtan, which is the act of praising divinity with chants and music is a powerful medium that can move souls - repeated listening of which can help keep devotees stay on the righteous path. Like minded devotees also form clusters and exchange information on social and community development issues.

Beyond religious congregations, the company of virtuous people can also instil and strengthen the sense of righteous virtues - honesty, fairness, courage, justice, etc. in members of the cluster. Going back further we can recall how our parents were particular that we kept good company. A good company, not only in our early days, but in later days as well has a lot to contribute to shaping our character. In Hindu religion the tradition of Guru-Shishya (pupil) is an age old one. In olden times in a Gurukul (Guru's residence), parents sent their children to acquire education. Pupils lived and intermingled with each other, learning from in-house and visiting Gurus and saints as the tradition was in those days. One can also imagine pupils learning from each other. Some pupils became Gurus in due course. It is no exaggeration to say that the company we keep greatly influences our character.

In modern times and parlance *Satsang* should mean the seeking of company that can enhance and enrich our virtuous lives. With modern communication channels it should not be difficult to find, form and strengthen the like-minded clusters around us and anywhere in the world. Access to virtual means of communications has made this very much possible - i.e., if we have the will to do so.

Five Human Weaknesses

As stated earlier, the end goal of 'Set of Personal Values' #1, #2, and #3 should be to work towards controlling five human vulnerabilities - 'Unwarranted sexual urges', 'Anger', 'Greed', 'Excessive attachment to family and worldly objects', and 'Ego'. The emotional, social, and financial costs of these vices, if unchecked, can be overwhelming. Let us briefly examine these in turn.

Sexual urges are the feelings that result from the urge to satisfy sexual desires. In the present day we are surrounded by provocative sexual material and porn sites. A Google search of 'adult websites' yielded hundreds of sites ranging from porn, escorts, fetish, to country specific sites. Around 4% of internet is porn related. Globally, each day 5% of the time of adults is spent watching 30-60 minutes of it[179]. The off-shoot of this is enhanced sexual desires - fulfilment of which can result in extra-marital affairs, cheating on partners, separations, divorces, contracting infections some of which are still not treatable and in extreme cases homicides.

In open societies, up until the marriage vows are exchanged, couples have had relationships. These relationships, if continued post-maritally or when one gets addicted to thrills of extra-marital affairs, can turn nasty and

---

179 https://www.psychologytoday.com/gb/blog/all-about-sex/202010/how-much-time-does-the-world-spend-watching-porn (Accessed 13-12-2021).

result in massive emotional cost. These costs can be particularly severe if children are involved. Financial costs for men in terms of support can also be strenuous. It is tempting to provide a list of Do's and Don'ts to have a fulfilling family life, However, until and unless we have imbibed in ourselves certain spiritual/virtuous elements, restraining oneself will never be an easy job - this is what the scripture says. Aforesaid caveats apply to both spouses, and both are equally responsible for the peace and tranquillity in the home. That said, there is specific mention of women in the scripture as central players in home making. Old-fashioned this may sound, but in this author's opinion, this belief is still firmly embedded in the psyche and wisdom of Hindu and Muslim culture dominated countries of the world.

Anger, especially uncontrolled, needs to be kept under check. It has the power to damage us more than it does others. It can be the cause of high blood pressure, headaches, insomnia, even stroke. A 2015 study conducted in the US on 34,000 adults found 'strong associations between anger and bipolar disorder, drug dependence, psychotic disorder, borderline and schizotypal personality disorders (p.2)'[180]. In addition to damaging our health, anger can also result in strained relations which can be fatal at the workplace. Attempts towards inculcating virtuous habits can help control and channel anger into productive causes. Nowadays help is available to deal with anger issues and a myriad of courses are run on how to regulate it. Such help should be sought to supplement one's own efforts to combat it.

---

180 https://www.ncbi.nlm.nih.gov/pmc/articles/PMC4384185/ (Accessed 13-12-2021). Published in CNS Spectr. 2015 April ; 20(2): 130–139. doi:10.1017/S1092852914000182

Lobh or Greed is next in the line of vices which needs to be kept under check. Greed is excessive desire for wealth and power. Unchecked Greed can make a person oblivious to others' needs and comfort - callousness can also set in in the character. In addition, it can give rise to jealousy, anxiety, and unwarranted rivalry. These in turn can impact negatively on health. A key message repeated in the scripture is that 'no matter how much wealth we amass nothing goes with us to next life.' As a result, we should inculcate in us the virtuous habit of sharing our wealth with fellow human beings. The theory is that learning to share can also keep greed under check. An act of sharing can also add a great deal to our happiness.

Moh or excessive attachment to material things and relations is next in line to keep in check in the making of a virtuous life. Attachment to material things refer to liquid (cash, stocks, bonds e.g.) and non-liquid assets (home, plant & machinery, a vehicle). Subjective excessive attachment to relationships is taken to be with one's spouse, children, parents and relatives, but can also include attachment to non-family members such as friends and community members. Attachment to material and non-material things is not a vice in the strict sense of the term, but something that borders on vice and can be a hindrance to a virtuous life. 'Moh' which is a common and well understood word in the Sikh world can be kept under check by this reminder to ourselves; the advice imparted to us in the scripture - advises that we all are destined to perish one day (as is also said in the Christian world 'dust to dust, ashes to ashes') hence it is futile to be excessively in love with worldly objects. Keeping oneself detached from 'Moh' is a job though that is easier said than done; hence, a spiritual approach to deal with it requires strong convictions in the wisdom of the scripture.

'Haume' or 'Ego' is the inflated opinion about oneself. People with an inflated ego can push others away from them and as people withdraw, gradual isolation may set in. In theory, unless an egotistic person has power (e.g., in a work environment) people soon begin to shun him into isolation. An isolated person can start to live in his own world - both in his mind and in the community as well. This can result in him i.e., an egotistical person, behaving odd and irrationally without him realising it. The scripture repeatedly warns us to be on guard of this vice which can subtly creep in on us from a variety of sources - when we start to acquire wealth or power, e.g., sycophancy can also inflate our egos the scripture warns. The way to combat Ego is to stay humble, bearing in mind that everything in this world is relative - there are always people of power, wealth, and influence below us as well as above us[181].

Five Mediums of Interface with the World

The five avenues of interface with the world are our vision, hearing, smell, taste, and touch (skin). How can we make them virtuous so that they are of assistance to us on our *Road to Nirvana?* Fortunately, this connection is rather simple but often eludes our attention.

What we see with our eyes depends mostly on the choices. If we decide to log in to a porn site or visit a nightclub to watch adult shows, or go to see an illegal dogfight, then we are not only *choosing to see* something that is not conducive to building a devout life, but we have also chosen to *hear* lewd and violent emotional outbursts. In live shows we can also *smell* drink, *taste* (food) and often

---

[181] Epitaph in Urdu on a gravestone read '*Main Aham Tha; Yahi Vaham Tha*' (translated it reads: 'I was important; this was *the* misconception').

end up with a sensation of *touch. In other words, most avenues of interface with the world are correlated* and operate in tandem with each other. No wonder in ancient Hindu mythology we find Hermits meditating with their eyes closed with still bodies to focus and find their connection with the divine. If we pause and think, we will realize that in places of worship - (church, mosque, temple, gurdwara, synagogue) all our five senses of interface with the external environment are in a calm stable position - we see, hear, smell and feel divine; true devotees will vouch that they also feel at one with the heavens. If we have worked through #1 to #4 in our model of *Road to Nirvana,* then dealing with the final set of variables in #5 described below should not be difficult to conquer.

Rationale of Set-B   Family Virtues

The importance of family is immortalised in Mother Teresa's words "if you want to change the world, go home and love your family."

Family virtues consist of teaching children religious virtues, loyalty to their spouse and care for elders. The principal responsibility for this lies with the parents. Research shows that a child's personality begins to take shape as early as age 3-5. A child begins to internalise whatever he sees and experiences with parents. A common site for a visitor to a Sikh gurdwara would be parents coming in with children of all ages, including new-born. As soon as it is comfortable, parents carry the new-born with them to the gurdwara. As a result, early on in their growth, they see, feel, smell (incense), touch, taste (langar) and sense the religious atmosphere. Hence, it is not surprising for this author that he has not come across any Sikh who says he is not religious or that he does not visit a gurdwara.

By the time a Sikh child reaches his teens he is immersed in the culture of the Sikh religion, even if he/she is not a regular gurdwara attendee. This author does not have the data to prove this, but I believe a great deal of loyalty to your spouse and a sense of care for parents stems from frequent visits to gurdwaras from an early age. As stated elsewhere, gurdwaras also function as social clubs where community information is also exchanged and bonding between families takes place. Often on key dates such as birth and death anniversaries, families organise religious events at home where families meet, and the cycle of interface and bonding carries on.

For non-Sikh families, the model as described above may only be partially valid. Research shows that 'the most religious countries are in Africa, the Middle East, South Asia and Latin America, while people generally are less religious in Europe, North America, East Asia and Australia'[182]. There is evidence that shows that religious couples' divorce rate is lower in religious countries than the rest[183]. This impacts positively on the upbringing of children and the care of family elders. Often the negative impact of divorces and separations, after several years of co-existence, is under-estimated.

In a 2021 study, the World Health Organisation (WHO) assessed that depression is a common mental disorder and about 5% of adults worldwide suffer from this ailment; depression is also the leading cause of disability worldwide and is a major contributor to the global burden

---

182 https://www.pewforum.org/2018/06/13/how-religious-commitment-varies-by-country-among-people-of-all-ages/ (Accessed 14-12-2021).

183 https://ifstudies.org/blog/regular-church-attenders-marry-more-and-divorce-less-than-their-less-devout-peers (Accessed 14-12-2021).

https://www.dupagecountyfamilylawfirm.com/naperville-divorce-lawyer/why-are-divorce-rates-rising-around-the-world-1 (Accessed 14-12-2021).

of disease; more women are affected by it and it can lead to suicide[184]. Although the WHO did not establish the link between depression and divorces, the link between the two is obvious - anyone who has gone through the process of divorce will vouch for the stress it can cause and financial uncertainty it can create, particularly (for supporting) men. In addition, access to children is a major issue, not to mention the sense of deep social shame it can bring in, still as-yet, relatively conservative societies. No wonder, therefore, the scripture lays such a high emphasis on the positives of loyalty and religious virtues in families and the care for elders - neglect of which is still frowned upon in many societies. Given the pace and complexities of a modern lifestyle, it is not uncommon to come across males (particularly in conservative societies) caught between loyalty to elders (parents) and spouse when there is a conflict between the two. A solution to such problems is never easy, but sane advice from virtuous company and one's own conscience based on justice can help.

Rationale of Set-C Community Virtues

> *The purpose of life, as far as I can tell, is to find a mode of being that's so meaningful that the fact that life is suffering is no longer relevant.*
> *(Jordan Peterson)*

Finally, we come to a set of community virtues held in the highest of esteem in the Sikh scripture and culture[185].

---

184 https://www.who.int/news-room/fact-sheets/detail/depression (Accessed 14-12-2021).

[185] A reviewer pointed out to me that community interactions as a virtue is often a hallmark of a relatively young religion or group. Apart from the advantages

Community virtues encompass within them the voluntary unpaid services for the community. Such services connect us with the community, raise our awareness of society, aids in physical and mental health and can be particularly of immense benefits to youth (Youniss, Mclellan, Su, & Yates, 1999, p. 248); a comprehensive treatment of social work theory can be found in Howe (Howe, 2009). We listed that following community services in the Figure 6.1 above - donations in cash or kind; physical help in community works; help in times of crisis such as a pandemic. All three services should be imparted with no discrimination of caste, creed, or colour.

Service to community begins with donation in cash or kind to gurdwaras and charitable organizations where it is put to a variety of uses. A good example of Sikh charitable work is presently the ongoing COVID pandemic in which help with cash, food and medicines is offered to families in need. In addition, without regard to their own safety, Sikh volunteers offered and performed funerals of infected victims whom most people - in some cases even the families of the deceased were petrified to conduct cremation responsibilities. One cannot help one's mind wandering into the scripture where at several places, the stark reality of this world and the fact that 'in the final analysis no one stands by you' is so clearly stated in more than one place. In numerous gurdwaras around the world the community kitchen offered langar is run 24/7. In the

---

listed here, its promotion may have an implicit strategic importance - that of keeping the group together. New religions would generally widen their following by weaning people away from existing belief systems into their fold. There can be serious pressure from society and family to abandon the new religion and revert to the old belief system. Community service and continuous interaction with people of the same new faith serves to reinforce their commitments and serves to 'keep the flock together'. Muslims also have similar practices (but confined to Muslims only) - 'Tablighi Jamaat's are examples.

West, Sikh charitable trusts are also offering food packages and other necessities for the homeless and needy. In this author's opinion, one reason for the cheerful nature of Sikhs is the help they proffer to the needy - as stated previously, research has shown that helping others makes us happy in return - as this happens, the cycle of community service and mutual happiness reinforcing each other continues.

Remarkable evidence of generosity and camaraderie of farmers from Punjab, Haryana, UP, Rajasthan, and other states in India, came to light in the recently ended farmer's agitation over three farm bills in India. For 14 months (August 2020 – December 2021) thousands of farmer families from affected states camped at the Singhu and Tikri border villages of Haryana. Singhu, on the northwest side is 20 km from Delhi; Tikri on the west side is 16 km from Delhi; the distance between the two is 34 km. Farmers from Punjab, Haryana, UP, and Rajasthan who formed a major chunk of sit-in protest on these borders, brought food grains and groceries in trollies pulled by farm tractors and set up temporary homes.

From day one farmers set up community kitchens in which they cooked food not only for themselves but for *whosoever* came in to eat - no questions asked. Hundreds of poor families who lived adjacent to the camps also got fed - for several poor families, in particular children, eating in the community kitchen became almost a daily feature[186]. Well-wishers of farmer communities also set up temporary medical facilities and stores of daily necessity items which were dispensed free of cost to anyone who came to collect

---

186 In an interview one farmer stated that stray dogs, cats, and monkeys also got fed in the process!

the required items[187]. Financial and material help poured in from all over India and overseas. When the agitation ended, tents and a plentiful supply of daily use items were donated by farmers to locals. Watching farmers and their families - mostly in their old age go through this harrowing time - sometimes in atrocious weather, was heart wrenching and heart-warming at the same time[188] (owing to the cheerful nature of farmer families despite hardships).

In order to inculcate the community service virtue in us we can begin small and then build on it. For instance, we can put aside a small portion of regular earnings for charitable purposes and at the end of a certain period the accumulated amount can be given to a charity of our choice. Similarly, we can look around and see where we can contribute directly e.g., working at charitable trust shops, backroom sorting (e.g., of food items), and cleaning of community spaces. Once we begin the cycle of community help, we can build on it, as ideas and connections would pave the way forward. Soon we will find that inculcating this virtue in us is beginning to make us eternally happy.

Chapter Summary

The goal of us human beings is to be happy in life. The apex state of happiness, when we are in intrinsic peace with ourselves, and the world is *Nirvana*. In Indian religious vernacular, *Nirvana* is reached when we are freed from the repeated cycles of birth and death - a state of ultimate bliss. Either way, for us to achieve a state of *Nirvana*, in *this* world or *beyond*, we need to adopt certain

---

[187] These included everyday items of garments, blankets, medicines, shoes, turbans, body warmers, food items including dry fruits and such.
[188] Around 700 farmers - male and female, died in the protest owing to accidents, illnesses, exhaustion, suicide, police high handedness.

virtues and become a virtuous person. The adaptation of virtues puts us on the *Road to Nirvana*.

The principles of Sikh moral philosophy, embedded in their scripture and shown by real life examples of their ten Gurus, reveals to us a simple way for us to be on the *Road to Nirvana*. The 'system' that emerges from the study of virtues in the scripture and the lives of Sikh Gurus and clarified by Sikh scholars in a written code of conduct (cf. Appendix to this chapter) is remarkably logical and simple in its approach. It goes something like this.

Our 'mind' is the driver of everything we do in our lives. It is essential that we keep our mind healthy and populate it with good virtues. Since a healthy mind is very much linked with a healthy body, the 'system' urges us to work towards habiting ourselves in a healthy body. This begins with an early rise, cleansing ourselves, undertake exercise, meditation and prayers, before setting out to work.

The 'system' then urges us to practice and inculcate in us, on a day-to-day basis, making it a habit and a part of our disposition, the virtues of humility, obedience, equity, service, self-sacrifice, justice, mercy, purity of service, calmness, and courage.

For us to get a gradual mastery over these virtues, the 'system' urges us to seek the company of virtuous people and keep a control over underlying human weaknesses - sexual urges, anger, greed, excessive attachment to worldly objects and ego. We can do this by keeping a check on our mediums of interface with the world i.e., what we choose to see, hear, smell, taste, and touch.

Alongside, to be a truly virtuous person, we also need to pay attention to our family life, by teaching good, religious, and non-religious virtues to our children, by being faithful to our spouse and looking after family elders. The final stage to become a truly virtuous person and a candidate for *Nirvana*, we should also serve the community we live in. We can do this by donating part of our earnings for charitable purposes and by extending physical help whenever required.

The rationale and ingredients of the *Road to Nirvana* dictated by the Sikh 'system' of virtues becomes clear and begins to make sense when we ponder a little deeper into its suggestions. Making an honest effort to perfect, as best as we can, each element of the 'system' takes us a step closer to *Nirvana*. The system also tells us that the journey towards it should begin from an early age - this is the reason it urges us to pay attention to our family life. As we grow older and enter into the complex web of the modern world, we need strong and consistent moral virtues and convictions to see us through a peaceful journey into work life, retirement, old age and final departure from this world. If we have led a virtuous life in *this* world, we have done well to achieve a state of *Nirvana* in *this* as well as in the *next* world. The best, the 'system' tells us, is that to achieve *Nirvana* we need not renounce anything and go over to forests or mountains to live in solitude; *Nirvana* can be achieved by being in the midst of family and community. Good luck to us all.

For those who are numerically oriented and wish to know, say on a 10-point scale (10 highest), *their* score on reaching *Nirvana*, appendix chapter 'Modelling *Nirvana*' has the answer. This chapter has been written for students who wish to undertake research work in this area. A non-technical reader can still read it omitting the technical part.

*

EPILOGUE

Build the raft of meditation and self-discipline to carry you across the river. There will be no ocean and no rising tides to stop you; this is how comfortable your path shall be
(Guru Nanak)

Peace and happiness shall fill your mind deep within if you act according to truth and self-discipline
(Guru Gobind Singh)

We began the journey of this book with the intention of arriving at answers to the big question of life i.e., can we free ourselves from the cycles of re-births and land in a state of ultimate happiness and bliss known as *Nirvana* in Sikhism and its sister religions - Hinduism, Buddhism, and Jainism.

The journey took us to an understanding of the facets of Sikh history, lives and teachings of 10 Sikh Gurus, growth patterns of the Sikh religion following the lives of its Gurus, key messages in the Sikh scripture, written and unwritten Sikh ethos and code of moral conduct and its close connection with 1800 year old wisdom on moral principles granted to us by Greek philosopher Aristotle.

This is the conclusion of our study.

In this author's opinion, our aim in life should be to first reach *Nirvana* in *this* world. If we are successful in this, the *Road to Nirvana* in the 'heavenly world,' for those who worry about it, sometimes too much, is made easier.

I invoke the famous sermon of Lord Krishna on *Karma* to explain how to reach *Nirvana in this world first.* You'll recall that *Karma* is equivalent to action, and every action, physical, mental, or emotional will lead to results at some time in this or later life. Krishna famously has said that *Karma* is in the intention: the intention behind the action is what matters. We should keep intentions behind our actions good. Intentions will be good when they are driven by a mind that has been populated by good virtues.

The Sikh way of life helps us to do good *Karma*, driven by good intentions in *this* world. Once this talent is perfected, we have cemented the pebbly *Road to Nirvana* (as the book cover picture shows) to the next world, and we should be able to fly into it as the birds in the picture above shows.

To be able to do good *Karma*, the Sikh way of life urges us to be disciplined in our day-to-day life and be honest about our sense of right and wrong i.e., our moral principles. Discipline in daily life requires that we have *control* over our mind which is the focal point of origin of all we do; it is our mind that drives us into good or bad *Karma*. Control over the mind is easier if we inhabit ourselves in a healthy body. To have a healthy body with a healthy mind in it requires discipline. Discipline in life begins with rising early, cleansing ourselves, saying our prayers and going out to make an honest living by dint of honest means, return home in the evening and stay loyal to our conjugal and family responsibilities.

When we are out and about, we should endeavour to be in the company of pious people (i.e., avoid dubious company; strive to be in the company of people from whom we can learn something good), take care not to hurt anyone, and not indulge in acts considered sacrilegious - stealing or hurting someone for instance. On the contrary, we should help the needy in whatever way we can - to the extent of protecting them, if protection is sought. Paying attention to such acts of moral principles would make us intrinsically happy, in addition to also keeping us occupied.

The Sikh way tells us to gradually work towards enriching our lives with good *Karma, in this* life, without expecting anything in return or worrying about the outcome, since good deeds lead to good outcomes. Continuing such attempts and keeping our mind content, filled with thoughts of good deeds also helps us control negative thoughts of anger, sexual urges, excessive greed, attachment to worldly objects and ego. Being in pious company further helps our physical and sensory interactions (through eyes, ears e.g.) with the outside world.

In a nutshell then, the Sikh way to *Nirvana* rests in making ourselves virtuous, within and outside our bodies and mind, in *this world first.* Once this is accomplished, the *Road to Nirvana* has been paved - how well paved, strong, and lasting this road leading to the next life is, will depend on the **purity of our virtues and soul,** of which **we are the sole judge,** - as, it is **only we** who can see inside us to gauge how pure we have made ourselves. I would say, on a 10-point scale, with 10 highest, if we award ourselves close to 10, we are doing well like the bird ahead in the picture

above – if we are far from it then we need to work harder.
Good luck.

**

APPENDIX CHAPTER MODELLING NIRVANA

I cannot teach anybody anything.
I can only make them think
(Socrates)

Introduction

In chapter 6 figure 6-1 we outlined a virtuous model of Sikh life that encompasses within it two sets of 'personal virtues', one set of 'family virtues' and one set of 'community virtues.' The question we can ask is: 'is it possible to determine how close or far off a person is on his index of virtuousness, which in turn can determine his proximity (say on 1 to 10 scale - 10 closest) to reaching *Nirvana*? The answer to this question is 'Yes'. It is statistically possible to arrive at co-efficients that can tell us a person's proximity to *Nirvana*, which is the focus of this chapter. This chapter is directed to a researcher - most likely an MSc, MPhil, or a PhD student, contemplating a thesis in part fulfilment of his degree in Sikh/religious studies.

In order for our researcher to arrive at the answer to the question he is seeking, primary data, with the help of a survey instrument (SI) (or Survey Questionnaire as it is sometimes called) will need to be collected and subject this data to statistical modelling. Our researcher shall require two sets of skills to complete the job - first, the skill of drafting a good SI, and second, the skill to analyse the collected data statistically. We shall briefly discuss the basic components of these two sets of skills in this chapter to help our researcher[189].

All research projects begin with a conceptual model of the research, arrived at after a literature review. We ask our researcher to keep in mind Figure A-1 which is such a conceptual model. To illustrate the SI drafting skills, we shall pick up one component - 'Personal Virtues - 2' and re-draw the conceptual map as in figure A-1. We shall show our researcher how to draft questions based on this set of virtues as an example. *The researcher then can draft similar questions for the other three components of the model outlined in the Appendix Figure.* Some overlapping between the questions may happen which should be dealt with.

Statistical models have independent variables, mediator variables, and control variables that impact on dependent variables. Figure A-1 lays these out. As stated, this is a sample which our researcher should modify to his requirements.

Drafting a Survey Instrument (SI) – the Basics

An SI consist of three parts: constructing the SI, administering it and analysing the data thereof. All three parts have their unique difficulties, hazards, and challenges. For instance, if a SI is ill-administered, it will bring in few responses; if the data generated by the SI is incorrectly analysed, say, by the application of wrong tests, the results

---

189 Material in this chapter draws from this author's unpublished monograph Singh (1999) *'Understanding and Analysing Data',* parts of which I have previously made available online to my students.

will be misleading. However, if the SI is ill-drafted in the first place, the successive two stages will yield few good results anyway. As a result, the onus of obtaining good results falls largely on a good SI.

Once a good SI has been drafted and primary data collected, a systematic analysis can begin. A decent SI has the following structure: a short self-explanatory title; a brief explanation of its aims; an introduction and contact details of the researcher; assurance to the respondent that the information provided will be used in strict confidence and for research purposes only (these are part of the ethical requirements of the project).

The opening section of a SI should contains 'Basic Information'. Data from this section is used for mediators and controls, such as the sex, marital status, and educational qualification of the respondent. Following this, five or six (or as required by the project), clearly labelled sections seeking information on the theme of the project should be drafted. A SI should end with gratitude shown for the completion of the questionnaire by the respondent.

Sections in the Survey Instrument (SI)
on Road to Nirvana

You'll recall that in chapter 2 we discussed the lives, attributes, and contributions of 10 Sikh Gurus. Table 2.1, Column-3 listed specific attributes of 10 Gurus as follows: Guru Nanak - Humility, Guru Angad - Obedience, Guru Amar Das - Equality, Guru Ram Das - Service, Guru Arjan Dev - Self Sacrifice, Guru Hargobind - Justice, Guru Har Rāī - Mercy, Guru Har Krishan - Purity of thought, Guru Tegh Bahadur - Calmness, and Guru Gobind Singh -

Royal Courage. Sikh philosophy embedded in the scripture and in the written and unwritten code of conduct of Sikhs, implicitly assumes, rather expects, that all Sikhs instil in them these qualities of their Gurus. Our researcher could take these ten attributes as the starting point of his research and draft his SI on the lines described here.

The SI of our researcher would have 12 sections beginning with section-I on 'Basic Information' as described above. The next 10 sections would contain questions on the 10 attributes listed above. The final section #12 would contain open ended questions. Before we make suggestions on the type of questions on the ten attributes that can be asked of the respondents, let us briefly review various question formats and wording styles which would come in handy to a researcher in his quest of a good SI.

Question Formats

There are five basic types of question formats described below. Each format has its own merits and limitations and should be used judiciously by the researcher for his questions.

1. Open ended formats: These are questions which invite respondents to write their responses in reply to questions.
2. "Yes" or "No" formats: These are questions to which the respondents can put a tick in reply to a question.
3. Rating-scale formats: In these questions, respondents rate between 1 to 5 (or 7 or 10) scale their answer to a

question. These are *Likert style*[190] questions that ask respondents to express their agreement or disagreement to a question.

4. Semantic formats: These questions also have scales like rating scale format questions but use adjectives such as receptive.........non-receptive, delightful..........not delightful from one end to the other to elicit responses.

5. Ranking formats: In ranking format questions, respondents rank their responses to a particular set of questions.

6. Check-list type format: In check-list type formats, the respondents tick or circle their choices. For example, in order to find which sport the respondent plays, the researcher may list a number of sports and ask the respondent to circle the sport or sports he/she plays.

---

[190] A Likert scale, named after psychologist Rensis Likert, is a statement that the respondent can evaluate by giving it a quantitative value, or subjective or objective dimension.

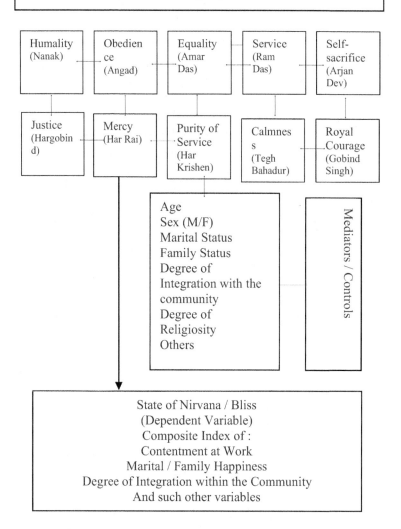

Figure A 1 Conceptual Road Map (for statistical modelling) to Nirvana Based on the Teachings of 10 Sikh Gurus
(Note: This partial model for illustrative purposes is drawn from full model of Fig 6.1)

Wording the Survey Instrument

Attention should be paid to the following points.

1. Keep the language of the questions simple. Avoid jargons and technical terms unless you *have to* use them. Bear in mind that a person not connected to your subject should be able to understand the questions.
2. Avoid long and complicated questions. If you have to have a question that is long, try and break it down into two or more sentences.
3. If you are going to have questions that end in a pure "Yes" or "No" answer, make sure that they cannot, alternatively be asked on a scale of, say, 1 to 5, 1 for 'strongly disagree' to 5 'strongly agree'. Questions on scales yield better results in terms of the beliefs of the respondents.
4. Avoid questions on which the respondent is likely to have only little or no knowledge of the subject. It is better to have no response than to have a wrong response. Similarly, we should avoid questions which could have a decided bias in response (e.g., a question on asking superiority of one's religion over others).
5. Avoid asking a question that is 'too direct'. Such a question may have to be broken down into two or more questions.

Additional Points

1. Leave enough space between questions.
2. If you are asking an open-ended question, leave enough space for the respondent to answer the question.
3. Instructions: Some general instructions can appear at the beginning of the SI. Specific instructions for a particular question should be crisp without sacrificing the essential details. If we are asking respondents to

skip a particular question, we should make sure that this is in bold or italics or shown by arrow marks.

4. It is a good practice not to ask difficult, or questions requiring write-ups, in the beginning of the SI.
5. The SI can be drafted using simple word processing tools such as Word. So, if you have not got access to a specialised software package to write questionnaires, it should not cause undue worry. You should make sure that the SI is balanced and not overly done in its presentation. It is the contents that matter most; it should suffice if they have been presented with clarity and simple layouts.

Indicative Questions for SI on Road to *Nirvana*

Based on the core messages of the 10 Gurus, we provide in this section a list of indicative questions that a researcher can ask respondents. The researcher is reminded that these are only suggestive and that he should carefully look into the aims and objectives of his research project and also discuss with his supervisor before arriving at the decision on questions to be included in the SI.

Section-1 Basic Information (Mediators and Control Variables)

This section should contain questions related to mediator and control variables that are critical in the analysis of the results. Sample questions are: (a) Sex (b) Marital status (c) Age (d) Education (e) Profession (f) Income (g) Ethnic affiliation (h) Religion (i) Location. For variables (c) to (f), provide some categories for the respondent to tick. For instance, for age, provide options with class intervals such as 16-20; 21-25.

Section-2 Contentment Index (Dependent Variables)

This section should contain a set of questions to gauge the contentment index of the respondents. A number of questions on a Likert scale can be asked about the respondents' level of contentment and happiness at work, home, family surroundings, society, within the community and at national level. Questions can also be asked about the inspirations and achievements the respondent had in life and their actual achievements, which would reveal the gap.

Section-3 Questions on 10 Core Sikh Values (Independent Variables)

(i)   Humility

Humility, which was the hallmark of first Guru, Guru Nanak, involves thinking of yourself as a humble and insignificant person ready to help others with no hang ups about your riches, status, or the position you may be holding. To elicit from respondents as to what is their index of humility, several questions can be put to them. The following is a selection of such questions. The nature of the questions is broad. This will help the researcher to find if the level of humility will change with a change in a person's fortune or family situation. In research, if one can, it always helps to procure a little more data, the analysis of which can enrich discussions. Most questions can be asked on a 10-point scale (1=not agree; 10=totally agree).

1. Do you consider yourself to be a person with utmost humility?
2. If your father asks you do a job, which he thinks is right to do, but you differ - how likely it is that you will still do the job?
3. If your elder brother asks you to do a job, which he thinks is right to do but you do not - how likely it is that you will still do the job?
4. Say you are leaving home and are just about on time to reach your office/place of business, when you see an elderly person in your building struggling to carry his stuff. How likely it is that you will stop by to help him?
5. You have a trainee join your office/place of work. How likely it is that you will teach him and also share most of your work secrets with him?
6. Assume you have a junior person join your place of work (office, shop, etc.) and that he is cleverer than you, even if you had been working in the same place and same job for many years. How likely you are to (a) accept this new recruit as your supervisor and cooperate, and/or (b) be open-minded to learn from him?
7. Say an elder in your community is briefing you on something but you already know about it; how likely it is that you will still listen to this elder patiently till he has finished telling you what he has to tell you?
8. Say you are in a queue in a hospital for an important meeting and there is a patient behind you. How likely it is that you will let that patient jump the queue if he says it is urgent for him?
9. Say you are in argument with an elderly person (assume he holds a post in a gurdwara) and that you

think you are right; how likely it is that you will come to agree with him?

10. Do you agree that if you become too humble it will harm you?
11. Do you agree that no one is born with an innate quality of humility? Humility is 'something' that can be cultivated?
12. Do you agree that family influences a great deal whether a person has humility or not?
13. Assume your financial situation has worsened. Do you agree that the changed financial situation will reduce humility in you?
14. Assume your family situation has worsened owing to say, a death in the family or your separation with your spouse. Do you think this will greatly affect the level of your humility?
15. If you notice the ego in others, how likely are you to talk about it to others?
16. How often do you say Grace (thank God for food; pray) before eating your meal?
17. In a formal or informal gathering of family and friends how likely it is that you would like to talk about you and your children's achievements?

(ii)   Obedience

Obedience refers to compliance, either owing to a request, order, or submission to someone's authority. Obedience can be particularly strong in the presence of legitimate authority granted either by the law or by the masses. Obedience is said to be the hallmark of the second Guru, Guru Angad Dev and it was particularly strong as masses had entrusted spiritual authority in Guru Nanak, who was Angad's mentor, before Angad was elevated to Guru-ship. For a researcher to fathom how obedient a person is, several questions can be crafted. The following is a suggestive list. Most questions can be asked on a 10-point scale (1=not agree; 10=totally agree) or in binary 'yes' 'no' form.

1. Do you consider yourself to be an obedient person?
2. Do you agree that obedience is essential for society to function smoothly?
3. Do you agree that dissent is always important?
   (a) In normal day-to-day discussions at home?
   (b) At the workplace?
   (c) In community meetings?
4. Will you obey a government law officer if he was not in uniform?
5. If you assess that no harm is going to come to you, will you:
   (a) Disobey a legitimate authority such as a policeman?
   (b) Disobey an elder privately?
   (c) Disobey an elder in a community meeting?
6. In a bus or a train, the officer asks you to give up your seat for another passenger. Will you: (a) give up your seat, (b) ask why you have to give up? (c) refuse to move?
   Do you always give a reason why you would not do a job?
7. Do you need to be reminded when you are doing a job?
8. Do you always question the instructions given to you for a job?
9. Do you ask for an explanation when your request for something has been turned down?

(iii)   Equality

Equality refers to a state of being equal in status, esteem, rights, and opportunities. In a social set-up, it is interpreted as treating people equal, irrespective of their social status, colour, ethnicity, and cultural background. By default, equality postulates equal rights and freedom for all the people. The researcher can ask several questions on the following lines to draw out the thinking of the respondents on the issue of equality. Questions can be on a Likert or binary scale. As stated previously, use a Likert scale wherever you can, as you can draw better results with them.

1.   Do you believe that all human beings are created equal and should *always* be treated as equal?
2.   Do you treat everyone - rich or poor with same respect and reverence when you speak to them?
3.   How likely are you to agree to reserving seats for the underprivileged for courses for which there is high demand, such as nursing, medicine, engineering?
4.   Are you in favour of a quota system for jobs for the underprivileged?
5.   Do you agree with same salaries for the job for able-bodied and handicapped?
6.   Are you for or against quota system that guarantees a fixed proportion of places for women in government jobs?
7.   Are you for or against a quota system which guarantees a fixed proportion of places for women to study in universities?
8.   Do you agree that there should be a quota system which guarantees a fixed proportion of places for women in executive positions?

9. How likely are you to agree with laws that promote equal salaries for men and women in the same position?
10. Do you agree that present divorce laws are not fair to men?
11. Do you feel that men and women have equal chance to get custody of the children when they divorce?
12. Do you agree with the view that it is alright for men to purchase sex?
13. Do you think it is appropriate for women to operate as sex workers?
14. Do you agree that most of the time in domestic violence, both wife and husband are equally responsible?

(iv) Service

The dictionary meaning of Service is 'the action of helping or doing work for someone.' The end result is the benefit a service creates for an individual, a group, a community, or it could be at the national level. The service provided could be voluntary unpaid work or paid work. A simple example would be a devotee doing work for the temple. An extreme paid example for service provision is the army personnel giving their lives for their country. A researcher can ask a number of questions on the Likert scale to a respondent to gauge his views towards service provision. The following are some examples. The questions can be asked on a Likert or binary scale.

1. Do you believe in the charitable work of free service to your community?
2. How happy have you felt when you have helped someone without expecting anything in return?

3. Say, as a devotee, on a regular basis you do a free service of cleaning your temple premises. Under a new rule you could be paid money for your work. How likely it is that you will accept the money?
4. What is the level of your satisfaction with the service level within your community?
5. How happy you will be to take the lead and give your time and money to improve the level of service in your community?
6. What hurdles do you face (e.g., time, money, motivation, family restrictions) when providing a community service?
7. Where does your motivation for serving others come from? (a) family (b) friends (c) from within?
8. What is your favourite form of service? (a) helping people in care homes (b) giving time in the local hospital (c) working with handicapped children (d) none of these?
9. How do you feel at the end of the day when you have helped someone? This question can be left either open ended for respondents to write their responses or some options can be provided.
10. What has been your most important act of service so far?
    With this question a researcher can elicit and categorise the preferred services of the respondents.

(v)   Self-sacrifice

Self-sacrifice is voluntarily giving up one's interests, comfort, and in extreme cases one's life to help and safeguard the interests of others. The party for whom you are making the sacrifice could be an individual, a group, a community, or nation. Self-sacrifice is an unselfish and benevolent act of the highest order if the person making the sacrifice has zero expectations in return of his sacrifice. A researcher can ask a number of questions on a Likert scale to gauge the depth of self-sacrifice in the respondent. Suggested questions that can be put to respondents are:

1. Self-sacrificing comforts:
(a) For strangers?
(b) One's family?
(c) Relatives?
(d) Friends?
(e) Community?
(f) Nation?

2. You find two persons in heated arguments on the verge of violence.
Most likely you will:
(a) Not get involved, and walk on?
(b) Wait and watch the situation, wondering if you should step in?
(c) Will step in to help reduce the tension between the arguing persons?

3. You are walking with two of your friends. On the way, a group of 4 old enemies of one of your friends comes up and are on the verge of harming your friend. How likely are you to get involved at the risk of yourself getting seriously injured?

4. What score would you give, if in the previous example, instead of your friend, it was your:
(a) Family member?
(b) Your temple priest?
(c) A relative?
(d) Stranger?
(e) European (foreigner) whom you have just met?

(f) Non-European, say, an African?

(vi) Justice

Plato argued in *The Republic* that justice is worthwhile - that just action is a good in itself and that one ought to engage in just activity (Lee D. , 2007). Such an action, he argued, should be pursued even when it does not seem to confer immediate advantage. This was a compelling insight from Plato. Justice refers to an act of being just and righteous in one's thoughts and actions.

At individual level this trait would aptly describe a person's character. The concept of justice is an abstract and a moral issue. People may interpret it differently depending on their cultural background; 'life for life' e.g., is still very much an accepted norm in the Arab world. At the state level, justice refers to applying e.g., the same legal codes for all to maintain law and order and the equitable distribution of resources in infrastructure facilities such as the provision of electricity, roads, and transport facilities and the provision of aid in times of natural disasters. There are several questions that can be put to respondents to draw out their stand with regard to justice. The following is a selected list which can be put to respondents on a Likert scale.

1. I believe the present political system justly treats all individuals.
2. There is social justice in our society.
3. I am fairly and justly treated at place of work.
4. I believe as a matter of justice that 'life should mean life'.
5. I believe for us to have a peaceful life, anyone who breaks the law should be treated strictly and put in prison for longer times.

6. Repeat offenders should be locked up for progressively longer times each time they repeat an offense.
7. I believe that juvenile laws are too lenient and should be made stricter.
8. I believe harsher punishments will discourage crime.
9. I believe longer prison sentences will discourage crime.
10. Justice should be swift and brutal for heinous crimes.
11. The application of the justice system for the rich and the poor is different, particularly in developing countries.
12. The justice system is mostly in favour of the influential people and people with money and power.

(vii) Mercy

Mercy refers to compassion or forgiveness shown to someone whom an individual has the power to punish or harm. Embedded in an act of mercy are the acts of ethical considerations of benevolence and kindness. Mercy can be showered in a social context between individuals or groups, or at national and legal level where a judge can take a lenient view towards an offender. In extreme cases death penalties have been converted into life imprisonments. Mercy shown could be towards animate as well as inanimate subjects. The former include animals and latter, plants and vegetation. Several questions can be put to respondents to gauge their take on mercy. Following are some examples that can be asked on a 10-point scale, or binary Yes/No formats.

1. Do you believe in showing mercy to criminals?
2. Do you believe in mercy to repeat offenders?

3. Do you agree that mercy should be shown to corrupt government officials?

4. Do you agree that mercy shown to animals in present day society is excessive and often at the cost of needy people?

5. Do you agree that there is too much emphasis on maintaining forests at the expense of people's needs?

6. Streets in countries such as in India are rife with stray dogs. Do you agree that all stray dogs should be put down?

7. Are you in favour of euthanasia - mercy death, for terminally ill patients?

8. To deal with the endemic issue of street crimes, Rodrigo Duterte, the president of the Philippines is accused of eliminating criminals, often on the spot without arresting and putting them on trial; but he did succeed in establishing law and order in drug ridden streets in the Philippines. Do you support his actions?

9. If a burglar is in your house with threatening gestures, would you go to any extent - to the point of killing him, to protect yourself and family?

10. If your pet dog is ill with only a small chance of recovery, would you wait until there is no option left but to put him down or would you be happy to put him down before time as well?

(viii)   Purity of Thought

This passage from the Holy Bible describes the purity of thought and soul: A chaste and pure person should be pure in body and soul, in his thoughts, senses, feelings, and even in his dreams and imaginations. A man should give careful attention to the purity of his thoughts as his thoughts also belong to God. As we take care of the purity of our hearts in order that God may dwell in them, so we must take care of our minds too. In the Holy Bible the Divine Inspiration says, "Hear, O Israel: …the LORD is one. You shall love the LORD your God with all your heart and with all your soul and with all your might" (Collins Anglicised ESV Bibles , 2012, p. 130).

Our thoughts influence our actions. In our efforts to become more like our Father in Heaven, it is important that we keep our minds clean and **pure**. Even though evil influences are all around us, we can control our thoughts and direct them in the right way. We must try to avoid things that encourage unclean thoughts"[191]. As we shall see later, similar sentiments are also echoed repeatedly in the Sikh scripture. Guru Har Krishan was the epitome of this virtue, his young mind in all earnest was full of pure thoughts of serving others. A researcher can ask several questions to gauge how pure the mind of the respondent is. The following are some questions that can be asked on a Likert scale.

1. When you are doing a job, how much purity of thoughts i.e., without distractions, are you engaged in?
2. Do you find that it is usually difficult for you to concentrate on a job?
3. When you sit down to meditate or pray how focused do you find your mind to be?
4. When a friend approaches you for help, with what degree of pure and pious thoughts you would help?
5. When a relative approaches you for help, with what degree of pure and pious thoughts you would help?

---

191 https://www.suscopts.org/resources/literature/210/purity-of-thoughts/ (Retrieved 29-9-2021).

6. When a family member asks you for help, with what degree of pure and pious thoughts you would help?
7. Do you think your intentions are as pure as your actions?
8. Have you ever attended special courses on how to purify minds?
9. Have you ever undertaken work for a charitable institution?
10. Do you agree with the view that when someone deals with people, he/she has to be shrewd, possibly a little cunning to get the job done?

(ix)   Calmness

The dictionary meaning of calmness is 'the state or quality of being free from agitation or strong emotion'. Calmness is an abstract mental frame of equanimity which is free from the commotions of life and its surroundings. A state of calmness depends on a person's temperament - how he has trained himself to deal with difficult situations. Calmness can be cultivated through meditation and breathing exercises. Some people born with exceptionally saintly traits have the innate gift of calmness in them. Guru Tegh Bahadur was one of them. Calmness is a trait that can yield rich results in creating social bonding and harmony. A researcher can ask several questions on the state of calmness of the respondent. The following are guide questions. As per the previous questions, a Likert scale can be used for most of the questions.

1. What score would you give to *your* state of calmness?
2. What score would you give to the following factors in distracting calmness in you?

(a) Internal environnement (family, social relations etc.)

(b) External factors (job, interacting with strangers etc.)

3. Do you regularly practice exercises to stay calm?
4. Have you ever attended or are planning to attend courses on calming or similar techniques?
5. If the answer to Q4 is 'no' - what is the likelihood of you doing so?
6. How concerned are you with your unsettled state of mind that it might land you in trouble one day?
7. Do you frequently get a guilty feeling that you could have controlled a situation better?
8. In sports, how unhappy are you if you do not win?
9. When people try to correct you, you do not like it, but you say nothing.
10. Do you get easily frustrated if you have to wait in a queue or in traffic?
11. Do you avoid difficult decisions because they cause you stress and disturb your calmness?

(x)   Royal Courage

Physical courage is the quality of the mind that enables a person to face up to a dangerous situation without fear or intimidation. Valour is the courage or bravery shown in a battle. Whichever situation a brave person faces and stands up to, he has an end goal which could be only for himself, or it could be for the common good of a group or community. Moral courage is the ability to do right in the face of uncertain circumstances that may tempt a person to back off from a situation or act in a way that is less than honourable. There is a high degree of correlation between the physical and moral courage - one may be the cause of the other and *vice versa*. Gurus, in particular Guru Gobind

Singh, was the epitome of physical and moral courage. A series of questions can be asked of respondents on courage. The following is a sample of questions that can be put to respondents on a Likert or similar scale.

1. What score would you give to your physical courage?
2. What score would you give to your moral courage?

How would you rate the following (on 10-point scale; 10 always)?

(a) Individual situations when you did not stand up to an uncertain or a dangerous situation when you should have.
(b) In a group, when you did not stand up to an uncertain or a dangerous situation when you should have.
(c) When discussing a situation in a group, how often did you agree to an uncertain situation when you actually wished a safer alternative should have been chosen?
3. Do you usually find it difficult to live with uncertainty?
4. Have you often failed to tap into your hidden strengths?
5. When you face daily challenges, do you sometimes struggle and feel stalled at the start?
6. Do difficult situations in your life make you feel frustrated or isolated?
7. Do you sometimes feel that you should have had more courage to stand up to difficult situations?
8. Do you sometimes forget to apply courage in difficult situations?
9. In your professional life do you feel that you are stuck in an unrewarding situation for a longer time than necessary?
10. When you react to a situation, do you recognize courage as one of your prominent virtues?

11. Do you sometimes feel that you are too complacent and have missed too many opportunities?

12. When in a group, have you ever given up on a difficult goal only to be disappointed afterwards at your behaviour?

13. In a group do you often hold back from speaking the truth for fear of annoying others?

14. Overall, do you easily 'give-up' when faced with a difficult situation?

Some General Points on Survey Instruments

Drafts and revisions: Once you have decided on the sections and their headings and have some idea as to what should be asked, the first draft should be written *at the earliest possible.* You may fine-tune it later; but at least you have something to work on. Feedback for improvements should be sought from a wider audience.

Pilot testing: After the SI has been drafted and sample chosen, what remains to be done is the administering of the questionnaire on a small part of the selected sample - i.e., the pilot study. The pilot study should be done on the same or similar set of sample respondents and feedback received incorporated. All notes and data from the pilot study should be preserved, as the piloting process needs to be explained in the report/paper/thesis.

Administering: The SI can either be administered by post or online with the help of tools such as 'Survey Monkey.' The SI can also be administered in face-to-face interviews or by a mixed method i.e., online and in person[192]. Online conducted SI's are cheaper than those conducted in person.

---

192 I have always advised my doctoral students to follow up the online survey with selected face-to-face interviews to fill in any gaps in their understanding of the subject or to clarify issues thrown up after the data has been put to analysis.

An online SI can also generate larger sets of data. The central problem with surveys is the poor response rate which often can get stuck between 10-20% of the total SI mailed, in which case it is imperative to check the data for sample biases. Sometimes a covering letter from an influential person or an institution is helpful in increasing the response rate.

Response rate of questionnaires = Number returned by the respondents ÷ Total number, N in the sample minus (questionnaires returned owing to, say, wrong addresses + questionnaires which are ineligible) x 100. As an example, consider that a researcher sent 100 questionnaires (N) and received back 30. Out of these 30, say 5 were improperly filled and are unusable; also, say, 10 came back because either the address was wrong, or the respondents had moved away. The response rate for the survey thus works out to be as follows:

Response rate = {30 ÷ (100 − (5 + 10))} x 100; = {30 ÷ (100 −15)} x 100 ; = {30 ÷ 85} x 100 = 35%.

SI Filled in face-to-face Interview: In this method, gaining access to respondents and fixing a suitable time for an interview is time intensive. If this method is to be adopted, then the researcher should pay attention to several issues: dressing soberly, keeping the appointment time, not lose eye contact too often, jot down only the most essential points at the time of the interview leaving the rest for the later write-up. Recording the meeting can reduce the quality of responses.

Telephone Questionnaires: This is a clumsy business and best handled by professional consulting firms with the help of trained female assistants.

Ethical Issues and Considerations: Ethical considerations have assumed great importance in present day survey work. Ethical requirements entail that SI's are drafted with integrity to collect information for which they are intended, with no hidden agenda, and that participants should, in no way, be coerced to respond to it. If so agreed, all data should be treated confidentially.

Data, Population, Samples and Variables

It is vital that the researcher fully understands with utmost clarity the concepts of data, populations, samples drawn from it, and the nature of variables emanating from the data. No matter how well a SI is drafted, if it is executed with a hazy understanding of these concepts, they will nullify the results. Hence it is worth a researcher's time to come to grips with these concepts.

The data is of two types - primary and secondary. **Primary data** is collected first-hand. **Secondary data** has already been collected by an individual or an institution and has been used for applied research, but which then is also made available to the research community. Most primary data is collected by means of a SI. A *survey* is a process which is designed to collect data, facts, or information about members of a group in a particular situation. A survey of a complete population, that is, about each and every member of the group is known as a **Census**. The **population** consists of all members of a group who are alike on at least one specified characteristic (e.g., all people with Sikh faith). A population can be finite (all people with Sikh faith) or infinite (people likely to adopt the Sikh faith in future). The population may be real or hypothetical. For instance, a preacher may be concerned with the efficacy of his sermons on both the present and future congregations. It should also be noted that the population may consist of animate (e.g., people, animals) or inanimate objects (e.g., ships, houses) or intangible events (riots, road accidents e.g.). Whatever the nature of the population, *it is specified by the investigator who aims to find something about it.*

Samples: there two types of samples: probability samples and non-probability samples. **Probability samples** include simple random sampling, systematic sampling, stratified sampling, cluster sampling, and multi-stage sampling. **Non-probability samples** include quota sampling, panel methods, judgement sampling, and convenience sampling. Randomly selected samples are considered ideal; if this was not possible than alternate methods may be considered. Whichever method a researcher uses he should provide a justification of its use. Convenience sampling should be avoided unless that is the only way left to collect the data.

If instead of surveying the whole population, which is often not feasible owing to time and financial constraints, a sample from the population is taken for the study then the process is known as a **sample survey.** In sample surveys it is essential to distinguish between the target population and the sampled population. The **target population** is the one about which we wish to make inferences (e.g., all people with Sikh faith). The population from where the researcher actually draws his sample is called the **sampled population** (e.g., the younger generation within the Sikh faith). These two populations will not always be the same. The essential point that arises in the case of these two populations is this: *can the researcher extend the conclusions arrived at from the sampled population to the target population?* The answer to this question lies in the judgement of the researcher and the proximity of the sampled population with the target population.

To reiterate, a sample is the portion of the population that is selected for analysis. Mostly researchers work with samples and the results derived from thereof can tell us about the characteristics of the population. The most important issue with regard to samples is that they should be of 'reasonable size' and 'representative' of the population. A sample that accurately reflects the population from which it is drawn is called *a representative sample.*

Steps in Analysing Survey Data[193]

Survey data that has been painstakingly collected should be handled with care in a systematic fashion. Collected data is input on a spreadsheet such as Excel or SPSS which is a commonly used software for analysing data in social sciences. After the data has been input in a spreadsheet, it should be checked for any inaccuracies commonly known as 'data cleaning process'. Once it has been established that the data is error free, backup copies should be made. The following logical steps should be taken in analysing the data.

Step-1 Diagnostics

1. Run frequency tables and graphs on the entire data set. Visually examine the soft copy for a quick check and feel of the data.
2. Detect any missing data and outliers - outliers are data figures that lie beyond the expected bounds. For instance, if a question has five options 1-5 and you notice a 6 or some other digit. Most errors occur while inputting data.
3. Test for any bias from non-responders in the sample. Statistical tests exist for this.

---

[193] Part of the material in this section is drawn from (Singh S. , 1999).

4. Descriptive statistics such as mean, median, mode, standard deviation, range, skewness, kurtosis, zero-order correlations and graphing etc should be carried out to get a good feel of the data. Sometimes errors are detected at this stage.
5. Run selected cross-tabulations to see the initial connections between variables.
6. Apply appropriate tests to check for normality of the data.
7. Check for the presence of any multicollinearity and homoscedasticity in the data.
8. Check the level of reliability with the help of appropriate measures such as Cronbach's alpha.
9. Carry out an all-important Exploratory Factor Analysis (EFA) and Confirmatory Factor Analysis (CFA). It has been suggested that variables should meet six assumptions in order to obtain factor analysis: large sample size, normality, lack of outliers, continuous data, absence of extreme multicollinearity and low percentage of missing data. (Mendenhall, Beaver, & Beaver, 2019).
10. Principal Components Factor Analysis (PCFA) and Factor Loading. The PCFA is targeted to cut-off a minimum set of variables accounted for the maximum variance in the data. To decide on how many factors we need in order to represent the data, Eigen Values and Scree Plot are used. The determination of the number of factors is usually done by considering only those factors with Eigen values of greater than 1.

Stage-2 Parametric and Non-Parametric Analysis of Data

After the data has been checked for accuracy and diagnostic tests have been run, the researcher can apply a number of parametric and non-parametric tests such as *t-tests, z-tests, ANOVA, chi-square,* on the data to test preliminary hypotheses. A list of such tests is provided below. There are essentially two types of tests - *tests to find the Association between the data and tests to find the differences between the data.* Some of these tests such as the Mann-Whitney U test is a powerful alternative to the *t-test* when data is not normally distributed. The researcher should take particular care in applying these tests depending on the nature of the sample and data e.g., whether it is categorical, non-categorical and the size of the sample.

(i)   Tests of Association: Correlation and Association

(i)   Pearson Product Moment Correlation Coefficient
(ii)   Spearman Rank Order Correlation Coefficient; Kendall's Rank Correlation   Coefficient
(iii)   The Point Biserial Correlation Coefficient
(iv)   The Mantel-Haenszel Chi-square
(v)   The Phi Coefficient
(vi)   The Contingency Coefficient *C*
(vii)   Goodman and Kruskal' *Gamma*
(viii)   Partial Correlations ; Partial Correlation for Ranked Data

Tests of Difference

(ii)   Categorical Data : Unrelated:

Testing for 1 proportion; Testing for 2 proportions; Testing for *k* proportions

(iii)   Categorical Data : Related:

2 Groups : McNemar change test; k Groups : Cochran Q test

(iv)   Non-categorical Data : Unrelated: Single Sample tests:

1 sample Z test; 1 sample t test; 1 sample variance test

(v) Non-categorical Data: Unrelated: Multiple Sample tests:

(i) 2 sample Z test, (ii) 2 sample t test, (iii) 2 sample variance test (iv) k sample means test plus Multiple range test, (v) 2-way ANOVA test (vi) Kolmogorov-Smirnov test, (vii) Mann-Whitney U test, (viii) Kruskall-Wallis 1-way ANOVA

(v)   Non-categorical Data : Related

(i) T-test for a related pair, (ii) Wilcoxon-Signed Ranks test
(ii) Friedman *2-way* ANOVA by ranks test

(vi)   Chi-square tests:

Chi-square test of independence;   Chi-square test of independence with Yates' correction;   Chi-square as a goodness of the fit test

Stage-3 Multivariate Analysis of Data

There are a number of multivariate tests a researcher can run on the data to test his hypotheses and test his conceptual model. Most likely, the researcher will resort to multivariate regression analysis including Probit (or Logit) regressions, Ordinal and Multinomial regressions. These are briefly described below. The comforting part is that the researcher only needs to understand the ethos of these techniques as they are in-built in modern software such as SPSS and are easy to use.

Multivariate regression is a powerful multivariate technique of the following type that can also include categorical variables (questions in the SI for which answers were 'Yes' 'No' type).

$$Y = \beta0 + \beta1X1 + \beta2X2 + \beta3X3 \ldots\ldots + \varepsilon \equiv X\beta + \varepsilon$$

In the multivariate regression equation above, dependent variable Y is a continuous variable; independent variables $X1, X2, \ldots\ldots X_n$ *could be continuous variables, interval, or on a ratio scale or dichotomous variables assuming the value 1 or 0 accounting for the categorical responses in the SI.*

If the dependent variable Y is constrained to say 1-5 (e.g., if the responses have preferences on 1-5 scale - 'ordered dependent variable') then we can make use of ordinal regressions. In an ordinal regression the link function is a transformation of the cumulative probabilities of the ordered dependent variable that allows for estimation of the model.

If we decide to use a categorical variable as dependent, then we can make use of Probit or Logit regressions. Both these models are commonly used regressions. You can use both these models and choose the one that gives you better results. However, difference between the two is mostly notable in small samples as Probit assumes normal distribution of the probability of the categories of the dependent variable; and Logit assumes the log distribution.

Negative log-log link function $p(z) = -\log(-\log(z))$ is recommended when the probability of the lower category is high. Complementary log-log function $p(z) = \log(-\log(1 - z))$ which is the inverse of the negative log-log function is recommended when the probability of higher category is high. If extreme values are present in the data, then Cauchit Link function $p(z) = \tan(p(z - 0.5))$ is recommended.

Multinomial Logit regression is a generalized linear model used to estimate the probabilities for the n categories of a qualitative dependent variable Y, using a set of explanatory variables X. The independent variables can be either dichotomous, interval or in ratio scale. For instance, in the conceptual model when the researcher is asking 5 qualitative questions to gauge the index of happiness in respondents, our researcher could convert each of these 5 qualitative responses into five binary dependent variables and run 4 equations (following *n-1* rule to avoid dummy trap) as a function of independent variables. Alternatively, and preferably, he can take recourse to *multinomial regression approach* choosing one category as the base to get his results.

These are powerful techniques with which a researcher can test his hypotheses. Experience shows that in addition to these widely used tests, *Structural Equation Modelling* (SEM) is another well-established technique among researchers as the software to run SEM models have come a long way. In SEM, coefficients multiple hypotheses can be worked out simultaneously.

There are additional multivariate techniques such ANOVA, MANOVA, Discriminant Analysis, Custer Analysis, which can be tapped into, if need be, depending on the requirement of hypotheses. The researcher is advised to consult a good book on multivariate techniques of the following kind (Tabachnick, 2020); (Hair, Black , Anderson, & Babin, 2018).

Chapter Summary

The 10 Sikh Gurus had several common traits between them. They all worked tirelessly for the upliftment of the masses by teaching them to be pious, truthful, hardworking, and by sharing part of their earnings with the community. In addition to these common traits, each one also had a unique individual code of conduct by which they lived and died, and for which they are known and revered within the Sikh community. These 10 codes of conduct were: humility, obedience, equality, service, self-sacrifice, justice, mercy, purity of thought, calmness, and royal courage. Each one of these traits when practiced diligently contribute to blissful living and collectively they could put a person on the road of *Nirvana*.

In this chapter I have proposed that with the help of a survey, it is possible for a researcher to find out the level at which we all are operating on these traits. As a simple example if we all are in the proximity of 10 (on a 1-10 scale; 10 highest) then we are doing well on our journey to *Nirvana*. The scores are liable to be influenced by the age, sex, marital, status, and other attributes of the individual. The (partial) conceptual model in Figure 6.1 lays out the plan for survey work considering the mediator and control variables. The coefficients from statistical models on the collected data would reveal the collective stand of the respondents with regard to their proximity to the state of *Nirvana*. Individual scores can be obtained by substituting the numbers a respondent has provided in the survey.

Open-ended questions can provide subjective material to supplement the objective scores. In first part of the chapter, along with a brief description of the traits, a sample of selected questions that can be put to respondents are listed. A researcher can build on these suggested questions. The experience of this author as supervisor to doctoral students shows that all three parts of a survey - drafting a good survey instrument, administering it and analysing data thereof are essential components and it is easy to make mistakes if the basics of these components are not clearly understood. As a result, I have also provided basic terminology attached to these three components. I strongly urge the researcher to read through this material and also that in the appendix. This should be a good start and supplement to books on surveys including data analysis.

The following sections provide supplement material useful in survey research.

Supplement Material - 1 A Primer in Data and Variables

There are two types of random variable - qualitative random variables and quantitative random variables. They yield respectively two types of data: **qualitative** and **quantitative.** Qualitative random variables yield **categorical** responses. Quantitative random variables yield **numerical** responses. For example, the response to the question "Do you believe in God?" The choices are clearly "Yes" or "No." On the other hand, responses to questions such as "To how many magazines do you subscribe?" or "How tall are you?" are clearly numerical. In the first case the quantitative random variable may be considered as **discrete,** while in the second case it can be thought of as **continuous.**

Discrete quantitative data are numerical responses that arise from *counting process,* while **continuous**

quantitative data are numerical responses that arise from *measuring process.* "The number of magazines subscribed to" is an example of a discrete quantitative variable, since the response takes on one of a (finite) number of integers, say, 1,2,3 or 4. On the other hand, "the height of an individual" is an example of a continuous quantitative variable, since the response can take on any value within a continuum or interval, depending on the precision of the measuring instrument.

In addition to commonly understood dependent and independent variables (described below), knowledge of some additional variables, some of which are created by the researcher, is helpful in applied research.

Dependent and Independent variables: A dependent variable is one whose value is taken to be dependent on or affected by some other variables. For instance, if we wish to study the relationship between a family's monthly expenditure and monthly income, the monthly expenditure will be taken to be dependent on the family's monthly income. The equation for this may be written as $C = f(I)$ [read: consumption is a function of income]. The consumption expenditure is then the dependent variable and the income an independent variable. Independent variable is one which is used to predict the value(s) of other variables. Dependent variable is also known as **regressand** and independent variable as **regressor** or **explanatory variable.**

Alphanumeric variable: When data are being put on to a computer file, we give names to our variables. Normally, the variables are identified with the help of names that contain only characters. Examples are "Sex" to identify male and female respondents; "Age" to identify the age of the respondents. Occasionally we also give names to variables which are only numbers. Examples are "11" to identify the sex variable, or "12" to identify the age variable. It is also possible to combine the alphabetic characters and numeric numbers to create a name. When this is done the resultant variable is called 'alphanumeric variable'. As an example, we could call our age variable by the name "A11" or sex variable with the name "S11."

Background variables: Also known as 'classification' and 'subject' and 'difference variables', these refer to the backgrounds of the subjects taken for study. Examples are the subject's ethnic background, his job status, his sex, and age. The background variables cannot be manipulated by the researcher, but he can have some control on them while analysing his data.

Control variable: This is an extraneous variable which the researcher does not wish to examine in his study and hence leaves it out or controls for it. In regression analysis, a control variable is used to subtract its effect from other independent variables.

Dummy variable: Also known as binary variable, this variable is created by the researcher to capture the influence of categorical variables which cannot be used as they are in a regression equation or in some other statistical technique. Take an example where a researcher has collected data on the number of successful wage contracts negotiated by the Personnel Directors of companies over a 10-year period. After having collected the data for a large number of firms, the researcher hypothesises that, whether the Personnel Director is a male or female has some bearing on the successful negotiation of the contracts. To capture this 'gender effect', the researcher creates a variable called "gender" which takes the value 1 if the Personnel Director is male and 0 if the Personnel Director is female. He then writes his simple equation as follows: $N=f(G)$ i.e., the number of successful contracts negotiated is a function of the gender of the Personnel Director.

Endogenous variable: This is a variable which is an inherent part of the system (or scheme of analysis) and is determined from within the system. The endogenous variable is 'caused by' other variables. **An exogenous variable** on the other hand is one which does not belong to the system and may be the influencing factor on other variables. For instance, if variables x and y tend to z or influence z then x and y will be labelled as exogenous variables to the system and z as an endogenous variable.

Intervening variable: An intervening variable is one which provides a causal link or relation between two variables. It is also known by the name of **mediating** and **intermediary** variable. As an example, consider the fall in the mortality rates among young children. One could say that advances in medical sciences are a direct cause of this fall. But it is equally possible that the overall level of awareness among people has also increased owing to rise in the level of education. Therefore, between the two variables, (i.e., the advances in the medical sciences and the fall in the mortality rates) is the intervening variable, the education, which has intervened to cause a fall in mortality rates.

Lagged variables: Consider the following equation for a set of families: $C_t = f(C_{t-1}, Y_t, Y_{t-1})$. Here C_t = consumption expenditure for the present year, C_{t-1} = consumption expenditure for the time period $t-1$ i.e., last year, and Y_t, Y_{t-1} are respectively the income for the present and the past year. What we are trying to model here is that the current consumption is dependent on the level of the past year's consumption, present year's income level, as well as last year's income level. The reason behind this is that the consumption is partly habit forming (the level of present spending will be influenced by what was spent last year, for example) and the level of expenditure on it will be influenced by not only the current income of the families but also the level of the past year's income (families may spend from their past savings, for example). C_{t-1} and Y_{t-1} are called the **lagged independent variables.** Note that one can also have a **lagged dependent variable** in an equation. The lags may go back to more than one year.

Supplement Material - 2   Levels of Measurement

Nominal and Ordinal Scales: Data obtained from a qualitative variable are measured either on a nominal scale or on an ordinal scale. If the observed data are merely classified into various distinct categories in which no ordering is implied, a **nominal** level of measurement is achieved. Here the numeric values itself indicate the categories for the elements. On the other hand, if the observed data are classified into distinct categories in which ordering is implied, an **ordinal** level of measurement is attained. Here the numeric values permit us to rank the data. Nominal scaling is the weakest form of measurement because we cannot account for differences within a particular category or to specify any ordering or direction across various categories.

Ordinal scaling is somewhat stronger form of measurement because an observed value classified into one category is said to possess more of a property being scaled than does an observed value classified into another category. However, within a particular category no attempt is made to account for differences between the classified values. Moreover, ordinal scaling is still a weak form of measurement because no meaningful numerical statements can be made about differences between the categories. That is, ordering implies only *which* category is "greater", "better", or "more preferred - not *how much* "greater", "better", or "more preferred."

Interval scale: The first characteristic of an interval scale is that the difference or interval between two data values *is possible and makes sense*. Secondly, the data on an interval scale *can be ranked*. Thirdly, we can make *arithmetic operations* like division, addition, subtraction on data that is on an interval scale. Interval data are always numeric. Given these features, the interval data makes it possible for the researcher to do more statistical tests than the nominal or the ordinal data. For such data (in Celsius) we can make statements like "14th December was 4 degrees colder than 10th of December." With appropriate formula we can also convert this data into Fahrenheit. We can also rank this data in ascending order. But the ratio of two data sets will not make sense. Thus, although we can say that "14th December was 4 degrees colder than 10th of December," we cannot say that "14th of December was twice as cold as 10th of December." This is possible only in the case of ratio scale.

Ratio scale: Data on a ratio scale has all the features of the data on an interval scale. In addition, the ratio of two data points is meaningful. For data that is on ratio scale, ratios of values for quantities do have physical interpretations. For instance, we can say 'this cat is twice as heavy as that cat'. Distance, height, weight are further examples of ratio data. Ratio data represents the highest possible level of measurement because multiplication and division of data values as well as subtraction and addition have meaning. Ratio data is always numeric and has an inherently defined zero in it. *Data in ratio scale lends itself to a great deal of statistical analysis.*

Amount of information contained in various measurement scales

Now that we have defined the various scales of measurements in which the data can be presented, we can guess which scale contains the maximum information and is most useful. The lowest on the rank is the nominal scale, followed by ordinal, interval, and then the ratio scale. Arithmetic operations are possible only on data presented in interval or ordinal scales. Of these two, *ratio scale lends itself to maximum manipulations and use of statistical tests of hypotheses.* However, as a researcher we would not be necessarily collecting data on a ratio scale all the time. *The kind of data we collect will be dictated by the nature of the research project.* However, different statistical procedures exist for different types of data. Procedures that are suitable for ratio scale may not be suitable for data on nominal or ordinal scale and vice versa.

Supplement Material - 3 Selected Essential Terms

A priori and posteriori comparisons: A *priori comparison* (or a priori hypothesis) occurs when a researcher states the outcome of the results beforehand i.e., before starting to analyse his data. This may be based on a theory or on common beliefs or on past experience. Contrary to this, *posteriori comparisons* (or a posteriori hypothesis) are made after the data has been analysed. This may occur when the researcher has no idea of the outcome of the analysis or when the results have shown a new approach to data analysis.

Abscissa and Ordinate: Abscissa refers to the horizontal x-axis and Ordinate refers to vertical y-axis. While plotting variables, *the independent variable is usually plotted on the x-axis and dependent variable is plotted on the vertical y-axis.* Some built-in graph programs sometimes ask us to specify your variables this way.

Attribute: An attribute is a qualitative variable or trait. The sex of the respondent, for example, is an attribute (it is also a qualitative, categorical variable). *An attribute variable* which reflects the trait of a subject, for instance, whether the respondent is a male or female, can only be measured and not manipulated in a study.

Contingency table: Also known as cross tabulation, it is a table formed with two categorical variables. In contingency tables, *the dependent variables appear in the rows and independent variables appear in the columns.* The table is called a contingency table because the row variables are contingent on or dependent on the independent column variables.

Note that a contingency table may contain more than two variables. When contingency tables contain more than two variables, they are called **multivariate contingency tables.** Thus, for instance, we could have further categorised the "Male students" and "Female students" by their age or their course status - under-graduates or post-graduates. If we had done so, we would have further subclassified the two independent variables.

Interaction effect: Interaction effect occurs when two independent variables interact to influence a dependent variable. Consider for example that we hypothesise that the rate of road accidents is a function of the age of the driver (young or old) and the fact whether at the time of accident he was under the influence of liquor or not. We set up the following equation $y = a + b1x1 + b2x2$ where y is the recorded number of road accidents, $x1$ is the age of the driver, and $x2$ is the dummy variable which records whether the driver at the time of the accident was under the influence of liquor ($x2=1$) or not ($x2=0$). This regression equation when run will give us some idea about the validity of our hypothesis. However, it is equally possible that the driver who had an accident was *young as well as drunk* at the time of the accident. The two variables $x1$ and $x2$ will then interact to influence y and ideally then we should have another dummy variable which will capture this effect (say $x3$ which takes the value 1 if the driver who had an accident was young as well as drunk; and 0 if otherwise). When two variables interact, there is said to be **first-order interaction**, when three variables interact there is said to be **second order interaction** and so on. The simple effect of independent variable(s) on the dependent variable is called the **main effect.**

Likert scale: Likert scales, so called after Rensis Likert, are widely used scales in questionnaire surveys. They can go from the highest levels to the lowest levels on which the respondents mark their answers. As an example, consider the following question from a questionnaire sent to a random selection of respondents to seek their opinions on the late-night opening of pubs: 'Would you support a petition for pubs to stay open late at night?'. The choices to answer this question are: 'I would strongly support', 'support', 'neutral', 'may be', 'would never support'. Likert scales or the derivatives thereof are widely used to capture the attitudes of the respondents. Such scales also lend themselves to statistical tests and as a result are popular with researchers.

Parameter: A population parameter is a summary measure that is computed to describe the characteristic of an entire population.

Statistic: A statistic is a summary measure that is computed to describe a characteristic from only a sample of the population. They are used as estimates of corresponding quantities in population called parameters. Examples of statistics are the sample mean, the sample median, and the sample mode. While sample values are computed from observed data, parameters remain unknown.

**

Bibliography

(n.d.).

Abu-l-Fazl. (2002). *The Akbar Nama (3 Vols)*. Delhi: Low Price Publications.

Aijen, I. (2005). *Attitudes, Personality and Behaviour*. Buckingham: Open University Press.

Ajzen, I., & Fishbein , M. (1980). *Understanding Attitudes and Predicting Social Behavior*. London: Pearson.

Allport, G. W. (1963). *Pattern and Growth in Personality*. San Diego: Harcourt College Publishers.

Annas, J. (1993). *The Morality of Happiness*. Oxford: Oxford University Press.

Aquinas, T. (2018). *Summa Theologica (originally written 1265-1274)*. Claremont: Coyote Canyon Press.

Aristotle. (2009). *The Nicomachean Ethics*. (D. Ross, Trans.) Oxford: Oxford University Press.

Aristotle. (c.335-323BC). *The Metaphysics [Kindle edition 2004]*. (H. Lawson-Tancred, Trans.) London: Penguin classics.

Azzi, C., & Ehrenberg, R. (1975). Household allocation of time and church attendance. *Journal of Political Economy, 83*(1), 27-56.

Badauni, A. A.-Q. (c.1590-1615). *Muntakhabh-ut-Tawarikh* (1990 ed.). (G. S. Ranking, Trans.) Calcutta: Bib.India.

Badā'ūnī, A.-Q. (1898). *Muntakhabu-t-tawārīkh, Volume 1.* (G. Ranking, & W. H. Low, Trans.) Asiatic Society of Bengal.

Barnes, M. (2011). *Interreligious Learning: Dialogue, Spirituality and the Christian Imagination.* Cambridge: Cambridge University Press.

Bass, B. M. (2009). *The Bass Handbook of Leadership [Kindle edition].* New York: Free Press.

Becker, G. S. (1978). *The Economic Approach to Human Behavior.* Chicago: University of Chicago Press.

Becker, G. S., & Murphy, K. M. (1988). A Theory of Rational Addiction. *Journal of Political Economy, 96*(4), 675-700.

Bellah, R. N. (1991). *Beyond Belief: Essays on Religon in a Post-Traditionalist World.* Berkeley: University of California Press.

Bloomfield, P. (2014). *The Virtues of Happiness.* Oxford : Oxford University Press.

Brent, M., & Dent, F. E. (2017). *The Leadership of Teams: How to Develop and Inspire High-performance Teamwork [Kindle edition].* London: Bloomsbury Business.

Bryman, A. (2011). *The SAGE Handbook of Leadership.* Thousand Oaks, California: SAGE Publications.

Burns, J. M. (1978). *Leadership.* NY: HarperCollins.

Burton, R. G. (2008). *The First and Second Sikh Wars: An Official British Army History (first published*

1911). Yardley: Westholme Publishing (Kindle Edition).

Cahn, S. M., & Vitrano, C. (Eds.). (2008). *Happiness: Classic and Contemporary Readings in Philosophy.* Oxford: Oxford University Press.

Cambridge University. (2017). *Global Definitions of Leadership and Theories of Leadership Development: Literature Review.* Cambridge: University of Cambridge. Retrieved 2 9, 2022, from https://www.cisl.cam.ac.uk/resources/sustainabilit y-leadership/global-definitions-of-leadership

Chrystal, G. W. (1902). *Meditations by Marcus Aurelius [Kindle edition: Original written c. AD 171-175].*

Clarke, P. B. (1891). *The Melanesians:Studies in their Anthropology and Folklore.* Oxford: Clarendon Press.

Clarke, P. E. (Ed.). (2009). *The Oxford Handbook of The Sociology of Religion.* Oxford: Oxford University Press.

Codrington , R. H. (2005). *The Melanesians: Studies in Their Anthropology and Folk-Lore (Originally published 1891).* Brookline: Adamant Media Corporation.

Collins Anglicised ESV Bibles . (2012). *Holy Bible: English Standard Version (ESV) Anglicised Edition (Kindle Edition).* Honley: Collins.

Cort , J. A., Dundas, P., Jacobsen, K. A., & Wiley, K. L. (2020). *Brill's Encyclopedia of Jainism*. Leiden: BRILL.

Cunningham, J. D. (1918). *A History of the Sikhs.* Oxford: Oxford University Press. Retrieved 2 8, 2022, from https://rarebooksocietyofindia.org/book_archive/1 96174216674_10153455457621675.pdf

Dalrymple, W. (2020). *The Anarchy: The Relentless Rise of the East India Company.* London: Bloomsbury Publishing.

Daniélou, A. (2003). *A Brief History of India (Kindle Edition).* (K. F. Hurry, Trans.) Rochester: Inner Traditions.

Das, R. (2019). *The Illustrated Encyclopedia of Hinduism.* Leicester: Lorenz Books.

David, S. A., Boniwell, I., & Ayers, A. C. (Eds.). (2013). *The Oxford Handbook of Happiness.* Oxford: Oxford University Press.

Dhavan, P. (2011). *When Sparrows Became Hawks: The Making of the Sikh Warrior Tradition, 1699-1799.* Oxford: Oxford University Press.

Dhillon, D. S. (1988). *Sikhism, origin and development.* London: Atlantic Publishers.

Dulebohn, J. H., Bommer, W. H., Liden, R. C., Brouer, R. L., & Ferris, G. R. (2011). A Meta-Analysis of Antecedents and Consequences of Leader-Member Exchange: Integrating the Past With an Eye

Toward the Future. *Journal of Management, 36*(6), 1715-1759.

Durant, W. (1935). *The Story of Civilization:Our Oriental Heritage Vol-1 Kindle edition (total 11 vols).* New York: Simon and Schuster.

Durkheim, E. (1915). *The Elementary Forms of the Religious Life: A Study in Religious Sociology [Kindle Edition].* (J. W. Swain , Trans.) Whitefish: Kessinger Publishing.

Ebaugh, H. R. (Ed.). (2005). *Handbook of social institutions.* Berlin: Springer.

Elphinstone, M. (2014). *The History of India (2 vol).* Plano, TX: Normanby Press [Kindle edition 2 vol 2014) (Originally published by John Murray, London, 1841).

Encyclopaedia Britannica. (2005). Encyclopaedia Britannica (UK) Ltd.

Evans-Pritchard, E. E. (1965). *Theories of Primitive Religion.* Oxford: Clarendon Press.

Fenech, L. (1997). Martyrdom and the Sikh Tradition. *Journal of the American Oriental Society, 117*(4), pp. 623-642.

Fenech, L. E., & McLeod , W. H. (2014). *Historical Dictionary of Sikhism.* Maryland: Rowman & Littlefield Publishers.

Feuerbach, L. (2021). *The Essence of Christianity [Kindle edition: Originally published in 1841].* (G. Eliot, Trans.)

Fiedler, F. E. (1978). The Contingency Model and the Dynamics of the Leadership Process. *Advances in Experimental Social Psychology, 11*, 59-112.

Flavel at. al. (2016). Lay Definitions of Happiness across Nations: The Primacy of Inner Harmony and Relational Connectedness. *Front. Psychol.* Retrieved 11 25, 2021, from https://www.frontiersin.org/articles/10.3389/fpsyg.2016.00030/full

Foot , S., & Robinson , C. F. (Eds.). (2012). *The Oxford History of Historical Writing: Volume 2.* Oxford: Oxford University Press.

Foot, P. (Ed.). (1967). *Theories of Ethics.* Oxford: Oxford University Press.

Frazer, J. G. (1890). *The Golden Bough [Kindle edition].* Boston: Digireads.com Publishing.

French, J. R., & Raven, B. (1959). The Bases of Social Power. In D. Cartwright , *Studies in Social Power* (pp. 150-167). Ann Arbor: Institure for Socail Research, University of Michigan.

Freud, S. (1920). *A General Introduction to Psychoanalysis [Kindle edition].* (S. Hall, Trans.) Horace Liveright.

Gautier, F. (2003). *Rewriting Indian History.* New Delhi: Indian Research Press.

Gerstner, C. R., & Day, D. V. (1997). Meta-Analytic review of leader–member exchange theory: Correlates and construct issues. *Journal of Applied Psychology, 82*(6), 827–844.

Gottfredson, R. K., Wright, S. L., & Heaphy, E. D. (2020). A critique of the Leader-Member Exchange construct: Back to square one. *The Leadership Quarterly, 31*(6).

Graham , G. (2010). *Theories of Ethics: An Introduction to Moral Philosophy with a Selection of Classic Readings.* London: Routledge.

Greenleaf, R. K. (2002). *Servant Leadership: A journey into the Nature of Legitimate Power and Greatness [Kindle edition].* (L. C. Spears, Ed.) NJ: Paulist Press.

Greenlees, D. (1952). *The Gospel of Peace according to Guru-Granth Sahib.* Wheaton, IL: The Theosophical Publishing House.

Grewal , J. S. (Ed.). (2011). *Sikh History From Persian Sources.* New Delhi: Tulika Books.

Grewal, J. S. (2008). *The Sikhs of the Punjab.* Cambridge: Cambridge University Press.

Griffin, L. H. (1898). *Ranjit Singh and the Sikh Barrier Between our Growing Empire and Central Asia.* Oxford, Clarendon Press. Retrieved from file:///C:/Users/singh/Downloads/1898%20Ranjit %20Singh%20and%20the%20Sikh%20Barrier%2

429

0between%20our%20Growing%20Empire%20and %20Central%20Asia%20by%20Griffin%20s.pdf

Grossman, N. (2014). *The Spirit of Spinoza*. Princeton: ICRL Press.

Gupta, H. R. (1984). *History of the Sikhs (Vol 1)*. New Delhi: Munshiram Manoharlal.

Haidt, J. (2006). *The Happiness Hypothesis*. London: Arrow Books.

Hair, J., Black, W., Anderson, R., & Babin, B. (2018). *Multivariate Data Analysis*. Boston: Cengage Learning.

Hamermesh, D. S., & Soss, N. M. (1974). An Economic Theory of Suicide. *Journal of Political Economy, 82*(1), 83-98.

Harris, I. (2009). *The Illustrated Encyclopedia of Buddhism*. Leicester: Lorenz Books.

Heil, J. (2013). *Philosophy of Mind*. London: Routledge.

Hinnels, J. R. (Ed.). (2005). *The Routledge Companion to the Study of Religion*. London: Routledge.

Hofstede, G., Hofstede, G. J., & Minkov, M. (2010). *Cultures and Organizations: Software of the Mind [Kindle edition]*. NY: McGraw Hill.

Hogarth, R. M., & Reder, M. W. (Eds.). (1987). *Rational Choice: Contrast Between Economics and Psychology*. Chicago: University of Chicago Press.

Howe, D. (2009). *A Brief Introduction to Social Work Theory.* NY: Red Globe Press.

Hunter, W. W. (1907). *A Brief History of the Indian Peoples.* Oxford: Clarendon Press.

Hutchison, J., & Vogel, J. P. (1933). *History of the Panjab Hill States (Reproduced 2008).* Noida: Books for All.

Jackson, R. (2011). *The God of Philosophy.* Durham: Acumen.

Jahangir, M. S. (c.1622). *Tuzuk-i-Jahangiri [Kindle edition].* (H. Beveridge, & A. Roger , Trans.) New Delhi: Prabhat Prakashan.

Jaques, T. (2006). *Dictionary of Battles and Sieges: A Guide to 8500 Battles from Antiquity Through the Twenty-first Century.* CT: Greenwood Press.

Kant, I. (2014). *Religion within the Boundaries of Mere Reason [Kindle edition. Original published in 1793].* NY: SparkNotes.

Kenny, A. (2011). *Aristotle The Eudemian Ethics [Kindle edition 2011 Originally published 340BC].* (A. Kenny, Trans.) Oxford: Oxford University Press.

Khan , H. I. (1990). *The Shah Jahan Nama (Originally completed 1636; Editors W.E. Begley; Z.A. Desai).* Oxford: Oxford University Press.

Klein, M. (2003). *The Courage to Act: Five Factors of Courage to Transform Business.* CA: Davies-Black.

Kohli, S. S. (1961). *Guru Granth Sahib: An analytical study.* Amritsar: Singh Brothers.

Kohli, S. S. (1997). *Travels of Guru Nanak.* Chandigarh: Punjab University.

Kolvereid, L. (1996). Prediction of Employment Status Choice Intentions. *Entrepreneurship: Theory & Practice, 21*, 47-57.

Kulke, H., & Rothermund, D. (2016). *A History of India.* London: Routledge.

Kunin, S. D. (Ed.). (2006). *Theories of Religion: A Reader.* Edinburgh: Edinburgh University Press.

Laffont , J.-J., & Martimort, D. (2002). *The Theory of Incentives: The Principal-Agent Model.* Princeton: Princeton University Press.

Lal, K. S. (1973). *Growth of Muslim Population in Medieval India.* Delhi: Research publications. Retrieved 2 7, 2022, from https://ia801602.us.archive.org/21/items/in.ernet.dl i.2015.129758/2015.129758.Growth-Of-Muslim-Population-In-Medieval-India-ad-1000-1800_text.pdf

Lane-Poole, S. (1903). *Medieval India Under Mohammedan Rule (A.D. 712-1764).* New York: G.P.Putman's Sons (2019 edition published by Alpha Editions).

Latif, S. M. (1891). *History Of The Panjab.* New Delhi: Gyan Books.

Lawson, H. (1986). *De Anima (On the Soul) [Kindle edition: Originally written by Aristotle c.350BC].* (H. Lawson, Trans.) London: Penguin classics.

Lee, A. (2020). *From Hierarchy to Ethnicity: The Politics of Caste in Twentieth-Century India.* Cambridge: Cambridge University Press.

Lee, D. (2007). *Plato: The Republic (Original published c.375BC).* London: Penguin Books.

Leitner, G. W. (n.d). *History of Indigenous education in The Punjab since annexation in 1882.* New Delhi: Master Printers. Retrieved 2 5, 2022, from file:///C:/Users/singh/Downloads/HISTORY%20OF%20INDIGENOUS%20EDUCATION%20IN%20THE%20PUNJAB_D-2624.pdf

Levenson, L., & Dwoskin, H. (2020). *Happiness is Free.* Minnesota: Sedona Press.

Lyubomirsky, S. (2010). *The How Of Happiness: A Practical Guide to Getting The Life You Want.* London: Piatkus.

Macauliffe, M. A. (1909). *The Sikh Religion: its sacred writings and authors (6 Vols) [Kindle edition: Vol 1].* Oxford: Oxford University Press.

Machiavelli, N. (2021). *The Prince [Kindle edition: Originally published 1513].* Karnatka: Tru Sign Publishing House.

MacKinnon , B., & Fiala , A. (2017). *Ethics: Theory and Contemporary Issues.* Belmont: Wadsworth Publishing.

Madra, A. S. (Ed.). (2004). *Sicques, Tigers or Thieves: Eyewitness Accounts of the Sikhs (1606-1809): Eyewitness Accounts of the Sikhs (1606-1810).* London: Palgrave Macmillan.

Majumdar, R. C. (2018). *Ancient India (first published 1952).* Delhi: Motilal Banarsidass.

Malinowski, B. (1979). The Role of Magic and Religion (first published 1925). Retrieved 2 21, 2022, from https://yale.imodules.com/s/1667/images/gid6/edit or_documents/flick_readings/flick_sup_readings/ malinowski-the_role_of_magic_and_religion.pdf?sessionid=bb be4390-b202-421d-a61c-8fd130ead74b&cc=1

Mandair, A.-P. S. (2013). *Sikhism: A Guide for the Perplexed [Kindle Edition].* NY: Bloomsbury Academic.

Mann, G. S. (1993). *The making of Sikh scripture.* Columbia: Columbia University. Retrieved 2 23, 2022, from https://www.proquest.com/openview/84f540c6703 d1fc16ea9522feb1a5e0a/1?pq-origsite=gscholar&cbl=18750&diss=y

Mann, G. S. (2001). *The Making of Sikh Scripture.* Oxford: Oxford University Press.

Marschak, J., & Radner, R. (1972). *Economic Theory of Teams.* New Haven: Yale Umiversity Press. Retrieved 2 4 , 2022, from https://cowles.yale.edu/sites/default/files/files/pub/ mon/m22-all.pdf

Maslow, A. H. (2014). *A Theory of Human Motivation [Kindle Edition].* Sublime Books .

McDermott, T. (2008). *Acqinas: Selected Philosophical Writings* . Oxford: Oxford University Press.

McLeod, W. H. (1989). *Sikhs: History, Religion, and Society.* Columbia: Columbia University Press.

McLeod, W. H. (2003). *Sikhs of the Khalsa: A history of the Khalsa Rahit.* Oxford: Oxford University Press.

Mendenhall, W., Beaver, R. J., & Beaver, B. M. (2019). *Introduction to Probability and Statistics.* Boston: Cengage Learning.

Mittal, S., & Thursby, G. (Eds.). (2009). *Studying Hinduism: Key Concepts and Methods [Kindle Edition].* London: Routledge.

Mone, K. R. (2021). *Hindustani Classical Music: An Appreciation [Kindle Edition ASIN: B095722DHL].*

Monro, R. H. (2020). *Benedictus de Spinoza. Ethica [Kindle Ed. Original published 1677).* Kyiv: Strelbytskyy Multimedia Publishing.

Mowbad, M. (2010). *The Dabistan (orignal published c.1645).* (D. Shea , & A. Troyer, Trans.) Montana: Kessinger Publishing.

Mueller, M. (1878). *Origin and Growth of Religion.* London: Longmans. Retrieved 3 22, 2022, from https://ia802605.us.archive.org/26/items/lectureson origi05mlgoog/lecturesonorigi05mlgoog.pdf

Mulligan, R. W. (1952). *St. Thomas Aquinas, The Disputed Questions on Truth (Originally written 1256–1259)*. Washington: Henry Regnery Co.

Neumann , J. V., & Morgenstern, O. (1943). *Theory of Games and Economic Behavior.* Princeton: Princeton University Press (Kindle edition 2007).

Nohria, N., & Khurana, R. (Eds.). (2010). *Handbook of Leadership Theory and Practice.* Boston: Harvard Business Press.

Ohrnberger, J., Fichera , E., & Sutt, M. (2017). The relationship between physical and mental health: A mediation analysis. *Social Science & Medicine*, 42-49. doi:DOI: 10.1016/j.socscimed.2017.11.008

Oppy, G. (Ed.). (2017). *The Routledge Handbook of Contemporary Religion.* London: Routledge.

Padam, P. S. (2005). *Bansavalinama (Dasan Patshaian Ka. In Gurmukhi).* Amritsar: Singh Brothers.

Pandey, R. B. (2018). *Samveda (Hindi language) [Kindle Edition].* New Delhi: Diamond Pocket Books.

Parsons , T., & Clark, K. B. (1966). *The Negro American.* Boston: Houghton Mifflin .

Petersen, A. (1999). *Dictionary of Islamic Architecture.* London: Routledge.

Qanungo, K. R. (1965). *Sher Shah and His Times.* Hyderabad: Orient Longmans.

Radnitzky , G., & Bernholz, P. (1987). *Economic Imperialism The Economic Approach Applied Outside the Field of Economics.* Oxford: Blackwell.

Reuer , J. J., Matusik, S. F., & Jones, J. (Eds.). (2019). *Oxford Handbook of Entrepreneurship and Collaboration.* Oxford: Oxford University Press.

Robinson, F. (2007). *The Mughal Emperors.* London: Thames & Hudson.

Rostow, W. W. (2017). *The Stages of Economic Growth: A Non-Communist Manifesto (first published 1960).* CT: Martino Fine Books.

Rousseau, J.-J. (2015). *The collected Works of Jean-Jacques Rousseau.* Oxford: PergamonMedia.

Russell, B. (1993). *The Conquest of Happiness (First published, 1930).* London: Routledge.

Russell, B. (2004). *History of Western Philosophy [Kindle edition. Originally publsihed in 1946].* London: Routledge.

Russell, B. (2022). *The Problems of Philosophy (First published 1912).* Natrona Heights, PA: General Press.

Ryan , R. (Ed.). (2019). *The Oxford Handbook of Human Motivation (2nd ed.).* Oxford: Oxford University Press.

Sarkar, J. (1932-1938). *The Fall of the Mughal Empire (in 4 volumes).* Calcutta: M.C Sarkar and Sons.

Sartre, J.-P. (2003). *Sartre: Being and Nothingness (originally published in 1943).* (H. E. Barnes, Trans.) Abingdon: Routledge.

Schopenhauer , A. (2010). *The Essential Schopenhauer: Key Selections from The World As Will and Representation and Other Works.* NY: HarperCollins e-books.

Segal, G., Borgia, D., & Schoenfeld, J. (2005). The motivation to become an entrepreneur. *International Journal of Entrepreneurial Behavior & Research, 11*(1), 42-57.

Sen, A. (1990). *Poverty And Famines: An Essay on Entitlement and Deprivation* (Reprint ed.). Oxford: Oxford University Press.

Sen, A., & Foster, J. E. (1997). *On Economic Inequality (Radcliffe Lectures)* (Enlarged ed.). Oxford: Oxford University Press.

SGPC. (2019). *Sikh Rahit Maryada (in Gurmukhi).* Amritsar: Shiromani Gurdwara Prabhandak Committee -SGPC. Retrieved from https://sikhbookclub.com/Book/Sikh-Rahat-Maraiyda-Published-By-SGPC

Shackle , C., & Mandair, A. (Eds.). (2013). *Teachings of the Sikh Gurus: Selections from the Sikh Scriptures.* London: Routledge.

Shapiro, I., & Green, D. (1996). *Pathologies of Rational Choice Theory: A Critique of Applications in Political Science.* CT: Yale University Press.

Singh, D. (Ed.). (2004). *Guru Granth Sahib Among Scriptures of the World.* Patiala: Punjabi University.

Singh, F., & Singh, K. (1991). *Atlas: Travels of Guru Nanak.* Patiala: Punjabi University.

Singh, G. (1690). *Dasam Granth*. Retrieved from https://ia600902.us.archive.org/16/items/DasamGr anthAll/Dasam%20Granth_All.pdf

Singh, G. (Ed.). (1960). *Sri Guru Granth Sahib (8 volumes: translated and annotated in English).* (G. Singh, Trans.) New Delhi: Allied Pubishers.

Singh, G. (1965). *A Select Bibliography of Sikhs and Sikhism.* Amritsar: SGPC.

Singh, G. (1974). *The Sikhs and Their Religion.* CA: The Sikh Foundation.

Singh, G. (2000). *Punjab ute Angrezan de Kabja (In Gurmukhi).* Patiala: Punjabi University.

Singh, G. (n.d.). *Last Days of Guru Gobind Singh.* Amritsar. Retrieved from https://www.sikhbookclub.com/Book/Last-Days-of-Guru-Gobind-Singh-By-Dr-Ganda-Singh

Singh, G. (n.d). *Twarikh Guru Khalsa (In Gurmukhi: for 10 Gurus).* CA.

Singh, H. (Ed.). (1992). *The Encyclopaedia of Sikhism (4 Vol 1992, 2011, 2011,2014).* Patiala: Punjabi University.

Singh, K. (2004). *A History of the Sikhs: Vol 1 1469-1838*. Oxford: Oxford University Press.

Singh, K., & Singh, P. (2019). *The Sikhs [Kindle edition]*. New Delhi: HarperCollins.

Singh, M. (2009). *Sri Guru Granth Sahib: English & Panjabi Translation (8 vol)*. Amritsar: SGPC.

Singh, P. (1994). *Community Kitchen of the Sikhs*. Amritsar: Singh Brothers.

Singh, P. (2003). *The Guru Granth Sahib: Canon, Meaning and Authority*. Oxford: Oxford University Press.

Singh, P. (2006). *Life and Work of Guru Arjan: History, Memory, and Biography in the Sikh Tradition*. Oxford: Oxford University Press.

Singh, P. (2019). *The Book of the Ten Masters*. Amritsar: Singh Brothers.

Singh, P. (Ed.). (2021). *Exploring Sikh Traditions and Heritage*. Basel: MDPI AG.

Singh, P. (2022, 3 11). *Understanding the Martyrdom of Guru Arjan Dev*. Retrieved from https://punjab.global.ucsb.edu/sites/default/files/sit efiles/journals/volume12/no1/3_singh.pdf

Singh, P., & Fenech, L. E. (Eds.). (2014). *The Oxford Handbook of Sikh Studies*. Oxford: Oxford University Press.

Singh, P., & Rai, J. (2013). *Empire of the Sikhs: The Life and Times of Maharaja Ranjit Singh*. London: Peter Owen Publishers.

Singh, R. (2015). *State Formation and the Establishment of Non-Muslim Hegemony: Post-Mughal 19th-century Punjab*. New Delhi: Sage Publications.

Singh, S. (1961). *Sri Guru Granth Sahib Darshan (In Gurmukhi)*. Patiala.

Singh, S. (1962, November). Guru Ram Das ank (in Gurmukhi). *Punjabi Duniya*.

Singh, S. (1972). *Sri Guru Granth Darpan (in Gurmukhi)*. Retrieved 3 31, 2022, from file:///C:/Users/singh/Downloads/GuruGranth%20 Darpan%20by%20Prof%20Sahib%20Singh-THIS%20IS%20PRINTED%20(1).pdf

Singh, S. (1996). *About Compilation of Sri Guru Granth Sahib*. (D. Singh, Trans.) Amritsar: Lok Sahit Prakashan.

Singh, S. (1999). *Understanding and Analysing Data (Unpublished Monograph)*. Reading.

Singh, S. (2004). *Divine Revealation*. New Delhi: Sikh Foundation.

Singh, S. (2005). *The Sikhs in History*. Amritsar: Singh Brothers.

Singh, S., Simpson, R., Mordi, C., & Okafor, C. (2011). Motivation to become an entrepreneur: a study of

Nigerian women's decisions. *African Journal of Economic and Management Studies, 2,* 202-219.

Singh, T., & Singh, G. (2006). *A Short History of the Sikhs Volume one (1469-1765).* Patiala: Panjabi University.

Sodi, H. S. (1995). *Ram Das Jeevan te Rachna (in Gurmukhi).* Patiala: Panjabi University.

Solomon, C. R. (1999). *Handbook to Happiness.* Illinois: Tyndale House Publishers.

Srivastav, H. (1980). *Raag Parichay (3 Vols in Hindi).* Allahabad: Sangeet Sadan Parkashan.

Stausberg , M., & Engler, S. (Eds.). (2018). *The Oxford Handbook of the Study of Religion.* Oxford: Oxford University Press.

Stausberg, M. (Ed.). (2009). *Contemporary Theories of Religion: a critical companion.* Oxon: Routledge.

Swedberg , R. (2020). *Economics and Sociology: Redefining Their Boundaries: Conversations with Economists and Sociologists [Kindle Edition].* Princeton: Princeton University Press.

Tabachnick, B. G. (2020). *Using Multivariate Statistics.* London: Pearson (India).

Thackston, W. M. (2002). *Baburnama: Memoirs of Babur (1483-1530).* (W. M. Thackston, Trans.) New York: Modern Library Inc.

Thapar, R. (2002). *Early India: from the origins to AD 1300.* Gurgaon: Penguin Random House.

Tharoor, S. (2016). *Inglorious Empire*. London: Penguin Books.

Timur, E. (1830). *The Mulfuzat Timury, Autobiographical Memoirs of the Moghul Emperor Timur*. (C. Stewart, Trans.) Retrieved 2 10, 2022, from https://rarebooksocietyofindia.org/book_archive/1 96174216674_10154691199226675.pdf

Tredennick, H., & Waterfield, R. (1990). *Xenophon: conversation of Socrates (Original written c.399BC)*. London: Penguin Books.

Tylor, E. (2016). *Primitive Culture Volume 1 (Originally published 2 Vols 1874 1891)*. Mineola NY: Dover Publications Inc.

Uchida, U., Ogihara , Y., & Fukus, S. (2015). Cultural Construal of Wellbeing – Theories and Empirical Evidence. In W. Glatzer, L. Camfield, V. MøllerMarian, & M. Rojas , *Global Handbook of Quality of Life* (pp. 823-837). Springer.

Unknown. (n.d.). *Puratan Janam Sakhi Sri Guru Nanak Dev Ji*. Retrieved 3 9, 2022, from http://www.panjabdigilib.org/webuser/searches/dis playPage.jsp?ID=3330&page=1&CategoryID=1

Vasant. (1990). *Raag-Kosh: Analysis of 1438 Raags*. (L. Gurg, Ed.) Hathras: Sangeet Press.

Whitehead, A. N. (1979). *Process and Reality (Edited by David R Griffin and Donald W Sherburne: Kindle edition)*. NY: Free Press.

WHO. (1997). *Islamic Ruling on Animal Slaughter.* Report of a Seminar Organised by the Muslim World League and the WHO. Alexandria: Regional Office for the Eastern Mediterranean. Retrieved 3 11, 2022, from https://applications.emro.who.int/dsaf/dsa49.pdf

Wickramanayaka , E. (2020). *Indian Raag Datils [Kindle Edition: ASIN B086833KJS].*

Williams , C., & Gurtoo, A. (Eds.). (2020). *Routledge Handbook of Entrepreneurship in Developing Economies.* London: Routledge.

Woodard, C. R. (2004). Hardiness and the Concept of Courage. *Consulting Psychology Journal: Practice and Research, 56*(3), 173-185.

Young, L. A. (Ed.). (1997). *Rational Choice Theory and Religion.* London: Routledge.

Youniss, J., Mclellan, J. A., Su, Y., & Yates, M. (1999). The Role of Community Service in Identity Development: Normative, Unconventional, and Deviant Orientations. *Journal of Adolescent Research, 14*(2), 248-261.

Yukl, G. (1989). Managerial Leadership: A Review of Theory and Research. *Journal of Management, 15*(2), 251-289.

INDEX

Brief CV of the Author

Dr Satwinder Singh retired in 2020 as Professor of International Business (IB) and Strategy at the University of Dubai (UAE). Previously he worked for the University of Reading (UK), Brunel University London (UK), United Nations in Geneva. He is an Associate Fellow at *The John H Dunning Centre for International Business*, University of Reading, UK.

Dr Singh holds an MA (Distinction) and PhD in Economics and has taught International Business (IB) and Strategy-related subjects to MBA and PhD students. He has conducted training programs in India and in Africa for MEFMI (Macroeconomic & Financial Management Institute of Eastern and Southern Africa), UNCTAD, and COMESA (Common Market for Eastern and Southern Africa) to help build the capacity to interface with international companies.

An award-winning teacher he has successfully supervised 15 doctoral students. Two of his students won Brunel University Vice Chancellor award for best thesis (2012 and 2018). He was awarded best Brunel Business School staff award in 2013.

Author to about hundred papers and book chapters, he has published widely in the area of IB, Strategy, and International Human Resource Management in reputed journals including *Human Resource Management, International Journal of Industrial Organization (IJIO), R&D Management, International Journal of HRM, Industrial Marketing Management, and British Journal of Management*. He has also researched and published work in *Entrepreneurship,* and *Corporate Governance* in which he recently published a book with Palgrave-Macmillan*.

His papers published in *IJIO* and the *African Journal of Economics and Management Studies*, have respectively won 'Emerald Literati Network 2012 Outstanding Paper Award' and 'ANBAR Citation of Excellence Award'. Additionally, his paper Measuring Organizational Performance: A Case for Subjective Measures, *British Journal of Management,* Vol. 27, 214–224 (2016), was a top cited paper for that year.

Google Scholar Index:
https://scholar.google.co.uk/citations?user=3wqkKH0AAAAJ&hl=en
ResearchGate Index: https://www.researchgate.net/profile/Satwinder-Singh-6

*(2018) Corporate *Governance and Organisational Performance: The Impact of Board Structure.* Palgrave Macmillan.

He Who Regards All as Equal is Religious
(Guru Nanak)

(Source: photo purchased from i stock)

Printed in Great Britain
by Amazon